VERA BRITTAIN (1893–1970) grew up in provincial comfort in the north of England. In 1914 she won an exhibition to Somerville College, Oxford, but a year later abandoned her studies to enlist as a VAD nurse. She served throughout the war, working in London, Malta and at the Front in France. In 1933 Vera Brittain published *Testament of Youth*, a haunting autobiography which conveyed to an entire generation the essence of their common experience of war. In 1940 she published *Testament of Friendship*, in which she commemorated the life of Winifred Holtby. This was followed in 1957 by *Testament of Experience* which covered the years 1925–1950. These three Testaments are also published by Virago. A convinced pacifist, a prolific speaker, lecturer, journalist and writer, Vera Brittain devoted much of her energies to the causes of peace and feminism. She travelled widely in Europe and lectured extensively in the USA and Canada. She wrote twenty-nine books in all: novels, poetry, biography and autobiography and other non-fiction.

WINIFRED HOLTBY (1898–1935) was born in Rudston, Yorkshire. In the First World War she was a member of the Women's Army Auxiliary Corps, and then went to Somerville College, Oxford where she met Vera Brittain. Winifred Holtby was a prolific journalist, writing for the *Manchester Guardian*, the *News Chronicle* and *Time and Tide* of which she became a director in 1926. She also travelled widely as a lecturer for the League of Nations Union. Her first novel, *Anderby Wold*, was published in 1923, followed, in 1924, by *The Crowded Street* (both published by Virago). She wrote five other novels: *The Land of Green Ginger* (1927), *Poor Caroline* (1931), *Mandoa, Mandoa!* (1933) (all published by Virago), *The Astonishing Island* (1933) and *South Riding* (1936), published posthumously after her tragic death from kidney disease at the age of thirty-seven. She was awarded the James Tait Black Memorial prize for this, her most famous novel. She also published a critical work, *Virginia Woolf* (1932); a study of the position of women, *Women and a Changing Civilisation* (1934), and numerous essays.

Vera Brittain and **Winifred Holtby** met at Oxford in 1919 and so began a friendship which lasted until Winifred Holtby's death in 1935. Many of their books are famous; it is less well known that between the wars they became two of the most influential journalists in London. They wrote about feminism and pacifism, unemployment and fascism, theatre and music hall; they argued for political justice for Black Africans, and they wrote about their own lives. This impressive collection, never before published in book form, still speaks to us eloquently today – and commemorates 'a marvellous friendship'.

Paul Berry, writer, lecturer and teacher, was born in Leicestershire in 1919. A close friend of Vera Brittain's for twenty-eight years, he is currently writing her biography. He is also Winifred Holtby's literary executor. Paul Berry is the author of *Daughters of Cain* (with Renée Huggett) and *By Royal Appointment*.

Alan Bishop was born in Zimbabwe in 1937. Educated in South Africa and at Oxford, he taught in universities in both Zimbabwe and South Africa before his expulsion from the latter in 1966. He now teaches English at McMaster University, Ontario, Canada. Alan Bishop edited Vera Brittain's diary of the First World War, *Chronicle of Youth*.

Testament of a Generation

The Journalism of Vera Brittain and Winifred Holtby

Edited and introduced by
Paul Berry and Alan Bishop

Published by VIRAGO PRESS Limited 1985
41 William IV Street, London WC2N 4DB

Copyright © 1985 by Paul Berry and Alan Bishop

British Library Cataloguing in Publication Data

Testament of a generation: the journalism of
    Vera Brittain and Winifred Holtby.
    1. Anthologies
    I. Brittain, Vera   II. Holtby, Winifred
    III. Berry, Paul, *19*   IV. Bishop, A.G.
    082   · PN6014

    ISBN 0-86068-439-3
    ISBN 0-86068-444-X Pbk

Photoset in North Wales by
Derek Doyle & Associates, Mold, Clwyd
and printed in Great Britain by
Anchor-Brendon, of Tiptree, Essex

Contents

CONTENTS

Acknowledgements

Thanks are due to the editors of the following newspapers and magazines for their courteous permission to include in this book certain articles and reviews by Winifred Holtby which originally appeared in their columns: the *Yorkshire Post*, *Good Housekeeping*, the *Women's International League for Peace and Freedom*, the *Guardian* for the *Manchester Guardian* articles, the *Daily Mail* for the article and review originally published in the *News Chronicle*, the *New Statesman* for the *Nation and Athenaeum* articles, the *Standard* for the *Evening Standard* article 'Is Family Life a Handicap?', and to Lovat Dickson for kindly agreeing to the use of 'Mother Knows Best', which first appeared in *Lovat Dickson's Magazine* in December 1934.

Articles and reviews by Vera Brittain, originally published in the following newspapers or magazines, are also printed here with approval or permission: the *Manchester Guardian*, *Peace News*, the *Yorkshire Post*, *Reconciliation* and *Christian Century* ('Massacre Bombing – The Aftermath', 1 August, 1945, © Christian Century Foundation). Previously unpublished material by Vera Brittain appears with the permission of the William Ready Division of Archives and Research Collections, McMaster University Library, Hamilton, Ontario, Canada. 'The Kind of God I Believe In' first appeared in the magazine *Kingsway*, and is reproduced with the kind permission of Lord Soper and the West London Mission.

Every effort has been made to locate the owners of the archives of now defunct journals, and we apologize to those we have been unable to trace.

Our thanks are due, too, to the Local History Collection of Hull Central Library, the British Library at Colindale and

Bloomsbury, Midhurst Public Library, the Public Information Office at the House of Commons, and the Fawcett Library, London.

The generous help of many individuals is warmly acknowledged – especially of Charlotte Stewart, Bruce Whiteman, Dr Kathy Garay, Dr Yvonne Bennett, Dr Deborah Gorham and Dr Fred Bottley.

We are very grateful to Carmen Callil for so enthusiastically encouraging the original suggestion for this book, and we are deeply indebted to Ursula Owen for her patient and perceptive editorial guidance, and for her kindness and encouragement.

P.B.

A.B.

January 1985

PART ONE

The Friendship

A Marvellous Friendship

Friendship is a strangely difficult and complex theme to investigate and write about. We are born into our families and love is something that happens to us. Friends are what we choose for ourselves and they have an important and special place in our lives. In her biography *Testament of Friendship*, Vera Brittain relates the brief life of Winifred Holtby, the brilliant journalist, the successful public speaker, the author of the classic Yorkshire novel *South Riding*, and she portrays, too, a woman of wit and humour, and of infinite kindness and compassion. Against this background she tells the story of a deeply affectionate and remarkable friendship between two women writers and reformers of exceptional industry, talent and courage.

Yet this sixteen-year friendship had developed from inauspicious beginnings, and when they first met at a shared coaching session on European history at Somerville in the Michaelmas term of 1919, Winifred and Vera did not like each other at all. Vera was then nearly 27, and had been away for four years serving as a VAD nurse in military hospitals in London, Malta and France. Her fiancé, her only brother, and two close friends were dead, and she returned to Oxford lonely and embittered. Winifred, after a year at Somerville, had enlisted in Queen Mary's Army Auxiliary Corps in the summer of 1918, and served first as a domestic worker in a New Zealand officers' club in Mayfair, and later as a hostel forewoman in France. She was five-and-a-half years younger than Vera, and returned, her friend Hilda Reid recalled, 'to a hero's welcome'.

The majority of their undergraduate contemporaries had come

straight from school. Perhaps defensively justifying the considerable age gap, Vera antagonized many of them by talking excessively about her experiences in the First World War in which they had been too young to participate. In a moment of high-spirited impetuosity the Somerville Debating Society hit upon an ingenious plan to curb these reminiscences by prevailing upon her to propose a motion 'That a life of travel is a better education than a life of academic experience'. Unaware of the Debating Society machinations, Vera accepted, and spoke of her nursing service abroad as a painful yet richly rewarding experience. She ended with what she describes in her fictional reconstruction of the episode (in *The Dark Tide*) as 'a stinging indictment of her fellow students' limitations'.

Speaker after speaker opposed the motion, and Winifred joined in by pointing out that it was possible to discover the comparative value of travel and a University career only by looking at the kind of person they each produced. 'Now I don't see the object of going in for something that's only going to make one unhappy and a general cause of depression to the people one associates with', she concluded, with more exuberance than tact. 'In the words of Rosalind in *As You Like It*, "I had rather have a fool to make me merry than experience to make me sad, and to travel for it, too!"'

The proposition was crushingly defeated, and, wounded by the personal attacks, angry and distraught, Vera was convinced that the debate had been purposely contrived publicly to mock and mortify her. Winifred had regarded it as no more than a light-hearted academic exercise, but Vera believed that she was in some way personally responsible for her humiliation. Winifred listened in pained disbelief to Vera's stormy protests, murmured that she was sorry, and arranged for the Debating Society to send a letter of apology. Acutely sensitive to other people's misfortunes, she suddenly understood that beneath the mature, self-confident façade, Vera was vulnerable and unhappy, and that returning to Somerville after a four-year absence had been a lacerating ordeal.

The following term Winifred heard that Vera was in bed with a chill, and appeared at the door of her room with a bunch of grapes. She returned next day; they talked of their course, spoke about their families, and discussed their wartime experiences. It was the beginning of a remarkable friendship between two women which is now part of our literary heritage.

When she returned to Somerville, Vera was in fact on the verge of a nervous breakdown. She had severe attacks of migraine and sleepless nights, and when she slept she had dreadful nightmares. 'I suffered for months from the delusion that my face was disfigured', she wrote several years later. 'It always looked disfigured when I saw it in the glass, until I got into a state where I almost screamed if I went into a room where there was a mirror.' Volatile and tempestuous, she frankly acknowledged that their friendship was largely Winifred's achievement, and owed most to her patience and infinite compassion.

Winifred's childhood on a Yorkshire farm was a carefree adventure. As the cherished younger daughter of elderly parents – both her mother and father were nearly 40 when she was born – life's calamities and controversies seem scarcely to have touched either her life or her consciousness. Looking back she described herself at 21 as 'a creature of completely uncritical piety and sentimental convention'.

The disappearance of the Holtbys' adopted son, George de Coundouroff, who had returned to Russia as an interpreter with the Allied intervention force after the Bolshevik Revolution, was a source of unalleviated grief to his young wife and the Holtby family. But Vera, talking about Roland, Victor, Geoffrey and Edward, brought home to Winifred in stark personal terms the brutality, the sacrifice, and the insanity of war. Among Winifred's papers when she died were studio portraits which Vera had given her of the four boys killed on the battlefields of France and Italy.

Vera's deepest grief was for her brother Edward, killed by a sniper on the Asiago plateau above Vicenzia five months before the war ended. Eighteen months her junior, musical, aloof and imperturbable, he was the perfect counterbalance to her edgy, apprehensive temperament. No one needed to be needed more than Winifred, and in her self-appointed role as Vera's surrogate brother she gradually became also her indispensable *alter ego*. 'I am your Deputy' she confidently asserted in her poem 'Symphony Concert' which she wrote 'For a Dead Musician'.

Winifred was a popular undergraduate, and whilst her friendship with Vera won the respect and admiration of some, there was also an undercurrent of chagrin and resentment. Their Somervillian contemporary, Lady Ogilvy, remembers Vera and Winifred walking up and down on the grass beside the tennis courts totally absorbed in their conversation and each other. 'It was', she remarked with gracious spontaneity, 'a marvellous friendship.' Dr Cecily Williams, the renowned paediatrician, was for a time a close friend of Winifred's, and had taken over her room whilst she was away with the QMAAC. At first she felt sorry for Vera, but she was mortified when, to use her own racy expression, 'she gobbled up Winifred'. It was the beginning of a pattern of criticism in which Vera was the inevitable scapegoat, and this antipathy was a constant source of sadness to Winifred. She wanted everyone to recognize that 'rare quality of goodness which is so strange a thing to find ... Katherine Mansfield had it, and Vera has.'

Winifred and Vera were absolutely sure of each other, honest and truthful, and it became a relationship of almost telepathic empathy. When they met at Somerville they were both struggling towards the dedication of their lives to writing, and the pursuit of peace, feminism and social justice. Their shared ambition and idealism made the process of dedication more conscious to both of them, and forged a bond that anchored their friendship through the changes and vicissitudes of life.

Winifred was linked to her parents by ties of love and loyalty but chafed against their feudal outlook and die-hard politics. They were, she admitted, 'separated by leagues mentally'. 'I would go mad in Yorkshire', she said, and only Vera completely understood and shared her resolution 'to work both ends – at one end with the individuals, and at the other with the "questions" '.

Impetuous and highly strung, Vera's fragile composure was easily shattered by criticism, setbacks, domestic crises and interruptions, but she fought resolutely to overcome the troubles arising from her inherent irascibility. Winifred calmed and reassured her, light-heartedly teased her and laughed, and was the indispensable ally in helping her to regain her equanimity. Writing to Vera from Monte Carlo in 1929 she described how she had listened to Jan Smeterlin, the pianist, and added affectionately, 'And when he gets cross he is so exactly like you, Vera, that I could kiss him. He says the same rampageous things ...'

Physically and temperamentally it was a friendship of opposites. Vera, slight, dark, very pretty and deceptively fragile-looking, was by disposition, Winifred tells us, 'wiry and fiery, full of sudden laughter and tears and petulance and affection'. Even in later years she retained an endearing aura of vulnerability, and Winifred's affection was in part protective, and of almost maternal solicitude. In 1933 she facetiously dedicated her novel *Mandoa, Mandoa!* 'To Vera Brittain V.S.V.D.L. irrelevantly'; a public offering in their private cipher to her 'Very Small, Very Dear Love'.

Winifred, nearly six feet tall with blue eyes and pale flaxen hair, described herself with ironic detachment as being 'as plain as a pikestaff'. Hilda Reid insisted she was beautiful, but Winifred laughed and pointed out that her nose was crooked, and that she still had baby hair which 'can only just be induced to stay on my head'. She conceded she had rather pretty feet but said that no one noticed because they were size eight, and all she could buy were low-heeled, broad-toed 'ward' shoes. She delighted in relating how in Paris once the young assistant in a shoe shop had thrown up her hands in despair. 'But Madame,' she cried, 'in France we do not gr-r-r-ow such feet.'

Winifred was deeply conscious of her good fortune in having had a stable, happy childhood, and in possessing a buoyantly optimistic temperament, a first-class brain, and a warmth of personality which made almost everyone she met her friend and confidante. She made a deep impression on the South African writer, Pauline Smith, whom she met briefly in 1926 during a lecture tour for the League of Nations Union. 'When I think of all that Winifred had in her of courage and real nobility of spirit,' Pauline Smith wrote to Sarah Gertrude Millin after Winifred's death, 'of how much she might still have done had she lived, and of how little *I* achieve with much less to contend against, I wish I could have gone for her. I know this sounds untrue, but it is not so.'

As soon as they could read and hold a pen both Vera and

Winifred knew with total certainty that they were going to be writers. Vera's earliest efforts consisted of five melodramatic novels written before she was eleven, whilst Winifred poured forth a spate of poems and verse of juvenile exuberance.

Vera and Winifred left Somerville with good second-class degrees in the summer of 1921, and Vera suggested that they should share a flat in London and embark upon their endeavours to fulfil their writing aspirations. Early in 1922 they rented a small studio apartment on the ground floor of a house in Doughty Street, a broad Bloomsbury thoroughfare within easy walking distance of the British Library. That autumn they moved to a more spacious flat on the top floor of 58 Doughty Street, and discovered to Vera's horror that they were plagued with mice which ate their apples and chewed their candles to the wick.

Brought up in well-to-do middle-class environments at a time when maids, cooks, charladies, manservants and gardeners were plentiful and cheap, neither Vera nor Winifred had any inclination for housekeeping or domestic chores. At first they had no help, and Winifred reports having spent the morning cleaning the kitchen and arguing with Vera over the O-Cedar mop and dusters about 'What is Individualism?' At 58 Doughty Street they engaged a charlady who regarded them as two highbrow young ladies busily engaged in writing books, but she decided she had been badly hoodwinked when she found them dressing up and setting out at five o'clock and not returning until nearly midnight! She took her leave in a flurry of moral indignation, and shortly afterwards Vera and Winifred moved to a large, unfurnished flat in Elgin Avenue, a long, tree-lined street leading from Harrow Road to Maida Vale, and conveniently close to Paddington Recreation Ground for fresh air and exercise. They bought furniture and carpets, engaged a full-time housekeeper, and were now absolved of most of the domestic responsibility.

Allowances from their fathers cushioned them against financial constraints, and with phenomenal energy they taught part-time and lectured for the Six Point Group and League of Nations, wrote articles and short stories, and completed the novels they had begun at Oxford. Winifred was 24 when *Anderby Wold* was published in March 1923. Vera was less fortunate and her novel,

The Dark Tide, was returned by innumerable publishers until in desperation she agreed 'to subsidize the publisher (Grant Richards) to the extent of £50 which the royalties did not reach'. Both women had their feet on the bottom rungs of the literary ladder, and the acceptance of their articles by the *Yorkshire Post*, the *Manchester Guardian*, and *Time and Tide* soon followed. This period of their shared literary apprenticeship, Vera remarked many years later, included some of the happiest days of her life.

A major strength of the Holtby/Brittain friendship was the constructive and practical help they gave each other with their books, articles and lectures. Early in their freelance careers, when Winifred's articles were, she reported, 'but homing pigeons', Vera tried to help by pointing out little errors of prepositions and heavy-handed punctuation. On the carbon copies of several of Vera's articles she has added a manuscript note 'Typed by W.H.' – yet Winifred hated typing and found it exhausting. At home in Yorkshire after her father's death Winifred reported disconsolately that she was 'a sort of factory of post-mortem activity ... tired and stupid ... the result of dealing with incessant swarms of people'. Vera wrote at once urging her to return to London as soon as possible and spend two days in bed. 'You need see no one, not even me. You can get your publicity stuff together there and I can type it.' They discussed their writing projects and read each other's work. 'There is no reason why we should not have, as you suggest, a holiday in Cornwall or Devon and "talk out" ', Winifred assured Vera in a letter from Pretoria in 1926. 'I should love it. I want to discuss my play, too.'

Vera's marriage to George Catlin in June 1925 led inevitably to a period of practical and emotional adjustment. After a six-week honeymoon travelling in Europe, Vera and George sailed for America early in September, and settled in a small furnished apartment on the top floor of a three-storey house in Ithaca on the campus of Cornell University, where George was engaged as a Professor of Politics.

Vera's departure was a dislocation that Winifred had anticipated with some trepidation; she had confessed to Jean McWilliam the previous year that 'No one will ever know what I owe to her during these five years'. Writing to Vera in America she was careful to provoke neither compunction nor concern. She told her that Lady Rhondda, the founder of the magazine *Time and Tide* to which both Vera and Winifred, and many other well known women contributed, and Mrs Archdale (the original Editor of *Time and Tide*) were being 'quite charming to me because they know that I miss you. And so I do – and don't. I cannot describe it. I am, as I said, very, very happy, but it's a sort of autumn empty happiness. I miss the feel of your fingers round my left arm when I walk through the evening streets ...' But, 'fierce for work', she was sustained by her belief in 'the big permanent values which nothing can affect – courage, loyalty, caritas in the Latin sense of love, responsibility'.

For Vera the stimulus of marriage and living in America at first mitigated their separation. In her letters to Winifred she discussed with the same intimacy and frankness her writing projects and the purchase of two georgette frocks and two summer hats, the trials of being 'a faculty wife', the lecture she gave for the League of Nations Non-Partisan Association in New York, the beauty of an April day walking along the banks of the Potomac River. But the following July as she was preparing to return to England she was assailed with doubts. Had Winifred changed? Would she want to go with her to the League of Nations meeting in Geneva? Did she intend, as her mother implied, to leave the Maida Vale flat for a place of her own? 'I am *longing* to see you', she told Winifred, 'more than I dare allow myself to, till I am actually within sight of Southampton'. When the *Majestic* docked in the middle of August, Winifred was on the quay to greet her. They had been apart for almost a year but the friendship remained as strong and steadfast as it had always been. 'You are sweeter and more foolish than ever', Winifred reassured Vera in a hasty note from Yorkshire three days later.

For Vera, the year in America had been 'a mixture of pain and pleasure, of delight and disappointment'. She 'would not now for the world not have married G', but there was the realization, too, that she needed as much as ever the warmth and understanding of Winifred's perfect companionship.

Until Winifred's death nine years later, Winifred, George and Vera shared various homes. In December 1928 they left Maida

Vale for a maisonette in Earls Court, and eighteen months later, after the birth of Vera's son, they bought jointly a house in Glebe Place, Chelsea, just off the Kings Road.

On the whole the unorthodox Brittain/Catlin/Holtby household worked well. They respected each other's individuality and separate interests, and their absorption in their work was the antidote to petty jealousies and emotional tension. But on each of them the three-way relationship imposed restraints and adjustments.

Winifred handled her position as the odd woman out with discretion and tact. 'I like to be with you both', she wrote to Vera shortly after her marriage. 'You give me exquisite joy'. She assured her that though their lives had changed, her friendship remained immutable. 'As for you, do you not realize that I don't care twopence whereabout in the scale of your loves I come, provided that you love me enough to let me love you, and that you are happy? I love you in a way that part of me has become part of you. When you are troubled, so must I be, whether I like it or not. When you are happy, part of me is happy, whatever else befalls. I who am part of you, can only gain by your gains.'

Perhaps partly to give Vera and George time alone together in their own home, Winifred was often absent from Glebe Place. She travelled frequently to Yorkshire to be with her parents, she spent holidays in Monte Carlo and Agay in the south of France with Lady Rhondda, and in Ireland with Stella Benson, and she lived alone for several months in 1934 and 1935 in lodgings in Withernsea and Hornsea writing *South Riding*. In London she led a strenuously independent life. She worked in the *Time and Tide* office and attended board meetings, often lunched or dined with friends or colleagues, lectured, and battled continuously with the insistent demands of her Friends of Africa organization. And yet, and yet … to the chagrin of her family and Lady Rhondda, Vera remained at the centre of her life. They discussed with the same intimacy their plans, their writing, their personal problems. Amy Burnett, their housekeeper at Glebe Place, recalled innumerable occasions on which the two of them sat round the fire after supper drinking coffee and deep in discussion. 'I would be as quiet as I could,' she said, 'and I don't think they even knew I was in the room clearing away the dishes.'

When Vera was away, Winifred took charge of the household and looked after the children, accompanying them to parties, on visits to their grandparents, and on excursions to the park where once they found great mounds of leaves and 'we all crept home looking like sweeps'.

At the end of 1931 Winifred had collapsed with high blood pressure, racking headaches and nausea. With limited knowledge, and none of our technological resources, her doctors were baffled, and she spent almost eight inconclusive months in nursing homes in London, 'convalescing' in Sidmouth, and in lodgings in a quiet country cottage at Monks Risborough in Buckinghamshire, until at last a specialist diagnosed that she was suffering from progressive renal sclerosis. He told her that she might live only two years, and taking no chances, Winifred immediately made a brief, simple will in which she appointed Vera as her literary executor, and left her 'my one-third ownership of 19 Glebe Place during her use of it'.

Between 1927 and 1933, Winifred became a highly successful and much-sought-after journalist, and in addition published three novels and a critical study of Virginia Woolf, while for most of that time Vera, preoccupied with her home and family, laboured with the manuscript of *Testament of Youth*. Often depressed, and disturbed by constant interruptions, Winifred sustained her resolve. She discussed, she suggested, she advised, and she read what Vera had written. 'What can I say to make you believe in your book as I believe in it?' she entreated in 1932 when Vera was facing a crisis of boredom and lack of confidence. 'When I read those early chapters of the *Testament*, I felt "This is *it*. This is the thing she has been waiting to do. This is the justification of those long years of waiting."'

It was obvious to all who knew them that it was a friendship of rare nobility. Monica Whateley, their feminist friend and a Labour Parliamentary candidate, was deeply impressed, but like many of their friends and acquaintances she could not believe that it was not a lesbian relationship. After Vera's marriage to George Catlin the speculation grew. In *Testament of Friendship* Vera briefly refuted the lesbian imputations, but in doing so, she said, she was anxious not to stigmatize homosexuality with an opprobrium she did not feel, and aware that if she protested too vehemently she was less likely to be believed. When her book was published, she was chagrined – and exasperated, too, she admitted – when 'many correspondents wrote me enthusiastically as a fellow homosexual'. And since her death the myth has continued to circulate.

Except to those vicariously titillated by other people's sexual idiosyncrasies, the individual's sexuality would seem to be important only as it affects his or her life and work, but to understand fully the friendship between Vera and Winifred it is none the less necessary to recognize that it was not a lesbian one.

Phyllis Bentley stayed with them for several weeks after the publication of her best-selling novel *Inheritance*, and dismissed the allegation as completely groundless. 'Certainly there was never any of that feeling between Vera and Winifred', she wrote. Hilda Reid knew them better and longer and denounced the rumour as 'utter nonsense'.

Small, vivacious and very feminine, Vera was extremely attractive to men. 'I am a markedly heterosexual woman', she wrote to her pacifist friend and colleague, Sybil Morrison, 'whose relations with men have been many and complicated, but who has had none with women.' As if anticipating the revival of the lesbian speculations after her death, she left among her papers a scarcely legible pencilled note written when she was ill and knew she was not going to get better. 'I loved Winifred,' she had scribbled on a leaf torn from a small pocket notebook, 'but I was not in love with her.'

Winifred had a minimal interest in sex, declaring that she took too much mental and bodily exercise 'for the physical to have much pull over me', and that her sexual drive was largely sublimated by her creative passion. She once suggested to Vera 'that we may perhaps make too much of the "enrichment by sexual relations". What if we find with Shaw's Ancients that the true adventure is right outside sex? ... I fall in love with different minds yearly.'

The sexual philosophy she expressed in *Women and a Changing Civilisation* must have appeared outrageously heretical to her more reticent contemporaries of fifty years ago. 'We do not even know,' she wrote, 'though we theorise and penalise with ferocious confidence, whether the "normal" sexual relationship is homo-, bi- or heterosexual.'

This tolerant attitude has led to a suspicion that she may have been, at least embryonically, bi-sexual. Phyllis Bentley, Hilda Reid and Amy Burnett were convinced that this was a misconception, and that Winifred's emotional feelings were inhibited by her long, stultifying entanglement with Harry Pearson. He was the son of a Driffield bank manager, and Winifred had loved him since she was a young girl, but Harry Pearson, feckless and footloose – a forerunner of our latter day 'drop-out' – had no intention of settling down, and Winifred philosophically accepted the limitations of their erratic relationship. In one of her few references to this inconclusive affair she admitted that Harry Pearson was charming, lovable and unstable, and added poignantly, 'I have loved him too well and long to feel no heart-burning'.

The renal sclerosis that led to Winifred's collapse was temporarily arrested, but she continued to have high blood pressure, and sometimes days and nights of sickness and pounding headaches. 'The only poor way I ever repaid her', Vera wrote remorsefully after Winifred's death, 'was that having been a war nurse I *could* hold the basin when she was sick without embarrassing her. I honestly believe that was why she went on living with me. I was the only one of her friends in whose house she could be ill comfortably, and where – having known me for so long – she could completely unbutton her personality when the strain of being the bright daughter or the efficient sub-editor became too much for her'.

Amy Burnett, their housekeeper, and Charlie, Amy's husband and handyman at Glebe Place, were also devoted to 'Miss Holtby', and when she was ill anxiously carried trays of food and pots of tea to her room at the top of the house. 'Oh, Charlie, you shouldn't do this', Winifred protested. 'It's much too much to expect.'

She enjoyed living in a family environment tossed about on its professional and domestic preoccupations. Any prospects she cherished of having children had vanished with her illness, and she delighted in being 'Auntie' to Vera's son and daughter – and in the opportunity it gave her of serving Vera. 'I love the children', she wrote from France in August 1935 as Vera battled at home with the aftermath of her father's suicide. 'They warm my heart and refresh my spirit, and who knows what sort of an academic busybody I might be without them.'

Above all the friendship was an affinity of kindred spirits, and, as Montaigne observed, affinities of this transcendent nobility defy analysis. 'If any man should importune me to give a reason why I loved him, I feel it could not otherwise be explained than by making answer, "Because it was he; because it was I."' Vera might at times be tactlessly outspoken or rampageous, at others reserved, anxious or depressed, but suffering had taught her to look upon the world with a passionate yearning for peace and justice and the happiness of mankind, and with love. 'If Winifred could make her will again in Heaven,' said Hilda Reid discussing the Vera/Winifred friendship, 'I'm sure the first thing she'd do would be to start a Vera Brittain Foundation'.

Winifred returned from France at the end of August, and died in the Elizabeth Fulcher Nursing Home on September 29. Vera was with her the previous day as she struggled to focus her elusive thoughts. 'Remember that I love you dearly', Winifred entreated. 'I'm intensely grateful to you; you're the person who's made me. You've got a mind like steel. It's the most honest mind I've ever known.' Would Vera, Winifred begged, go back that night and help to straighten out the tangles in her mind? 'I think we've discussed everything for the moment', she said as Vera kissed her and went to find Harry Pearson. 'Of course, I can always say I love you, but you will come back tonight, won't you?'

Winifred's death left Vera with a permanent scar. 'For sixteen years we had lived together, with rare intervals, under the same roof', she told Sarah Gertrude Millin ten days later. 'No one has ever been mentally and spiritually nearer to me, nor ever now, I imagine, will be again.'

This shared volume of their selected journalism is a tribute to two outstanding women writers. It commemorates also a wonderful friendship of magnanimity and love.

Winifred's and Vera's journalistic output is astonishing. The bulging files of photocopies of their articles are formidable evidence of their fertility of ideas, their industry and interests, and in making this selection it has been a melancholy task to consign the bulk of their work to the obscurity of the publications in which it first appeared.

Vera and Winifred's friendship was also a partnership of shared ideas, idealism and endeavours. They were both dedicated and active supporters of the women's movement. Part Two, *Feminism*, concentrates upon their individual contributions to continuing and consolidating the work of their suffragette predecessors, and Winifred's lively, satirical articles are a striking contrast to Vera's trenchant, polemic style.

Vera, like Winifred, was a dedicated 'Reformer-sort-of-person', and was well aware that this was how she would be remembered. 'I shall be written off as a pursuer of "causes," ' she wrote a few years before her death, 'which is an insulting way of describing a passion for justice.' The loss of her fiancé and her only brother in World War I, and her nursing experience among the mutilated and dying soldiers from the battlefields of France, precipitated her pacifist convictions, and remained the driving passion behind her lifelong commitment to the fight for peace. Winifred had returned from South Africa in 1926 seething with indignation at the social and political injustice, and worked tirelessly to publicize the plight of the Africans, and to secure effective trade union representation. Many of the articles in Part Three, *Politics*, reflect these predominating themes, whilst others provide an indication of their wider concerns, opinions and beliefs.

Both Winifred and Vera somehow found time for other interests, and the selection of articles in Part Four, *A Writer's Life*, have been chosen to illuminate the personalities of two courageous women whose journalism is not only an eloquent epitaph to their ideals and endeavours, but is also a remarkable testament to the lives and times of a generation.

Paul Berry, West Sussex, 1985

Introduction to Winifred Holtby's Journalism

In her glowing tribute to Winifred Holtby, Lady Rhondda, the founder and editor of *Time and Tide*, revealed how one day she was discussing Winifred's work with 'a famous man' – whom irritatingly she fails to identify. 'That is the most brilliant journalist in London', he told her. 'Why don't you get her for your literary editor?'

During her lifetime Winifred achieved a prestigious position as an influential journalist, and through this work she reached a far wider audience than through her novels. Her ceaseless flow of ideas, her versatility and humour, the perfect amalgam of thought and feeling, gave her work a highly individual and popular appeal. To these talents was added the rare gift of satire, the power to hold simultaneously in the mind conflicting and inconsistent points of view.

Since her death in 1935 it is not as the brilliant journalist that she is remembered, but as the author of *South Riding*, her classic Yorkshire novel in which she captured for future generations the mood and feeling of a particular place at a particular time. In 1981, with clairvoyant faith in Winifred's work, the Virago Press embarked upon the reissue of her five previous novels published between 1924 and 1933. Now that these are again available it is a fitting complement that a selection of her journalism should once more see the light of day.

Winifred's first journalistic success was entirely fortuitous. On a grey December morning in 1914 she was sitting down for breakfast with the other boarders at Queen Margaret's School in Scarborough when a shell fired by a German destroyer landed on the town with a reverberating crash. Such an attack had been anticipated, and, acting upon a warning letter from the head mistress, three-quarters of the pupils had been recalled home. The forty or so girls remaining were precipitately evacuated in orderly if wildly excited crocodile formation. The following day Winifred wrote a graphically exuberant letter to the head girl giving her an account of their adventures. In a flurry of maternal opportunism, Mrs Holtby extracted the letter from the head girl, copied it out, and at her instigation Winifred's eyewitness report was not only prominently featured in the *Bridlington Chronicle*, but was also syndicated in Australia.

From an early age Winifred never doubted that one day she would become a writer. Her unexpected journalistic success boosted her confidence, but as she acknowledges in her autobiographical article 'Mother Knows Best', it was at Somerville that she learned that an essay, and an article, should have a beginning, a middle, and an end, with the facts and arguments clearly and concisely divided in chronological sequence. After leaving Oxford, Winifred and Vera embarked upon their literary apprenticeship. In London, in a whirl of activity, they taught and lectured, they worked for feminist organizations such as the Six Point Group and Open Door Council, and somehow found time to write novels, stories and articles.

As a journalist Winifred was not an overnight sensation. 'The journalistic stunt does not seem to have leaped into success', she informed her friend Jean McWilliam in South Africa. ' … Though I keep on sending out stories, articles and poems they are but homing pigeons.' She didn't have 'the article gift', she told her, and analysed her style as being either too pedantic or too colloquial. She attempted unsuccessfully an article on Charlotte Brontë, but 'I couldn't get it down well enough'. Vera then tried her hand, and to Winifred's delight it was accepted. But Winifred persisted and in 1924 she submitted to *Time and Tide* an unsolicited article entitled 'The Human Factor'. Lady Rhondda, outspoken and dominant, had a sharp eye for gathering around her people of talent and ability, and she realized immediately 'that Winifred Holtby was someone to be reckoned with … I knew that here was someone who counted and whom I must at once get hold of'.

By the autumn of 1918, when it was evident that the war would not last much longer, Lady Rhondda had been speculating on what she would do when her work with the Ministry of National Service came to an end. She had been 'enormously interested' in the birth of the *New Statesman* in 1913, and in a moment of truth she knew that her overruling ambition was to found a weekly review of her own. Before the war she had been an active suffragette, and had gone to prison for setting fire to the contents of a pillar-box in Newport, South Wales. Her magazine, she decided, would be run by women; it would be a forum for feminist opinion and a spearhead of the feminist movement, but, in addition, it would be sufficiently broadly based and authoritative to attract a wide and influential audience. *Time and Tide* was founded in 1920, and her purpose, Lady Rhondda tells us in her autobiography, was 'to mould the opinion, not of the large crowd, but of the keystone people, who in their turn would guide the crowd'.

Lady Rhondda knew Winifred and Vera as speakers and supporters of various feminist organizations, and especially of her own Six Point Group. She was a formidable and lonely woman, and Winifred, she discovered, was one of the younger generation whose company gave her vivid pleasure. She describes her as 'almost always happy, full of humour and gaiety, and with a delicious satiric feeling for life and all its oddities that was a sheer joy to listen to'.

On an overcast January day in 1926, Winifred sailed from Tilbury on a six-month lecture tour of South Africa for the League of Nations Union, and during her absence Lady Rhondda realized what an invaluable colleague and friend Winifred would be on the staff of *Time and Tide*. Shortly after her return to London in July, Lady Rhondda invited Winifred to become a director, and she accepted.

Winifred was by temperament fifty per cent a politician and publicist. 'I shall never quite make up my mind whether to be a reformer-sort-of-person or a writer-sort-of-person', she confided to Lady Rhondda, and this insoluble dichotomy pursued her to the end of her life.

As a journalist she did invaluable propaganda work, and her

position on *Time and Tide* was of great importance in providing unfettered scope for her reforming zeal. She often contributed several items to one issue; a leading article, an essay or story, a book review, and, as an enthusiastic theatre-goer, she was for almost a year the paper's dramatic critic. More of her work appeared anonymously than under her own name. She had a fundamental belief in the value and sanctity of the individual. She did not seek to transform people, but applied herself to the work of setting them free from squalor, ignorance and oppression, from discredited conventions and the insanity of war.

Her articles in the first two sections, 'Feminism' and 'Politics', bear witness to the principal causes to which she devoted her talent, energy and money. Paradoxically, until she returned to Somerville in 1919 at the age of 21 after serving for a year with the Women's Army Auxiliary Corps, she appears to have been almost unaware of the suffragette struggle, or of the continuing feminist demand for equality.

As the precocious, favourite daughter in a comfortably-off middle-class farming family she accepted her idyllic childhood as a matter of course. All the accounts of the Holtby family are dominated by her forceful, dynamic mother; David Holtby is mentioned only fortuitously, almost as if to establish that Winifred was not illegitimate! But if Winifred inherited much of her mother's vitality and public concern, she shared with her father a sense of humour and fun, and a delight in the riotous absurdities of life, which gave her work and personality an exuberant exhilaration. Margaret de Coundouroff, the daughter of Winifred's adopted sister, lived with the Holtbys at Cottingham for many years, and remembers David Holtby as 'a lovely person'. 'I'd call him an amusing saint', she writes, and adds in words that might as aptly be applied to Winifred, 'I used to think that God must be like him, gentle and serene.'

Grace, her older sister, was pliant, undemanding and self-effacing, and there was no brother vying for parental preference. Winifred freely acknowledged that Vera first aroused her allegiance to the feminist cause, and when her book *Women and a Changing Civilisation* was published in 1934 she inscribed on the flyleaf of the copy she gave Vera, 'For Vera, who taught me to be a feminist'. Winifred's support for the feminist cause never wavered, but in *Women and a Changing Civilisation* she looked forward with idealistic longing to a wiser world. 'The real object behind our demand is not to reduce all men and women to the same dull pattern ... We might, perhaps, consider individuals as individuals, not primarily as members of this or that race, sex and status. We might be content to love the individual, perceiving in him or her a spirit which is divine as well as human and which has little to do with the accident of the body. We might allow individual ability rather than social tradition to determine what vocation each member of our community should follow'.

Winifred's absorption in the rights of the Africans stemmed indirectly from her friendship with Jean McWilliam, the officer in charge of the WAAC unit at Huchenneville where Winifred was the hostel forewoman. In 1920, Jean McWilliam was appointed a lecturer in English at Rhodes University, and the friendship was continued with long, uninhibited letters. In her novel *The Land of Green Ginger* Winifred transposes her own emotional feelings for South Africa to her 8-year-old heroine, Joanna. 'To find – the day before Christmas Eve and by lamplight too – the Land of Green Ginger, dark, narrow, mysterious road to Heaven, to Fairy Land, to anywhere, anywhere, even to South Africa ... '

When Winifred visited South Africa in 1926 its beauty enchanted and bewitched her. She was spellbound by the vast blue bay of Cape Town, the dazzling white sand, and Table Mountain towering above the modern city; by sunrise and sunset on the veld; by ostriches dancing among flowering geraniums; by pastel-blue plumbago, and oranges and orange blossom on the same tree. But overshadowing the beauty was the menacing brutality, injustice and oppression. Vera was with her husband at Cornell University at this time, but Winifred knew she would share her indignation and distress. 'The situation here is quite terrible', she told her. 'A huge mass of absolutely helpless people; a few half-educated black leaders, bewildered by modern industrial conditions and perplexed by an inbred inferiority complex when dealing with white men; a large indifferent or hostile white population ... ' She described lodging houses in Johannesburg where men died of phthisis among the drunken brawling of their fellow lodgers, prostitutes spreading syphilis from foul hovels in the back yards of elegant houses, squalid native shacks patched together with paraffin tins, the natives deprived of all legal rights, shut off from industrial expansion, segregated in areas uninhabitable by whites, and performing the most menial, degrading occupations for starvation wages.

For the last nine years of her life Winifred passionately committed herself to the fight for the rights of the five million Africans and 500,000 Coloureds. With the same clarity of vision as Olive Schreiner she recognized the elemental truth that the freedom of all human beings – irrespective of sex, race or colour – is the first essential for the full development of life on earth.

Winifred made two major contributions to the South African struggle. First, she sought to bolster and give new impetus to the Industrial and Commercial Workers' Union, the ICU, which had been founded in Cape Town in 1919. By 1926, under the erratic leadership of Clements Kadalie, this native trades union was drifting towards financial chaos and disintegration. In London, Winifred enlisted support for the ICU from a few sympathetic socialists, and in 1928, largely at her instigation, William Ballinger, a 34-year-old Scottish trades unionist, was selected to go to South Africa as its technical adviser. Winifred was convinced of the need to make Ballinger financially independent of the ICU, and shouldered almost single-handed the onerous task of raising the money to pay his modest salary and expenses. She sought contributions from the Trades Union Congress, the Co-operative Guilds, and the International Federation of Trade Unions. When the Ballinger Fund was exhausted in 1932 she prevailed upon a collection of distinguished sympathizers, including H.G. Wells, Josiah Wedgwood, Bertrand Russell, Bernard Shaw and Archbishop William Carter, to sign an urgent appeal which was published in *Time and Tide* and the *New Leader*. Financing Ballinger's work was a continuous and uphill struggle, and it is now impossible fully to know the extent of Winifred's personal commitment. She paid Ballinger's passage out, and the Fund's only regular income appears to have been her guaranteed support of £100 a year. Vera was one of the few people who recognized Winifred's heavy financial burden. In 1934 she half-seriously suggested giving the Fund ten per cent of the profits from her prospective American lecture tour in return for Winifred's supervision of the children and the Glebe Place household during her absence, and she was surprised by the alacrity with which Winifred accepted.

As well as fund-raising, Winifred took every opportunity to place articles publicizing the native cause, but this was a difficult assignment. Traipsing unsuccessfully from hotel to boarding house in an endeavour to obtain accommodation for Clements Kadalie when he visited London in 1927, she was acutely conscious of the racial prejudice that existed in Britain, and the African cause was not a topic to find favour with the readers of the large circulation dailies. *Time and Tide* provided an invaluable springboard for her work, and as her reputation grew she made the most of her opportunities to place articles with socialist publications such as the *Nation and Athenaeum*, the *Co-operative Review*, and the *New Leader*.

Winifred Holtby was a courageous pioneer in the fight for social and political justice for the black people of South Africa, and at the instigation of her friends in England, supported by the Non-European and Native Affairs Department, the Johannesburg City Council agreed to provide the financial resources for the erection of a Winifred Holtby Memorial Library, 'which would serve native women as well as native men'. Opened in December 1940 in the Western Native Township, it was the first library to be built and equipped solely for the use of non-Europeans. Vera dispatched all Winifred's books on South Africa, and an oil painting of her inscribed 'A Friend of Africans'. Twenty years later most of the Bantu living in the township were moved to Moroka, a suburb of Soweto, and as the library was intended for the people and not for a specific location, it was transferred to a building opposite the Post Office in Moroka in 1963. Sadly, it was destroyed in the unrest and rioting in 1976, and has not yet been rebuilt.

Feminism and South Africa were the major causes to which Winifred devoted constant time and effort. They are the consistent themes running through all her journalism, but her political involvement and wide-ranging sympathies were too catholic to confine her work to these two topics. Until her health broke down in 1932, her personal assignment on *Time and Tide* was to gather home news, and to report on contemporary events and controversies. In the second part of this book, 'Politics', Winifred's opinions of the life and times of the 1920s and 1930s are reflected. They found expression not only in articles, but in leaders and book reviews and, especially, in her inimitable 'Notes on the Way' column in *Time and Tide*.

'Notes on the Way' was a weekly feature of personal commentary on the contemporary scene, and was for several years the prerogative of the playwright St John Ervine. Each article was prefaced with the editorial rubric that 'We must not be taken as necessarily in agreement with the opinions expressed'. When St John Ervine relinquished this commission in January 1932, the column was written for a month at a time by a galaxy of distinguished writers, including E.M. Forster, Stella Benson, Bernard Shaw, Rose Macaulay, Rebecca West, Aldous Huxley, Ellen Wilkinson and T.S. Eliot. Winifred was a regular contributor, and these articles contain some of her most trenchant journalism.

Winifred became a committed socialist only after considerable thought and experimentation. At Somerville, to the amusement of her friends – as Hilda Reid recalled – she was for a term a member of all three political parties, and with magnanimous impartiality attended a Conservative dinner, a Liberal dinner, and a Labour tea! In 1923/24 she worked for Percy Harris, the Liberal MP for Bethnal Green, but her growing awareness of widespread poverty and unemployment and the degradation of the Means Test, of appalling housing conditions, the inadequacies of the social services, and the inequalities of education, led her to support the more radical Independent Labour Party.

Winifred abhorred the deeply entrenched class system, and the assumption of inherited privileges. On one occasion when lecturing for the League of Nations she had a violent argument with her hostess as to whether maids should be treated with haughty reserve or a free and easy camaraderie. Her hostess heartily disapproved of Winifred's liberal attitude, and told her that, as an older woman, she knew better. Winifred retorted spiritedly that she didn't see that age made much difference. 'I've lived among young people, I am one, and I know what they feel like.' 'The hunting and luxury life vexed her,' Mrs Holtby conceded after reading one of Winifred's short stories in which she had satirized with caustic wit some family friends whose idle lifestyle she deplored. 'She criticized their mode of life freely to us,' her mother admitted reluctantly.

In *Time and Tide* Winifred was able freely to express her opinions on contemporary affairs, unhampered by editorial idiosyncrasies, or the necessity to tailor her work for a particular public. As her reputation grew the requests for articles from other newspapers and periodicals increased, and in 1934 from Withernsea, where she was writing *South Riding*, she wrote to tell Vera that the *News Chronicle* had just wired her for a topical article entitled 'A Woman Looks at the News'. 'I'm going to our Post Office to ask the pretty but rather fluff-headed girl if she can rap out a thousand-word wire without fainting', she added. 'They have the old-fashioned tap-morse instrument here and it seems rather cruel.'

Over the years Winifred contributed to more than twenty newspapers, magazines and periodicals. Her miscellaneous work alone would fill several volumes, and making a selection of a mere nine articles for the final section of this book has been a painful task. For several years she wrote a weekly front-page feature for *The Schoolmistress*, the journal of the National Union of Women Teachers, and in one of these she expressed the opinion that for the exalted few 'journalism is an art as well as a profession'. From among her contemporaries she pinpointed Sir Norman Angell, Rebecca West and H.N. Brailsford, an influential leader writer, as her nominees for this particular accolade. On the evidence of the articles included in the last section on 'A Writer's Life' Winifred Holtby herself seems a worthy claimant for the same distinction.

The *Yorkshire Post* and *Manchester Guardian* were the first newspapers to accept Winifred's freelance journalism, and she continued to write for them throughout her life. Later she contributed to the *News Chronicle*, and more intermittently to the *Daily Herald* and the *Evening Standard*. She wrote also for a wide range of periodicals, including the *New Leader*, the *New Clarion*, the

Nation and Athenaeum, the *New Statesman*, the *Realist*, *Nash's Magazine* and *The Quiver*.

She was a regular feature writer for the *Radio Times*, contributing popular scholarly profiles of among many others Chopin, H.G. Wells, and Robert E. Lee – 'The Hero on the Wrong Side' – as well as flippant squibs such as 'Football in the Dining Room' after listening to the 1930 Cup Final, and 'The Secrets of Sago'. 'Her work has the sagacious perception of her native Yorkshire', the editor commented. 'Her only fault as a journalist is that she never gets her manuscripts typed!'

As one of the leading book reviewers of her time the two examples in the final section are a good indication of her penetrating and informative criticism. As well as reviewing regularly for *Time and Tide*, the *News Chronicle* and the *Yorkshire Post*, Winifred succeeded Clemence Dane in 1933 as the literary critic on *Good Housekeeping*, and each month reviewed from 15 to 20 books in discerning articles of more than 3,000 words. She completed her last review the week before she died, and it appeared posthumously the following month.

The seven general articles in the final section reflect vicariously her philosophy and enjoyment of life. 'Mother Knows Best' is included for the Winifred Holtby enthusiasts who have requested any autobiographical work available.

In her Prologue to *Testament of Friendship* Vera relates how five months before Winifred died at the early age of 37 they were discussing the proposal put to her by three separate publishers to write her autobiography. 'I never feel that I've really had a life of my own', Winifred declared. 'My existence seems to me like a clear stream which has simply reflected other people's stories and problems.' On the surface this appears an incongruous statement. She was a brilliant journalist, successful novelist, lecturer, and indefatigable worker for numerous causes; few people have lived fuller or richer lives. And yet, and yet … as Winifred would say. Did she feel, perhaps, that her intense preoccupation with her work, the constant concern and support for her family and friends, had left her no time for a private life or the personal interests which sustain the autobiography?

Most of her contemporaries are dead, but in letters and

conversation a few have left vivid personal vignettes. 'Quite simply', Phyllis Bentley wrote, 'Winifred was the best person I have ever known. When she entered the room it felt as if all the lights had been turned up to blaze higher.'

Norah Martin was engaged by Vera as nanny for her young son, John, and found Winifred 'tremendously friendly and great fun'. She had a lot of African visitors, and 'there were always roars of laughter when they were there'.

Winifred had a gramophone in her bed-sitting-room on the first floor of Nevern Place, and regularly each morning she did exercises to Rimsky-Korsakov's symphonic poem *Sadko*, and the music from the 1928 Drury Lane production of *Show Boat*, including Paul Robeson's famous recording of 'Ol' Man River'. Frequently she collected the 18-month-old toddler from the nursery to do the exercises with her.

In 1930 Amy and Charles Burnett took over the management of the domestic side of the Brittain/Catlin/Holtby household. Amy was the eldest of twelve children of whom only five survived, and her story of poverty and lost opportunities suggested to Winifred the character of Lydia Holly in *South Riding*, the girl from 'The Shacks' who is called upon to sacrifice her scholarship and return home to look after her younger brothers and sisters when their mother dies in childbirth.

Everyone who knew Winifred felt she was a very special person, and Amy was devoted to her. 'I feel very proud to have known her. She was always so kind and gentle, never bad-tempered, and she had a sweet smile for everyone. She wasn't supposed to eat meat but whenever there were guests she wouldn't hear of me cooking something specially for her, and insisted on eating whatever I sent up.'

The Burnetts were married on a bitterly cold day in February 1934. As Amy stood shivering outside the church Winifred stepped forward and, taking off her fur coat, put it round Amy's shoulders. She lent the Burnetts money to buy furniture, and gave them her review copies of books she thought they would enjoy.

'She always seemed to know when I was feeling a bit depressed', Amy confided, 'and would ask me to go to her room to have a heart-to-heart talk, and I felt so much better for it.'

On the morning of Winifred's Memorial Service at St Martin-in-the-Fields several guests were to return to Glebe Place, and Amy was bitterly disappointed at being left behind to prepare the lunch. 'I was in the kitchen feeling very sad and depressed when suddenly I heard Winifred calling me in her lovely soft-toned voice, "Amy, are you there?" I went to the foot of the stairs and looked up. Somehow I felt her presence and I was very happy.' When Amy's daughter was born several years later she christened her Winifred.

Winifred was one of those rare people who gave all those who knew her the uplifting feeling that the world was a better and happier place for her existence. 'She was such fun', people said, almost with one voice.

This gaiety of spirit, like scintillating conversation, is an elusive quality to recapture, and her wit and exuberance are probably best reflected in her novels. Mrs Holtby loathed her daughter's almost Rabelaisian touches of humour, and one can imagine her shuddering on reading Winifred's light-hearted article 'Ssh! Do You Dream About Lions?' in the *Radio Times*. One morning, Winifred related, she innocently remarked at the breakfast table that the previous night she had dreamed of lying on board a boat outside Las Palmas, and eating sixteen bananas before breakfast. 'Instead of saying "Did you? How nice it sounds!" they cried "Bananas? Did you say *bananas*? Oh, my dear!"'

Amy Burnett remembered Winifred rushing from Glebe Place one morning to keep an appointment but reappearing five minutes later to change her hat, and making very ribald comments about the local pigeons and their need for lavatorial training!

On one occasion when Winifred was at home in Cottingham she sympathized with Margaret de Coundouroff, the young daughter of her adopted sister Edith, for the unreasonably low mark she had been given for one of her school essays. 'Never mind', she consoled her, 'I'll write one for you and we'll see how I get on', and they were both highly amused when the essay elicited an almost equally critical assessment.

'What I remember above all', Lady Rhondda declared, 'was that sheer radiance of happiness', and, confusing sanctity with goodness, she said that in her opinion Winifred was a saint.

Vera perceived more clearly than anyone Winifred's valiant fight against illness and pain, and her knowledge of a premature death; her happiness, Vera maintained, was not simply a matter of inherited good fortune, but a spiritual quality which Winifred wrested from life with extra-sensory perception and enormous courage.

Amy Burnett, a woman of perspicacity and total honesty, always referred to Winifred as 'an angel', and an angel the Oxford Dictionary tells us is 'a divine messenger'. In 1985, half a century after her death, Winifred's articles on feminism and South Africa, on war, Fascism and the unemployed, are still relevant, and they reflect Amy's ingenuous definition with uncanny significance.

Paul Berry, West Sussex, 1985

Introduction to Vera Brittain's Journalism

Vera Brittain's career as a journalist was long, prolific and successful. It began before 1921, the year she and Winifred Holtby left Oxford and took a flat in London, and ended in 1968, two years before her death at the age of 76. During those fifty years she published well over a thousand articles, book reviews and open letters (including the two hundred 'Letters to Peace Lovers' of the Second World War), and achieved a reputation as one of England's most effective writers on topics connected with feminism and pacifism, the two causes to which she was most fiercely committed.

From the beginning, her journalism and her political activism were closely linked. In 1925 she told her husband-to-be, George Catlin, that

There is less division than you perhaps think between my literary and political work. The first – as my articles at least must make plain to you – is simply a popular interpretation of the second; a means of presenting my theories before people who would not understand or be interested in them if they were explained seriously.

'The artist and the crusader were inextricably combined' – as she was later to remark about Olive Schreiner, the great 'pioneer' whose pervasive influence on her life and work is so often evident.

Although her first professional article appeared in 1920, Brittain's career did not begin in earnest (she later said) until 1926. 'For the first two or three years of my onslaught upon editorial offices, my journalism, like Winifred's, remained persistent and hopeful rather than progressive.' But they were both also very busy in other directions. Between 1922 and 1924 they published two novels each, and established themselves as dedicated political workers and platform speakers for the League of Nations Union and the feminist Six Point Group – in the process making useful journalistic contacts (notably with Lady Rhondda, founder of *Time and Tide*). During those years, too, they observed League of Nations Assemblies at Geneva and travelled extensively in a Europe still suffering from the ravages of the First World War – experiences embodied by Brittain in the half-dozen articles she published in 1924-25.

Then, just as she was becoming known as a promising new journalist, her marriage to George Catlin, a political scientist and academic, removed her from England to the United States. After she had endured a year of professional frustration there, they decided to attempt 'semi-detached' marriage, and towards the end of 1926 she returned to London to resume her career. 'The work which I had vainly sought in America immediately appeared in embarrassing profusion. ... in six months not one freelance contribution [was] refused.' She was now publishing regularly in *Time and Tide*, and in two major Northern newspapers, the *Manchester Guardian* and *Yorkshire Post*, as well as occasionally in socialist magazines like the *Nation and Athenaeum* and *Foreign Affairs*. A series of articles for the magazine *Outlook* on 'Prospects in Women's Employment' became the basis of a short book, *Women's Work in Modern England* (1928); which in turn led to the commissioning of articles on similar topics for London newspapers like the *Daily Mail* and *Daily Chronicle*. It was a period when journalism, and journalists, flourished.

In later years Brittain published in a very wide range of British newspapers and periodicals (from the *Daily Mirror* to the *Daily Telegraph*, from *Good Housekeeping* to the *Congregationalist Quarterly*), and in other English-speaking countries (especially the United States). Priding herself on being a freelance 'popular' journalist, Brittain sought as wide and varied a readership as possible; but among her finest pieces are some directed necessarily to specialist audiences, or published in 'coterie' magazines to which, unpaid, she would often contribute. For all this diversity, however, she maintained throughout her career the three associations inaugurated in the twenties: with the *Yorkshire Post*, for articles and reviews (1920-67), with the *Manchester Guardian*, for articles (1927-66), and with *Time and Tide*, mainly for reviews (1923-66); adding *Peace News* (then the organ of the Peace Pledge Union) later, for articles and reviews (1938-64). These central, enduring professional associations define the consistency – socialist, feminist, pacifist – threading her journalism from beginning to end.

Her output very quickly reached its peak, in the years 1927-29 (in the latter year alone she published nearly a hundred pieces); and during the following five years (1930-34) she consolidated her reputation with a steady flow of articles and reviews, at an average of over forty a year – despite the very hard work of writing *Testament of Youth*, and the demands of two young children and a busy household. But in 1935, the year of Winifred Holtby's death, Brittain's output suddenly fell to eighteen, its lowest for ten years; and only once during the remaining thirty-four years of her career did it rise above twenty. In fact, considerably more than half of all her articles and reviews were published during the decade 1926-35, although that period is only a fifth of her entire career.

Some reasons for this disparity are obvious enough. From the early thirties her energy was increasingly directed to the writing of long books – like the ambitious novel *Honourable Estate* (1936). She also became ever more deeply involved, from the mid-thirties, in political action – especially in committee-work and speech-making for the peace movement. In April 1937 she complained in her diary: 'Four invitations to speak at peace meetings, two to send messages to "Peace Weeks" ... My life is not my own – and everyone all over the country is doing their best to prevent me being the writer which alone makes me of value to their cause!' Moreover, there was the 'continuing effect of the slump upon freelance journalism': in the thirties 'the once frequently commissioned articles which represented a substantial part of our livelihood' became 'difficult to obtain'. But it also seems very likely that Winifred Holtby's death – depriving Brittain of the loved and respected companion with whom she had worked so closely and creatively for over fifteen years (friendly skirmishes over their articles and reviews had been one of the joys of their relationship) – led her to place less emphasis on journalism.

It is notable, in particular, that the great majority of Brittain's three hundred feminist pieces – which compose the largest thematic group of her articles and reviews – were written before 1935. Though she published two long historical studies – *Lady into Woman* (1953) and *The Women of Oxford* (1960) – in later years she wrote comparatively few articles on feminist topics. This trend had begun before Holtby's death: with the threat of a second world war looming ever more darkly over Europe in the thirties, she wrote more and more frequently about war and peace until, in 1937, pacifist articles outnumbered feminist for the first time – a predominance that continued to the end of her career.

The obvious difficulty of making a representative but necessarily minimal selection from Brittain's thousand articles, reviews and open letters (only about five per cent of which could appear in this volume) was compounded by the very different nature of the two main categories of her journalism. Many of the feminist pieces, written close together early in her career, overlap extensively. They also show, as a group, no striking shift or development of thought – probably less as a result of the narrow time-span than of Brittain's very firm, long-held feminist convictions, and a general decrease of concern and dissension over 'the position of women' in the decades after the vote had been won (an apathy she attacked). On the other hand, they have impressive range, both in topic and tone; and it therefore seemed best to allow theme a stronger role than chronology in determining their arrangement.

Brittain's pacifist journalism, unlike the feminist, runs almost the length of her career: it is the only other extensive thematic category, exceeding the feminist journalism by about fifty pieces if one includes the two hundred 'Letters to Peace Lovers'. Since they show a clear evolution of thought which is of considerable historical as well as personal significance, the selected pacifist pieces have been printed in strict chronological order.

The final group consists of articles, reviews and letters written throughout her career, and on various topics. They are of the type she sometimes called 'a personal impression', and define her complex personality, formative experiences and important relationships; so they have been arranged to outline the course of her life.

The text of each previously-published article has been collated where possible with Brittain's typescript. In a very few instances I have omitted or restored short passages; but I have otherwise resisted all impulses to gild the lily, beyond adding notes to provide additional information intended to be useful.

Vera Brittain was a very careful, orderly writer whose academic training both as literary critic and historian is often perceptible in the manner as well as the substance of her journalism. Her best pieces have a lasting strength and interest. Their characteristic combination of meticulous documentation, firmly logical development, and forceful (sometimes – even now – provocative) opinion, has left an impressive record of her sensitive, intelligent, noble engagement with two of the most important political and social issues of her, and our, time – the subordinated position of women, and the urgent need to achieve lasting peace before irremediable disaster overtakes us and our planet. On both issues she was ultimately (and, at first glance, surprisingly) an optimist – a realistic optimist who, after a full look at the worst, yet believed that the better can prevail.

Her best journalism surely deserves to be placed beside the other literary achievements (very different, but closely related) for which she is now admired around the world: it survives its occasions triumphantly; it offers new readers serious enjoyment, intellectual challenge, and wisdom.

୬

I FEMINISM –
'Why Feminism Lives'

Two linked questions are likely to occur to modern feminists as they read Brittain's selected feminist pieces. The first can be quoted from her fine article 'The Whole Duty of Woman': Have we really advanced so much further today? The second: How *could* she have been so optimistic?

While some of the social and political reforms she advocated in the twenties and thirties have been achieved, others undeniably have not – and change has been slower than she appears to have expected. For instance, equal pay irrespective of sex is still not a reality throughout the workplace, and governments still recoil from enforcing it; and some measures, like the welfare provisions for mothers and children that Brittain considered essential for the full liberation of all women, are now vitiated by cutbacks and the 'new conservatism'. More broadly, some political and social attitudes have altered little, so that women remain under-represented in international, national and local politics, and are still generally expected to bear a heavier familial burden than are men.

On such matters Brittain was neither naïve nor weak, as 'Why Feminism Lives', her trenchant statement on behalf of the Six Point Group, proves. But she was of course a product of her background and experience. A child of the late-Victorian and Edwardian eras, growing up in a suffocating but wealthy home, she assimilated, however unwillingly, some of the opinions and expectations of the privileged middle class. In later life, she set out to understand the much harsher restrictions of working women, and had herself seen the typical accommodation of the 'wage-earning classes' that she excoriated in 'I Denounce Domesticity!' – 'badly-planned, inconvenient little houses which harbour dirt, involve incessant labour, and are totally unequipped with the most elementary devices for saving time and toil'.

But her sincere and informed desire to ameliorate the circumstances of lower-class women cannot conceal the fact that her feminist vision, like that of many feminist leaders in her time, was essentially middle-class. Her comfortable surroundings (with servants to help run the household), her liberated life-style and professional success, all made it difficult not to find hope and assurance in what had already been achieved. And this tendency was strengthened by both a positive, pragmatic temperament and a historian's inclination to measure the present against the past. But her optimism was also characteristic of the 'second-generation' feminists; and we should not discount its benign effects – without it, would she have worked so well for the cause?

When the 'pioneers' won for women the right to vote, the feminist movement, Brittain saw clearly, 'changed its character and became economic' – a natural and logical development, she thought, since women's ability to exploit their new-won political opportunities would depend largely on achieving economic independence 'in a world where money means power'. But persistent social prejudice still pressured women to be subservient, and most women were ignorant about the professions now opened to them (at least theoretically) by the Sex Disqualification (Removal) Act of 1919. So in article after article she urged women to 'overcome their oldest and subtlest enemy, the inferiority complex', and provided helpful practical information about job opportunities and conditions.

While concentrating on this 'economic' feminism – the second phase of feminism, as she saw it, succeeding the suffragists' 'political' feminism – she also worked to promote the third phase, 'social' feminism. This would centre on the social and legal reform of marriage and motherhood, and would become the primary focus of the next wave of feminists. Helping to prepare the ground for 'social' feminism, she published articles (and the short book *Halcyon, or the Future of Monogamy*) attacking traditional views of the institutions of marriage and motherhood, and forcefully advocating reform. To tolerate continuance of the traditional 'career of the home-worker' – unpaid servant of husband and children, in a badly-designed, labour-intensive house – was not only to deprive the woman of her right to self-fulfilment but also her community of the benefits she could bring it through work outside the home.

Here, as so often in her feminist thought and practice, Brittain was echoing Olive Schreiner's *Woman and Labour*. Like Schreiner, too, she recognized the importance of internationalizing feminism – not only to help achieve the liberation of women in other parts of the world, but also to try to secure women's rights through international legislation. She and Holtby had joined Lady Rhondda's Six Point Group in 1922, approving of its very specific 'economic' and 'social' feminist goals (which included equal pay for women teachers and improved legislation for the unmarried mother) and its internationalist orientation. In 1929 Brittain helped to compose, for presentation before the League of Nations Assembly, a Treaty for Equal Rights which aimed to ensure that 'there shall be no discrimination against women in either national or international law'. An enthusiastic member of the Labour Party from 1924, she was also confident that socialism would prevail, nationally and internationally, and would help feminism to its final goals.

But by the end of the twenties Europe was already beginning to darken under the shadow of Fascism and Nazism, and during the thirties Brittain's main endeavours shifted to the urgent task of working for peace. She continued to write occasional feminist pieces, but by 1936 she had become more an observer and recorder of feminist activity than a participant. She warned of the renewed energy of 'anti-feminism' in Hitler's Germany and Mussolini's Italy, and even in her own country; but the few feminist articles she wrote during the war show her confident that, as during the First World War and its aftermath, feminism would continue its advance.

Brittain's feminist theory and practice were clear and direct. For a decade hers was one of the most influential voices attacking prejudice against women (her wittily scathing review 'Men on Women' is representative), and contributing forcefully to public debate on feminist issues. In her 1927 article 'Women in Industry' she straightforwardly but constructively tackled an issue causing controversy and division in the movement; and that article also makes very plain her respect for 'clear and hard facts', her conviction that the effort of digging up information, analysing it, and using it to develop persuasive argument was fundamental to the success of feminism.

Very effective as public speaker and committee worker, she was also, within the movement, a moderate who avoided identifying herself closely with factions involved in disputes that threatened the common cause. During the conflict in the twenties between the so-called 'new' and 'old' feminists (associated respectively with Eleanor Rathbone, the Labour MP, and Lady Rhondda), Brittain was sympathetic, as many of her articles indicate, to the ideals of the 'new' feminists (who stressed women's special needs and aspirations, especially as mothers, rather than the demand for equal rights with men); but she continued to work hard for the Six Point Group. Her feminism represented a creative reconciliation of 'old' and 'new' feminist priorities, both of which she forwarded. Judiciously pragmatic, eclectic, and independent in her judgement, she made a notably positive contribution to the feminist movement of her time and, particularly through her journalism, greatly influenced her successors.

∽

II POLITICS –
'No Compromise with War'

In *Woman and Labour*, Brittain commented, Olive Schreiner had 'emphasized that the women's cause was also the cause of peace' because she recognized that 'women's values were usually, because biologically, creative and constructive'. This conjunction of feminism and pacifism (reasserted recently at Greenham Common) was present in Brittain's life and thought from an early age. When, in her last year at school, she read, 'with an ecstasy still living in retrospect', *'We take all labour for our province!'*, she also read *'We pay the first cost on all human life'* – 'No woman who is a woman says of a human body, "It is nothing!" '

But while her feminism was unwavering from then on, her pacifism evolved slowly, painfully, uncertainly. As a girl of 20 at the outbreak of the First World War, she was swept, like most of Europe, into patriotic militancy: just before Great Britain declared war, she feared that 'our bungling Government will declare England's neutrality', and a few days later she was encouraging her 18-year-old younger brother Edward to join the army. Yet almost simultaneously – and long before the deaths of her fiancé Roland Leighton, two close friends, and Edward – she lamented, in words that echo a passage in *Woman and Labour*, 'I am incapable of feeling glad at such a wholesale slaughter of the Germans ... I can only think of the 25,000 mothers who reared these men with toil ... '

As a VAD nurse from 1915 to the end of the war, she learned in hideous detail about the effects of modern combat:

... I went back to the Hospital – back to one or two dressings that make even me almost sick – that of the man with the hand blown off & the stump untrimmed up, & the other man with the arm off, & a great hole in his back that one could get one's hand into, & other wounds on his leg & sides & head. Poor, poor souls!

She never forgot the suffering she had witnessed – above all, the 'blinded eyes and scorched throats and blistered bodies' of the gassed German soldiers she had nursed at Etaples; and she never forgot, also, how easily she had been caught up in the initial euphoria. But it was not until nearly twenty years later – in 1937, when she joined Canon Dick Sheppard's Peace Pledge Union – that she finally and fully became a pacifist.

In the intervening years, she had of course worked for peace, but until 1928 without any urgency. Then, after publishing the article 'Our Backs to the Wall' (which, despite its flashes of bitterness, is essentially nostalgic), she began a series of Armistice Day meditations in the *Manchester Guardian*; with increasing emphasis, as the international situation deteriorated, using these to warn of the need to work for the prevention of another world war. In this period, too, she wrote *Testament of Youth*, her great 'vehement protest against war'.

Together with Winifred Holtby, she was also working for the League of Nations Union, convinced, like so many in her generation, that the League was the world's great hope for the preservation of civilization; that, through international co-operation, war would be outlawed and outmoded. With the rise of Fascism and Nazism from the late twenties, that hope gave way to disenchantment and fear. The articles Brittain published during 1933-34 are panicky, matching the prevailing mood of the time; she appealed desperately to women, and in 'Why Not a Peace Crusade?' suggested public action of the type used a few years later by the PPU.

By 1937 she had finally abandoned the League of Nations, despairing of its efficacy, and rejecting its increasing reliance on the policy of collective security – a policy exacerbating rather than reducing international tension. In the long article 'No Compromise with War', she persuasively exploited her historical knowledge to bludgeon collective security as a 'compromise with militarism' which 'can lead us nowhere but the edge of the abyss'. She was now 'an uncompromising pacifist', utterly convinced that 'any kind of peace is better than any variety of modern war'. This faith led her into unpopularity and contumely (she said later that it blighted her literary reputation); but she never seriously regretted it.

As Great Britain entered the Second World War, she wrote – angrily, bitterly, but also with characteristic candour, practicality and optimism – to inspirit her colleagues; 'Lift Up Your Hearts!' is perhaps the most moving and deeply felt of all her articles. And throughout the war she worked indefatigably for the pacifist cause, arguing that this was made all the more important by the pacifists' failure to avert the war. During the early period, including the Blitz, she was mainly in London, and quickly published a personal account entitled *England's Hour*: timely and patriotic, it also firmly expounded the 'special function' of pacifists in maintaining 'rational judgements and charitable values' threatened by the conditions of war. From 1939 her 'Letters to Peace Lovers' communicated her views to some two thousand subscribers; and in 1942 she published *Humiliation with Honour*, a pithy exposition of pacifism in the form of letters to her son.

Two particular issues became the focus of her pacifist work: a campaign to 'persuade the Government to allow small quantities of special food to pass through the British blockade to the children, mothers and invalids of the German-occupied Continent'; and a campaign against the saturation-bombing of German population-centres (a policy sanctioned, though never officially, by Churchill and the War Cabinet, and carried out by the RAF's Bomber Command under Sir Arthur Harris). Both of these indiscriminate forms of combat caused widespread death and suffering among defenceless civilians, and Brittain saw them as expressions of the moral decay endemic in war. She became chairperson of the PPU's Food Relief Campaign, and was a founding member of the Bombing Restriction Committee formed by Corder Catchpool; apart from committee-work and speaking-engagements on behalf of both organizations, she wrote articles and pamphlets, and with her booklet *Seed of Chaos* (1944) succeeded in making saturation-bombing a matter of considerable public concern in the United States.

Brittain's pacifism, like her feminism, is very forcefully articulated in her journalism; but within the pacifist community, as within the feminist movement, she was a moderate. Under the stress of war, sharp differences of opinion soured relations, not only between pacifists and some of those who, though not pacifists, worked hard for the same causes, but also among pacifists themselves. The campaign against saturation-bombing was a major cause of such friction, 'absolute' pacifists arguing that war must be opposed absolutely and that opposition to one aspect of it conceded acceptance of the whole. In the midst of this dissension, Brittain was able to work creatively both with 'absolute' pacifists and with those whom she called 'peace-lovers' (like Dr George Bell, the Bishop of Chichester, a leading worker against both the blockade and saturation-bombing). Her arguments in favour of 'humanizing' war are succinctly presented in her reply to George Orwell's attack on *Seed of Chaos*, and are implied, in many articles, by her advocacy of amelioration on the basis of commitment to humane values, and above all to compassion. It was, again, a reasoned and pragmatic position, which allowed her to avoid dissension and to work positively.

As the war ended, she looked both forward and back: forward to urge, passionately, the reconciliation that had not been attempted after the First World War and that was essential, she believed, if a third world war was to be prevented; and back, to the appalling destruction wreaked by saturation-bombing and the blockade, warning of the likely consequences of such profoundly inhumane behaviour. The dropping of atom-bombs on Hiroshima and Nagasaki (preceded by the little-remembered saturation-bombing of Japanese cities) came shortly after she wrote 'Massacre Bombing – The Aftermath', horribly justifying her forebodings – just as recent assessments of the saturation-bombing of Germany have tended to agree with her in rejecting that policy. 'Civilization's Rubicon,' she wrote, 'was crossed when the indiscriminate destruction of persons living within a specified area became a recognized feature of military policy'; once that policy was accepted or tolerated, the use and proliferation of nuclear weapons 'lay in the logic of history'.

But she remained hopeful, during the final two decades of her life, that human beings could still achieve peace in time to forestall a nuclear holocaust. In 1948 she became an energetic chairperson of the Peace Pledge Union (PPU). Ten years later, she welcomed the advent of CND (a movement with philosophical similarities to the campaign against saturation-bombing) as a popular peace movement which might radically shift government policy; and in her seventies she was one of the prominent supporters carried away by the police from a CND sit-in demonstration at Trafalgar Square. In 1961 she defended the aggressive methods used by the Committee of 100 to 'capture public imagination' – methods similar to those she had advocated in the thirties, and reminiscent of the successful campaign waged half a century earlier by the suffragettes.

She knew, none better, how urgent is the cause of peace in our time; and she knew that, as in the long battle for women's rights, optimism and confidence, not pessimism or despair, were needed for success. Always capable of adjusting creatively to changed circumstances, she maintained for nearly thirty-five years, with the support of a strengthening religious faith, the vigorous certitudes of her pacifism. It can be peace: no compromise with war.

∽

III 'A WRITER'S LIFE'

And what was she like? Her husband remembered her as 'shy and withdrawn, preferring one or two friends to many acquaintances'; as 'one of the most single-minded and conscientious women I have ever known'. And Winifred Holtby saw her as 'a person whom life has battered':

… but never for a moment does she give way, nor lose her sweetness, nor her tenderness for suffering, nor an imagination which is constantly trying to devise ways for protecting other people from the sorrows she has known.

Those of us who could not know her, and admire deeply her

42

courageous, principled life and achievements, can of course learn much about her from her autobiographical books, and can 'infer much from her other writings. Among these, her journalism is most revealing, since it ranges through her writing-life and contains, scattered amongst it, a number of explicitly autobiographical or semi-autobiographical pieces. These describe various experiences (some traumatic, others in themselves trivial), define the importance of particular influences and friendships, and imply a character of great complexity.

It is no accident that the word 'friend' recurs frequently, even in the titles of these pieces. Although her shy intensity sometimes made her seem abrasive or remote, she gave herself throughout her life in close friendships. The article 'Christmas and Friendship' sympathetically, unassumingly, and with typical practicality implies her joy in her friends.

Always central in Brittain's character, as Winifred Holtby recognized, was a strong sense of social duty – an extension of friendship to the wider community. This is certainly apparent in her journalism (for instance, in the forceful but balanced indignation of 'Tragic Watershed'). But other important characteristics are also present: a sense of humour, less frequent and ebullient than Holtby's, but well illustrated in 'The Seeing Eye' – where it is directed against another characteristic, her 'instinct for tidiness'; a warm appreciation of humane behaviour and devotion to duty in her fellows (from King George VI in 'Memorial Queue' to the taxi-driver of 'Casualty'); and this list could easily be extended.

But most striking of all, I think – and most fundamental – are the linked characteristics of optimism and religious conviction. Brittain wrote of Winifred Holtby's work for peace that it 'rested upon a deeply religious principle'. The same must be said of her own work to ameliorate the human condition. As a girl she had been intensely but rebelliously religious, believing that Christ 'was man, even as we are, and that his divine nature is the same in quality – though greater in degree and realization – as our own'. 'The Kind of God I Believe In' expounds her unorthodox but strongly held faith in its final form. God, she asserts, is not an 'anthropomorphic Old Testament deity' but an immanent force of wisdom, 'the indwelling spirit of truth and goodness'. This belief justifies an ultimate optimism, since, in spite of 'such evil deeds as obliteration bombing and the starvation of Europe', human beings have within them 'essential goodness – a goodness which could transform the world if they worked with the God within them instead of blindly joining His enemies'. It is a faith that finely harmonizes her life, personality and achievements.

Alan Bishop, 1985

PART TWO

Feminism

Winifred Holtby

'FEMINISM DIVIDED'

On returning this week from South Africa, my attention was directed to several significant signs of a reawakening of Feminism from the six years' lassitude which followed the partial success of 1919. Among other things, I was shown Mrs Hubback's interesting article on 'Feminism Divided,' in the *Yorkshire Post* of 12 July. Mrs Hubback sees among feminists two schools of thought – the Old Feminists, who view with misgiving any 'decline from the pure milk of the word' of 'equality of liberties, status and opportunities between men and women,' and the New Feminists, who believe that 'the satisfactory solution of these points is undoubtedly in sight,' and that 'the time has come to look beyond them.' They have, therefore, included in their programme reforms such as family allowances, birth control, and similar policies affecting the lives of 'women who are doing work that only women can do,' together in some cases with causes of more general interest such as peace by arbitration.

The division concerns both the aims and policy of the feminist movement, and superficially the New Feminism appears more tolerant, sane and far-sighted. Old Feminism, with its motto, 'Equality First', and its concentration upon those parts of national life where sex differentiation still prevails, may seem conservative, hysterical, or blindly loyal to old catchwords. This is not the real truth. The New Feminism emphasizes the importance of the 'women's point of view', the Old Feminism believes in the primary importance of the human being.

Of course, sex differentiation is important; but its influence on human life is unlikely to be underestimated, and the Old Feminists believe that hitherto it has been allowed too wide a lordship. It belongs to the irrational, physical, and emotional part of a man's nature, where it holds almost undivided sway; but the experience of the past six years alone has taught us that in politics and economics, W.S. Gilbert was as good a psychologist as Freud. Politically, every child born into the world alive appears to be a little Liberal or a little Conservative, irrespective of sex. Educationists have proved that their inclinations are towards science, arts, sport, and manual work. The economic history of the war proved the same disrespect of persons, male and female, for industrial efficiency. Hitherto, society has drawn one prime division horizontally between two sections of people, the line of sex differentiation, with men above and women below. The Old Feminists believe that the conception of this line, and the attempt to preserve it by political and economic laws and social traditions, not only checks the development of the woman's personality, but prevents her from making that contribution to the common good which is the privilege and the obligation of every human being.

Personally, I am a feminist, and an Old Feminist, because I dislike everything that feminism implies. I desire an end of the whole business, the demands for equality, the suggestions of sex warfare, the very name of feminist. I want to be about the work in which my real interests lie, the study of inter-race relationships, the writing of novels and so forth. But while the inequality exists, while injustice is done and opportunity denied to the great majority of women, I shall have to be a feminist, and an Old Feminist, with the motto Equality First. And I shan't be happy till I get it.

The Old Feminist policy of concentration appears, therefore, to have three great advantages. It is not so sanguine as that of the New Feminists, who believe that 'the satisfactory solution of these points is undoubtedly in sight.' I have read Lord Birkenhead's speech during the debate on the admission of peeresses to the House of Lords. I have just returned from South Africa, where women have no vote for members of the Legislative Assembly. I have followed the policy of the International Labour Organization with regard to 'protective' legislation for women workers. We shall find our satisfactory solution if we work for it, work hard, work with sacrifice, and buy our freedom with untiring vigilance. The Old Feminism, as conceived by such societies as the Six Point Group, the National Woman's Party in America, summons us to this work.

Secondly, Old Feminism has the merit of the definite object. Two-thirds of the failures and tragedies of political life come from divided loyalty. For a single cause, the defence of their country, the destruction of tyranny, and so forth, a million people may venture life and limb. But for an extended programme of reform it is not easy to evoke loyalty. Men will either hate the one and cleave to the other, or they will give a tepid acquiescence to all, which is worth nothing. Political parties necessarily present unwieldy programmes. They succeed when they discover one really good war-cry. The great value of societies, whether they work for international peace, family endowment, equality between men and women, or the rest, lies in their disentanglement of a single issue from the complexity of political and economic interests. They make sincerity possible.

And, thirdly, the Old Feminism restricts to as small a field as possible the isolated action of women, in order that elsewhere both sexes may work together for the good of the community. When liberty and equality of action and status for men and women has been obtained, then all other reforms, including those rearrangements of domestic life, such as family allowances, concern sons and husbands as well as mothers and daughters. It would be a grave mistake if they appeared to an easily misguided public as purely women's reforms, in which a few kindly and philanthropic men took a measure of gracious interest.

The Old Feminists have also looked ahead, beyond the achievement of the reforms for which they are now working. They also have their vision of society, a society in which sex-differenti- ation concerns those things alone which by the physical laws of nature it must govern, a society in which men and women work together for the good of all mankind; a society in which there is no respect of persons, either male or female, but a supreme regard for the importance of the human being. And when that dream is a reality, they will say farewell to feminism, as to a disbanded but victorious army, with honour for its heroes, gratitude for its sacrifice, and profound relief that the hour for its necessity has passed.

Yorkshire Post, 26 July 1926
Reprinted in Time and Tide, 6 August 1926
(By courtesy of the Yorkshire Post)

❧

LADIES FIRST

When a publisher recommends the 'strong human interest' of a new novel, its readers may be warned that they are unlikely to encounter cheerful fiction. The Annual Report of the Chief Inspector of Factories and Workshops for 1923 has 'strong human interest', and the warning holds good. A record of accidents, poisoning and crowded workshops is inevitable when only the exceptional is recounted in detail, and bears witness to good already achieved as well as to reforms still needed; but here and there an ominous passage occurs, which arouses attention by its very lack of emphasis. Especially is this true of the section devoted to women's employment. Here the report states: 'There is a general consensus of opinion that the reversal of the process which was so striking a feature of war-time industry is now practically complete. Women have returned to women's industries, and very few of them are to be found even in those sections of men's trades for which war-time observation showed them to be peculiarly well fitted. Those who do remain have been retained as survivors of a vanishing period, and, although they will not be dismissed, they will be succeeded as they marry or retire, by men.'

The distinction between men's and women's trades is peculiar. It does not apparently depend upon the amount of physical exertion required. The Report itself testifies that women are still being employed upon the manufacture of slag wool and sanitary pipes, the former being an unpleasant, the latter an exhausting process, involving the lifting of heavy weights. On the other hand, women are disappearing from the lighter and better-paid processes, such as certain operations in glass works and oil-cake

50

mills. The explanation lies, not in the work itself, but, like the whole problem of women's industrial position, in the history of the past hundred years.

During the Industrial Revolution men, women and children were employed indiscriminately in fields and factories, mines and mills. The Factory Acts and the changing social conscience of the nineteenth century, removed the women not only from those industries for which they were physically unfitted, such as mining, but, again indiscriminately, from nearly all the better-paid branches of skilled manufacture. At the opening of this century a movement was taking place by which women were slowly returning to certain processes for which their greater delicacy of touch and manual dexterity were required, but the custom of paying them at a lower rate than the men operatives caused them to be, however unwillingly, a danger to the solidarity of organized labour, and prevented their participation in the full advantages of trades unionism. During the war the absence of many of the men and the reorganization of industry upon a new basis opened a door through which the women were implored to enter. They entered. The war lasted for four years. War-time industrial conditions lasted for nearly six. Then, almost as quickly as they had arisen, they came to an end. The door shut again, and women are vanishing from 'men's trades'.

The reversal process is due, not to a single cause, but to a fourfold movement. First of all, in 1919 the demand for munitions, army stores, equipment and so forth, came to an end. War-time industries had to be reconverted to their original condition. Disorganization caused an inevitable fluidity of labour, during which many women lost their work, when their employers, in arranging staff reductions, acted upon the old courtesy adage of 'Ladies First'.

Secondly, those men who had been drafted from industry into the fighting forces returned to civilian life. Here was a perfectly clear issue. The man who had fought was entitled to the work that he had left. Nobody grudged to him this obvious justice, though it was perhaps recognized a little less clearly in the case of the ex-service woman.

The return of the soldier was, however, only one and

comparatively small contributory cause of the exclusion of women from industry. There followed, thirdly, upon the disorganization of industry and the return of ex-service men, the trade slump and the consequent general decrease of demand for labour. Both men and women found their work endangered, even among those who had obtained places in the reconverted peace-time industries. The unemployment affecting both men and women, brought about by the trade slump, was the cause of far more loss of position to the women than their replacement in some cases by returned soldiers, a point frequently overlooked.

During former crises of similar nature, a slump in trade has been followed by a general reduction in real wages; but the organization of the workers through trades unionism has acted upon the principle that it is less disastrous to the community as a whole for a few people to be employed at high wages, than that many should be employed at a starvation rate. Here entered the fourth issue. The trades unions having decided upon a perfectly sound policy of a few workers and well paid, had to determine who those workers should be. The unions had been formed at a time when women's part in industry had been small. They were organized, inspired and led by men who had struggled and sacrificed for labour solidarity. The women in most cases only entered them by courtesy after the foundation work had been done. In those cases where women, such as Miss Bondfield, have attained to great eminence in the Labour world, they have done so as the representative of the trades union movement as a whole, and not of the women in the unions. Consequently, when the question arose of who was to stay in and who to go out of the industries, it was almost inevitable that the cry should again be raised of 'Ladies First'.

The women had no organization to strengthen their position. They could not claim that by their rate of wages they were maintaining the 'standard of life'. They had not the leaders to make their position clear.

They had, instead, to fight upon an issue clouded continually by sentiment and prejudice. The real claim of the ex-servicemen became the stalking horse for hundreds whose national service had been no more exacting than that of the industrial women, but who, like the women, found themselves in jeopardy through the trade slump. The old, deeply-rooted feeling that women ought not to be in industry at all, combined with the perfectly justifiable, but indiscriminately applied, sense of gratitude to the ex-soldier; together they formed an effective smoke-screen behind which many men gained places which, in open competition, they could not hold against the women. The delusion that women have merely lost their places to ex-service men is completely shattered by the words of the Report where it refers to the substitution process as being continuous, since those women who 'have been retained as survivors of a vanishing period ... will be succeeded as they marry or retire, by men.'

The way out of the difficulty seems to have been found by another class of women, although they have yet by no means succeeded in reaching their goal. The doctors, teachers, lawyers, civil servants and other professional women whose position was improved during the war, have not now lost all their advantages, in spite of a scrupulous recognition of the claims of the soldier. They realized that while men and women start upon an unequal basis, the same organization is unfitted to deal with both their needs. While women are paid lower than men in mills and factories, their competition must be a danger to be combated by the unions, in spite of continual and sincere attempts at co-operation. They entered the unions late, and entered them weak, and modern economics do not recognize the law of the eleventh hour.

The professional women realized that they must form their own unions. The National Union of Women Teachers, the Union of Women Civil Servants, were the result of continued failure of women to make their voices heard effectively in unions established and controlled by men. They were formed, not because the interests of men and women in industry are antagonistic, but because their present position is so unequal that the same organization will not hold both. Directly men and women within an industry stand upon an equal footing, their interests will be identical, and one union can include them both.

Really, the whole position hangs again upon the old problem of equal pay for equal work. While women accept lower wages and humbler positions for equal work, the unions must fear their competition and condone their exclusion. When they have obtained, through persistent organization, an effective recognition of the principle that work must be rewarded simply according to its merits, then the grounds for sex-differentiation and consequent sex-antagonism in industry will have been eliminated.

Time and Tide, 8 August 1924

ᔊ

COUNTING THE COST

Chance threw into my hands yesterday two journals published by women's organizations: a Women's Institute journal from England and the Journal of the American Association of University Women. Turning the pages of the English paper I came across an indignant letter signed 'A Mere Man', in the way that indignant men will sign when they wish to indicate that they are something so much more than mere. 'Mere Man' was furious with the Women's Institute because in his district 'there are thirty-seven engagements in six months, and no mention is made of committee meetings, classes for folk-dancing and for handicrafts. In a little country town the Institute has held a summer fête, a jumble sale, a tombola, and a two-day indoor fête within six months.' He says that this is all very well for the wives. 'I know how much the Institute has meant to the average country woman.' But the things which the husbands say about the Institute are 'unprintable'. 'Surely a married woman's place is at home when the man comes home from work. If I came home from work at six (which I don't) and had to get my own tea, things would happen.'

He really is very cross indeed. He makes you feel that the first of those things which would happen would be a very bad tea. Bad temper never fries good bacon. He is one of that still extensive number of husbands who feel themselves entitled to the full-time services of whatever woman they have married, and if wives aren't waiting in the home with tea ready at the very moment when their husbands appear at the door they'll larn 'em.

Local authorities, private employers, and wives themselves

frequently encounter similar stalwart champions of the Cause of Husbands. Theirs not to reason why: theirs but to demand that the wives do or die, lest six o'clock tea, carpet slippers, and the warm wifely welcome should perish from the home. And, indeed, it may be true that a man who marries a woman on the express understanding that he will pay for her if she will be his housekeeper has a grievance when he finds the housekeeping neglected and the wife at a tombola. It may be so. Yet I rather think that 'Mere Man' gives the case away when he confesses that he knows how much the women's institutes have done for women. If they have satisfied a need among the country women something must have been lacking in their lives before, and no woman leading an incomplete, stunted sort of life is going to make a really admirable wife.

It happened that in the American University Women's Journal an article appeared which provided an interesting comment upon this wrathful husband. It was a summary by Anne Byrd Kennon of reports collected by the Research Department of the Women's Educational and Industrial Union of Boston on college wives who work. The union had set about its job in the thorough, unsentimental fashion typical of the modern American university. No nonsense here about the finer shades of ethics or the domestic traditions of a great nation. It put facts first, theories afterwards, and conclusions very far behind, instead of shouting out the conclusions first and filling in the subsequent gaps with bluster. From four big groups of university women the union collected evidence about 11,474 women graduates; 3,833 of these had married, and 12 per cent of the married women worked outside the home. There follow imposing statistics of the degrees held, hours of work, and types of employment. Office managers, teachers, insurance salesmen, chemists, dressmakers, research workers, welfare supervisors, doctors, scenario writers, and bookkeepers are among the cases examined. Some women have children; some have not. Some work with their husbands, as college teachers, doctors, lawyers, and business partners. Others pursue entirely different activities.

But beside these figures, useful and interesting though they may be in showing salaries, jobs, and chances of promotion, the union has collected a considerable body of material based upon opinion. How far has the combination worked? How far is it satisfactory? What is the price paid by those households for the liberty of wives to work?

There are some mothers who find it difficult to give adequate attention to young children. One writes: 'This is not a satisfactory way of living. It is detrimental to my little girl. However, we manage better since she is in school.' One mother gets up early, bathes and dresses two babes, gives them their breakfast, and leaves at eight o'clock, when the nurse arrives. She gets her own breakfast in town, teaches all day, eats supper in town, and returns at seven to find her nurse with her wraps on ready to leave. These are the mothers who have not been able to evolve any very practical arrangements for their nurseries. A resident nurse would solve the second problem; the first seems to be answered by a mother of six children who teaches in the music department of a college. She writes: 'I enjoy teaching music, and I am not a brilliant success as a housekeeper. I have an excellent Bohemian woman to do the cleaning and cooking. I think perhaps the children enjoy the music more than they would enjoy me if I had let my music slip and devoted myself mainly to housework.'

As for the husbands, their opinions seem to vary. Of course there is a difference between the wife who devotes herself wholly to her husband's comfort and the wife who is following a career of her own. One Boston teacher says that though she could teach and look after her child quite easily she could not do this and play bridge and amuse her husband and his men friends in the evening. The report concludes that for a happy combination of a professional pursuit and married life six things are necessary – the husband's active co-operation, health, adequate household assistance, training before marriage, adjustable hours of work, and various arrangements for the children; and of these perhaps the most important is the husband's co-operation.

Why should he co-operate? our angry he-husband might inquire. Why should he voluntarily lose a hostess, an entertainer, a devoted slave? Probably because he has counted the cost and found it well worth while.

If the cost of these joint marriages includes less leisure for the mother to spend with her children, on the credit side must be reckoned the advantage to the father. The husband of a full-time mother rarely goes near the nursery. It is wholly his wife's department; it is her job in life. And thus he looses much joy in his own children. But the husband of a professional woman has great fun in the nursery. He often becomes proficient with baths and toys and prams and drying-rails. He may even be the first discoverer of a newly cut tooth, the first to hear a newly spoken word. He can hold forth learnedly on Montessori methods, Freudian theories and educational experiments.

No change in our social or economic habits is made without some loss. As every year more wives in England and America go out to learn their living, as those who are housekeepers by profession find more interests outside the home, we may at first pay by loss of some airs and graces of social intercourse, some elegance, some comfort. It is absurd to ignore the cost. The real question to ask is: Are the gains worth while? Freedom to develop individual talents, the use by society of the best minds to serve her, co-operation in intelligent work, equality of the sexes, the gradual disappearance of the whole system of snobbery created by the hierarchy of leisured women? Are not these worth a little discomfort, even to the 'Mere Man' whose six o'clock tea may sometimes be a few minutes late?

Manchester Guardian, 23 November 1928

∽

SHOULD A WOMAN PAY?

This article is not what it appears to be. My vision of the Woman Who Pays is not your vision; at least, it is not yours if yours is the same as mine was twenty years ago. I remember the idea. A snowstorm outside a baronial castle. Seen through the lighted windows, the young heir drinking champagne with his haughty family. Outside, the heroine, in a shawl, preferably holding a baby, with the snow falling on her upturned face, and a voice singing somewhere in a Cockney accent:

It's the same the whole world over,

It's the poor as gets the blame;
It's the rich as gets the pleasure,
    Isn't it a blinking shame?

'The Woman Pays', they told us on posters outside the Repertory Theatre, on the early cinema screen, in the novelette.

Today, though the problem has nothing to do with babies and baronets, it still really touches the deep springs of human instinct. Today the vision evoked by the phrase is certainly different. Jack and Jill, young, smart, efficient, he from a motor agency, she from an office, meet for lunch in a city restaurant. Her salary is probably quite as large as his. It may even be steadier if he works largely on commission. They order the lunch, eat it, enjoy themselves, call for the bill. She produces her bag. 'No, no, my dear Jill; certainly not. I asked you.' 'But, Jack, you paid last time; it's my turn.' 'I couldn't possibly. Put your bag away; I shall be dreadfully offended.' 'But look here, Jack. This is absurd. I like meeting you at lunchtime. It is much more fun than lunching alone. But I can't let you pay for my lunch every time. It isn't fair and it isn't right. It embarrasses me horribly. Please, please, be sensible, and just let us meet as friends and each pay for our own, or else take it in turns to pay for both.'

But no, he will not. All his masculine honour is affronted. He grows dignified, sulky, obstinate, and she becomes desperate, cynical, reckless. He says he does not know what women are coming to. She says that men are quite impossible and that their friendship is spoilt and that she won't be treated as a parasite. And so they part, and he tramps back to the motor showroom, and drops a nut into the intestines of a car, while she boards her bus back to the office, makes two mistakes in a report on the last General Purposes Sub-committee; and they both hate everything.

Something has got to be done about it. All over the country, in schools, work-shops, offices, and showrooms, girls are earning, some quite as much as their brothers, friends, and husbands, some much more, some only a little less. The demand for 'equal pay for work of equal value,' incorporated into the Peace Treaties as a fundamental principle of economic settlement, does not merely concern the pay roll of a Government or private firm. However little the principle is yet practised, however hard the feminists have still to fight before they see the ideal of the Peace Treaty incorporated fair and solid into the four corners of a statute-book or the budget of a private company, the thing is coming. Women have gone out into the labour market. They are asking that they shall be paid according to their achievements, not according to their sex, and certainly one day they will get what they demand.

Meanwhile the ethics of social encounter reflect the economics of an earlier epoch when all women were theoretically dependent upon masculine finances. It is not an immemorial custom. In the Old Testament women are hostesses. It was Jael who entertained Sisera, and Deborah who sang of them, 'He asked water, and she gave him milk. She brought forth butter in a lordly dish.' Remembering what Jael did next, we may say that the precedent was not wholly fortunate; but the fact remains that in the ancient East, and in mediaeval Europe, women quite frequently entertained their friends.

The system of masculine entertainment came in with the industrial revolution, the introduction of factory labour, the divorce of women from domestic industry, and the consequent subjection of ill-organized unskilled labour in mines and factories and private houses. The woman who worked had no money to spare for entertainment. The middle-class woman who did not work had no money at all. Again and again we encounter stories of the extraordinary situation of women living in large houses, with armies of servants, tremendous meals, and wardrobes full of clothes, and not two sixpences to rub together for their own use. Arnold Bennett's brilliant short story, 'The Murder of the Mandarin', tells only too truly of Mrs Cheswardine, with her 'elaborate and costly frock', her champagne, her adoring husband, 'the best-dressed woman in Bursley', who in order to buy a silver belt to decorate her ball-dress – price one guinea – has to attempt the murder of a mandarin.

When women possessed no money, men, of course, had to pay for them. And the men liked it. It made them feel strong and protecting and benevolent and gave them most agreeable sensations of superiority. These are excellent psychological reasons why it is more blessed to give than to receive. A waitress, recently asked why she always handed the bill to the man in a mixed party, said 'Oh, but it's the man's privilege to pay.'

But not all men liked it. Mr Shaw has said that one of the results of the new economic position of women is to disclose the fact that quite a number of men prefer to be kept by somebody else also. Among people of both sexes are the independent, who like to pay for themselves and to entertain others, and the dependent who are quite content to be kept and petted and paid for. Carried to extremes, both types are tiresome. The only sensible way out of the difficulty is to drop this sentiment about 'a man's privilege'. If some women still think that any man, however ill he can afford it, ought to pay all bills for entertainments, it is time they learned the new code. If some men feel affronted, insulted, and dishonoured every time a woman pays, it is time that they dropped their ridiculous pride and prejudice and learned to share and share alike.

We are eating increasingly at restaurants. Men and women are increasingly free to go about together. It is absolutely necessary, unless we want to live in a nightmare world, to drop these anachronisms of custom. Differences of income will continue to exist; they may continue to complicate entertainment. But it is quite time that we recognized the irrelevance of sex to the question of 'Should a woman pay?'

Manchester Guardian, 21 December 1928

∾

THE MAN COLLEAGUE

Sir Alfred Hopkinson, MP, retiring member for the English Universities, has delivered himself of a profound valedictory statement. 'In many ways,' says he, 'I think the modern girl of today is brilliant ... But in spite of her brains I cannot somehow ever imagine a woman Prime Minister. There is something lacking in her which a man leader has. It is perhaps what I should call mental tact. She is too interfering and unable to take things as they come without a lot of fuss as a man will ... It is this rather obstinate interference which I rather dread.' Sir Alfred represents a constituency where men and women co-operate as colleagues.

Before Oxford and Cambridge opened their administrative offices and councils to women both sexes enjoyed the freedoms of the younger universities. Men and women there work together in the laboratories, follow each other to the lecture-halls, and discuss examination questions in the senior common rooms.

But there has not yet been a woman Vice-Chancellor of Manchester or Sheffield University, and Sir Alfred does not think that there will be a woman Prime Minister of Great Britain. The wish is probably father to the thought.

All over England today men and women are working together in factories and on farms, in shops and offices and theatres and consulting-rooms. But it is nearly always the man who sits at the big desk with the telephone and the woman who sits at the little table with the typewriter. The company director employs a woman secretary, the male doctor an assistant, the lawyer a clerk. The butler lords it over housemaids and laundresses. The chemist has a girl dispenser and another girl at the cash desk. And so long as the men give the orders and the women obey them all goes well. There are, of course, still occasional outbursts of absurdity, as when recently certain London hospitals declared that the presence of women medical students upset the aspiring male doctors and put them off their football; but on the whole the co-operation of men and women seems to work well enough.

Very few men even today admit openly that they enjoy working with women, though at heart quite a number think it rather pleasant to have tea brought into the office by a nice little typist, or to see the charming irrelevance of flowers on the desk, or a daffodil-coloured hat hung behind the door on a spring morning. Generalizations are here, as ever, foolish. Some men still obviously feel profound embarrassment in the presence of a woman who is neither wife nor housemaid. But these are increasingly the exception. For the most part women enjoy working with men. They feel no shame in their confession. Women have never disliked men as men have quite often seemed to dislike women. They find the men kind, ready to give advice, competent, conversational, and, on the whole, discreet. But not silent. The myth that women are more talkative was invented by the garrulous sex to cover their own extravagances. I have worked with men in offices and on committees, and it has never been my women colleagues who held up my work while they argued furiously about the cup-tie or the possibility of Absolute Law until just ten minutes before we had to dispatch the mail. When during the war I worked for a short time with a mixed land gang, it is true that at first the girls talked rather more than the men as we mended roads or cleaned turnips; but after one of the young men had been crossed in love the slow stream of his grievance flowed from sunrise to sunset, over the broad backs of the ewes or the bent heads of his colleagues indiscriminately. As for academic men, their lectures to their students have a predetermined end, but their lectures to their women colleagues go booming along from the first moment of introduction till the final hour of parting. This passion for imparting information to females appears to be one of the major male characteristics.

Still, it is quite possible to hazard the generalization that nice men make agreeable colleagues if – and here the proviso is so big that it changes the whole aspect of the situation – they are in a position of unquestionable superiority. Directly the possibility arises of having to take orders or money or criticism from a woman the friendly atmosphere evaporates and a chill raw breath from the Old Cave creeps in, fetid with decaying prejudices and the blood and bones of old conflicts. It takes a man of almost superlative civilization and intelligence to accept orders gracefully and naturally from a woman.

Why are women, in spite of the promises of governments, still debarred from all executive posts in the Civil Service except those rare ones which leave only women under their command? Why has only one woman been made head of a department in the League Secretariat at Geneva, and that only under protest and at a lower salary than her male colleague? Why are the heads of mixed council schools almost invariably men? Why are women business directors almost wholly confined to the proprietors of acknowledged 'women's' businesses, such as dressmaking or catering? Because men find it beneath their dignity to regard a woman as their superior. They find something a little comic about it. The woman boss is a matter for comic pictures and music-hall jokes and sly banter. Even among the most generous and civilized of men the consciousness of ignominy in accepting money or orders from a woman makes itself felt in the most unexpected places. The Old Adam is continually breaking out and making both sides self-conscious.

A prejudice so old and so deeply rooted is not easy to explain. Its deepest roots undoubtedly lie in the sex instinct, which demands an active, dominating male and a passive, accepting woman. Until intelligent men are prepared to face this fact, and to recognize that their dislike of 'women leaders' arises largely from their encouragement of the sex instinct to cross over from its proper place into what should be the neutral ground of the office or the parliament, we shall get no farther in removing the most fundamental difficulty. But besides this there is the prestige game, which men play with so much more interest than women. Generations of struggle and dignity and ambition lie behind the man, who likes to give high-sounding names to his position, to surround it by impressive ritual, and to assume an attitude of grave circumspection towards it. Not so the woman, with generations of getting the housework done and the children fed without much trouble about appearances behind her. And it is tiresome for the dignified male to work under the woman who cares more for the job than for its dignity.

So men like Sir Alfred Hopkinson find that women lack mental tact and are too fussy; and women find that men are absurdly pompous even when they are not jealous. But every mother who brings up a son in a nursery ventilated by the fresh air of equality does something to remove these difficulties, and every woman who does her work so well that honest men are forced to respect it does something else. Men and women colleagues have much to learn from each other, and need all their honesty and intelligence to win the battles of this sex war – a war not of one sex against the other, but of both sexes against the hidden instincts and prejudices which spoil their free relationship.

Manchester Guardian, 24 May 1929

THE WEARER AND THE SHOE

Our proverbs have a habit of playing us false. They are at best the aphorisms of a rough-and-ready philosophy which may or may not be appropriate to the occasion on which we make use of them. 'Look before you leap' has been an excuse for inaction as often as it has been a protection against folly. 'Blood is thicker than water' – a singularly irrelevant consideration – has served as a justification of that clannishness which puts family interests before social sense. Because proverbs represent folk-wisdom they echo the sentiments of mediocrity and the guides for a rule-of-thumb conduct. They do not take the long view or the broad vision, and it would be stupid to expect these of them.

We should remember this limitation of proverbial wisdom when listening to the wiseacres who comment on the result of the ballot announced this week by the Civil Service Clerical Association. Nearly seven thousand girls, mostly in the lower grades of the Civil Service, answered the questions submitted by their association relating to the problems now vexing the Royal Commission on the Civil Service. To the question 'Are you in favour of the retention of women in the service after marriage if the marriage gratuity thereby is forfeited by all?' 4,795 women replied that they were not in favour, as against 138 who voted for the retention of married women. To the question 'Are you in favour of the retention of women in the service after marriage in the event of the gratuity being retained for those who retire on marriage?' 3,537 voted against the retention of married women as against 1,396 who would let them stay on.

Now, say the wiseacres, you see what happens. The feminists have been making a desperate fuss, protesting against the enforced resignation of women teachers and civil servants upon marriage. But when we ask the women themselves what they want to do they vote by overwhelming majorities in favour of retirement whether their marriage gratuity is retained or not. Only the wearer can tell where the shoe pinches. Only the girl in an office can tell whether she wants to give up her work and marry. The man – and the woman – on the spot is the person really qualified to tell the truth. In the words of Mr W.J. Brown, MP, secretary of the association,

'The normal woman looks forward to marriage, and knows that whether she retires on marriage or not retirement will be inevitable as soon as the children come. I think most women, therefore, who contemplate marriage know that sooner or later they will have to make the choice between their home or a business career, and therefore they are less inclined to vote for the raising of the marriage bar than would otherwise be the case.'

All this sounds very settled, comfortable, and decisive. The women civil servants want to retire on marriage. The wearers know where the shoe pinches. Let the feminists go home and hide their heads under the old purple, green, and white banner of the Suffrage days. Their doctrinaire enthusiasms are out of date.

But are they? Or is there by chance a slip in the reasoning of the wiseacres? Is the proverb by any chance defective as a guide? Sometimes only a chiropodist can really tell whether pain is due to an ill-fitting shoe or a corn on the foot, and in any case proverbs embody their own short-sighted wisdom, which is not always infallible.

Who are the girls who have voted for the marriage bar? Nine out of ten swing daily to their offices in suburban trains and trams and buses, carrying in their suitcases a powder-puff and a love-story or *Home Chat*. They are the public which creates the demand for light fiction in libraries, the public for which the advertisers write: 'Every woman sees a home through her engagement ring', the public reared on the fairy stories of 'Cinderella' and 'Beauty and the Beast'. They think, on foggy mornings when the alarm-clock goes, that they loathe above everything the scramble to the office. They think that if only they could marry and have a little home of their own all would be well. They forget that even in married life there are alarm-clocks and bills to be met and crying babies at night. The love stories so wisely stop on the sound of wedding-bells and the scent of orange-blossoms.

A marriage gratuity enables one to pay the first instalment on one's furniture. The Civil Service acts as a kind father presenting his daughter with a cheque before her wedding day. Who wants to give up a marriage gratuity? Then, what about chances of promotion? Most of the seven thousand are in the lower grades of the profession. Their work is not exhilarating. If they are writing-assistants they have little chance of improving their position. Clerks and typists are not often filled with vaulting ambition. The pretty, attractive girls say, 'Well, we'll keep slogging along until he comes.' The plain and sad ones say, 'Well, if the others clear out, they'll leave more room for me.' The fear of unemployment creates a wish for fluidity, for the constant reopening of posts, for the desk emptied of one girl so that another can take her place.

Boredom and dull routine work, splashed stockings, the alarm-clock, the fear of unemployment, and the desire for escape – these are the forces that have defeated the feminists when the women civil servants answered their questionnaire. But have the girls who voted for the marriage bar really analysed their position? What did that little body of 138 see when they voted for the abolition of the marriage bar, even if the gratuity went with it?

I think they saw the prospect of marriage before them, but not marriage demanding that cruel alternative – a home or a career. I think they saw themselves and their husbands working apart during the day and meeting together at night, able to put aside a little money for harder times, to enjoy their additional income, and to save for their children's education. They probably saw a Civil Service organized more flexibly, so that married women could retire temporarily while having their family, a Civil Service which regarded children and the experiences of childbirth and a nursery as assets, not as disadvantages, to the individual worker and to the State. I think they saw women's work raised from its status at the bottom of the labour market, where it lies now largely because of this tradition that it ends on marriage and that girls are wasteful creatures who will squander a technical education on the care of a little house. They saw the temporary sacrifice of the marriage gratuity repaid a hundredfold in the improved standard of average remuneration paid for women's work. And they saw through the nonsense of criticizing, 'two incomes going into one home', knowing that this argument is never applied to father and son or to two brothers working together.

There were only 138 of them, but they saw more clearly than the others, not only immediate advantage, but ultimate good. We need not be surprised at the smallness of their number. The wonder is, what with the twopenny women's magazines, the English winter which makes getting up early for work so hideous, the fog of economic fallacy dulling our vision, and the rigid and short-sighted attitude of so many employers, both public and private, toward maternity concessions, that there were even 138 feminists in the Civil Service Clerical Association. Most of the feminists have already, I believe, joined the Federation of Women Civil Servants, which stands for the abolition of the marriage bar. Perhaps the 138 will join them also now. If so, good luck to them! The wearer may know where the shoe pinches, but the chiropodist and shoemaker alone know how to set it right.

Manchester Guardian, 31 January 1930

✍

LADIES IN RESTAURANTS

I have just been handed a notice of a meeting, which I shall certainly attend if I possibly can, to be held in Kensington Town Hall on 4 April, to protest against 'the refusal of certain restaurants, cafés, and other places of refreshment to admit women unaccompanied by men, after certain hours.' The reason why I do not want to miss this meeting is not so much because I see that Lord Balfour of Burleigh is to be in the chair, and that Mrs Cecil Chesterton, Mrs Abbott, of the Open Door Council, and Miss Alison Neilans are among the speakers. It is not even because the meeting is organized by St Joan's Social and Political Alliance, the Roman Catholic Feminist organization. It is for a personal and particular reason of my own.

One night, four or five years ago, I went to the theatre in a big north-country town with an old friend of the family, a middle-aged woman who was the matron of one of the houses of an old and famous boys' public school. I doubt if there is among my whole acquaintance a more admirable and respectable person or one whose looks inspire more confidence in her tact, wisdom, moderation and morality. Her face, her bearing, even her hats emphasize the strong sense of responsibility towards the young which has developed during her life's work. She has also, mercifully, a sense of humour, a knowledge of human nature, and many other pleasant qualities.

We went to the theatre. I cannot remember now what the play was, but it must have been a long one, because it kept us until the usual theatre train had gone. There was one other due to leave for the suburb where we were staying, but not until nearly midnight. It was a cold evening. It was raining. The fire in the ladies' waiting-room had gone out. The refreshment-room was closed; but that did not matter, for I remembered that the Station Hotel, an old-established and respectable institution, opened right on to the platform. I had often been there with my family when I was a child. We used to stay there after rare visits to the opera or after weddings and other festivities. I restored the drooping spirits of my companion with promises of a seat, a fire, and coffee, and went boldly in through the revolving doors. On we went to the quite familiar lounge, with its deep pleasant sofas, its huge fire, and waiters moving about with trays of light refreshments. We sat down. My companion sighed with relief, for she was rather tired, hated the cold, and declared that she was just dying for a cup of tea.

I beckoned a waiter, gave my order, and did not notice at the moment his puzzled look. It was my friend who said, 'I think there's something wrong.' And she was right. The waiter went off and fetched a fussy little man whose face was quite familiar to me. 'I'm sorry,' he said, 'but are you residents?' 'No,' said I. 'We're waiting for the 11.45 train, and just want some tea.' 'I'm sorry,' he said, 'I'm afraid you can't stop here. We can't serve you. You must go.' 'But it's not after hours,' I protested. 'We only want some tea. I've often been here before.' I told him my name, which he knew. He was regretful, but rules were rules. We were females entering the hotel without a man after a certain hour – I forget the hour – and we were not going to stay the night. Out we must go.

And out we went. We walked up and down the bleak, chill, damp, draughty platform until our train arrived – twenty minutes late. Next day my companion was in bed with a bad cold and acute rheumatism. When I made inquiries about the hotel regulations I was told that it was a pity, but nothing could be done. The rule had been made in order to safeguard public morality, and no exceptions could be allowed.

Of course, I was an idiot. I should have taken the course of a more courageous woman whom I know in London. She is a political organizer and social worker, a person of great experience and initiative. She had been to the House of Commons to follow the fortunes of a bill in which she was greatly interested, and having sat, as one does sit in the House, till late at night, she came out and walked up with one or two friends to Piccadilly Circus. They, too, were tired; they, too, were thirsty; they, too, saw an open café, and, longing for tea or coffee, they went in. They, too, were refused admission because they were unaccompanied by a man. 'Well,' said their leader, 'that's easily remedied.' It was. In two minutes they found their man and brought him in triumph to the café door. Nothing is easier to find than an accommodating man in Piccadilly Circus. This time they were admitted. The man was fortunately both sporting and sympathetic. He appreciated their plight and played his part perfectly. They had their refreshments and went on their way rejoicing.

Another woman whom I know, once prominent in the suffrage movement, has told me that she actually broke down the rule itself by threatening to go out and collect a sandwichman drearily promenading the street outside a restaurant which forbade her to enter. But best of all, I think, is the public protest to be made on April 4 which asks for the abolition of the rule itself.

For what sort of protection does such a regulation offer to the public? It is already possible, without it, for an innkeeper or restaurant proprietor to order out customers who behave improperly. Are women unaccompanied by men the only people to menace public propriety? Does the refusal to serve women with tea or coffee, to give them shelter and warmth for which they are prepared to pay, really protect male customers from temptation? And is it not, perhaps, rather insulting to presume that every unaccompanied woman who enters a café after ten o'clock does so for purposes of prostitution?

For that, after all, is clearly the purpose of the rule. Women are dangerous. Especially women after ten o'clock at night. All women who go about the streets alone at this hour may be suspected, in spite of the growing army of women doctors, political secretaries, programme sellers, office cleaners, midwives, actresses, members of Parliament, rescue workers, night-school teachers, journalists, hospital nurses, and all those other workers whose lawful pursuits may keep them up late at night – to say nothing about the millions of ordinary people who sometimes stay up late to see a play or go to a dance or visit a friend.

Is it not time that we insisted upon the removal of a regulation which really offers a considerable insult to our sex? There is no reason behind it. If women want to behave badly they can do so at any time of day. Temptation cannot be confined within hours like the public sale of alcoholic liquor. Bad behaviour is not limited to women who go about without the restraining companionship of a man. On the contrary, women alone, or in twos and threes, are on the whole rather more likely to behave in a decent, orderly manner, perhaps, than women with men. There is no rule, so far as I know, that men unaccompanied by women should not be served.

Indeed, the longer I think of it the more furious I am with myself for not going on to the platform, that night four or five years ago, finding a nice, friendly porter and bringing him back to the hotel. That would larn 'em!

Manchester Guardian, 28 March 1930

∽

ANECDOTAGE: THE MASCULINE MISFORTUNE

There are, I know, people who declare that 'anecdotage' is not a misfortune but an accomplishment. That is the cause of the whole trouble. If only we would once agree that this habit of collecting stories, remembering stories, telling stories and repeating stories, yea unto seventy times seven, is no merit, but a disease to which the elderly and inert are specially liable, then we might hope. But that is not so. The victims cherish their malady, and, having no regrets, will seek no cure.

Anecdotage is a British malady and a masculine misfortune. It is British, because the conversation of a true Briton still walks lamely. His national taboo closes to him so many fruitful subjects discussed by other races. It is masculine for reasons which I shall show.

I recently had an argument with a friend of mine, one of those recurrent arguments which break out quite amicably every time we meet. He begins by scolding me for failing to make use of my opportunities. I hear good stories and I do not remember them. Far from repeating them till they are worn quite flat, I fail to repeat them once. They come in at one ear, as the saying is, and go out at the other. Or, as the saying isn't, they fail even to make an entry, but go buzzing about in space, making air-waves or sound-waves, or whatever other commotion meaningless sounds do make, and fade away into silence. If I tried to remember now a single good story to illustrate my point, quite seriously I could not. I have in my head at present only two anecdotes. One stays there because I have never quite understood it, and I keep it hoping to see the point. The second is improper.

Now this, says my friend, is all most reprehensible. A fund of good anecdotes, says he, is as important a part of social equipment as a clean handkerchief. Conversation without anecdotes, says he, is like refreshment in a Dry country; it lacks stimulant. Anecdotes are the cocktails of conversation. Like alcohol, they provide a pleasant relaxation. We cannot, says he, be talking all the time of politics, or the Stock Exchange, or the insides of motor cars, or religion, or the weather, or other serious subjects. We cannot, when meeting strangers for the first time, confide in them our religious difficulties, or tell them how we have been crossed in love. So let us tell anecdotes, which are at least impersonal, universal and humorous, less dangerous than gossip, and less boring than the technicalities of golf or racing.

I am quite certain that my friend has revealed one of the real reasons why Englishmen tell anecdotes. They are a form of self-defence. They prevent a man from 'giving himself away'. They help him to retain his self-confidence when meeting strangers in an hotel lounge or chance acquaintances on board a ship. Men wish to talk, but they do not wish to say anything. So they turn themselves into little human gramophones and put on another record – another story. The records drown all silence, provide something to say, and make an effect of conversation without communication. It is a harmless form of entertainment.

The need for this anecdotal armour seems to be specially felt by the British man. Members of other nationalities appear to feel less difficulty in protecting themselves during casual encounters. I remember, for instance, while rattling along the dark road between Florence and Siena, meeting a charming young creature who informed me as his first, or almost first sentence, to a complete stranger, unseen in the unlit bus, that 'the soul of the Italian is as pure as the crystal spring'. After that interesting piece of information, there was no need of anecdotes between us. We plunged into a most elegant conversation which lasted, not only throughout the journey to Siena, but throughout five delightful days spent wandering about that city. By the time we parted we had disclosed to each other, in broken French, all our ambitions, hopes, desires, fears, and, I believe, our loves. I can today, with a tremendous effort, just recollect his name. His appearance I have entirely forgotten. But I always look back upon Siena with peculiar pleasure.

With Italians and with Russians, anecdotes are superfluous. I once went to call upon the Russian relative of a friend of mine in Switzerland. I found him in a large garish room, his small family playing about the floor, his wife and sister doing their social duty in the background. We exchanged greetings, and immediately he plunged into a discussion upon the doctrines of free-will and predestination. I found him quite delightful. We parted with mutual expressions of affection, deepened by our almost complete inability to understand each other's French.

Now anecdotes ... The anecdote is, I believe, a British masculine expedient, because the British male fears all communication. Not so the British female. British females in buses, trains, and hospital waiting-rooms, are perfectly ready to discuss their private affairs, their family fortunes, their domestic misfortunes, their religious beliefs, and even their affairs of the heart. They enjoy making confidences, as their acquaintances enjoy receiving them. They are less afraid than men of giving themselves away.

To make a confidence is to risk one's dignity. Women have, as a rule, less sense of dignity than men. They have not been trained by many generations of ceremonial and pomposity to mind making a fool of themselves more than they mind a murder. Women have, by their domestic responsibilities, been forced to abandon the pose of impersonality. You cannot be impersonal while suckling a child or bathing a baby, or leading home a drunken husband. You cannot be impersonal while managing the affairs of a small house. You cannot mind more about your dignity than your efficiency while attending to small children. And now that women have gone out into the world, and meet casual acquaintances as colleagues among aviators, surgeons, or commercial travellers, they still carry the atmosphere of free-and-easy intimacy with them.

Yorkshire Post, 12 September 1930

෨

WOMEN AS THEY USED TO BE

'Millicent Garrett Fawcett' by Ray Strachey (John Murray)

On Tuesday, 9 November, 1929, a large and remarkable congregation crowded Westminster Abbey. Representatives of the State and Church were there, distinguished politicians, publicists, writers; women in splendid academic robes, older women who looked as though they had not moved in crowds for a very long time, and young girls with eager, interested, respectful faces.

They had gathered in the Abbey to commemorate the passing of a great national figure. The spirit of the ceremony and of the congregation was solemn, but triumphant. I saw no tears, but I saw much dignity and reverence. Above everything, the gathering was impersonal. No name was mentioned, no sermon preached.

A stranger entering the Abbey would have recognized that honour was being done to wisdom and public service, but could hardly have guessed what manner of human being was thus commemorated, nor what achievement Church and State acknowledged.

The service was the Memorial Service for Dame Millicent Fawcett, who had died the previous August. And while I felt the serene impersonal beauty of the occasion, I could not help comparing it with another Memorial Service held the previous year. Dame Millicent had lived to enjoy the aftermath of triumph for the cause to which she had devoted her long working life; Mrs Pankhurst died on the eve of victory. The same day that saw the final passage of the Equal Franchise Bill through the House of Lords saw the funeral of the leader who had done more than anyone to secure it. That death was characteristic – dramatic, poignant, linking personal loss for ever with impersonal triumph.

The service in the big church in Smith Square was crowded to overflowing by women moved by deep personal emotion. All night before in the shadowy church, relays of watchers had knelt beside the coffin. The roads leading to the cemetery were thronged with men and women to whom Mrs Pankhurst's name had been a byword – for infamy or heroism. The crowds she had swayed in her lifetime followed, many among them weeping, to her grave.

I do not know of two commemorations that could have been more different – or more characteristic. I never knew either woman personally, though I had seen both on platforms and heard each make a brief speech once. Both, when I saw them, were a little detached from active work for the feminist movement which had been inseparable from their personalities before the war. But I knew, when I compared the poignant, dramatic funeral in Smith Square, and the memorial service, removed by time from personal grief, official, dignified, in the Abbey, that the difference was perfectly appropriate and right. Mrs Ray Strachey's biography confirms my feeling.

Dame Millicent Fawcett was one of the great figures of our age. She was the perfect constitutional statesman. Her life was devoted, with good sense and constancy and courage, to public service, and particularly to the achievement of justice for women. There was no passage in her life which was not moderate and admirable. What she set out to do, she ultimately accomplished, and until she accomplished it, neither personal grief nor public disapprobation would deter her from her purpose. She had every virtue but wildness and almost every talent except genius. The world is a better place because she lived in it.

But to write a biography of so essentially moderate and sensible a person is a far more difficult task than to write of an agonized and passionate heroine. Mrs Ray Strachey was a friend of Dame Millicent; she loved and admired her; she followed and shared in the later part of her public activities for women's suffrage. She believed in her policy of constitutional action.

She writes easily and intimately and with wide knowledge, not only of Dame Millicent's life, but of the whole background of the woman's movement. Yet even so, she cannot make this a completely satisfying story, for the truth probably is that neither Mrs Strachey nor her leader saw the suffrage movement quite as history will see it. They did not leave out, but perhaps they misinterpreted, the part played by that sharp and violent militant struggle which ended only on August 4, 1914.

The whole life-story has a characteristic unity. It was fitting that Mrs Fawcett should come from the Eastern counties, associated as they are with Puritanism and independence. It was fitting that her ideals of justice and reason should be shared by her family; that Elizabeth Garrett Anderson, the great doctor, and Agnes Garrett, pioneer house decorator and suffragist, should be her sisters; that her entry into political life should begin with her splendidly successful and devoted marriage to Henry Fawcett, the blind don and politician who was to become Postmaster-General. It was fitting that her daughter at Cambridge should be placed 'Above the Senior Wrangler'. For her life was an essentially happy and triumphant one. The death of her husband brought her sorrow, faced with characteristic courage, but her work seems to have been a source of enjoyment and interest to her rather than of agony.

The bitterness of Florence Nightingale, the anguish of Josephine Butler, the tortured courage of Mrs Pankhurst seem strangely alien to this cheerful and optimistic woman, who refused to lose her sense of proportion, attended concerts and parties and domestic gatherings in the thick of the fight, and told comical little tales to soothe distressed committee meetings. She was rarely troubled by doubts. Confident of her own integrity and good sense, and her calm assurance, she went straight forward.

So Mrs Strachey writes of her, and so, it seems, she was from youth till age. If her lack of perplexity led her sometimes to make decisions which history has not justified, such as her support of

Liberal Unionism, her distrust of the Militants, and her assurance of the nobility of the war, it also gave her qualities of leadership which served her well.

News Chronicle, 2 July 1931

❧

FOR SERVICES RENDERED

A star interest of the Beaverbrook press has been the serial publication, beginning last Sunday, of Mr Somerset Maugham's new play, *For Services Rendered*. 'The play is being acclaimed as a masterpiece, the *Journey's End* of the peace days', says the caption. It is, of course, a brilliantly competent play; the cast acts together as though its members had been born for that purpose, and one performance at least, Flora Robson's, touches genius. But I do not think the play a masterpiece, in spite of its technical perfection. It seems to me to contain one magnificently right achievement, and one assumption so subtly false that it vitiates the merit of the drama. The good thing is the character of Leonard Ardsley, the country solicitor, father of the war-devastated family, superbly written by Mr Maugham, and excellently played by Mr C.V. France. For that part alone, the play would have been worth writing, worth acting, and worth remembering. For Leonard Ardsley, white-haired, venerable, and jolly, shines in the radiant supremacy of his crass insensitiveness. He is the sound man, the man of common sense, the man who 'sees things in their right proportion', and who made England What It Is. During the war he gladly Did His Bit; he was a Special Constable; he Gave his son – to be blinded – a great sorrow to him, because now Sydney cannot follow him into the business; he has kept his three daughters; he has been a Good Husband to his wife; he gave sensible advice to the ex-naval Commander, garage-proprietor Collie Stratton, refusing, naturally, to do more than give advice; and he looks round his family circle in the last act, and congratulates himself and them that, really, there is very little to worry about; they have not done so badly; all is, if not for the best, at least well ordered and controlled by his own practical common sense. And under his nose his wife is dying of cancer, one daughter married to a drunken oaf, another about to elope with an elderly married roué, the third crazy with frustrated longings; the Commander has been driven to suicide, and his son transformed by pain into a callously selfish cynic. He embodies the huge army of mellow optimists who refuse to look upon the disquieting face of reality, who happily tell us that the country's heart is in the right place because it continues to elect National Governments and keep the flag flying at Geneva and elsewhere; who blandly invite others to sacrifice themselves upon the altars of domestic order or business propriety, and who on the outbreak of the next war will again pride themselves on their readiness to offer services which they are quite certain will not be demanded. The Leonard Ardsleys, excellent good fellows, are responsible for more suffering, folly, waste, ugliness, and injustice than all the criminals in our gaols together. Ibsen himself has not exposed more formidably a typical apostle of the Great God Bunk.

Yet Mr Maugham, for all his wit, his competence, and his splendid impatience with the complacent sentimentality of Leonard Ardsley, has himself strangely succumbed to a sentimental assumption which wrecks the validity of a great part of his play. With graphic ferocity he draws the three daughters of Leonard Ardsley, like the three daughters of M. Dupont, doomed to ruin. One marries disastrously, because 'any marriage is better than none'. One wastes her youthful beauty on the golf links till, in a panic, she flies to her elderly admirer, and one, whose lover was killed in the war, offers herself in vain to the bankrupt Commander, and goes crazy when he prefers death to her desperate generosity. The picture, as a picture, is true enough, though I cannot believe that a woman with the character of Mrs Ardsley would have let it remain so. 'A good mother', they call her, and Mr Maugham obviously agrees. A hopelessly incompetent mother, I suggest, or she would have driven Eva and Lois out into the world years ago. For there are homes like this one – make no mistake. In pleasant country towns stand pleasant red-brick houses, with cars in the garage, and puppies on the lawn, and drawing-rooms full of silver photograph frames and chintz, where girls today are rotting away their youth, hag-ridden by the fear of middle age, of futility, of frustration. Mr Maugham seems to attribute this to the war. He is wrong. These women are victims of another evil, the Leisured Lady tradition, that still keeps middle-class girls behind their father's tea-tray until they can sit behind their husband's. The terror of old age that walks by night, the nagging fear, are not found among competent and ambitious professional women, keen on their jobs. Long before the war, long before *The Times* published its articles on the Superfluous Woman, women like Eva cried out in desperate humiliation, and girls like Lois ran off to elderly admirers. And they will continue to do so after the next war, too, unless in sweeping away our civilization, it destroys also this, among other superstitions.

For Mr Maugham not only blames the war for evils it did not cause. He falls into that odd masculine illusion which would be a little touching in its naïve vanity, if it were not so dangerous, that women can only climb out of prison by aid of a strong male arm. There are not enough men to go round, this play implies; therefore, Lois must endure an old man's illicit ardours, and Eva sacrifice herself till her endurance snaps. But let a woman only find the right lover, and all her problems will be solved ... We have no right so to mislead the suggestible and accommodating young. All of us over thirty, who have not completely closed our eyes through life, know that this is not true. Celibacy may suit few of us – though it probably suits more than social traditions allow us to believe. Enforced celibacy always is an evil. To love and be loved is an experience exquisitely worth the pain that inevitably accompanies its pleasure. But to suggest that marriage simplifies everything, and even in itself constitutes a reason for living, is flatly immoral. There are as many wasted and frustrated lives among the married as among the unmarried. And to suggest that, in our present state of society, an unorthodox affair will not raise more problems than it solves, shows a lack of sophistication quite fantastic in a writer pretending to know his world. Each of us has to find his or her work in life, and that thing greater than ourselves which gives life its meaning. The question of our virginity or otherwise has its own importance, though this is too frequently exaggerated; but really it is irrelevant to the main issue, and the sooner we recognize this, the better. The romanticism shown here by Mr Maugham is typical of a social tradition which may retain a certain old-fashioned charm, but is a luxury which I hardly think that our contemporary society can afford.

Time and Tide ('Notes on the Way') 19 November 1932

✌

UNEMPLOYMENT AND THE WOMEN WHO WORK

No topic yet perished from public discussion because it was already stale. One might think that everything had been said on the old subject of women's employment in the professions and industry; but Sir Herbert Austin's ingenious suggestion revived the whole thing again when, at the Oxford Conference of Works Managers, he commended Herr Hitler's solution of the unemployment problem by the dismissal of female employees. Of course, mathematically considered, there is something to be said for it. The problem of female unemployment was solved, not so long ago, by sending our able-bodied males to kill each other off in France and Flanders. But the process was not thorough enough. Some men came home and expected to re-enter their old employments. Babies were born and have grown up to expect jobs for themselves. Now if Sir Herbert could devise a female European war and send the women out to kill each other off, keeping just enough at home to replenish the stock of male babies, with legalized practice of female infanticide, that might be a good idea. Or, if he does not like that notion, here is another. I was recently interested in the foundation of an African newspaper. Part of the capital required for its foundation was to be put up by a certain chief in Swaziland. I heard last month that he had changed his mind and decided instead to use the capital for increasing the number of his wives from 72 to 200. Now if Sir Herbert would start a campaign among industrialists for this form of public-spirited and large-minded polygamy – he might arrange that each female employee, when dismissed, should be married by her ex-employer, who would automatically then become responsible for the support of all her dependents in the war of crippled brothers, invalid parents, fatherless children, and whatnot – he would, as they say, be talking. Solomon did it, you remember, more or less.

Time and Tide ('Notes on the Way'), 7 October 1933

✍

A CONSPIRACY OF SILENCE

Invasion of private decency, against which Mr St John Ervine made an able attack in his address to the Institute of Journalists, is not the only evil from which the modern press suffers. Equally serious is the repression of inconvenient knowledge. Some months ago a friend of mine attended an enormous meeting in the Queen's Hall. It was packed. It was rampageous. It was exciting. It concerned a topic of undoubted public interest. She came home full of entertaining anecdotes about it. Next morning I looked through the London papers, and could I find a word about it? No. Not one, anywhere. So last week, having a free evening, I dropped in to a meeting conducted under the same auspices in the Essex Hall. The speaker was one of the few people whose names are familiar to practically every English-speaking person; her work, for good or evil (I personally think for good) is one of the most revolutionary, far-reaching, and important pieces of individual pioneering in our century; the changes effected by her on society are impossible to ignore even by her opponents. Yet during the course of her lecture last week she told us that not one London daily paper had a report of her big Queen's Hall meeting; that not one had reviewed her latest book; that they would not even accept paid advertisements of any conferences or meetings, for which her name was used. The reason she gave us was that the Free State censorship had declared her and her work to be anathema, and that, because it might endanger its Irish circulation, no London Protestant daily dare mention her name or work. I give the explanation as she gave it. The woman is Dr Marie Stopes.

Time and Tide ('Notes on the Way'), 28 October 1933

✍

FEAR AND THE WOMAN WHO EARNS

On Monday in the Central Hall, Westminster, a mass demonstration of women's organizations is being held to uphold the claim of Equal Pay for Equal Work.

It is typical of our muddle-headed world that the protest should have been left to women, for the real injustices of inequality affect men just as much.

Not long ago when the *News Chronicle* published its series of articles on the woman secretary, one correspondent angrily replied: 'Yes. Better pay and smart clothes for the girl typist. Unemployment and patched pants for men.'

It would be foolish to deny that undercurrent of fear, resentment and antagonism running through current comment upon the position of the woman wage-earner. 'Pin-money girls', 'two incomes for one family', 'married women taking men's jobs instead of letting their husbands keep them' – these are the targets for protest, and not only from men.

Their fiercest critics are often the wives of men who live in hourly fear of unemployment; mothers of beloved children whom they dream of in nightmares as suffering under the hardships of the Means Test and 2s. a week allowance; daughters of professional men battling to 'keep up appearances' on dwindling incomes.

This opposition is not confined to private opinion. In some countries it has given rise to a definite public policy of trying to remove women from the general labour market, wherever she comes into competition with men.

In this country we have had individual employers saying that they would like to replace all women in industry by men. Local authorities have inserted the thin end of the wedge by refusing to employ married women; but at the moment, taking it by and large, it is easier for a woman to obtain employment – of a kind – in England than for a man.

In Germany up till last year this was also true. But Hitler began his drive 'back to the kitchen'. Wherever possible women in administrative positions have been replaced by men. In certain factories women are 'invited' to hand over their jobs to their fathers or husbands, or to sweethearts whom they can then marry, claiming the government marriage-loan.

Last October one woman, Alice Rilke, courageously suggested in the *Vöelkische Beobachter* that: 'A woman without private means and without work is also one of the unemployed and a charge on the public. To turn away a woman who has to find work and to replace her by a man is not the creation of work.' But her protest had little effect.

In Germany this drive against the industrial and professional employment of women is justified as a recognition of the importance of her maternal functions and real domestic interests; but that is not the true reason. Wherever there exist two sections of a community, one of which is for some extraneous reason paid at lower rates than the other for equal work, the same antagonism, the same fear, the same campaign for prohibitions exists.

It is perfectly understandable. The blackleg – for whatever reasons – remains a danger to society. It is true that today women are often used to undercut men's wages – just as in South Africa blacks have been used to undercut white employees.

In spite of Government promises of equality Civil Servants are still paid at differing rates. The general grade of clerkships start at the rates of 30s. a week for men and 24s. for women. The Burnham Scale for teachers stands at the proportions of five-fifths for men to four-fifths for women. Except in certain professions, such as medicine and the stage, where women have fought for and secured equality, in most cases, at least of monetary payment, private employers have followed the Government's example.

The effect of this upon the men is to arouse justifiable suspicion, fear and sometimes something worse. In actual fact women 'black-leg' little enough. They are still by custom or trade union regulation excluded from many ranks of better paid labour – as the black workers are segregated in South African industry by the operation of the Colour Bar.

But the fear is there; the cases of hardship have occurred; the sense of a reservoir of low-paid labour waiting to overflow and swallow all the jobs keeps men awake at nights. And few emotions are so destructive of the happiness of communities as fear. It breeds injustice; it breeds antipathy; it prevents the candour of good comradeship.

But the effects upon the women are no better. Conscious that they are paid less, they feel their work to be less important. That reduces their incentive to undertake long or arduous training; it reduces the incentive of their parents to encourage or permit such preparation. Actually, therefore, some girls become less efficient, and being less efficient than they might be, lose interest in their work and respect for themselves.

It is notable that low payment of itself diminishes the prospects of efficiency. Few causes contribute more effectively to the traditional 'feminine' disabilities of weaker muscles and nervous instability than the anaemia and fragility following malnutrition. The world marvelled at the strength and eagerness of war-time munition workers – fed and paid as industrial women workers had rarely been fed and paid before; but it did not always connect these two facts.

'The degradation of woman and womanly labour,' the psychologist Adler wrote, 'is further indicated by the fact that women are paid less than men, regardless of whether their work is of equal value … so long as we cannot guarantee every woman an absolute equality with man we cannot demand her complete reconciliation with life, with the facts of our civilization and the forms of our social life.'

That is going far; but does it go too far? Looking round on a world where resentment and suspicion so often exist when there should be only mutual respect and understanding, where antagonism too often replaces co-operation, and where a hot emotion of anger overcomes the men who see girl typists crowding City buses, while the girls resent what they feel to be masculine patronage and jealousy, can we deny that the Austrian psychologist has some claim to be heard?

It was a woman, Josephine Butler, whose main concern was not with economics but with the sanity and kindliness of the relationships between the sexes, who replied once to a questioner: 'You ask me what I think the most important thing to place before the electors. I think the most important thing is the principle of equality, equality and equality.'

News Chronicle, 9 March 1934

BLACK WORDS FOR WOMEN ONLY

Any constant reader of Fascist literature must have been impressed by the frequent if uneasy references to the Importance of Woman.

Our island breed of blackshirts forms a fairly reliable barometer to Continental thought upon this subject. When Sir Oswald Mosley found the Labour Party too small to hold his 'New Hellenism' and broke away to create the new party, he established a weekly paper entitled *Action*.

Some of us may remember how, in October, 1931, we were urged from walls and hoardings to 'Take Action', and how, when we took it, we learned that it stood for Volt, and 'What does Volt stand for? It stands for Vigour, Order, Loyalty, Triumph'.

Tucked away, on the twenty-fourth page, after Gardens, but before Architecture, was a section called 'Listen, Women', devoted to female interests. What women were to listen to were, first, reflections upon the possible fall of the pound and how little this immediately concerned housewives; and, secondly, an exhortation to follow French styles of cookery by making *ragoûts* and *bouillons*.

Next year Sir Oswald founded the British Union of Fascists and delivered his soul of its burden of conversion in a book entitled *The Greater Britain*. Here, in one section of one of the twelve chapters, he said what he had to say about 'Women's Work'.

'It has been suggested,' he began modestly, 'that hitherto in our organization too little attention has been paid to the position of women.

'It is true that in our political organization we have hitherto concentrated on the organization of men. This was not because we underrate the importance of women in the world; but because our political experiences have led us to the conclusion that the early stages of such organization are a man's job ...

'The part of woman in our future organization will be important, but different from that of the men; *we want men who are men and women who are women*.'

The italics are Sir Oswald's; they are, I think, important. They seem characteristic of that Fascist inclination to dream of an eclectic Olympus of virile he-men (Romans, Britons or Teutonic-Aryans) separated sharply from all lower forms of being.

'Fascism,' he continues, 'in fact would treat the normal wife and mother as one of the main pillars of the State,' and is gently sportive about 'professional spinster politicians' whose one idea is to escape from the normal sphere of woman.

Two years later, in *The Fascist Week*, he returns to that attack, and declares, 'it will not be surprising to those familiar with *this distressing type*' (the italics are mine) 'that the interests of the normal woman occupy no great place in the attention of Parliament.'

When one remembers how 'this distressing type' has fought for maternity and child welfare services, improved education and better housing, one is driven to wonder precisely what Sir Oswald visualizes as the interests of 'normality', and how he proposes to deal with them in his corporate state.

It is not irrelevant to compare what Sir Oswald promises with what Herr Hitler has performed.

The German Constitution of 1918 granted equality before the law to all citizens. Women entered politics, the professions, the civil services. Between thirty and forty-two sat in each of the various Reichstags as deputies between 1919 and 1933 – a higher proportion than in any other country. They held high executive and municipal offices.

But the Nazi movement has reversed all that. Women may vote, but none stand on the lists as candidates. Their associations are now directed by men; since July, 1933, all the girls' high schools have been controlled by men. Professional women are finding themselves compelled for one reason or another to resign from work. Married women are persuaded to leave their employment, and unmarried workers are often asked to surrender their jobs to men, as in one Hamburg tobacco factory, where 600 girls were asked to hand over their work to fathers, brothers or husbands, or to retire, marry, and claim the State marriage loan.

There is little hope for ambitious young women in Nazi Germany, where the brightest contribution of constructive economic thought towards the solution of the unemployment problem appears to have been the expulsion of large sections of the community from paid work, as a penalty for being women, Socialists or Jews, and their replacement by unobjectionable loyal male Aryans. Individual women have protested against this mass campaign to restore their economic dependence and drive them back to the kitchen. But protests are penalized; public influence is strong, and there are women who have been temporarily persuaded to believe that Hitler's policy really serves their interests.

One such wrote recently to the *Manchester Guardian* declaring: 'The German people, led by their great Führer, are today labouring for the rebirth of the nation and of morals. They know perfectly well that this task invests women with at least the same importance as men. The young generation obtain their first nourishment and teaching from their mothers …

'Woman has again been recognized as the centre of family life, and today it has again become a pleasure and an honour to be a mother.'

No explanation is offered of why or when motherhood ceased to be a pleasure and honour – perhaps when children were driven to concentration camps?

But what is significant is the emphasis laid on the exclusively feminine functions of wifehood and motherhood. Throughout history, whenever society has tried to curtail the opportunities, interests and powers of women, it has done so in the sacred names of marriage and maternity. Exalting woman's sex until it dominated her whole life, the State then used it as an excuse for political or economic disability. The moment those disabilities were removed, women began to urge the claims of children, of health, of domestic welfare for consideration before the law; until they spoke, these claims were rarely heard.

Today, whenever women hear political leaders call their sex important, they grow suspicious. In the importance of the sex too often has lain the unimportance of the citizen, the worker and the human being. The 'normal' woman knows that, given freedom and equality before the law, she can be trusted to safeguard her own interests as wife, mother, daughter, or what you will.

Clarion, 24 March 1934

THE BEST OF LIFE

A Woman's Best Years by W. Béran Wolfe (Routledge)

From an American paper which reaches me here in a small town on the Yorkshire coast, I learn that Dr Béran Wolfe's book, *A Woman's Best Years*, is a best-seller across the Atlantic. I am not surprised; for its appealing sub-title is *The Art of Staying Young*, and if there is today a universal emotion, it would seem to be a terror of female middle age. The press suggests it; magazine stories suggest it; advertisements suggest it; even the local paper here, an assiduous organizer of beauty competitions, has had prizes for the prettiest outdoor girl, smiling girl, and beauty queens for this or that carnival. Once it ventured as far as a 'mother and baby' beauty competition, but that really sailed pretty near the bleak wind of middle age, since women in their forties can sometimes produce exquisite babies, and it did not inspire repetition.

Advertisers of face creams, corsets, patent medicines, and slimming systems unite in eulogizing secrets of keeping middle age at bay. W.S. Gilbert's Katisha in *The Mikado* was only one in a long line of repulsive middle-aged and desperate stage spinsters. The disgust, the dread, are not confined to our sex. Lady Rhondda recently aroused vehement controversy in the correspondence columns of *Time and Tide* by calling attention to what she described as the 'cold mutton' attitude towards women over forty, displayed by some of our most gifted gentlemen novelists. It is difficult to say whom the 'tell-tale wrinkle', so much quoted in advertisements, alarms more – the woman who perceives it in her mirror, or the man who recognizes it on his dinner-partner's face.

As a spinster of 36 (with a hip measurement of 42 – I measured it this morning after reading an unusually apocalyptic and terrifying corset catalogue) I am naturally interested in this business. All the propaganda in the world has not yet persuaded me that life grows less interesting as one grows older. I am increasingly of the opinion that I reached the right side of 30 just over six years ago, and that in another four years I shall be on the right side of 40; but I admit that after reading the more luscious advertisements in the daily and weekly press, I feel my convictions a little shaken. Can I really be living in a fool's paradise? Shall I one day, and very shortly, wake up to find myself upon the frontier of a cheerless country, a no-man's land in which the almond tree shall flourish only to provide me with unguents for my fading skin, in which the grasshopper shall be a burden because I am no longer agile, 'and fears shall be in the way ... and desire shall fade'? So powerful, so skilful and so universal is the propaganda, stabbing our most tender vanities, stirring our most sensitive secrets, hitting all the most delicate susceptibilities of our nature, that I think she must be a robust woman who is not occasionally stricken by these qualms. Hence the demand for *The Art of Staying Young*; hence the salutary stimulants which it provides for those that need it.

W. Béran Wolfe is a psychiatrist. He has a wide experience of human nature at large and the female nervous system in particular. And he, with an uncompromising and racy pen, unmasks this turnip-ghost of middle-aged misery.

He does not deny the difficulties. He accepts as good things the pleasures of physical energy and sexual attraction which are the usual advantages of youth; yet he concludes his thesis with the sentence, 'If she lives them fully and courageously, the middle decades should be a woman's best years.' His book, quite apart from its invigorating common sense, makes entertaining reading. It is full of case-histories of Miss A. or Mrs T., of pithy aphorisms and briskly controversial statements. Many readers in this country may be shocked by the calmly objective attitude which Dr Wolfe adopts towards maternal solicitude, lesbian love, the custom of the gigolo, and relationships outside marriage. His approach to conduct is purely pragmatic. He does not ask, what do moralists say? but how, in common experience, does this work? Sometimes, I feel, his suggested remedies are a little too glib or facile, his confidence too bright. But I welcome warmly his insistence upon the damage of egotism, his demand that to be lived fully, life must be shared bravely, and his courage in putting sex in its proper place – and that a considerably less important one than has been accorded by many less practical psychologists; very few people could quarrel with his final recipe for a happy middle age. These are the qualities that he demands: tolerance, courage, readiness to risk mistakes, imagination, the art of playing, self-esteem, social contacts ('the only real safety that exists in this world is the safety that comes from being thoroughly connected with men, women, and children'), avoidance of neurotic traits, a sense of humour, and the quality of zest. All very sensible, bracing and suggestive – if it can be done. Yet sometimes when reading Dr Wolfe's book I felt myself looking round a world where as many good causes seem doomed as won, where lives are thrown fruitlessly away, liberties curtailed and hopes defeated; and I wonder whether it is all quite such a cheerful business, this 'social solidarity', this sharing of other people's lives; but I was always driven back to the thought that if it seems bad when shared, it would be worse in isolation. After all, there is a profound psychological truth in that observation: 'We are members one of another'.

Good Housekeeping, May 1935

✍

KING GEORGE V JUBILEE CELEBRATIONS

A short while ago I received a letter from a left-wing organization asking me to sign a resolution protesting against the Jubilee celebrations; the war and the unemployment figures alone, it said, made any jubilation for the past twenty-five years inappropriate. Now I was reared conscientiously as a Protestant, and have spent a good part of my thirty-six years protesting ever since. But on this occasion I refused – not that I fail to share the organization's attitude about the war and unemployment; not that I am a royalist or think it any matter for congratulation that two individuals should have been exposed for twenty-five years to the ordeals to which we submit our royal family. It is possibly worse to be an unemployed riveter on the Tyne-side than to be a king or prince of England; but I am not sure. I think the riveter has the greater chance of happiness. What we can congratulate ourselves upon is the public spirit with which an unusually unselfish royal family has fulfilled its role. But those were not the reasons which I gave for refusing to protest against the Jubilee. I looked back on the past twenty-five years and decided that these were, on the whole, the most propitious that women in this country have ever known.

I know that this is an unpopular subject. I am constantly reprimanded for 'flogging the dead horse of Feminism'. All right. Personally, I do not think the horse is dead; but if it were, that would prove my point superbly. Twenty-five years ago forty thousand women marched through the streets of London in what was known as the Women's Coronation Procession. It was a protest against desires unfulfilled. It represented arts, sciences, authorities, powers; lawyers and doctors walked there, the prototypes of peeresses and abbesses; and they were led by women carrying banners who had been imprisoned for insisting upon women's right to use their abilities in such service. 'It will not come in my time,' Mrs Pankhurst said. But do I not remember the extraordinary service at which Mr Baldwin unveiled Mrs Pankhurst's statue under the shadow of Parliament, in which he, the constitutionalist, honoured her, the rebel, for having 'set the heather on fire', at which Dame Ethel Smyth in the robes of a doctor of music led the police band playing *The March of the Women*, which she had once conducted with a tooth-brush through the bars of a window in Holloway Gaol to a chorus of exercising prisoners? I have seen a woman cabinet minister walking through the lobby of the House of Commons; I have seen a woman architect chosen to design the Shakespeare Memorial Theatre; I have seen my own mother applauded by a county council when she was elected as its first woman alderman; I have myself been heckled as an agitator at Marble Arch, demanding the vote in the equal franchise campaign of 1927 and 1928; and I have been enfranchised. I have voted. And I know that those people who say that the world is no better off since 'women have been let loose in it' simply do not know what they are talking about.

I have seen a revolution in social and moral values which has transformed the world I live in. It is a direct result of that challenge to opinion which we call the Women's Movement. I do not just mean that legally married mothers are now allowed to be their children's guardians, that grounds for divorce (though still ridiculously and indecently inadequate) are equal for men and women, that birth control is no longer an unmentionable horror but an accepted instrument of civilization, that maternal mortality is no longer a rather obscene joke but a matter for national regret and persistent effort, that the salvaging of human failure, which at the beginning of the century was regarded as a matter for hushed voices and private committees of a few heroic women, is now a widely recognized and sensibly conducted social activity, so that in a small Yorkshire town I was recently asked to appeal at a public meeting (in front of my own male cousins and uncles – ask yourselves, Edwardians!) for money to supply a Girls' Sheltering Home not only with food and furniture, but with pictures and gramophone records and occasional tickets to the cinema. I mean that a world has changed.

I am well aware of the imperfections of the movement. I have seen what has happened in Germany, where the pendulum of reaction has swung back so violently that all that had been gained seems lost again. I know that Great Britain has dependencies in Africa and the Far East still untouched by any sense of the humanity of women. I have recently visited a meeting of the National Union of Women Teachers in Manchester, where that valiant body was protesting against the unequal payment of equal work for men and women under the Burnham Scale; I have visited an immense conference of the National Union of Teachers at Scarborough, where unequal pay was deprecated, but not very actively opposed; I have visited a conference of the Open Door Council at Ashton-under-Lyne and heard of the mean and humiliating injustices imposed upon the least articulate and powerful women in the country – those in unorganized industries or unemployed, and the wives of men in similar plight. I know that we still have plenty to do. I know too that we have gone so far in some directions that we seem to have fallen over backwards. Take (since it is no use being over-delicate) this vexed question of virginity. When I was a child an unmarried woman who had compromised her reputation for strict chastity was an outcast; she was called fallen, unfortunate or wicked, according to the degree of charity in those who mentioned her. Today, there is a far worse crime than promiscuity: it is chastity. On all sides the unmarried woman today is surrounded by doubts cast not only upon her attractiveness or her common sense, but upon her decency, her normality, even her sanity. The popular women's magazines, short-story writers, lecturers and what not are conducting a campaign which might almost be called the persecution of the virgins. In the course of my business as a journalist and book reviewer I encounter it daily. For instance, this week I was sent for review an American detective story, *Murder Without Weapon*, by Means Davis – slick, clever, erudite. In the course of conversation in a hospital, relative to a most unpleasant murder, this pretty piece of dialogue occurs:

'Across the room the pediatrician was saying to the psychiatrist: "It is the nastiest thing in the world!"

… "What's that, Simpson?" the pathologist upon his right asked.

"Life-long virginity!" '

Quite. I would not quote that little exchange of wisdom were it not for its constant reiteration in varying forms. There have been times when I have almost regretted that I did not accept the foreign gentleman who once proposed to me in a basement flat in Maida Vale while the gramophone played *No Rose in all the World*, and who next wrote to me from Wormwood Scrubs asking me to be good enough to send him some woollen undergarments because, while serving his sentence for forgery, he found the English climate rather cold. Seriously, it takes considerable vanity, self-respect and periodical inoculations of flattery for the unmarried woman of what was once considered unblemished reputation to stand up to the world today.

I think this is a temporary phase. I think we shall one day get over this somewhat adolescent preoccupation with the human body and its miscellaneous experiences. Meanwhile … meanwhile I realize that I have other reasons to rejoice for these twenty-five years. I am a countrywoman. I remember a village in which was no artificial light, no telephone, no telegraph, no health insurance system, no transport beyond the private dog-cart or carriage of the well-to-do farmer, or the weekly carrier's cart with its slow horse which took an hour and a half to drive to the nearest shops. I remember the alarms of sickness by night, the long, painful hours of waiting for the doctor, the babies that died unnecessarily, the monotony of winter, the rigid class divisions. I remember my father, the gentlest of men, whose beloved memory is today a legend in the village where he lived, opposing the Saturday half-day off for his farm labourers. I remember the village idiots, once a recognized feature of the countryside. And I think today of the raised wages, the improved housing, the health services, buses, women's institutes, the regulated hours of work, the wireless, the young farmers' clubs, the playing-fields, the extremely well-run homes for mentally defective children, the rural community councils ... No, no, no. As a countrywoman I cannot protest against Jubilee celebrations.

Time and Tide ('Notes on the Way'), 4 May 1935

∽

A GENERATION OF WOMEN'S PROGRESS

When our king and queen came to the throne, a Women's Coronation Procession marched through the London streets. It consisted of forty thousand women, carrying banners and clad in symbolic costumes, representing a pageant of Empire, of the arts, the sciences, of labour and learning and authority and motherhood. Five abreast they walked, and in the place of honour at their head went seven hundred ex-prisoners who, since Sir Edward Grey's Manchester meeting on 13th October 1905, had suffered imprisonment during their campaign for women's suffrage.

The reign opened in the middle of that controversy which startled all, divided homes, and sent delicately nurtured and protected ladies, young and old, to chalk pavements, interrupt meetings and experience the humiliations of gaol sentence which till then had seemed a nightmare totally remote from such as they. But the suffrage movement and its brilliantly conducted advance guard, the militant campaign of the WSPU, were only part of a great revolution which was during the next twenty-five years to change the entire position of women in this country, and to influence public opinion and political action throughout the world.

In this year of Jubilee, an international congress under the chairmanship of an Englishwoman is being held at Istanbul 'to secure the enfranchisement of women of all nations; to establish equality of liberties, status and opportunity between men and women; to educate women for their task as citizens and to further their influence in public life'. There, in the traditional centre of the most tyrannical servitude of women, in the stronghold of the harem system, newly elected Turkish women members, who took their seats in the parliament at Angora for the first time this spring, are meeting contemporaries from the old and new worlds, from Far East and Far West alike, in open discussion of their common interests. That nobody seems to think this very strange and particularly exciting marks the real measure of the advance of women during the past twenty-five years.

It is often complained that in spite of their enfranchisement, their opened opportunities of public service, their new authority as cabinet ministers, members of parliament, aldermen, mayors and justices of the peace, women have made little impression upon the national politics of this country. It is true that certain standards of value remain too little unchanged. We still spend on battleships what we need for bathrooms, still tread the ways of international co-operation with one eye turning back to watch the humour of the fighting services; but at least all women's non-party organizations stand for peace.

The laws passed since women obtained political enfranchisement in this country include a series of measures for the protection of children, such as the Criminal Law Amendment Act of 1922, the Bastardy Act, the Adoption of Children, Legitimacy, Infant life (Preservation), Age of Marriage and Children and Young Persons Acts; they include the Widows, Orphans and Old Age Contributory Pensions Act; they include the safeguarding of maternity by the Registration of Midwives and Maternity Acts and they have been supported by campaigns for the reduction of maternal mortality, for school feeding, nursery schools, for birth control and for infant welfare. These matters, once of vital importance to individuals but hardly mentionable in public, have, during the past twenty-five years, become important issues of national policy.

Their influence on public affairs is only one indication of the transformed position of women in the world at large. One of the few good features of the war of 1914 was that it gave an opportunity for women to prove their individual capacity. Running hospitals, conducting operations, holding high positions in the Civil Service, working as farmers, engineers and bus conductors, driving lorries, making shells, cleaning windows, and finally replacing soldiers at the base in Queen Mary's Army Auxiliary Corps, they threw down a challenge to those who had hitherto relegated them to kitchen, nursery or drawing-room. Today we take it for granted that women should become surgeons, engineers and ministers, that a woman electrician should obtain the contract for rewiring Winchester Cathedral, and that a woman architect should design the Shakespeare Memorial Theatre at Stratford-on-Avon. There are still certain prohibitions: English women are not ambassadors, bishops or members of the Stock Exchange; there is a prejudice against their rise to the top of most professional trees; the slump has revived jealous antagonism to women wage-earners, and many girls are still discouraged by their 'only a woman' complex. But these decrease yearly.

The change of attitude has been helped by the part played by women in sport. When an Amy Johnson breaks flying records, a woman driver wins races at Brooklands, or a woman carries off the King's Cup for marksmanship at Bisley, the legend of women's delicacy and instability loses force. The actual discovery of her muscles has affected the contemporary woman's mentality, too. It was always realized that the poorer classes had limbs, that housewives could carry coal buckets and turn heavy mangles, that country women could make hay and load wagons, that factory women could lift heavy weights and handle levers; but when this reign opened, though the secondary schools for girls had initiated hockey and lacrosse, we still were unacquainted with the bronzed, muscular young athlete, hiking, swimming, cycling, jumping, known today as 'the out-of-door-girl'.

But the profoundest change of all, perhaps, is that which has affected individual minds and social habits. The qualities of independent judgment, self-reliance, candid companionship and spirited initiative are not novel; certain rare individuals have always had them; but that they should have been substituted for the docility, squeamishness, subservience and triviality, which were the earlier foundations of genteel upbringing for young ladies, does indeed mark the revolution of values which has made the reign of His Majesty King George V the most notable in the whole history of British women.

Yorkshire Post, 6 May 1935
(By courtesy of the Yorkshire Post)

Vera Brittain

WHY FEMINISM LIVES

The feminist movement of the present day is not very popular. It has a good many openly declared enemies, all of whom appear determined to misunderstand its true aims and meaning, and to misrepresent its personnel. The opposition to it chiefly finds expression in the contemptuous indifference of women under-graduates at universities, in the complacent lethargy of the mass of unoccupied or semi-occupied middle-class married women, and in the open hostility of certain sections of the press.

The press opposition is of course the most vocal, and may be said to represent the sentiments of the other two sections of opinion. Part of it is gently patronizing, lightly chaffing those women who share in feminist activities, and jocosely suggesting that their enthusiasm is just a bit behind the times. Another part, turning a conveniently blind eye on the charm and elegance of the average modern feminist, delights to publish little contemptuous phrases about 'masculine women' and 'virulent wives'.

Yet a third part – and this to the woman's movement of today is the most dangerous part of all – maintains that feminism is merely hysterical, since it is now quite unnecessary. Feminists are told, in the words of a weekly paper, that 'all the strongholds of the enemy have been taken, all the big battles fought and won. Nowadays there is nothing left for the fighting feminist but to magnify minor grievances … into some semblance of the grand old causes.'

To rational women with occupations, who have certainly no time to waste on 'minor grievances', but who still take part in the feminist movement, it seems strange that any intelligent journalist should look upon the vote, which has never been other than symbolic, as in itself a 'grand old cause', and at the same time so completely disregard the still unfulfilled endeavours and aspirations that lie behind it. The vote, both before it was gained and after, was merely the symbol of equal rights and opportunities for men and women in all departments of life; it gave women for the first time the means of asking for what they wanted, but it did not thereby fulfil those demands. Feminism still lives in England today because the incompleteness of the English franchise represents but one symbol among many others of the incomplete recognition of women as human beings.

It is now generally agreed that the work of a human being is something dignified, something which deserves adequate remuneration and conditions that promote the utmost efficiency. On this principle a whole political party, which certainly would not describe its motives as 'minor grievances', has taken a firm stand, maintaining that anything which deprives a man of such remuneration and such conditions is a denial of his human rights. But this principle, now theoretically admitted in the case of men, is still far from acknowledgement in the case of women, who are frequently regarded as a class apart, vaguely sub-human and not quite entitled to the same opportunities as men in education and in the professions.

For the moment we may put aside the raging controversies in various occupations as to whether women really do equal work with men and are entitled to employment after marriage – questions which, incidentally, involve not 'minor grievances', but such fundamental human problems as the possibility of marrying and the wisdom of having children. More specific examples than these exist of the general undervaluation of women's achievements. Not long ago, for instance, the Civil Service post of 'Draughtsman in the Hydrographic Department of the Admiralty' was advertised as 'open to men and women'. Only one post existed and the best applicant presumably would get it, yet if the chosen candidate chanced to be a woman she would receive a lower salary than a successful man.

Nor do these invidious distinctions operate only at the beginning of a career. At present the majority of eminent women – such as our woman representative at the League of Nations

Assembly – go through life as substitute-delegates, vice-chairmen, sub-editors and assistant-secretaries; they are human beings with a hyphen, never quite complete.

This sense that the dignity of woman's work has never been wholly acknowledged inspires such remarks as that of Miss Margery Fry during the discussions on the Oxford statute which limited the number of women undergraduates: 'Women do their best work when they are allowed to do it, not as women, but as human beings.' It is the urge behind woman's growing demand for employment unhandicapped by inadequate pay or unnecessary restrictions as whether she is married or whether her husband has an income. The right to separate her public and private affairs as every man is allowed to separate his is no 'minor grievance', but the test of a fundamental distinction – the distinction between a social chattel and an independent, responsible individual.

Thus the issue behind the suffrage movement and behind the subsequent agitations over 'equal rights' is, and always has been, the same; it is not so much a demand for the vote, which in itself might well be described as a 'minor grievance' rather than as a 'grand old cause', but a demand for a satisfactory answer to the fundamental question: 'Should a woman be treated as a human being, and if not, why not?'

Woman herself, long conscious of complete humanity, today desires only that others shall recognize it and honestly accept the implications of such recognition. The fight for aknowledgement now bores rather than enthralls her; its postponement seems illogical, an anachronism, a waste of precious time. Her goal is the work of citizenship which awaits her as soon as she is allowed to play her full part in the making of civilization; she continues to agitate, often a little wearily, only because she desires to abolish the need for agitation.

The word 'feminism' – a much maligned word, which has come to stand for many irrelevancies, such as dowdiness and physical abnormality – still adequately expresses her true desire, a desire that might well be summed up in one sentence addressed to mankind: 'Recognize our full humanity, and we will trouble you no more.'

Pamphlet published by the Six Point Group, 1927

MRS PANKHURST AND THE OLDER FEMINISTS

I saw Mrs Pankhurst only once, and only once heard her speak. That was at a polite little meeting less than a year ago, when much of the old force was spent, and the old fires were beginning to burn dimly. Under such circumstances it may seem an impertinence to lay claim to any impression at all. Yet it is, I suppose, true enough to say that those who impress us most in life are less often our friends and relatives, dear as these may be, than the makers of the movements of which we become members, and in which we remain when they are gone.

The name of Mrs Pankhurst was a familiar echo in my schooldays – an echo that became louder as her exploits gathered publicity and I grew to the self-important maturity of a prefect. Our headmistress was an ardent if discreet feminist, and some of the older girls were occasionally taken to village suffrage meetings of a suitably moderate type. During the holidays rumours of imprisonments, church burnings, forcible feedings and the Cat and Mouse Act drifted through the unsympathetic columns of the morning papers to the prosperous and complacent Midland town in which we then lived. At bridge drives and other forms of social diversion, Mrs Pankhurst and her 'screaming sisterhood' formed suitable subjects for that vocal variety of witch-burning in which provincial tea-parties so very often indulge.

I remember being taken to those tea-parties, my feet clad in the stout low-heeled walking shoes of pre-war scholastic convention, and my youthful ankles decorously concealed by the tight folds of a skirt just twice the length of the one I wear now. I listened to the sweeping indictments of 'those awful suffragettes' in a critical silence which became more silent and more critical as the time approached for a battle royal with a recalcitrant family for permission to go to college. (How often, I wonder, do the supposedly emancipated girls of our 'leisured classes' still wage these battles in the smaller towns of this country? More often, I suspect, than most of us imagine.)

The affair of the Rokeby Venus, so my diary informs me, temporarily disturbed my growing sympathy with the despised and derided 'suffs'. School-girls feel – or at any rate used to feel –

a disproportionate reverence for the contents of the museums and picture galleries round which they are – or were – escorted in well-behaved crocodiles. But not for long was my allegiance diverted; even then the voluptuous dorsal curves of Velasquian females appealed but little to my sense of the beautiful and agreeable. The fragile prettiness of Mrs Pankhurst, depicted in effigy at Madame Tussaud's, attracted me far more. Finally, however, it was Olive Schreiner's *Woman and Labour* – lent to me, as head girl, by that same discreet but feminist headmistress – which supplied the theory that linked my personal resentments with the public activities of the suffragettes.

And now that Mrs Pankhurst is dead, though her life was tragic in so many ways, I cannot help but feel that she and the women who followed her were luckier than we. They were luckier, mainly, for two reasons. They fought, first of all, for a clear-cut issue, which was popular in the sense that it was easily understood. Before 1914 you wanted a vote or you did not, and though you might differ as to methods, your object was the same. Suffragists and anti-suffragists were, on the whole, so much less complicated than feminists and anti-feminists.

Today half a dozen things – equal pay, equal opportunities, the right of married women to work, freedom from restrictive legislation, the retention of nationality on marriage – remain to be fought for. They are no less urgent than the franchise merely because less obvious. Yet it is difficult to work for them all at the same time, and even more difficult for all of us to agree that they are all necessary and to decide which matters most. Their common denominator is, of course, that of equal humanity – is or is not a woman a human being in exactly the same sense as a man? But humanity is not a concrete, attainable qualification; it is an abstract idea. As such it is hard to transform into a slogan, and it has an academic flavour that renders it anathema to the present-day youngest women, with their horror of anything that sounds heavy or 'pious', and their self-conscious individualism which regards self-sacrificing devotion to any cause as 'pre-war' or 'démodé'. The woman's movement of today requires a high degree of intelligence and reason in each one of its followers; the feminism of the suffragettes demanded such intellectual standards only from their leaders.

In the second place Mrs Pankhurst was fortunate in being the protagonist of a cause that was won. Even had she not lived to see virtually the victory, she must have known after the Act of 1918 that full enfranchisement was merely a question of time and perseverance. The satisfaction that the realization of an ideal must bring can in this generation be fully appreciated – and envied – only by those of us who left the schoolroom to be told that our king and country needed us; whose naïve young enthusiasms were caught by the false gods of war, drained of their purity and vitality, and five years later flung back, empty and useless, in our disillusioned faces. It is given to few men and women to dedicate themselves, wholly and selflessly, more than once.

But the older feminists, unlike the majority of human pioneers, have seen their dreams come true. More certainly than Latimer in the days of Mary, Mrs Pankhurst lighted a candle in England which neither change nor circumstance is likely to put out. The forms of religious expression change, and one sect follows another into oblivion, but a race or a class or a sex, once liberated, never returns to its old condition of servitude. The candle which Mrs Pankhurst lighted at the beginning of this century has flared into a torch, and the women of today and tomorrow will see that it burns on for ever.

Manchester Guardian, 20 June 1928

᭡

THE SUFFRAGE EXHIBITION

The Suffrage Exhibition recently held in London by the Six Point Group provided a strange comment upon the rewards of human endeavour. In recalling to some of us the political excitements and public heroines of our schooldays, it reminded us also how seldom the vicissitudes of time permit men and women to wage war on society for their own advantage.

Those photographs, letters and relics of prison battles left an oddly mixed impression of triumph and humiliation, of heroism and bathos. A picture, curiously inspiring in its challenging fearlessness, of Christabel Pankhurst as the young Siegfried hung almost next to a chubbily derogatory cartoon of 'St Christabel' at the same period, while close beside these a series of picture-paper snapshots, footed with rather patronizing captions, showed the youthful suffragist leader, clad in an ankle-length hobble skirt, self-consciously posing for the enterprising reporter who had 'discovered' her during her exile in Paris. Portraits of the sad and lovely face of Mrs Pankhurst, the cheerfully resolute countenance of Mrs Pethick-Lawrence and the determined bulldog form of 'General' Drummond touched old press photographs of these same champions kicking and struggling in the arms of hefty policemen.

These, one reflected, looking with a retrospectively impotent anger at the smirking photographed faces of those jocular passers-by for whom the sadistic spectacle provided a free 'show', were the women who fulfilled the supreme test of courage and self-sacrifice by putting their object before their dignity. Thanks largely to those scenes which revealed so clearly the incompatibility of women's clothes with women's claims, the very possibilities of equal humiliation, despite a regrettable return to longer skirts, have vanished with white lace petticoats, spotted veils, curled ostrich boas, and hats on which birds of paradise in full feather rested in overwhelming nursery gardens of flowers and fruit. The pre-war press attitude of contemptuous ridicule, always so much harder to fight than firm political opposition, reappeared in some of the old posters preserved since 1910 and 1911. 'Suffragette Outrage in London', they reported; 'Wild Women at the Palace'. And finally one's eye was caught by one loftily hung evening-paper poster, which seemed to strike the note of the whole exhibition with its huge black-lettered query: 'Where is Christabel?'

Where, indeed, is she? Where are they all whose militant names had acquired international fame when our mothers were the age that we of the war generation are now approaching? If we seek them in the Cabinet, in Parliament, on County Councils, in the once-closed professions that they have opened for us, or at the heads of big businesses that but for them would still be exclusively in the hands of our fathers and brothers, we shall seek them in vain. Mrs Pankhurst, like Emily Wilding Davison and Lady Constance Lytton, lies in her grave. Christabel Pankhurst, leaving other women to fight for those barrister's triumphs which would have come so easily to the quick brain and ingenious tongue of the young suffragist advocate, wanders in the mystic by-paths of Seventh Adventism where her old friends cannot follow her. Annie Kenney, 'Charlie' Marsh and Vida Goldstein no longer draw eager crowds to hear them in Hyde Park or on Peckham Rye. Mrs Pethick-Lawrence, though her feminist ardour still shines above the eclipse of other reputations, remains unrewarded by office or place, while among the young girls of 1910 and 1911 who left the schoolroom to walk with bright eyes and flaunting banners in suffragette processions, Monica Whately is one of the very few to become even a candidate for Parliament. Political eminence has gone, only too often, to women once bitterly hostile to 'The Cause', or has been accepted, with a pretty show of reluctance, by others, not even sufficiently interested to oppose the militants, who were content before the ultimate triumph of the suffragette campaign to leave national and social problems to their husbands.

Reflecting, as I left the exhibition, on the baffling irony of life which reserves its best prizes for those who did not compete, I suddenly remembered Olive Schreiner's allegory, in *The Story Of An African Farm*, of the hunter who died exhausted holding only one white feather of the bird of Truth which he had pursued over deserts and mountains throughout a lifetime. In the hour of death came the vision which told him that he, who appeared to have won so little, had after all his reward. 'Where I lie down worn out,' he said, speaking for all whose war is waged for posterity, 'other men will stand, young and fresh. By the steps that I have cut they will climb; by the stairs that I have built they will mount. They will never know the name of the man who made them. At the clumsy work they will laugh; when the stones roll they will curse me. But they will mount, and on *my* work; they will climb, and by *my* stair!'

The suffragettes, like the hunter, had their reward.

'When I remember those great days', I heard an old militant who had come to the exhibition to revive exhilarating memories remark to the friend who accompanied her, 'I almost wish that we still hadn't got the vote!'

For comrades who have shared the inspiration of any great campaign for an ideal end, the attainment of their object may well bring with it a flavour of Dead Sea fruit. But even sadder is the case of their successors who reap the benefits without having shared in the struggle. The age of consolidation now reached by the feminist movement requires qualities of organization and common sense very different from the courage and heroism demanded by the brief and brilliant epoch of militancy. To those of us who love a fight and find a literary holiday in political polemics, the Suffrage Exhibition came as a rueful reminder that, although we wear the laurels, it was others who won the victory.

Manchester Guardian, 28 October 1930

COMMITTEES VERSUS PROFESSIONS

A few weeks ago I was a guest at a very pleasant house-party which was largely composed of pre-war and post-war members of the women's movement. One evening a discussion arose between those two groups with regard to the value, purpose and duration of committees.

'I like my committee meetings to go on all day,' remarked a feminist leader who had been associated with the movement many years before the war. 'You really feel then that you've got something done.'

One of the younger guests, who has already won considerable success in her own profession, appeared quite scandalized by this statement.

'All *day*!' she exclaimed. 'But when do you do your *work*?'

The older feminist regarded her with a half-amused yet half-rueful expression.

'But you see,' she explained after a pause, '*I* think committees *are* work!'

Nothing, it seemed to me, could have summed up better than this little conversation the essential difference between pre-war and post-war feminism. The pre-war movement was almost exclusively political and legal. It involved, as all political movements do, the expenditure of endless hours in committee rooms, in conferences, in public speeches, in lobbying recalcitrant MPs – hard, incessant, but almost entirely unpaid work of a type for which, until recent years, even the Members of the House of Commons were themselves not remunerated. It would be interesting to estimate how many hours of the lives, for instance, of Mrs Pankhurst or Dame Millicent Fawcett were passed in this way.

After the war, owing partly to women's success in war careers and partly to the limited triumph of political feminism, the movement changed its character and became economic. The significance of this change is still incompletely realized by those older feminists who now complain that the young woman of the present day takes no interest in the progress of her sex. A yet further stage, incidentally, remains, for within the social unit of the family the protected status of woman as wife and mother is still very widely taken for granted. But the gigantic task of making feminism social as well as political, legal and economic belongs to the future; it is with the essence of the new economic feminism that we are here concerned.

It lies, I think, in the acceptance by the younger women of the idea of self-support as a moral principle, a duty as obvious as it has hitherto been for men. In the eyes of the post-war feminist, to live on money entirely supplied by someone else is ignoble and humiliating, however socially useful one's activities may be. The obligation of financial self-sufficiency appears to be equally strongly felt by those who possess either husbands or private incomes or both; in these cases it becomes an obligation to earn in addition sufficient money to guarantee independence should husbands or private means fail. 'My first duty', says the post-war feminist in effect, 'is to do sufficient professional work of some kind to supply me with a living wage or salary. After that I'll see what time I have over for committees and speeches.'

It is not altogether surprising that the women's organizations which arrange morning conferences and 3 p.m. committees do not see as much as they could wish of this professionally-minded young woman. They have not yet sufficiently understood that in her eyes 'leisure' is identified with anti-feminism, and that 'leisure', strangely enough, does not mean idleness, but the failure or inability to earn money.

'Oh, I couldn't possibly join *that*!' exclaimed a hard-working young journalist when asked the other day why she did not belong to the oldest and largest of the feminist societies. 'It's entirely composed of leisured women. They wouldn't understand my point of view.'

It would certainly have astonished Dame Millicent Fawcett and Mrs Pankhurst and most of the other pre-war feminist leaders to hear themselves described as 'leisured', and to be regarded as not-quite-complete feminists because they had no standard professions from which to draw their economic support. Yet this attitude is the logical result of the doctrines that they themselves preached. They knew that woman could not change the world for herself until she was politically free and possessed a vote of her own. Their successors have realized that her freedom must be still limited until she possesses money of her own and need account to no one for the way in which it is spent. Indeed, the need for women who can and will supply funds for new educational institutions and new social experiments by means of which to complete the liberation of their sex was never so great as it is today.

This difference between political and economic independence is the measure of the gulf between pre-war and post-war feminism. It is a gulf which can and should be bridged. The young professional woman should realize that her own happy situation would never have come about if for over half a century women had not been prepared to spend, without remuneration, the greater part of their lives in committee rooms and on public platforms. She will soon learn, too, from experience, that the need for a limited number of such women still exists, as it has always existed for a limited number of such men. Reforms, of whatever kind, are seldom accomplished until one or two persons are prepared to devote their lives to them without reward. Voluntary work is not necessarily amateur work, though the post-war feminist is apt, with youthful scorn, to identify the two.

The effort in toleration demanded of the pre-war feminist is even harder, for she has to try to understand a point of view which is a little contemptuous of those volunteer achievements that she rightly regards as remarkable. She will find, perhaps, most comfort in the realization that this self-sufficient young woman, with her ardent belief in the primary moral obligation to be economically independent, is the logical product of a movement that has aimed from the beginning at putting women on their own feet in a world where money means power.

Previously unpublished: 1929

∾

WOMEN IN INDUSTRY:
RESTRICTIVE LEGISLATION AGAIN

Now that the right of women to the franchise on the same terms as men is acknowledged at least in theory by all three political parties, the next problem of the first importance to women is likely to be that of equal occupational rights. It is true that the advantages and disadvantages of differential legislation for women in industry have been debated at intervals since the close of the Industrial Revolution, but ten years ago the investigations of the War Cabinet Committee on Women in Industry vigorously revived the question, and during the past twelve months the subject has seen the limelight in one fierce debate after another.

The signatories of the majority report of the War Cabinet Committee, though on the whole in favour of restrictive legislation, appeared to find some difficulty in making up their minds whether such regulations were really an advantage to women in those instances where they did not apply to men also. Special sex restrictions were, however, emphatically condemned in the minority report, compiled by no less distinguished an industrial specialist than Mrs Sidney Webb, who expressed her opinion 'that the consolidation of the Factory Acts should be made the occasion of sweeping away all special provisions differentiating men from women'.

The question was again revived at the end of last year in the discussions on the Lead Paint (Protection Against Poisoning) Bill, which virtually closed the painting trade to women, in spite of the fact that wartime and subsequent experience has tended to show that, where pay and conditions are approximately equal, lead as a racial poison is no more dangerous to women than to men. Lord

Phillimore, speaking in favour of an amendment to the Bill in the House of Lords in November 1926, pointed out that the previous classification by Factory Acts of women and young persons in one category no longer represented the real situation, and was resented by women as likely to handicap them in their contest with men in trades and professions for which both were equally fit. Lord Balfour of Burleigh remarked on the same occasion that the humanitarian grounds put forward by trade unions on behalf of these regulations were too often a camouflage for the desire to do away with women's competition.

Two conferences on the subject at about the same date, one summoned by the Standing Joint Committee of Industrial Women's Organizations and the other by the National Union of Societies for Equal Citizenship, showed, as did a debate between Miss Doris Stevens and Miss Wilkinson organized by the Consultative Committee of Women's Organizations early this year, that the problem is one of the most vital confronting industrial women today. Many women workers appear to be troubled by the very natural fear that opposition to restrictive legislation will play into the hands of diehard employers anxious to seize any excuse to delay improvements in factory regulations, and that a demand for equality may lead to the loss of advantages already gained. The whole question is bound up with that of equal pay for equal work, since protection is likely to be offered as a substitute for equal pay, which by improving the health and conditions of working women would tend to remove the demand for special legislation.

The latest discussion of the subject was organized by the Six Point Group on 6 December, when the chief speakers were Mrs Elizabeth Abbott, the President of the Open Door Council, and Dr Marion Phillips, the well-known Labour Party organizer. The chair was taken with great energy and acknowledged partiality by Mrs Barbara Drake, author of the distinguished economic study, *Women in Trade Unions*.

It was scarcely to be expected that either party would succeed in convincing the other, but during the course of the evening several points emerged which illustrated both the difficulties and the scope of the controversy. Mrs Drake raised the first in her opening address, in which she showed that the opposing views on the subject were really based on different sorts of values, of which the one is concerned with the immediate practical advantages of a class, and the other with the completed future triumph of a sex. As so thorough a student of economics herself, Mrs Drake might well have added that only scientific research can really determine the respective merits of the two positions.

In her strong and well-informed speech, Mrs Abbott, who always shows a sound reliance upon reports and documents, spoke of the four evils which the investigations of the Open Door Council have found to handicap the woman wage-earner as the result of differential sex-legislation. 'Protection', she contended, 'invariably lessens a woman's chance of earning more than the lowest wage; it leaves her open to wage-exploitation by employers; it encourages other and extra-legal restrictions; and, last but by no means least, it deprives her of the status of a free and responsible adult human being.' The condemnation of a whole sex, she further argued, was based, not upon investigation, but upon unproved assumptions; for instance, no scientific inquiry into the respective liability of the sexes to poisoning had been undertaken either by the International Labour Organization or by a specially appointed medical commission before women were shut out of the lead paint industry.

The equally clear and reasoned address of Dr Phillips seemed to be based on the supposition that women's past and present disabilities are inevitable and must continue; she neglected the tendency of such limited inquiries as have been made, chiefly in America, to show that woman has hitherto been not so much the inherently weaker sex as, for various economic and historical reasons, the weaker bargainer, which she need not remain. Again, the deep-rooted misunderstanding of feminist aims by industrial women was brought out very clearly; Dr Phillips appeared to be astonished and even confused by the whole-hearted applause which greeted her statement that in many industries protection was as desirable for men as for women. The present demand of feminists is not so much for a removal of safeguards as for a different machinery, such as men unionists have, for obtaining them. Maternity, for instance, may well be better protected by a

State grant-in-aid which enables the mother to take without anxiety as much rest as she needs, than by the cast-iron prohibition which forbids her to work for a specified number of weeks.

Finally, and most definitely of all, emerged the profound confusion in the public mind between restrictive legislation based on sex, and that demanded by feminists, which is determined by the nature of the work and not by the sex of the worker. Only clear and hard facts showing the results of both types of restriction can eliminate this confusion, and impartial scientific investigation is alone capable of eliciting such facts. The position of women in industry is unlikely to alter radically until this controversial problem is faced and studied, without prejudice, and above all without the class passion too frequently aroused by the apparent contrast between middle-class theory and working-class anxiety.

Manchester Guardian, 8 December 1927

∽

WORKING FOR A WOMAN CANDIDATE

Our candidate, with a fine record of public service and feminist achievement behind her, was fighting her first election. She was particularly well equipped for a Parliamentary contest, having a mind which worked with great rapidity, an unusual faculty for translating ideas into words, and a powerful voice which her supporters declared would carry over three counties.

The division itself, needless to say, was recalcitrant to the last degree. It consisted of a rural area surrounding a cathedral town not far from london – one of those hopelessly conservative districts which progressive women are so often made by their political parties to fight three or four times before a more encouraging prospect is permitted them. Such contests no doubt develop the courage and resource without which no woman – or man – would tackle them at all. Nevertheless it is often heartbreaking to see conspicuous talent making difficult headway against the dullness and obtuseness of clodhopping tradition, which is allowed for an unnecessary number of years to prevent this ability from reaching the House of Commons, where swift intelligence and vital speeches are by no means so general as they might be.

There are, all the same, consoling reflections to be salvaged from a cheerful defeat which raised the progressive poll by three thousand votes. These reflections, moreover, have a wider application than the limits of one political party, for in the mere fact of a woman addressing eight meetings a night and being both vociferously supported and heckled at all of them, lies the entire history of a century-old struggle.

What, I wonder, would the shades of our grandmothers, who were apt to faint or go into hysterics after the fatigue of walking half a mile, think of the vigorous woman whose most urgent desire, after her eighth meeting, is not brandy or sal-volatile, but to continue all the way home in her car the discussion precipitated by the last heckler? How would they, who accepted so unquestioningly the ready-made opinions of their menfolk, react to the sight of a woman converting by undaunted argument a public hall filled with hard-headed males?

Perhaps, when their first shock of incredulity was over, they would be carried away by the same wave of crusading enthusiasm which seized the feminist workers in that constituency whose support at earlier elections had been enlisted only on behalf of men. Instead of being the decorative but unimportant accessories of a serious campaign – a mere bevy of human flowering plants on the platform – they would realize that, because of the struggle and the sacrifice of a generation of pioneer women, they had become colleagues working for a colleague in whose footsteps they themselves might one day follow. The young women who cast, as did so many of us, their first votes at this election, must all have been conscious in their different ways of their predecessors who worked to create this recognition of equal political status that they themselves would not share – of Josephine Butler and Olive Schreiner and Mrs Pankhurst – as well as of others, such as Mrs Despard and Dame Millicent Fawcett, who are with us still. But to those of us who voted or worked for women candidates who themselves took part in their earliest youth in the struggle for the franchise, this reminiscence of unpayable debt came most vividly of all.

Numerous anomalies still, of course, remain in these contests between party men and women. Many an old Conservative candidate, such as the final victor in our country constituency, has for years voted in the House against woman suffrage, and only too often has based his arguments upon plausible reasons of chivalry. But when one of these disregarded women becomes his too-intimidating political opponent, confusion descends upon his old values and traditions. Uncertain where gallantry should end and politics begin, he will in one breath offer his opponent the use of a car because his supporters have punctured her tyres, and in the next denounce her without hesitation as a double-dyed liar.

These anomalies, however, though they provide an amusing psychological study for any feminist, are less important than that education of a constituency which a first-rate woman candidate can achieve. Most men are honest individuals who give honour where honour is due, and nothing so quickly inspires their respect as sound knowledge and a courageous readiness to retaliate when attacked – both of them qualities in which many county MPs of long standing are conspicuously lacking. The majority of male voters who came to our crowded meetings to scoff remained, like the parishioners in Goldsmith's 'Deserted Village', to pray. And I do not believe that it was only our imagination which saw in them a growing attitude of equal comradeship towards those wives and daughters who had not only become voters, but were, like themselves, voting for a woman.

Above all, our campaign has been an object-lesson to those hard-driven wives who have hitherto regarded themselves as the insignificant subordinates of their husbands. The sight of a woman effectively occupying a platform and winning widespread allegiance for her party provides the best evidence that life, as much for women as for men, may be a thing of dignity and beauty, of leadership and power. Anti-feminist prejudice, and that inferiority complex which is the most enervating influence that women have still to contend with, are alike disappearing in the constituencies where women candidates have fought.

Now that universal suffrage is achieved, it can only be a matter of time before such women are given seats in accordance with their talents irrespective of their sex. Those who, like our own candidate, are still young may well live to fight elections in that better day. In the meantime the service which they are rendering to their less progressive sisters, especially in the country districts, is beyond calculation.

Manchester Guardian, 5 June 1929

❧

WHAT TALKERS MEN ARE!

'But I never interrupt him,' said Mrs Black, concluding her tale of a dogmatic male acquaintance and his heretical opinions; 'I just let him go on and on, and try to fix my mind on something else.'

Lady Brown looked reflective and sympathetic.

'I know,' she admitted. 'It was just the same when Colonel X came to dinner at my old home. Sometimes I didn't agree with a thing that he and my father said, but I never rose to anything more than an "Oh, really?" '

'Well!' exclaimed Miss Grey. 'That *is* a confession! I know *I* find myself listening to the most infuriating male monologues without a murmur. But I should have thought that *you'd* have the strength of mind to protest!'

Now at first sight there is nothing unusual about this conversation that I heard the other evening. You could probably listen to its counterpart – in varying dialects and with different turns of phrase – at Mayfair luncheons, Village Institutes, and the tea-tables of Putney and Balham. The only thing that made it remarkable was the identity of the speakers, for Mrs Black, Lady Brown and Miss Grey are three of our leading feminists. Few men can equal them in public speaking, editorial ability and literary reputation. Yet even they, despite their opinions, confessed themselves overwhelmed by the still universal masculine tendency to tell women what they ought to think.

Since I heard this triple admission I have begun to wonder why it is that, in spite of the belief in sex-equality which most of us profess, men still hold the floor at the majority of social gatherings. For hold the floor they certainly do. Listen in to the average At Home, the typical dinner-party, the characteristic political function, and you will be obliged to admit that Mrs Dora Russell's description in *Hypatia* of the old-fashioned family – 'Conversation is a masculine monologue punctuated by assent' – has a wider application than she gave it. In fact the public meetings of a woman Parliamentary candidate appear to be about the only occasions to which it is inappropriate.

The explanation is due, I think, to a traditional difference in male and female education. Men have been brought up until quite recently to believe that women are nature's pre-ordained listeners because as a sex they have nothing sensible to say. 'Only Giotto could draw a perfect circle,' ran a 'comic' caption which I saw some years ago in a leading humorous journal, 'but how many women can argue in one!'

And yet, if we except the largely mythical henpecked husband, few men could seriously maintain that as talkers they encounter many rivals amongst women. Man, whether young or old, is notoriously the garrulous sex. He loves the sound of his own voice as dearly as chanticleer at dawn. Never is he so happy as when, in an after-dinner speech, he has a roomful of somnolent colleagues at his mercy. The public speeches made by women are invariably shorter and more to the point. So are their committee meetings. When I attend a women's executive I know for certain that I shall arrive home in time for dinner; but mixed committees, though they start at the same hour, often find me dinnerless at 10 p.m.

Man's inculcated contempt for woman's ideas would not, however, have established him so securely as the dominator of conversations had it not been accomplished by a simultaneous undermining of confidence in women themselves. Up to the twentieth century, and even, in some families, until the war, girls were brought up, like the good child of the Victorian era, to be seen and not heard. They were taught that their opinions, however well founded on facts, had no value because they emanated from a female intelligence.

Even today there is quite a number of 'mixed' organizations which are conducted on the assumption that the women members will not be worth hearing, and are to be tolerated, should they venture to express themselves, only out of politeness. I once belonged – only for a short time – to one such political association, which specialized in after-dinner speeches followed by debates. Never, throughout the period of my membership, was the set speaker a woman, and during the debate, according to conventional procedure, the women present remained silent until, late in the evening, the chairman remarked with a bland smile: 'Perhaps one or two of the ladies would like to contribute to the discussion.'

Once, with a tremendous exercise of courage, I forestalled this weighty permission in order to correct the mis-statements of a speaker with regard to a London slum area in which I had been a school manager, and had worked during two General Elections. The affronted courtesy with which I was heard might have been expressed in the celebrated words of Dr Gregory to his daughters: 'Be even cautious in displaying your good sense. It will be thought you assume a superiority over the rest of the company. But if you happen to have any learning, keep it a profound secret, especially from the men.'

It is not really surprising that, although women have won political victories, they have not yet overcome their oldest and subtlest enemy, the inferiority complex. Diffidence has been too long identified with womanly virtue to be an easy foe to conquer. Until it is routed and extinguished, I suspect that the uninterrupted male monologue will continue to be a conspicuous feature of every social function.

Daily Chronicle, 8 October 1929

ᢒ

MEN ON WOMEN

'Feminism: A Sociological Study of the Woman Question',
by K.A. Wieth-Knudsen (Constable)
(translated from the Danish by Arthur G. Chater),
and 'A Short History of Women' by John Langdon-Davies (Cape)

Professor Wieth-Knudsen, having had the somewhat depressing experience of being born and brought up a misogynist, endeavours in this solemn work to explain his reasons for this peculiar state of mind. The fundamental reason is of course – as he robustly declares through 320 close-printed pages – that Woman is the epitome of all the vices, while her arch-enemy Man is the 'spiritually perfectible' paragon of all the virtues.

According to Professor Wieth-Knudsen, a woman is useless to her husband except as a source of 'food, children and promotion', while such little personal initiative as she ever displays is directed towards 'the sweet hour of vengeance upon Man'. If she works, she is 'soured and anaemic' before thirty; when enjoying herself she makes a noise 'like an army of howling dervishes on the march'. She lacks mental stability and has a monopoly of 'duplicity, faithlessness, treachery and ingratitude'. By her shameless habit of going out of doors unattended after ten o'clock at night she has increased the number of prostitutes in Copenhagen from 1,500 to 20,000 (a fact, if true, which those less well acquainted than Professor Wieth-Knudsen with the wickedness of women might suppose to reflect adversely upon Copenhagen and even upon Man). In spite of these adventures she is, to the extent of 45 per cent of her number, 'erotically anaesthetic', while her tendency, if uncontrolled by her husband, is to 'lead the children dead against his wishes'. If he opposes her she endeavours to 'break his resistance', and to this end sets herself 'to rob him of regular sleep' by such methods as 'introducing animals into the bedroom, which, as is well known, is intolerable to higher natures'.

After reading all this and much more like it, we naturally feel that what Professor Wieth-Knudsen, who obviously cannot have studied at first hand the disorderly millions of Nordic females to whom he so roundly and continuously refers, knows about women is marvellous indeed. How, for instance, does he arrive at his estimate of 'erotically anaesthetic' women, upon whose sexual tepidity his main case against 'feminism' is founded? Enterprising as the professor is, neither he nor his colleagues can possibly have sampled all the women in Europe or even in Denmark. Nor does he supply us with such evidence as might, for instance, be obtained from a questionnaire addressed, through the instrumentality of some colossal organization, to all married women. We have it! His knowledge is, of course, based upon intuition – no doubt an infectious quality, liable to be caught very easily by one who is constantly reading what sympathetic male colleagues have written about women.

Assured as we now are of Professor Wieth-Knudsen's acquaintance with female depravity, we naturally expect him to deplore the fact that all children are left during their most impressionable years in the care of these perverse monsters, and even – since no biologist is as yet able to assure us that that noble animal, Man, inherits nothing whatever from his wicked mother – to suggest some way of continuing the human race without their regrettable intervention. But to our astonishment the Professor does none of these things. He actually regards child-bearing and child-rearing as the main functions of this personification of folly and ignorance, and even describes Woman as having 'moral and educational values for her home and children' – a somewhat surprising accomplishment for such an unstable, immoral, anti-social, extravagant and noisy creature.

Mr John Langdon-Davies, in his *Short History of Women*, takes care to dissociate himself from those authors – such as W.L. George, Anthony Ludovici (and, he might have added, Professor Wieth-Knudsen) – who produce what he rightly calls the 'literature of impertinence'. He is, however, an interesting example of the truth that undeniable historical facts can be made, by careful selection, to prove whatever a writer wishes them to prove. This is particularly noticeable in his treatment of medieval Christianity, which appears at the moment to be exceedingly unpopular amongst amateur biologists.

According to Mr Langdon-Davies, the three essentials of woman's happiness are the worship of fertility, the right to work, and the acknowledgment of rational equality with man. The second and third of these would now be admitted by all reasonable persons, and the first is true in so far as it implies our allegiance to the constructive and affirmative principles in life as opposed to those conventions which prohibit and deny. The author, however, appears insufficiently to acknowledge the tendency of fertility-worship to degenerate into the belief that women have no social value apart from their reproductive functions – a belief which immediately removes them from the category of human being. It is at least questionable whether, over those large tracts of the earth's surface, such as India and China, in which women are calculated only in terms of so much sexual capacity, they are any better off than in Ancient Greece, where, according to Mr Langdon-Davies, they were not, except in Sparta, valued even for this.

Again, it is undoubtedly true that few notions about women have been more universally degrading than the gross, perverted misogyny of the Early Fathers, such as Clement of Alexandria, who declared that 'every woman ought to be filled with shame at the thought that she is a woman'. Yet Christianity established the first social system which offered to women positions, as abbesses or prioresses, that gave them a value independent of their physical functions, and thus acknowledged humanity as something more than either manhood or womanhood. Mr Langdon-Davies does to some extent realize this fact, but he exaggerates the medieval reverence for virginity at the expense of that love of work and authority for their own sake which must have driven many women, who would today be headmistresses or the organizers of Civil Service departments, to take the veil as the only means of obtaining them.

The best part of the book is the author's perceptive analysis of the 'female character' – that monstrous myth, typified in the writings of Dr Gregory and Hannah More, which immured eighteenth and nineteenth century women in a stuffy prison of prudery and inertia. And few feminists can fail to be interested in Mr Langdon-Davies' prophecy of woman's future or in the conclusion of his argument: 'Once both sexes use their reasons equally, and have no unequal penalty awaiting the exercise of their emotions, then women cannot fail to dominate. Theirs is the stronger sex, once nature and art cease their cruel combination against them.'

Time and Tide, 22 June 1928

THE WHOLE DUTY OF WOMAN

There appears to be but little intrinsic connection between a Board of Education Report, and Mrs Gaskell's *Life of Charlotte Brontë*, yet between them the two have been responsible for some melancholy reflections on the whole duty of woman.

The other evening I was sitting beside my fire rereading the *Life of Charlotte Brontë*, when the post brought to me a request for a speech which involved a discussion of the differences still existing between the education of boys and that of girls. My correspondent suggested that, in preparing my speech, I should read the Board of Education Report on the Differentiation of the Curriculum for Boys and Girls in Secondary Schools.

Obediently I pursued with the Report its scientific inquiry as to whether any native inferiority in the female intellect determined that differentiation; so strangely appropriate a comment was it upon Mrs Gaskell's book, that my practical purpose in studying it was drowned in a poignant realization of Charlotte Brontë's bitter problem.

Her honest plan for earning her own livelihood had fallen away, crumbled to ashes ... Her poor father, nearly sightless, depended upon her care in his blind helplessness, but this was a sacred pious charge, the duties of which she was blessed in fulfilling ... I told her very warmly, that she ought not to stay at home; that to spend the next five years at home, in solitude and weak health, would ruin her, that she would never recover it. Such a dark shadow came over her face when I said, 'Think what you'll be five years hence!' ... She did not cry, but went on walking up and down the room, and said in a little while, 'But I intend to stay, Polly.'

A few weeks later, Charlotte herself wrote:

Meantime, life wears away. I shall soon be thirty; and I have done nothing yet. Sometimes I get melancholy at the prospect before and behind me. Yet it is wrong and foolish to repine. Undoubtedly, my duty directs me to stay at home for the present. There was a time when Haworth was a very pleasant place to me; it is not so now. I feel as if we were all buried here. I long to travel; to work; to have a life of action.

So Charlotte Brontë, bound by the gentle and negative virtues of modesty and resignation, stayed at home to care for a sick father, a drunken brother, and a sister whose proud independence of soul approached very nearly to something which at the present day we should probably describe as obstinate stupidity. She sacrificed herself and her genius, and the world is so much the poorer. She produced only three great books when she might have given us twenty. Yet her years of weary martyrdom at Haworth could save neither her father from sorrow, her brother from sin, nor herself and her sisters from premature death.

One wonders whether a calm and resolute refusal to remain in the dark house on the edge of the churchyard for the sake of an invalid might not have had the effect of removing both her family and herself to a healthier sphere, and thus of saving the lives of them all. But in the days of Charlotte Brontë not resolution but submission was the whole duty of woman.

Have we really advanced so much further today? The Board of Education Report on the Differentiation of the Curriculum is only part of a volume of evidence that we have yet far to travel. The idea that the duty of man concerns Things, but the duty of woman concerns Persons, is not the monopoly of reactionaries. We are living still under the shadow of an age which made a woman the first servant of her parents, with the usual alternative of standing in the same relation to her husband, and later to her children. Should unpropitious fortune withhold from her these objects of solicitude, she drifted into attachment to a relative, or possibly (the terms were frequently synonymous) to an invalid, as though woman resembled that type of larva which can only live with its nose firmly fastened to a stick.

This tradition of personal devotion was not confined to the limits of family life. It touched our literature; it inspired our art. Burd Ellen of the ballads might tramp through blood and fire for the sake of Childe Waters, but Joan of Arc, who led the men of Orleans in the sacred cause of France, was burned as a witch. In our pictures the eyes of the Infant Christ look out upon the world, but the eyes of Mary look only to her Son.

Our mothers were brought up to believe in this supreme duty of individual service; they have bound the consciences of their daughters to the same iron tradition. And what has been the effect upon the present generation? The Board of Education Report tells us a good deal; if its scope took it further it could tell us even more.

The talents of a boy are always a source of pride to his parents; they are held to justify him in any choice of life that he may make. When fully developed they commit him to the pursuit of a profession or to the service of a cause. But in the average middle-class family the talents of a girl are seldom the source of anything but domestic controversy. If she loses in the struggle she is obliged, for reasons very different from those of the unprofitable servant in the parable, to bury her talent in the earth. If she wins, she emerges from the contest with so much the less vitality for the arena of open competition.

Even if her claims are reluctantly acknowledged, and she is sent with her brother to training college or university, her handicaps are not yet eliminated. During the vacation the brother goes off cheerfully on a reading party which is by no means all reading. 'Let the lad have a bit of a holiday after grinding away all those weeks at those rotten books,' remarks the typical father indulgently. But the similar grind of his sister is no such excuse for relaxation. Her return for the vacation is regarded in most middle-class households as an opportunity for her mother to 'get a little rest now Mary is at home'.

Apart from the domestic round of every day, she is expected to help elaborately and without thanks in the preparations for every small entertainment, at which immense gratitude will greet her brother if he condescends even to be present. She is able to work uninterrupted for perhaps two vacations out of eight. And then we are told that the results of competitive examinations prove women to be less capable than men of achieving First-Class Honours!

The completion of her training does not even yet release the girl from the agitation of conflicting claims. If she remains at home she cannot give her whole time and thought to the profession in which the first rung of the ladder is always the hardest to climb. Let her be a doctor or a teacher, a lecturer or a writer, the first family illness, the first domestic crisis, will demand her immediate attention. She may be earning ten guineas a week, but in many homes she is still expected to tend her family for nothing and lose the ten guineas as well, in order to save her parents the three or four guineas which would pay for the services of a professional nurse. Only by leaving home altogether is she able to call her time her own. She is obliged to handicap herself in the struggle with the expenses of a separate establishment while her young brother still lives at ease under the paternal roof, indulged and waited upon like an honoured guest.

Even now the whole story of her disadvantage is not finished. There remains her well-trained conscience to be reckoned with, and her carefully learnt lesson of individual claims. Reason may tell her that she is of more value to her clinic of overworked mothers and ill-nourished children than to her invalid father for whom she pays a capable nurse-companion. Yet sentiment and tradition (to say nothing of her relatives) will murmur that selfishness alone urged her to leave the one for the many.

The more she is endowed with the sensitive imagination which adds so much to the value of her work, the more she is at the mercy of pity and of prejudice, the deadliest enemies of achievement. The better the woman, the more desperate the struggle, until she may well be driven to doubt whether her duty be the stern daughter of the Voice of God or the arbitrary creation of her grandmother. Her liberty, if ever it is finally achieved, leaves her with only half her vitality left for her profession. The other half has been exhausted by the battle between her insistent reason and her well-trained conscience.

Can we wonder that the prejudiced and the ignorant, who judge by surface values only, still have grounds for regarding the woman as inherently less capable than the man of holding her own in the race of life? In the home, at school, in the university, in the professions, it is only after a prolonged struggle that she reaches the place where he was able to begin.

Time and Tide, 23 February, 1923

෨

THE PROFESSIONAL WOMAN: CAREERS AND MARRIAGE

For many years the professional woman has waged war upon the convention that a woman's work is a kind of superior hobby, incidental to domestic claims and intermittent amusements. The results of the struggle are now beginning to reveal themselves in some of the newer occupations, where such essentially private considerations as marriage are no longer used as excuses for terminating a woman's career. In consequence many girls, before deciding what form their training shall take, are wisely asking which professions employ only spinsters or widows, and which are compatible with a normal married life.

Married women are at present discouraged from entering or continuing precisely those professional occupations which recent statistics have shown to employ the largest number of women – teaching, nursing, medicine and the Civil Service. The dismissal of women civil servants on marriage is a State regulation which operates throughout the service. In teaching and medicine the majority of women employed are under the jurisdiction of local authorities, of which only a few have seen fit to revise the conventional opinion that a wife's time should be entirely at the disposal of her husband and children. In nursing the position is somewhat different; the exodus of married women is probably to be attributed less to hospital regulations than to the inclinations of the workers themselves. Nursing is still poorly paid, and many of its duties are not dissimilar from the domestic occupations of a household. Less hardship therefore is involved in the transition from hospital to home than in professions where comparatively good salaries are obtainable and a highly-specialized training is required.

According to the Sex Disqualification (Removal) Act of 1919, a woman was no longer to be debarred by sex or marriage from entering any profession or holding any public appointment. In the three professions which would have been chiefly affected by this legislation, a small but vocal minority has protested for some years against the fact that, so far as marriage is concerned, its promises have remained a dead letter. The policy of the Federation of Women Civil Servants includes opposition to the persistent ban on the employment of married women. In teaching and medicine the question periodically becomes a question of controversy in various parts of the country. The dismissal eighteen months ago by Twickenham Higher Education Committee of Dr Isabel Turnadge, an exceptionally well-qualified headmistress, on the sole ground of her marriage and motherhood, aroused a discussion in which even Mr Bernard Shaw was moved to take part. More recently a successful battle against the dismissal of married women teachers was waged under the leadership of Mrs Simon among the members of Manchester City Council. Sir James Purves-Stewart's now famous objection to medical women students, on the ground that 50 per cent of them marry and abandon their work, was universally challenged by women doctors who could see neither logic nor justice in being compelled unwillingly to resign public appointments on marriage and then blamed for leaving their profession. Subsequent investigation of this random estimate showed the number of women doctors who marry and retire to be less than 10 per cent.

The opponents of compulsory celibacy among professional women find their soundest argument in the number of occupations in which married women are already accepted without criticism, and in which they successfully combine public duties with private obligations. There is no prejudice against married women, as such, in social work, in journalism, in advertising, in secretarial work and in all forms of independent business, while in the artistic and interpretative professions, such as the stage and the concert platform, the claims of a very hard and exacting life were fulfilled by married women with children long before the Sex Disqualification (Removal) Act was thought of. A regular eight-hour day at school or office is light compared with that of the actress who has rehearsals every morning, performances every evening, and matinées two or three times a week. Teachers, doctors and civil servants may well ask why the shadow of the cloister, which in the Middle Ages provided the only independent career for ambitious and intelligent women, should loom so heavily over three occupations.

The answer is that teaching, medicine and the Civil Service are long-established professions which inevitably harbour many ancient prejudices and assumptions. One of the most persistent of these assumptions is the belief that 'business' is the chief concern of a man's life but personal relationships the main interest of a woman's, and that marriage is therefore the be-all and end-all of her existence – a belief translated when women began to enter professions in large numbers into the theory that their work was only a 'meantime' occupation between school and marriage, and need be neither carefully studied nor adequately paid. Even a recent writer on careers for the young allows his advice to the parents of daughters to be shaped by this belief. 'Many girls', he remarks, 'are so obviously, and happily, destined for the married state that the parents need not very seriously consider an alternative vocation as a permanency.'

Suppositions of this kind, in a competitive society where marriage and motherhood are themselves at the mercy of economic forces, have already been responsible for too many of the disadvantages under which women suffer, such as the tendency of parents to economize on a daughter's education, her consequent low status as a second-rate worker, the persistence among women of a non-professional attitude, their resulting inability to organize, and, finally, the lifelong relegation of the girl who fails to marry to the ranks of the unskilled, the inefficient and the underpaid.

Teaching, medicine and the Civil Service will probably never fall into line with the newer professions, which utilize every available talent without regard to the private circumstances of the worker, until the safe rule is adopted that efficiency, and not irrelevant personal considerations, shall be the sole basis of selection. Women advertisers, actresses and journalists have already proved that the employment of married women leads to none of those evils, such as the disruption of family life and the introduction of an unstable element into the economic world, which its opponents have prophesied. In the United States one wife in every four is 'gainfully employed' without shaking the solid foundations of that prosperous democracy. The arbitrary regulations that close some of the main avenues of employment to the married woman are dictated by no real consideration for the needs of wife, husband or children; they are based on prejudices which, rooted as they are in the taboo-superstitions of primitive society, find their last refuge in the ancient institution of marriage.

Manchester Guardian, 27 September 1928

'KEEPING HIS LOVE'

The other day my attention was arrested by an article in one of those popular little magazines with coloured covers which are now appearing in such large numbers to tempt the slender purse of the 'home woman'. The article was entitled 'Keeping House for Him', and opened as follows:

The career of the homeworker is the finest in the world. If you can keep your husband's house efficiently, you can also keep his love … Every wife is ambitious for her husband, and, when you come to think of it, a lot depends on her. She has to do with his smart appearance and his punctuality, her cooking makes a great difference to his health, and if she is a cheerful, happy little woman as well as a careful manager, he will be able to go to work free of all home worries.

I can see thousands of 'little women' – to say nothing of their husbands and their critical mothers-in-law – reading over these sugary-sweet sentiments with murmurs of purring approval. Like the writer of the article, they gladly take for granted that, because the work and the objects of the woman-in-the-little-house coincide so exactly with the description here given, they always will and always ought so to coincide. How many of these readers, I wonder, perceive the flagrantly immoral assumptions underlying these childishly innocent paragraphs? Perhaps we can help them to see by a brief analysis.

The first and fundamental assumption made is that a husband, in relation to his wife, is not a rational human being but a peculiarly exacting animal, whose love, which at best is cupboard love, has to be 'kept' by good food, creature comforts, and the same kind of protection against all worries as a too-conscientious mother arranges for her child.

According to assumption number two, a wife is a person without a life of her own. All her activities are second-hand, directed to the career, the appearance, the health, and the punctuality of another person.

Assumption number three impresses upon the 'little woman' that home responsibilities – which include some of the most important problems of life, such as the health and education of children – are not mutual burdens to be lightened for each by being shared with the other. The husband is to be 'spared' them, and the wife, whether competent or not, has to shoulder them all.

Fourthly, the wife is never to be herself, at ease with her husband as one may be at ease with a good, understanding friend. She is always to be acting, pretending to cheerfulness, and concealing difficulties with which her husband has the first right to be acquainted. In other words, throughout her married life she is to play the part of a first-class hypocrite.

Finally, such a marriage can never even approach a happy comradeship based on mutual confidence and respect. It is an employer and employee relation of the worst type, in which the employer is irrational, impatient, unadaptable, and at the mercy of quite unpredictable moods, while the employee receives no wages beyond her keep, and is unprotected by trade union regulations in a most exacting task.

Such assumptions as these, of course, have their origin in our antiquated ideas of courtship – ideas derived from the artificial emotions of the ages of chivalry. These manufactured emotions played their part in the development of human relationships, but their continuance is fatal to that complete honesty of men and women in their dealings with one another which is a main object of the feminist movement and the keystone of the new morality. This dishonesty in the conduct of love dies hard, for we cling as pathetically to the forlorn expedients of insincere artifice as the medieval maiden once clung to her superstitious faith in the love potion. Nothing could prove the struggling survival of the old methods of husband-hunting more clearly than an advertisement, which I came across the other day, in one of the leading American newspapers, of a book designed to coach the would-be wife in the arts of fascination.

Jane Johns is one girl who felt that she was unattractive to men – but she really did something about it. She actually made a serious study of her most attractive girl friends. She observed thousands of tiny things about them that go to make up their great 'It' – and she practised them until she became the most popular girl in her set. She found that she had more 'It' than she ever dreamed of. Then she studied the men she knew and discovered for herself secrets which every unmarried girl would love to know. In short, she learned the mystery of being attractive.

Whether we are English or American it is surely time that our attitude toward the men with whom we work, the men that we marry, and the men into whom our sons will grow, acquired a dignity which is compatible with our political freedom, our present educational standards, and quite incompatible with the propitiatory, apologetic expediencies of bygone ages. To treat a lover or a husband as though he must be humoured like a naughty child or a pet dog is in reality the expression of a profound contempt both for manhood and for marriage. We have no right to select as a lifelong companion any individual for whom we feel so little respect. Tact is necessary in all personal relationships, but even tact becomes mere despicable manoeuvring unless it is based upon an assumption of reasonableness in the other person.

There is still too wide a belief that the art of wifehood – an art that should be studied before matrimony and not only after it – consists of mollifying a child or propitiating an employer. Actually nothing is further from the ideal expressed in our own marriage service than a mother-and-child or employer-and-employee relation. 'The mutual society, help, and comfort that the one ought to have of the other' implies an agreement entered into by loyal adult companions and based upon an equal love and reverence. Such love and reverence do not grow from protection or propitiation, but from the knowledge that one's partner is a respect-worthy and dignified person. To acquire dignity and reasonableness – that is the major task of every human being, whether male or female. The woman who is conscious of possessing these qualities, and who has wisely chosen her husband because he possesses them too, can safely leave the contemptible little expedients of husband-holding to be practised by the infantile-minded who have failed to understand what is meant by adulthood.

Manchester Guardian, 29 November 1929

'SEMI-DETACHED' MARRIAGE

Of recent years intelligent women in ever-growing numbers have been faced with an intolerable choice. This choice has been forced upon them by local government bodies, by education authorities, by the castes that make rules for the long-established professions, and by public opinion of the old-fashioned type. In effect, it is this: Shall a woman who loves her work for its own sake continue it throughout her life at the sacrifice of marriage, motherhood and all her emotional needs? Or shall she marry and have children at the cost of her career, and look forward for the rest of her days to an existence which, for a highly-educated woman, means intellectual starvation and monotony?

Few people appear as yet to understand how wicked is this alternative. They do not seem to realize that, because it involves a limitation, to an unknown degree, of human capacity, it amounts to a negation of human life and its vast possibilities.

Each normal person, whether man or woman, is endowed by nature with a mind and a body, and is intended in the course of his or her development to fulfil the requirements of both. When the natural functioning of either mental or physical powers is artificially thwarted, the individual suffers intensely and in the end becomes warped and bitter. This is especially the case if such frustration is the result of deliberate though unwilling choice. Public opinion is ready enough to acknowledge this fact when a woman refuses marriage in order that she may continue her profession. It is less ready to admit that the woman for whom mental atrophy has been the price of marriage, is no more normal and complete than she who has foregone husband and children for the sake of a career.

The solution of this complex problem is not, of course, beyond the ingenuity of civilized mankind. Man is a reasonable animal; in more than a few instances he is highly inventive and intellectual. The trouble is not that the difficulties of modern marriage are too great for remedy, but that, in everything pertaining to the married state, tradition is so strong that it would rather deny the existence of problems than see them faced and dealt with in a new fashion.

One of the strongest of traditions is that which regards marriage as a day-by-day, hour-by-hour, unbroken and unbreakable association. Our grandparents were wont to boast that they had been married for thirty years and had never spent so much as one night under different roofs. 'Never alone waking, never alone sleeping' appeared to represent the Victorian conception of marriage, and even today there are husbands and wives who would regard brief holidays apart from one another as almost immoral.

Such relationships quickly reached – and still reach – a point where suspicion developed in one partner if the other was long absent, or if every moment of his or her day was not subsequently accounted for. Under such circumstances marriage soon becomes a bondage, with mutual jealousy for chains. Nothing could be further from the free, generous and intelligent comradeship which is the marriage ideal of the finest young men and women of today.

To the extent to which we can succeed in liberating ourselves from these old bonds of jealousy, fear and suspicion, a more elastic arrangement becomes possible. Many recently married men and women have already realized that marriage has been too long the synonym for one domestic ménage, instead of symbolizing the union of two careers and two sets of ideals. They now understand that true comradeship means something more than being always in one another's company, that it signifies a deeply rooted sympathy of minds, an identity of aim though pursued by different methods, and that for this, perpetual association is unnecessary, though intermittent reunion is desirable.

Intermittent reunions, at weekends and during holidays, are often quite easy to arrange, especially for salaried workers with definite hours, such as teachers, secretarial and social workers, local government employees and men and women in most kinds of business. On the other hand, perpetual association, if forced before circumstances readily admit of it, means financial loss as well as complete upheaval for one of the married partners – usually, owing to the strength of tradition, the woman.

That is why many women, and many of the better type of men, who are not so ready as their forebears to sacrifice the interests of their wives to their own comfort, are beginning to practise the more elastic arrangement of 'semi-detachment' – with the children, for obvious reasons, cared for by their mother. They have found that the advantages of living under one roof do not outweigh the disadvantages of one partner being deprived of her chosen occupation, and being thereby made dependent, restless and discontented.

No one of course claims that 'semi-detachment' is as agreeable as a joint household and the constant mutual companionship of two individuals who are too fully and happily occupied to have any room in their lives for the old personal jealousies. Nor is it a solution adapted to every type of man or woman. But, at any rate until circumstances can be manipulated into suiting both parties, it has been found by those who have practised it to be by no means the worst of evils. The complete waste of a woman's training and the frustration of her ambitions is a far greater threat to the success of many marriages.

Evening News, 4 May 1928

✍

DIVORCE LAW REFORM

The large majority by which the House of Commons passed the second reading of the Matrimonial Causes Bill on Friday in effect recognizes that the traditional conception of 'guilt' in a broken marriage belongs to an outdated moral code which attached a special obloquy to sexual misdemeanours, and gave social sanction to vindictive conduct which is itself a form of sin. The passing of the double moral standard has brought with it a realization that hatred, cruelty, jealousy and exploitation are often as much 'guilt' as the matrimonial offence by which a despairing partner may terminate a marriage.

The House has endorsed the honest and merciful realism substituted by the Bill for the social hypocrisy which reserves a moral stigma for one form of wrong-doing while minimizing others. Many who are themselves happily married hope that, for the sake of those less fortunate, the Government will give all possible facilities to enable the Bill to become law, without necessarily rejecting the idea of a Royal Commission to deal with other anomalies.

Letter to the Editor, The Times, 10 March 1951

THE CARE OF MOTHERHOOD

'Save the Mothers', by E. Sylvia Pankhurst (Knopf)

In a letter to Miss Pankhurst, published towards the end of this volume, Mr Bernard Shaw remarks, with perhaps undue optimism for one so critical of our social usages, that 'a book by you exposing obstetric savagery and superstition in the British Isles might attract some attention'.

Whether the degree of interest prophesied by Mr Shaw will be taken, as it ought to be, in this important book, remains a matter for conjecture, but Miss Pankhurst has undoubtedly fulfilled her own part in exposing, very clearly and fully, the 'savagery' of this country's contemptuous indifference towards the needs of maternity and its consequent long endurance of haphazard obstetrical methods of which no condemnation could be too severe. Her study of maternal mortality is mainly based upon the opinions of gynaecological experts, the researches undertaken by Medical Officers of Health and facts given publicity in Government reports. Only seldom does she express her own views or make use of personal experience, while her soberness of statement and deliberate suppression of natural indignation may well surprise those many readers who have hitherto known her as the fervent and uncompromising advocate of unpopular causes.

This admirable restraint is more than the beginning of wisdom, for it renders her book the most damning possible indictment of these national values which permit an annual expenditure of £176¼ millions (the added estimates for the Army, Navy, Air Force and Ministry of Pensions in the last financial year) upon the causes and consequences of human destruction, and only £19½ millions (our contribution in the same year to the Ministry of Health) on the care of human life.

How little, moreover, of even this meagre allocation is reserved for the constructive purpose of maternity and child welfare is brought to light over and over again by this comprehensive survey. The disproportionate economies of which mothers have been too long the patient victims are more than sufficient to explain our present maternal mortality figures. Miss Pankhurst's proposed scheme, given in full constructive detail, for a National Maternity Service, appears an ideal difficult of attainment only because in all that pertains to motherhood and infancy we have fallen so far short even of normal human consideration and common sense.

Let us consider only a few of the amazing facts on which Miss Pankhurst comments. First, though the cruel regulation that mothers may not be admitted until in labour is common to most institutions, only a very few provide ambulances even at night. Thus the poor woman requiring hospital accommodation – usually because she is an abnormally difficult case – must undergo in severe pain the risks and humiliations of a long train or bus journey, though an ambulance is always forthcoming for the slightly injured victim of a trifling street accident. Secondly, the appalling mortality amongst unmarried mothers is largely due to the efforts of self-righteous persons, neglectful of the morality of mercy in the interests of other so-called morality, to punish the offender by excluding her and her helpless child from the benefit of such maternity schemes as may be available. An actual example is given from a Hampshire town. Thirdly, a person suffering from the smallest ailment unconnected with childbirth receives more aid from the National Insurance than a mother before, during or after her confinement. 'Motherhood and womanhood', Miss Pankhurst appropriately points out, 'were at a discount when the National Health Insurance Acts were passed.'

One could quote from this book innumerable further examples of the disastrous consequences which have befallen the race through motherhood and womanhood being 'at a discount'. They are so no longer, but the grave results of their long neglect remain. Only recently have a few pioneer women begun openly to condemn those false social values which have relegated maternity to an insignificant place in the scale of national importance.

Among these courageous critics of twentieth-century 'civiliz-ation' Miss Sylvia Pankhurst, once the eloquent champion of woman's suffrage and now the advocate of that better treatment of mothers which must be, sooner or later, the logical consequence of the vote, has played a conspicuous part. Her efficient and timely book is a challenge to all who care for the welfare of posterity to go and do likewise.

Clarion, November 1930

ও

THE UNMARRIED MOTHER

In these days of rapidly changing moral judgments, Mr St John Ervine's paragraph in your last issue, on Miss Sylvia Pankhurst and the right of unmarried women to be mothers, has a somewhat antediluvian flavour, particularly when he suggests that illegitimacy necessarily involves martyrdom for the child. The tendency of modern humanitarianism and justice is to minimize, rather than to emphasize, the difference between legitimate and illegitimate children. So far is this true, that it has been possible in recent years for individuals whose legitimacy was at least doubtful to rise to the highest offices of State; the late Minister for War in the first Labour Government was even, I believe, accustomed to boast of his foundling origin.

Mr Ervine, moreover, fails sufficiently to distinguish between unmarried motherhood by chance and by choice. The courage and initiative which leads a woman deliberately to undertake motherhood outside marriage is likely more than to atone in her child's upbringing for any disadvantage that it may suffer from initial lack of status. In the many instances, also, in which the child's parents live together, either because they cannot marry or because they disapprove of marriage on principle, the father's influence is no less than in the ordinary conventional home. Despite the modern advocacy of fathercraft, the average father's sense of responsibility towards a child in its formative – and troublesome – years still appears to be nil. It seems even possible that the father of a child deliberately produced outside wedlock may, like the mother, be roused by the knowledge of its possible handicap to a degree of conscientiousness which, when contrasted with the universal abandonment by 'respectable' fathers of the care of their small children to anybody but themselves, may render illegitimacy a positive advantage.

Letter to the Editor: Time and Tide, 18 October 1930

NURSERY SCHOOLS

The recent appeal in the Press by the Presidents of the Nursery School Association for the provision of more open-air nursery schools for children between 2 and 5 years of age has drawn attention to an experiment which provides a solution for many social problems. Child health and welfare, the difficulties of housing, women's unemployment and the combination of motherhood with paid work – all these are questions whose complications would be in varying degrees reduced by the universal establishment of nursery schools.

The nursery school movement, in which Miss Rachel and Miss Margaret McMillan were the famous pioneers, was a logical development of the infant welfare movement. Sir George Newman, in his book *Citizenship and the Survival of Civilisation*, tells us that infant mortality in Britain and the United States, which twenty-five years ago was 150 per thousand, has now been reduced to half that amount. But mere rescue from death is not enough; it is useless to save children for the nation if they are to grow into adults with deformed bodies or feeble constitutions, whose own offspring will contribute in their turn to the large mass of the C3 population. The nursery schools, limited in numbers though they still are, have already proved that such national loss and wastage is preventable.

The average of delicate and diseased children entering the elementary schools today at the age of 5 years is 30 to 40 per cent. The average among children who have attended a nursery school from 2 to 5 years is only 7 per cent. Though from 80 to 90 per cent suffer from rickets when they first enter these schools, these cases are all cured within a year by the open-air life and the careful dieting at the midday meal which is provided. Other 'minor ailments', such as scabies, ringworm and impetigo, have practically disappeared.

The foundation of physical health is, of course, of little value if mental health does not follow in its wake. In Dr Cyril Burt's tables, issued by the LCC to teachers, the distribution of intelligence is shown as follows: 46 per cent of all school children are normal, 20 per cent are bright or supernormal and a very small percentage stand even higher. This leave 30 per cent of dull or subnormal children, but Dr Burt reckons that of these 30 per cent are dull only through neglect in their earliest years. These unnecessary victims of bad housing, smoke-ridden towns and overworked parents are the first to be rescued by the regular routine, combined with the methods of awakening interest and intelligence, which the nursery schools provide.

From start to finish all the equipment of these schools is carefully adapted to a child's needs and capabilities. In the children's playroom, which is gay with plants, flowers and pictures, the books and toys are kept on accessible shelves or in low cupboards from which the children can help themselves. The chairs and tables are tiny and can easily be moved by small hands. A door in the wall opens into the garden, where seesaws, rabbit hutches and a sandpit are provided. Even the washbowls in the lavatory are tiny, and each peg of clothes is marked by a little picture which the child can recognize as his.

The day begins at 8.30 or 9, and ends at 4. The morning's work – chosen, as soon as they are old enough, by the children themselves – may consist in the alternation of singing games and rhythmical exercises with clay-modelling, brick-building, feeding pets or gardening. Twelve o'clock is dinnertime, and an hour's sleep follows. A nurse is there to attend to tiny ailments or accidents. At the midday meal the children are taught to serve themselves and one another. Nothing is done for them that they can do for themselves, and thus a foundation of mutual as well as self-discipline is laid.

Though the welfare of the child must be put first among the advantages of such a scheme, there are others which come only second in social importance. Teaching, we are told, is overcrowded: how are we to find work for all the girls who wish to enter this profession? Among would-be teachers there are many who would prefer, if only the work were available, to deal with tiny children rather than the more difficult and less attractive 6-to-14s. The establishment of a nursery school in every town or country district would provide a large number of posts for such girls. The superintendent of the school is in every case a certificated teacher specially trained and qualified for nursery school work, and she draws a salary equivalent to that paid in accordance with the Burnham Scale to all teachers of similar experience.

One final controversial question remains for which the nursery school provides at least a partial solution. The abandonment, still generally taken for granted, of paid work by a girl when she marries is the fundamental disadvantage of all women throughout the whole field of their employment. Whether she works in office or factory, or whether she is a university woman pursuing a profession, her payment and her limited opportunities for promotion are alike based upon the assumption that she is a temporary worker. We are told by women with long trade union experience that restrictive legislation, which helps to keep women at the bottom of the labour market, is unavoidable because they are more difficult to organize than men, and that this inferiority of organization is mainly due to the marriage and departure while still young of those vigorous women who if they remained at work would become leaders and organizers in early middle age.

No doubt a majority of women will always prefer the more personal work of a home to that of a factory or an office, but it is probable that women whose natural gifts entitle them to lead their fellows would be as eager to remain at work if they could as is a talented doctor or teacher or journalist to continue her profession. Present social arrangements mean a very hard life, which only women of exceptional character and ability are prepared to face if professional or industrial work is to be continued and the household well run at the same time.

Nursery schools are of the greatest possible assistance to women who wish or are obliged to combine motherhood with paid work. To be able to leave a child in good hands from nine to four is an inestimable boon to the mother and an advantage to the child, who requires companionship of his own age and specially adapted occupations and surroundings far more than he needs the constant society of his own parents. The nursery schools now so urgently needed for the children of the poor are likely to provide a way out of her difficulties for the professional woman also. The Nursery School Association is at work upon an experiment which should command the interested support, not only of mothers and social workers in poor districts, but of economists, sociologists, political scientists, and all other abstract thinkers who are studying how best to improve the organization of a complicated world.

Manchester Guardian, 29 March 1929

❧

I DENOUNCE DOMESTICITY!

I suppose there has never been a time when the talent of women was so greatly needed as it is at the present day. Whether great talent or small, whether political, literary, practical, academic or mechanical, its use is a social duty, for the simple reason that all ability is at a premium in our depleted generation.

Fourteen, fifteen, sixteen and more years ago, the men who are now between 30 and 50 – that time of life when promise blossoms into achievement, and the capacity for leadership grows into authority which holds sway in every department of human activity – were almost all engaged in war. When the fighting ended and they came home from France, from Italy, from Palestine, from Mesopotamia, they left behind them more than a million of their comrades who were destined never to grow older than 19 or 22, or 25.

In the case of some of the young poets, such as Rupert Brooke and Edward Thomas and W.N. Hodgson, whose work was published and acquired fame, we are able to calculate at least part of what literature lost with these men who never again took up the pen that they had exchanged for the sword. But in the fields of politics, of foreign affairs, of local government, of teaching, and in the more exotic spheres of music and art, it is less easy to estimate the extent of our misfortune, since ability in these directions is apt to develop late, and the opportunity to hold commanding positions seldom offers itself until early middle age.

We only know that in the white-walled cemeteries of France and the Italian mountains, on the desolate slopes of Gallipoli and beneath the shining sands of tropical deserts, lie the lost leaders who might have rescued us from the political and economic disasters which have recently made such a holocaust of hope.

139

As a nation we have sacrificed all this talent, and yet, with a singularly crass incompetence, we fail to make use of that which remains. Still, for all practical purposes, ignoring the fact that men form only half the population of any nation at any time, we forget that one sex remained almost unimpaired by that historic violence of death and mutilation. Women, as much as men, inherit the ability of the race – daughters, indeed, are popularly supposed to reproduce more often than sons the energy of capable fathers – and yet they have failed to replace even in part that sum-total of national power which disappeared between 1914 and 1919.

At a crisis in world history when every ounce of vitality, of initiative, is required to weight the scales against catastrophe, we may well ask why the social contribution which women's ability could and should make has somehow been stifled at its source.

The answer is that, with a few exceptions, the gifts of every woman who marries – and marriage naturally comes, and for the sake of the race ought to come, to those who are most vital, most able, most attractive – are dissipated and submerged owing to the stultifying persistence of an unadapted, anachronistic home life. I do not mean by this that the objects pursued in the home – the efficient care of the minds and bodies of its inhabitants, the maintenance of a happy marriage relationship, the rearing of children to be healthy and valuable citizens – are negligible objects. On the contrary, I believe them to be of the first importance. But I do maintain that the methods by which they are at present carried out are antiquated, wasteful, expensive, and infinitely destructive to the potential achievements of the women who shoulder the lion's share of domestic responsibility.

To this contention I can hear a number of readers objecting: Well, what, after all, does it matter if married life is exacting for women, if nearly all household duties take longer than they need, if most wives dissipate their energies from sunrise to sunset upon a hundred unrelated trifles? It is only the exceptional woman, the literary or artistic genius, who will be inconvenienced by civilization's failure to rationalize the home – and exceptional women are too few and far between to justify the alteration of social arrangements which suit the majority.

Here I would reply, with all the vehemence at my command,

that it is not merely genius that our country needs today, but all ability, in any shape or form, which is capable of being used for national purposes. What we lack so conspicuously is the normal proportion of conscientious, enlightened intelligence – of the type that our universities call 'good sound Seconds' – which make for efficient government, sincere internationalism, and progressive municipal authority.

The woman who washes dishes, knits woollies and makes junkets when she might be leading a local education committee from negative obtuseness to constructive activity, is as much an example of national waste as a brilliant playwright condemned to darn stockings. Of course, we cannot – as someone will undoubtedly object – use all our able women on work of direct national importance; the scope of politics, of local government, even of voluntary organizations, is limited, although that of creative art and of certain kinds of business is not. But we do want to make suitable use of the best women we have, and this article is written to point out that our present domestic system operates against that freedom of selection which alone brings the best to the surface.

Except for the comparatively fortunate owners of modern tenement flats, the wage-earning classes of this country still live in badly planned, inconvenient little houses which harbour dirt, involve incessant labour, and are totally unequipped with the most elementary devices for saving time and toil. Sometimes they are without electric light, sometimes without gas; frequently, in country districts or ancient slums, they are supplied with neither. Bathrooms are non-existent, and often there is no running water or indoor sanitation; every drop of water used has to be carried, and slowly or expensively heated in individual kettles. Though all the household laundry must be done at home, no modern apparatus for washing and drying exists; in the absence of scullery or washhouse, every object in the one or two small living-rooms becomes damp and dim with steam. Sinks are always of the wrong height and relegated to the darkest corner, while such conveniences as built-in cupboards, pulleys and fitted plate-racks are unknown. Even gardens or small yards, where infant children can sleep in the open, are the exception rather than the rule.

The melancholy tale of archaic planlessness could be continued indefinitely. It can be summed up by saying that the home is the one place upon which sufficient capital has never been spent, with the result that, in literally millions of households, women with poor tools and no modern equipment fight a perpetual losing battle against the ever-accumulating detail of domesticity. Year in, year out, they waste human energy and valuable intelligence upon tasks which machinery could perform more quickly, more easily, more cheaply and more efficiently.

All over the country, girls who have been usefully trained as secretaries, as teachers, or as social workers, are struggling to hold on to knowledge and intelligence beneath the burden of trivial but exacting organization to which marriage and motherhood automatically but quite unnecessarily bind the woman who undertakes them. The intimate and purely personal relationship of marriage has suffered unduly from the false identification of wifehood with domestic economy, for marital success does not, and should not, depend upon the economic occupation selected by either partner. Actually, the present nightmare of domesticity is, perhaps, the worst enemy of monogamous marriage in the modern mechanized world; it involves too great a contrast in the life of 'emancipated' woman before and after marriage, and chains her to trivial, irrelevant cares which arouse resentment in herself and automatically destroy fascination.

But even if it were possible by the wave of a wand to change our archaic homes into the clean, light and airy dwellings dreamed of by the utopian town-planner, we should still, without a change of heart and of education, suffer from our thraldom to the domestic tradition of the individually managed household. Most wives and mothers are still hypnotized by the belief that houses can be run and families reared only if a hundred separate little meals are cooked by a hundred women, and a hundred lonely children are escorted round streets and parks by a hundred isolated nursemaids. The idea that talent and energy can be diverted from the self-regarding home to the service of the State through co-operative effort and the pooling of responsibilities is still regarded as a species of unnatural and highly dangerous communism.

I happen to live in a spacious Chelsea street which is practically a blind alley; on either side of the wide road, writers and artists, living in flats or studios or little houses, pursue their exciting careers with zestful determination. Nothing, I imagine, would better please the women among these workers than to be released for ever from cleaning, housekeeping and shopping, yet their separate gas stoves still burn away in their tiny individual kitchens, and at spring-cleaning time a score of vacuum cleaners whine plaintively through the air. Only a very little reorganization would turn the street into a domestically self-sufficient community, with communal kitchens, laundries and nurseries, where two or three trained domestic organizers, paid by joint contribution, could supervise the activities of a much-reduced army of charladies and send round the communally-owned vacuum cleaner in accordance with a prearranged programme. Yet I fear that the studios and the flats will have vanished beneath the housebreaker's hammer before their owners devote their undoubted intelligence to solving in co-operation the urgent problem of their own freedom. The one hope of progress lies in the open-air nursery school on the corner, to which almost all the street's children run daily, in joyful eagerness to join their companions; it is, perhaps, a portent.

Labour-saving houses, well planned and well equipped, kitchens, laundries, day-nurseries and nursery schools established on a communal basis by joint effort for mutual benefit, trained specialists in domestic organization employed by each group to engage and supervise all the household 'helps' in the little community – these are some of the social expedients which will release married women to fulfil the public duties that await their ideas and experience. No doubt there will always be a few who cling to the old wasteful isolation and refuse to co-operate, since unnecessary domestic preoccupations offer to the socially irresponsible woman, who does not want to use her mind or to take any part in disinterested service, a way of escape from public obligation similar to that of the 'escape into illness' indulged in by the self-centred neurotic.

But every woman who has eyes for the world outside her four walls would welcome the elimination of widespread waste. Sparring with incompetent tradespeople, responsibility for the training and cleanliness of young maids, should not rest upon the political woman, the woman councillor, the woman journalist, the woman JP; the country needs her undivided attention to the national work for which she is suited. Even her children should not be permitted to destroy her social effectiveness, and it is no more to their advantage than to hers that they should do so. Babies and toddlers are far happier when they can enjoy the society of their contemporaries in properly equipped day nurseries and nursery schools, than living, lonely and constantly thwarted, in houses primarily adapted – in so far as they are adapted to anything – to the needs of adults. Moreover, a child's mentality derives no benefit from the growing consciousness of maternal sacrifice; modern psychologists now agree that the most satisfactory home is one in which both parents lead lives of their own and avoid that neurotic concentration upon their children which is noticeable in too many mothers.

Each generation has not merely to produce the next; it is at least as important to create a better world for its descendants to live in. There is no virtue in mere continuity. 'What's the use', as a friend of mine remarked the other day, 'of hammers making hammers, and never a nail knocked into the wall?'

The ability of women is nationally needed as never before, but it cannot be used until we acknowledge to ourselves the urgency of a fundamental reconstruction of married women's work and position. The three essentials of this reconstruction are the rationalization of the home, the elimination of wasted time and energy by co-operative effort, and a new emphasis in the education of women, which will stress the existence of responsibilities outside the family, and teach them that domestic work is not life, but merely a means to living.

Quiver, August 1932

WOMEN STILL WAIT FOR EQUALITY

Many young women to-day regard their mother's struggle for equality as a closed chapter of history. 'Why go on with that old stuff?' they inquire scornfully. 'It's simply flogging a dead horse!'

No doubt the young German women thought the same just before they lost, five years ago, almost everything that their woman's movement had won for them.

With Fascist influences rampant throughout the world, the time has not yet come for women to feel confident of their position. Only recently the closing of administrative posts to women in the Colonial and Dominions Offices has served as a reminder that 'eternal vigilance is the price of liberty'. It is true that, with the minor exception of the House of Lords, English women have achieved political equality. But they are still very far from economic equality. In many industries and professions they do not yet receive equal pay for equal work.

A woman teacher, for instance, receives by the Burnham Scale a salary which is four-fifths that of a man's. The alleged reason is that her expenses are less, though I have yet to learn of any commercial company which charges a woman four-fifths of a man's rate for gas, electricity, food, water and transport.

In 1921 the Civil Service gave official recognition to the principles of equal pay and equal opportunity, but years later it adopted scales of payment which meant more rather than less disparity between men and women. A year or two ago, when the women tax-clerks at Somerset House asked for salary equality with men, their request was refused.

For most women, equal opportunity is also an unsubstantial myth. Many jobs are still open only to spinsters. The example set by the LCC in raising its marriage bar has not been widely followed. Marriage is now reluctantly acknowledged as an asset to a woman doctor, but it still means dismissal for most Civil Servants, secretaries and teachers.

The risk of marriage is given as one reason for excluding women altogether from our Diplomatic and Consular services. Another is the supposed objection of men to serving under women, which in other professions supplies a popular excuse for refusing a woman promotion to the highest posts. She must not be a judge because she would have to direct male barristers and jurors. She cannot be appointed to an important administrative position in the Civil Service because a roomful of men would be working under her.

This objection to feminine leadership seems peculiarly characteristic of English manhood. It is much less pronounced in the United States, whose male citizens certainly do not lack virility. America not only admits women to her Diplomatic Service, but promotes them when they have served their apprenticeship.

Washington appointed Mrs Ruth Bryan Owen as Minister to Denmark, and quite recently sent Mrs Borden Harriman to represent America in Norway. In the United States women can be, and are, created judges. American women have successfully challenged the masculine monopoly which in England prevents most women barristers and solicitors from making a name or even a modest income. In 1880 America already had 75 women lawyers. Today she has over 3,000.

Even in England, the bias against women in responsible positions is confined to certain conventional occupations. I have never met a male author who objected to writing a well-paid magazine article because the editor was a woman, or an actor who refused a part in a promising play at a woman manager's theatre. In politics, also, the woman who has proved her value easily commands masculine support. I cannot imagine a constituency in which the men would not work as loyally for Ellen Wilkinson as for any male MP.

Why, then, should not women be diplomats, judges, chief inspectors and administrative officers? Today, when the training and experience of women has changed out of recognition since the time of our grandmothers, it is prejudice alone which prevents these appointments.

Numerically, perhaps, the group affected is not large. Millions of women workers can never hope to be highly salaried Civil Servants or successful lawyers, and may wonder why they should concern themselves with these limited middle-class claims.

The reason is that so long as one category of workers holds a lower status than another, the value of every member of that category is thereby reduced. Industrial women receive a lower minimum wage than men in many trades for precisely the same reason that women in professions are refused promotion or dismissed on marriage.

Those nations which cannot outgrow their prejudices are still living the dead life of the past. A society does not thrive in the long run by setting traditional limits here and putting irrational restrictions there. It fulfils its highest destiny by offering more opportunity and an ever-widening freedom to those vital qualities of energy and initiative which, whether found in men or in women, are alone capable of carrying forward the boundaries of civilization.

Daily Herald, 26 March 1938

✍

WOMEN WORKERS, TODAY AND TOMORROW

For the second time within a generation, England's women workers are deeply involved in a world war.

There is one thing, and perhaps only one, to be said in favour of these gigantic conflicts, which have dictated the history of our time. They are convulsions which shake all life to its foundations; and though they destroy too much that is good, they bring down antiquated traditions and prejudices as well. Because war is a time of testing, it is also a period of opportunity. Of no section of our society is this truer than of its women.

The last war completed the struggle of women to escape from the tyranny of Victorian homes. Before that war began, this country had witnessed such now historic conflicts as the fight for higher education, the struggle to enter hitherto masculine professions such as medicine and the law, and the campaign for the franchise. After so much preliminary spadework, the changes brought by the war came fast. Between 1914 and 1919, women had entered industry and the professions in large numbers. They had shown ability in fields hitherto regarded as beyond their powers. Being required to move as well as to think quickly, they had discarded the voluminous garments and complicated coiffures of Edwardian fashion. They had already achieved emancipation in practice when the partial franchise was bestowed on them in 1918, and in 1919 the Sex Disqualification (Removal) Act admitted them, at least theoretically, to the majority of professions.

So far as women exclusively are concerned, this war is unlikely to bring so many dynamic changes, but rather, by further establishing the right to equality and the capacity for full comradeship with men, to continue what the first cataclysm began. Women will find themselves part of a far greater revolution which will involve society as a whole in its results. As Ralph Ingersoll remarked of the dancers at the Dorchester in his wartime book, *Report on England*: 'What is about to expire is not the breath in their bodies but their property rights in banks and mortgages. What is about to end is life as they knew it.'

Students of history realize that we are now at the close of that epoch of modern European history which began with the Renaissance. We live in an era potentially as tremendous in its consequences as the fall of the Roman Empire. The first Great War started revolutionary changes in certain sections of society. The present war is likely to make them universal. A new page of history is about to be turned. How far are the women workers of today preparing for the chapters which they will share in writing?

Both industry and the professions clearly show the signs of the times. One of the most important developments has been the increasing use of compulsory powers by the Minister of Labour, culminating in the recent National Service Act which empowers him to direct women into the Auxiliary Services. The chief steps towards this compulsion have been the withdrawal of girls from 20 to 25 from the distributive trades (with the exception of the food trades), from the light clothing trade (women's underwear, children's clothes, millinery, etc.), and to some extent from the Civil Service. Since the Employment of Women (Control of Engagement) Order came into force on 16 February, women between 20 and 30 have only been able to obtain employment through the Labour Exchange.

In the great munition and engineering industries which now absorb so many women, there are three groups of female workers. These comprise the women doing work which was known as women's work before the war, the women who are doing men's work but are not recognized as thus engaged, and the women who are doing men's work, whether skilled, semi-skilled or unskilled. By no means all these women belong to what were commonly described as 'the working classes' before the war. Quite a number of middle-class girls from secondary schools, called up under the National Service Act, are now going into factories. Some hope to use their experience after the war to obtain posts as factory inspectors and welfare officers. Although important supervisory positions are reserved for women with previous experience, many of these girls get promotion to the category of 'charge hands' who supervise a number of workers.

There is now litle segregation in industry between men and women workers as such. Any practical working division between the sexes is dictated by the nature of the work and not by prejudice. It is recognized that distinctions between 'men's' work and 'women's' work are largely arbitrary. Many women are naturally talented on the mechanical side of industry, and are often regarded as better at precision work through having more patience.

This does not mean that none of the old inequalities remain. The attitude of official England towards women was shown at a recent meeting of the International Labour Organization in New York, when the British delegation did not include one woman even in an advisory capacity. Discriminations against women exist throughout the field of compensation and insurance. Under the Personal Injuries (Civilian) Scheme a woman is paid 7s. a week less than a man for civilian war injuries, and under the National Insurance system women's benefits and allowances are less than men's. For this reason a woman's recovery from sickness is often retarded, since she cannot afford to buy nourishing food or to take sufficient rest.

But on the whole the main handicaps from which women suffer in industry, as in the professions, are the two from which, despite frequent promises of amendment, they have suffered since the last war – limited opportunity and unequal pay. In wartime there is a tendency to exploit women and make patriotic appeals to them to sacrifice claims which have hitherto been regarded as excuses for denying them equal rights. Married women tend to be the chief sufferers from this policy. In many occupations, and notably in such professions as teaching and the Civil Service, women before the war were dismissed on marriage with the plausible excuses that the sacredness of family life would be impaired by a mother going out to work, and economic stability disturbed by two incomes coming into one home. But as soon as women's work is required on a large scale, both these excuses go by the board. The sacredness of family life has not prevented government pressure upon married women to enter industry, leaving their children with neighbours or, if they are fortunate, in day nurseries. Nor does anybody – except perhaps magistrates concerned with cases of juvenile delinquency owing to excessive spending power – worry unduly about not only two, but five or six, incomes going into one home.

In munition factories the women doing men's work receive about four-fifths of a man's wages. 'Munitions' now include every requirement of war in addition to the death-dealing and damage-inflicting weapons which are at present the main objects of production. Lorries, signalling sets, searchlights, the very tools themselves, all become munitions in wartime. Their makers are recruited from such 'non-essential' industries as dressmaking, cosmetics, jewellery, and the various branches of the tourist trade.

Under the Government Training Schemes, even more marked inequality of pay exists. Men of 21 and over receive a weekly wage of 65s. 6d., with a first and second increment of 5s., making a maximum 'male' rate of 75s. 6d. Women of 21 and over, though doing the same work, receive a weekly wage of 43s. with a first and second increment of 3s., making a maximum 'female' rate of 49s.

At a Training Centre for three hundred women in London, I talked to a girl who had worked at Harrods' Stores, to the ex-proprietress of a dressmaking establishment in South Molton Street, and to an actress who had belonged to a repertory company. Later the woman superintendent sent me a list of occupations previously pursued by the trainees at the Institute. It read as follows: 'Office workers, 58; housewife or no specified occupation, 138; dressmaker, milliner, tailor, 21; cutter or designer, 7; saleswoman, 23; teacher, 16; journalist, 13; beauty specialist, 11; supervisor, 14; artist, 10; actress, 8; catering or domestic, 17; ARP, 8; nurse, 5.' There are now about forty Government Training Centres in different parts of the country, as well as a number of Emergency and Auxiliary Training Establishments.

Owing to the enormous development of mechanized warfare and to the existence of these training centres, engineering is the profession in which the position of women has most markedly changed. A woman with a gift for engineering has a much better chance of success than before the war, when women were not employed in engineering shops, and pioneers such as Amy Johnson and Caroline Haslett had considerable difficulty in acquiring the necessary training or finding it for others.

But engineering is not, of course, the only professional field for women affected by the war. In the Civil Service a large number of women of all ages are being taken on as temporary clerks, and many women graduates on coming down from the university become Temporary Assistant principals (Administrative Grade). In September last the Woman Power Committee of the House of Commons, led by Miss Thelma Cazalet, MP, took a deputation to Mr Eden on the subject of women's exclusion from the Diplomatic and Consular Services. In a letter to the committee some time afterwards, Mr Eden explained that all regular entry into these services was suspended for the duration of the war, but agreed then to consider the appointment of a committee to examine the question again 'in the light of existing conditions'. Meanwhile, he said, as a wartime measure he was prepared to consider applications, 'through the normal channels', from women as well as men for temporary posts of the Administrative Grade in the Foreign Office whenever any vacancies arose.

Neither in the Foreign Office nor the Civil Service, judging from the wholesale demobilization of women holding clerical posts after the last war, does there seem to be much prospect for the future. The field of accountancy appears better; at present there is a great demand for accountants, and if a girl is articled to an accountant when she registers, she is allowed to remain and finish her articles.

All the professions which previously admitted women are still open, though the uncertainty of being allowed to continue their training is affecting the entry of women over 20. Owing to a change of outlook since the last war, women university graduates seldom go into the Services. One of the characteristics of the present younger generation, among men as well as women, is a desire to get out of uniform rather than into it. A specialist in the field of women's employment recently remarked that today the women anxious to wear uniform are mainly 'the less educated rather than the college type'.

We are still, perhaps, too far from the end of the war for any detailed prophecies about its effects upon the position of women as such. The chairwoman of a leading women's organization lately stated: 'I do not think that the position of women will be as bad as it was after the last war, as I do not think that the government or employers will care to drop back to the old attitude to the same extent. We can make more fuss, or rather a more effective fuss, than we could then.' The extension of the National Service Acts to women certainly includes all statutory safeguards, such as those of reinstatement or compensation on demobilization. If we lived in a wholly logical society it would seem obvious that one reply to Nazism, which regards women as auxiliaries, would be to treat them as equals.

After the last war, the often-repeated pious decision by public bodies – 'We must have *a woman* on this committee' – gave expression to the public opinion which, still with some surprise, was praising women's achievements. When the present conflict ends, popular sentiment, having long taken for granted the presence of women in public life, is more likely to say: 'We must have Mrs X on this committee because we need an expert accountant – or statistician – or legal adviser.' If women, by training, fit themselves now to fill positions open to those with special qualifications, they will be ready to play their part in that unknown, difficult but adventurous future which lies beyond the end of this war.

Quiver, May 1942

PART THREE

Politics

Winifred Holtby

SEX AND THE POLICEMAN

We are celebrating the centenary of Josephine Butler not inappropriately by a thorough awakening of national interest in the public aspects of sexual morality. We have been shocked by the Savidge case; indignant over the arrest of Miss O'Malley; uneasy about the two Scottish attempts to revive compulsory treatment for venereal disease; agitated by the controversy concerning public teaching about birth control; interested in the sessions of the Home Office Committee on Street Offences; perturbed by the revelations of Miss Mayo in India and Judge Lindsey in America; impatient over the delay in raising the statutory age of marriage; and enthusiastic over the action of the League of Nations against the international traffic in women. Yet we do not seem to realize that this final action lends an entirely new importance to our other preoccupations. The convention on the traffic in women goes no further than to admit that international commerce in women for purposes of prostitution is a crime; but by going so far it creates a precedent of immense significance. It establishes the first clause in a minimum code of sexual morality to be observed in all civilized nations. Undoubtedly there will be further developments. We are unlikely to stop at a single principle.

If the theories governing our laws about public morality were simply our own concern, we should do well to clear our minds about them, much as we dislike definition of general principles. But when it appears that we can no longer limit the responsibility for our actions to our own nation, it is even more necessary that we should take stock of our existing practice. Granted that we do not believe that men can be made good by Act of Parliament; granted that we learn to place increasing trust in educational methods of individual reform; granted that our private judgments upon sexual morality vary from the puritan standard of the devout nonconformist citizen, to the almost equally devout libertarianism of those who, like Dr Norman Haire, believe that boys and girls would do best to mate at sixteen and thenceforward live a complete sexual life; yet it is obvious that certain actions surmount the barriers of our private differences, and present themselves as matters for public intervention. In a nominally democratic State, directly we permit the invasion of the policeman into the private ground of personal morality, we can no longer disclaim a certain responsibility for the theories justifying that invasion. 'The Law', said Hobbes, 'is the public conscience.' By what principles is that conscience stirred? We read the evidence before the Home Office Committee on street offences; we read the parliamentary debates upon the Edinburgh Corporation Bill; the discussions of the Portsmouth Labour Conference upon public instruction in methods of contraception; and we come to the conclusion that we really do not know what we want.

It is important that we make up our minds, at least to a minimum standard of what is tolerable, because, whether we like it or not, we are committed to some kind of action. We have before us Lord Parmoor's Traffic in Women Bill, the Home Office promise to raise the age of marriage, the Committee on Street Offences at present considering its burden of somewhat confused and bewildering evidence, the tribunal appointed to inquire into the action of the police in interrogating Miss Irene Savidge, and the pressure by Edinburgh and Glasgow for parliamentary permission to examine, detain, and treat persons suspected to be suffering from venereal disease. We shall only scratch the surface of any reforms required of us along these lines unless before dealing with them we make up our minds to answer publicly two or three questions which already some of us have answered privately, but upon which our laws still give us no clear direction.

Are we or are we not prepared to embody in our common law an equal moral standard for both sexes? No revision of our law concerning street offences can be effective which continues to obscure this issue. Witnesses before the Home Office Committee realized this, yet seemed reluctant to acknowledge it. The Chief Constable of Manchester admitted that in his city – one with a good record in these matters – magistrates followed the practice common to both England and Scotland, and required evidence of soliciting by a man from a woman witness, but not of soliciting by a woman from a man; giving as his reason that it does not seriously affect a prostitute to be convicted of solicitation, but that it would ruin a man. Lord Balfour of Burleigh was questioned upon the Public Places (Order) Bill which he introduced into the House of Lords and which places offences of annoyance by soliciting committed by men or women on the same footing. Certain members of the committee obviously doubted his sincerity in regarding the Bill as a practical proposal. 'The committee will agree', said Lord Balfour, 'that an equal moral standard is desirable. The question is, whether it is possible. If so, we must get rid of the existing law.'

But is it possible? This would seem to be a question for the moralists. A second question, often confused with the former though really quite different, is rather a question for the scientists. Is some form of prostitution necessary? Mr R. Ross, Chief Constable of Edinburgh, told the committee that if the words 'common prostitute' were removed from the law, and, apparently, the prostitute herself from the streets, 'you remove one of the main safeguards of the virtuous woman.' But if the prostitute is indeed the protector of virtue, why is she not honoured for her necessary and noble work? Witnesses seemed to suffer from some confusion. One admitted that the institution was necessary yet would wish to 'turn prostitutes off the streets'; another referred to diseased prostitutes as 'dangerous animals'. Obviously if the healthy prostitute is a desirable member of society, we are foolish to oppose, as we have opposed at Geneva and elsewhere, State toleration of vice, the establishment of licensed brothels, and the compulsory inspection and medical treatment of prostitutes.

On the other hand, if the prostitute is unnecessary, then one of two things would appear to follow. Either men and women may live healthily in chastity or within the legitimate confines of monogamous marriage, or else some form of legitimized temporary partnership is desirable.

We appear to be singularly poor in our evidence of the former possibility; the latter has been suggested by several witnesses before the Home Office Committee, who agreed that public order had improved through the intervention of the 'amateur'. Judge Lindsey's picture of modern American youth confirms it for another continent; many of our contemporary novelists imply it for this country. If indeed men and women, freed by birth control from the unwilling conception of children, are living together as a common habit, should we not do well to recognize some form of 'companionate marriage'?

If we agree that certain actions are anti-social, however, upon what are we to base our definition of crime? Shall we prosecute only for offences which cause public annoyance? At present in this country, as in New York and other States, we punish sodomy and unnatural vice which may affect only two co-operating persons, or even one. The Savidge case arose out of an arrest for an indecent action which, even if it had been committed, took place in the twilight and without other witnesses than the police investigator, and which could therefore have caused no public annoyance, since the guilty parties might have been supposed to perform it for their pleasure, and the policeman saw only what he had gone forth to see.

If, indeed, we must set up the police as guardians of public morals, are we sure that we are recruiting the force from among the right people? It was Mr Forbes Lancaster, KC, Metropolitan Police magistrate, who said, not long ago, 'I yield to no one in my admiration of the way in which the police discharge their primary duty to the public in the protection and defence of the life and property of His Majesty's subjects, but I do not regard them as ideal custodians of public morality, and the sooner they are relieved of their duties in this respect, the better it will be for their own reputation and the safety of women lawfully using the public streets.'

The guardianship of sexual morality is a highly difficult, delicate, and controversial duty. For such a task, honesty and conscientiousness are not enough. We need for it human insight, judgment and experience in no small degree, some scientific knowledge, and very great powers of discrimination and good sense. Are we prepared to recruit, train, and pay such guardians adequately? If not, what do we really expect of our policemen?

What, indeed, are we going to do about the whole business? Let us, as Mrs Ray Strachey tells us, 'face the facts' by all means; but it is also desirable that we should face our theories.

Nation and Athenaeum, 23 June 1928

∽

THE VEGETARIAN MILLINER

I have recently come across a paragraph in the *Manchester Guardian* which gives me that particular satisfaction which comes to us when we encounter our old problems under a new guise. 'A branch official of the National Amalgamated Union of Shop Assistants', it runs, 'reports to his union that a woman who keeps a milliner's shop is insisting that her assistants shall be vegetarians like herself or they will have to leave.'

Now that at once suggests a complex situation. There may be people who are vegetarians for fun, but I have never yet encountered them. All the vegetarians whom I know – I am not one myself – are so because they believe the slaughter of animals for human food to be a barbarous and degrading custom. They are probably right. Every time I read one of Mr Bernard Shaw's stringent remarks about people who feast on corpses I wonder how it is that I can continue to eat roast pork and chicken with equanimity. In any case, I feel that in all probability the vegetarian milliner is a person of high and serious principle.

Nor do I believe that employers threaten their employees with dismissal just for fun. The kind of woman who is herself a vegetarian for humanitarian reasons is probably the kind of woman who lies awake for a week before deciding to dismiss an improver or an errand-girl. I know of few more wretched experiences among the minor miseries of life than the bad half-hour before the interview in which one has to tell someone to go. I am sure that the vegetarian milliner does not want to lose at one fell blow all her assistants. It will probably ruin her business.

Her orders will be late. The hats will not fit. The new girl will probably have adenoids, the matcher will lack an eye for colour, and the improver will have perfectly appalling ideas of her own; one knows how it can be in a workroom.

Still, the milliner has reached that stage of conviction when not only can she not endure to eat meat herself, but she cannot sit in the same house as a meat-eater. *Ecraser l'infâme.* She must become not only a practitioner of her own principles but a propagandist, and a propagandist by compulsion. We have met this kind of thing before in the landlord who cannot endure tenants on his property who do not vote Conservative in the general election, the manufacturer who cannot stomach trade unionists, and the nonconformist whose aversion to Papacy is such that he would not have a Roman Catholic on the town council if he could prevent it. There has been recently a growing tendency among political parties to demand conformity in matters which do not immediately affect party issues as well as in those which do. The Labour party has issued to its branches a list of societies with which they may not affiliate. Its candidates are subjected to a similar act of uniformity. Heresy-hunting has always been a popular human pleasure, but we are mistaken when we attribute all its activities to insincerity. Just as some otherwise courageous and normal people cannot bear a cat in the room, so others cannot endure the proximity of an Imperialist, a divorcee, a meat-eater, or a Jew.

The attitude is partly instinctive; there is the strong sense of repulsion. But it is also partly strategic. Solidarity gives strength. The fear of heresy as an undermining influence runs through the history of human organization. The group draws together against not only the stranger but the person of alien ideas. Even if those ideas do not mean direct opposition to the purpose for which the group is formed, they are felt to be dangerous. Curious habits and strongly held opinions combat the social forces of crowd feeling and docility. The milliner probably does not feel that her assistants will make any the worse hats for eating ham sandwiches in their lunch hour; but she probably does feel with good reason that ham-eating in a vegetarian establishment leads to criticism, and so to disloyalty, that it breaks up the corporate cohesion of the group, and that it is wrong in itself.

There comes the rub. What are we to do about this strong moral conviction which we have that some things are wrong in themselves and must not be tolerated? The Grand Inquisitor undoubtedly often felt the sentiment which Bernard Shaw attributes to him in 'Saint Joan' of strong desire to save the soul of the heretic. Love of the sinner as well as hatred of the sin illuminated some of the acts of intolerance which we unthinkingly rank simply among the tales of human oppression. The milliner probably wants to prevent her assistants from committing an evil and cruel sin upon her premises. She would rather have them unemployed, with all the moral and physical dangers attendant upon unemployment, than complacently countenance their commission of sin under her roof. The heresy-hunting parties which drive away promising candidates because of one unorthodox opinion which they hold, the churches which excommunicate inconvenient saints, the societies which shun the individual convicted of one specially feared type of unusual conduct or belief are moved probably by what they feel to be the highest moral motives.

But beside the conscious motive which declares its inability to tolerate sin there is the more often unconscious motive of hunger for power. We should all like to inflict our beliefs upon our fellows. We enjoy enforcing conformity. We harbour a misguided illusion that the world would be a better place if we could induce our fellows to accept our own ideas of it. I certainly fall into this error myself. I should like to see all my friends and acquaintances keen feminists, believers in the ultimate right of all persons to find their own level irrespective of sex or race. I should like to see them all with a taste for fine literature, charming clothes and houses, enlightened education (rather vaguely defined because I am not yet sure myself what is enlightened), for sea bathing, free discussion, weekly reviews, my own writings, and State-supported hospitals. But I believe that if I had my own way with them for a fortnight I should soon find my newly made world a tedious place.

After all, there is something in disagreement. I never admired my housekeeper more than on the night of the general election. I had been canvassing all day, and at night went to hear the results announced in the Queen's Hall with some strongly Socialist friends. When we came in we found supper laid on the table by our Tory housekeeper. She had decorated the room with cornflowers and blue ribbons. She had gone to the trouble of unearthing and putting up some old blue curtains. The colours of her political party greeted us every way we turned, and our only surprise was that she had not hung the Conservative candidate's poster in our window.

Now the world would be a dull place without that spirit. The candidates which a party refuses to endorse because of their unorthodoxy on some special point are probably the very people who could best serve the party. The assistants who refuse to exchange their ham for salads are probably the best hat-makers. 'Notions of liberty', Professor Laski once wrote, 'are always in a difficult case. For their very basis is an admission that men ... are united only by partial bonds.' But perhaps the hardest lesson for us to learn is that this world is a complex and not a simple place, that one man's meat is another man's poison, and that even good is relative, not absolute.

Manchester Guardian, 20 March 1930

THE LABOUR PARTY DILEMMA

I have been amusing myself recently by the acid cattishness of Mr John Scanlon's little book, *The Decline and Fall of the Labour Party*. It is full of crude and over-simplified economics – a sort of nursery Marxism; for instance, this, as an explanation of the ILP gospel:

They believed, rightly or wrongly, that any system which produced goods to the value of £1 and then hoped to have them consumed by giving the worker, who was also the consumer, 10s. to buy back £1's worth of goods, was bound to create gluts.

And he believes too much in 'the simple solution of making purchasing power equal productive power', which may be desirable, but only a simpleton would call it 'simple'. Yet the book is not only immensely readable; it contains a profound psychological truth. The real tragedy of the Labour Party since the war has been a tragedy of confusion of values. Its members did not know whether they wanted to make happy, complacent, middle-class citizens of us all, with a hierarchy of wealth, plus morning-coats, plus breeding, and the standards and social code of nineteenth-century society, with its leisured ladies, conspicuous consumption, social superiorities and all, or whether they wanted to establish an entirely new standard of human values. Mr Scanlon traces their decline through the abandonment of the second ideal for the first. I think he is right. We live by instincts and ideas, and ultimately our ideas modify our instincts. At present we act as though the gentleman whose sole aim in life is to reduce his golf handicap is a more reliable citizen than the driver of the Cheltenham Flyer. I do it myself, subconsciously suspecting the plumber, or the man who delivers the milk, of vices I should more justly attribute to bishops. We all, I think, except a few rare creatures, act as though possessions were more significant than personality, intelligence, or mere beauty. And our lives are starved and distorted, according to the measure in which we model them upon standards which are economically impracticable and spiritually contemptible. The loss is ours.

Time and Tide ('Notes on the Way'), 26 November 1932

✍

A SHOWMAN FOR PEACE

Cry Havoc! By Beverley Nichols (Cape)

The case for peace needs its Cochran. The trouble about so many appeals for common sense in world politics is that they are dull. Their arguments may be unanswerable, but the other side has all the emotional vitality; it has the news-value, the power and the glory. Of all institutions the Church alone can rival the Army in mastery of spectacle. It also has the ponderous weight of tradition behind it; its ritual has been consecrated by death. But choir boys are not drilled like drummer boys. At the Anglo-Catholic centenary High Mass, one ecclesiastical official succumbed to nature and put up an umbrella. No umbrella has ever broken the superb precision of the Trooping of the Colour. The Czecho-Slovak Sokols can achieve a brilliant perfection of mass movement; but the Army has the music, the banners, the prestige of ancient corporate memory. What can a League of Nations Union Garden Party, with a peace pageant organized by the vicar's daughter, do in the face of the Aldershot Tattoo? What phrase of music is more profoundly moving than the bugle call of the Last Post? How can the most enlightened speaker on, say, the political consequences of economic isolationism prevail against the skirl of pipes and the march of a Highland Regiment down the road?

'*La Patrie est en danger*', 'Your King and Country need you'; the old appeals, the old tunes, run like madness in our blood.

The instinct they arouse is not ignoble. It is only irrelevant. Our country *is* in danger. The menace of war is all too imminent and too real. But the call to arms in its defence is never again going to protect it. The Aldershot Tattoo, the Territorials' march, the OTC parade stir the old memories; but they have nothing to do with future safety. Worse; they give a sense of false security. The Hendon Air Pageant is a little less irrelevant, but its lesson is ambiguous. The case for fighting for one's King and Country is magnificent. The trouble is that it is out of date.

We have been warned. There was the sober and by no means ultra-modern Mr Baldwin's speech on air warfare and youth in the House of Commons. There was Mr H.G. Wells's remarkable broadcast address on 'Communications' last winter. There have been imaginative prophecies such as Zilzer's cartoons on gas warfare published recently in this paper. There have been multitudinous and authoritative reports by military and scientific experts.

But it takes a popular writer to popularize a subject. It takes a fashion expert to indicate to most of us when our instinctive reactions and preconceived opinions are old-fashioned. The grave authorities have been warning us that the nationalist-military idea was no longer practicable; soldiers as well as statesmen have impressed upon us that territorial frontiers do not run across the heavens. But we needed a Bright Young journalist of the Sunday press, a writer of revues and intimate confessions, a disciple of Mr

Cochran, to assure us of the undoubted truth that the military idea is out of date.

Let there be no mistake. The Beverley Nichols of *Cry Havoc!* is the same lisping sentimentalist who perpetrated *Prelude, Patchwork* and that crude Thackerayan imitation, *Self*. But he has done what few sentimentalists contrive to do. He has grown up. He has applied his quick wits, his facile and picturesque pen, his dramatic temperament and his wide experience in showmanship to a problem which is enormously important, difficult and urgent. The result is a book written upon the folly of war as an instrument of national policy, the influence of the armaments' manufacturer on politics, and the wild idiocy of our irresponsible, acceptance of outmoded forms of thought, which is a really valuable contribution to social sanity.

Cry Havoc! has the defects of its qualities. It is sometimes unnecessarily facetious. It is more often unnecessarily overwritten – as in the descriptions of the mountains above Geneva on page 135. It is exasperatingly self-conscious. There was, for instance, no need for Mr Nichols to write on page 32, 'I am a pacifist, honoured by nobody', unless he hoped for an eager contradiction from admirers crying, 'No, no, dear Beverley Nichols! We honour you!' The references about mothers are as faintly nauseating as most of Mr Nichols' references to mothers.

But let nobody be deterred. If the book has the defects of its qualities, it has the qualities of its defects. It is an admirable piece of showmanship. Mr Nichols has made the pacifist's pilgrimage in search of a creed exciting. He has acted as producer to eminent authorities, Sir Norman Angell *versus* Lord Beaverbrook, Major Yeats-Brown *versus* Mr Robert Mennell, Mr G.D.H. Cole *versus* Sir Arthur Salter – and no 'turns' in a Cochran revue have been better staged. Mr Nichols' apprenticeship in the theatre has served him well. Whatever else is wrong with this book, there is not a dull page in it. It has done what a hundred more sober arguments could not do. It has shown the anti-war apologists how to popularize their case. And the case it states is the true one.

The book is first of all exciting. There are descriptions of a visit to a munition factory, an amusingly vain attempt to inspect the great French armaments centre at le Creusot; there are details, in a chapter characteristically called *To Make Your Flesh Creep*, which suggest what gas warfare will mean to a civilian population, that really achieve their indicated intention. Mr Nichols took trouble. He himself put on a gas mask and entered a poison-testing chamber. He did not like it. No one would have liked it. 'I walked up the stairs. Into the chamber. The world, now, was only a whirling of grey veils, a choking and a gasping, a foul nightmare. It was not that one was afraid, for there was nothing whatever to be afraid of. The mask was working perfectly ... No ... it was the psychological effect (to quote my friend) which was so appalling. One felt so helpless, like a trussed animal in a burning building.' Quite. Mr Nichols asks us to imagine what that would be like continued for twenty-four hours. 'Twenty-four hours is a long time. Supposing the raid came at four o'clock in the morning. By four o'clock in the following afternoon you would be wanting your tea, to say the least of it. Your head would be bursting, your brain on fire' ... 'In the most recent defence of London air manoeuvres, out of a total of 250 aeroplanes which took part in a night attack on London, only sixteen were even discovered by searchlights, let alone shot down', Mr Nichols reminds us. But when he visited Marlborough, his old school, and asked the Corps Commander of the OTC 'Do the War Office supply you with gas-masks or do you have to buy them yourselves?' the reply was 'Gas masks? We don't have any gas-masks! Nor any gas training ... ' 'But surely it's fairly generally admitted that the next war will be decided in the air?' 'It is not admitted *here*.' OTCs, like national armies, are out of date.

One of the admirable qualities in the book is its honest admission that it is derivative. Mr Nichols borrows freely from such reports as *The Secret International*, published by the UDC, *What Will Be the Character of a New War?*, published by Gollancz, and *The Menace of Chemical Warfare to Civilian Populations*, by A.J. Gillian. Where his own knowledge fails, he calls in experts to help him. Sir Norman Angell's challenge to Lord Beaverbrook, which he quotes at length, is as devastating as Lord Beaverbrook's failure to reply. Cole and Salter make an admirable pair of duellists. Mr Nichols' final indictment of school histories comes well after the preparation of the ground by better qualified authorities.

It is the function of a popular publicist to be quotable, nor does Mr Nichols fail here. The cake is full of plums. 'Mr Asquith ... made very pretty play with his unsheathed sword on more than one occasion in August 1914. But if, instead of the phrase 'we shall not sheathe the sword' he had used the phrase, 'we shall not desist from gassing babies', the emotions of his audience might not have been so exalted.' 'It is precisely because man is insular that he should be international ... When I first walked into the hall of the League of Nations I saw so many unpleasant foreigners that I felt that Englishmen were, by comparison, gods. I saw Italians whose faces oozed with grease. Japanese with such fixed and irritating smiles on their faces that I wanted to bash them, Frenchmen who smelt of *violette de parme* and looked as though they had just come from a rather slippery orgy with pink and white mistresses, Spaniards of abominable arrogance, elbowing people about ... I bustled with Brittanic zeal. For this very reason, I prayed for greater strength to the League of Nations as a curb to my own British instincts.' That is recognizably true. So is the description of the digestive and atmospheric handicaps of delegates to the Disarmament Conference. But even more striking is the entire chapter called *The League and the Liars*, and the final anecdote of the journalist in the chapter called *The City of Hope*. This journalist roused Mr Nichols from uncomprehending despair and showed him the real value of the League's work. ' "If only the *people* could be made to realize that," responded Mr Nichols. "If only the press of the world would not always sneer. Now, *you're* all right. I don't read your newspaper, but I imagine you'll cable back a pretty encouraging report?" ... He drew a crumpled wad of manuscript from his pocket and began to read. "Another staggering blow was dealt to the moribund League of Nations this afternoon when ... " He grinned. "You see," he said, "my paper doesn't like the League of Nations." ' For that story alone Mr Nichols deserves our thanks. It explains much.

But there are other stories, equally illuminating. Behind Mr Nichols' occasional vulgarities his self-consciousness, his over-apologetic whimsicality, is the *flair* of a first-rate producer. Read this book. Be irritated, annoyed, or stirred to contradiction if you like. I promise that, unless mentally defective, you will not be bored.

Time and Tide, 12 August 1933

❧

HITLER AND THE GERMAN RELIEF COMMITTEE

Talking of enthusiasm, I attended last Friday evening the meeting in Kingsway Hall organized by the German Relief Committee, and saw there displayed two copies of the German edition of the *Brown Book of the Hitler Terror*, and one copy of the prohibited German paper, *Die Rôte Fahne*. The Brown Books were printed in microscopic letters, bound in plain yellow paper, about two inches by three, easily slipped from hand to hand and into pockets. The paper was printed on four flimsy sheets, the size of ordinary book pages, easily rolled into the shape of a cigarette. These books, these newspapers, are carried by men and women who know that discovery means instant death, or life in a concentration camp, which may be less tolerable. They know that the traffic in prohibited literature endangers not only themselves but their families and their friends. They have no thought of gain, and no reward but the consciousness that with each book distributed, each newspaper slipped into a cigarette case, one or two more German citizens may learn a few of the facts, which never appear in German newspapers, about the foundations on which the Hitler régime has been built. At the meeting we were assured that there are hundreds, no, thousands, of men and women calmly taking these risks, distributing banned information, distributing food parcels to families of men in the concentration camps and prisons, distributing relief to the dispossessed. Their names, their performances, will never and can never be known publicly. Their activities stir beneath the surface of German national life. I remember as a child on our tranquil farm reading of the fictitious escapades of the Scarlet Pimpernel during the French Revolution, and of the real escapades of the Carbonari during the Italian Risorgimento of the nineteenth century, and thinking that such daring, such devotion, belonged to a remote, romantic world. Yet here are the little secret books, the five-mark food parcels, the meetings in London, the rough vigorous community-singing of that depressing tune which can yet stir the heart when shouted with conviction, the *Internationale*; here are the heroism, the tragedy, the waste. I know well enough that in Berlin the Horst Wessel song is being chanted with equal sincerity by young Nazis as disinterested as those Socialists who in London cheered on the efforts of their German comrades by singing the *Internationale*. It is not valour which humanity lacks; what we really seem to need at this juncture in our affairs is enlightened common sense. It is the old lack, the old sorrow ... 'If thou hadst known, even thou at least in this thy day, the things which belong unto thy peace!' ... But we do not know. They are still hid from our eyes; and with the best intentions in the world we terrify, imprison, torture and oppress each other.

Time and Tide ('Notes on the Way'), 21 October 1933

✍

UNEMPLOYED IN 1934

'Memoirs of the Unemployed'
Edited by Lance Beales and R.S. Lambert (Gollancz)

I implore readers to buy, borrow or steal this poignant book. It is readable, though not what is called 'easy reading'. Here are twenty-five accounts, collected originally for publication in *The Listener*, of what it actually feels like to be a skilled artisan, whose ability is rotting for want of practice, an ex-officer who tries to sell tennis rackets on commission, a village carpenter hanging round the house and garden unable even to invent an odd job to keep him occupied, a South Wales miner 'too old at 49'. These people have told their own stories. The ring of truth strikes through their bitter sentences. Here is the carpenter: 'I don't intend to see my wife or boys starve, and I don't intend to starve myself. I've got a good pair of hands on me and I mean to use them. If I'm not allowed to earn bread I shall take it'. Here is a Scottish hotel servant, self-respecting, fastidious and intelligent: 'Ministers all over the country deplore the great craze for gambling which has sprung up within recent years. What is the chief cause? The natural desire of decent men and women to obtain for themselves and their children those absolute necessities of life, such as boots, warm clothing, proper food, which the wage formerly provided but which the dole denies.' Here is a Derbyshire miner's wife: 'My husband ... is a changed man ... He never complains, but I wish he would. It makes me unhappy to find him becoming quieter and quieter when I know what he must be feeling. If I had someone to talk to about my troubles I should feel better ... We quarrel far more now than we have ever done in our lives before. We would both rather be dead than go on like this.' In all the records there is a craving desire for work as the one thing that makes life worth living. In some there is a burning hatred of injustice and the patronizing 'charity' which is supposed to mask it. In some there is humour and sturdy pride, as in the rulleyman who explains that he cannot do dock work or building, which mean climbing ladders, as he has no head for heights; 'but give me a rulley and a good horse and I'll hold my own with anybody. I'm as well known in the carting world as Lloyd George is in parliament.' These are real people, human and decent and aware. If their book is heart-rending it is also important. These are the men and women of 1934.

Good Housekeeping, March 1934

❧

SHALL I ORDER A BLACK BLOUSE?

I recently saw a healthy, vigorous-looking specimen of Fascist youth striding down the King's Road, Chelsea, to that grey pseudo-Gothic ex-theological college which is now rudely dubbed 'Ecstasy Castle' to distinguish it from the more sober 'Transport House'. This young Fascist was a tall, well-built woman in the early thirties, with close-cropped black hair, black beret, black blouse and party badge. I had to admit that her uniform was business-like, her walk determined, her air pleasantly self-confident.

She had probably attended a Fascist rally and thought, with the optimism of inexperience, that a mass meeting denotes mass conversion. Perhaps she saw the British Blackshirts, and herself among them, as pioneers and crusaders, marching to sweep away from their beloved country decadence, lethargy and confusion. They would smash the foul slums and build a new Jerusalem; they would take the unemployed youths, rotting their lives away in squalid by-streets, the bored, indifferent or neurotic leisured women; they would take the lonely, the devitalized, the cynical and give them a part in the corporate state, a faith, a hope, something to live for. The Fascist leaders have at least learned this lesson, that it is not the invitation to prosperity and ease, but the call to sacrifice, labour, pain and effort which wins the finest followers.

Thinking all this, I was almost tempted to walk into the Fascist headquarters and inquire how I too could qualify to wear a black blouse. Then I wondered. After all, I recalled, that enviable sense of exaltation is not the exclusive property of the Blackshirt movement. It has been observed in Catholic converts, Salvation Army recruits, militant suffragettes, Communists, Jacobites, Jingoes and pacifists alike. A thousand different enthusiasms have illuminated dawns in which it was bliss to be alive and very heaven to be young. And if I choose one, will it be Blackshirtism? There are, I feel, disadvantages about it.

From what has occurred in Germany, Italy and Japan, it seems to me that Fascism is too closely related to nationalism to be comfortable. Though Sir Oswald Mosley has repudiated repeatedly the charge of chauvinism, I cannot believe that his semi-military organization, his stress of national and racial distinctions, and the things which he permits his followers to say, really make for peace and international confidence. Though I can recognize the austere satisfactions of intolerance, I have seen enough to suspect the civilization of the concentration camp. I do not relish a country in which men are afraid to speak their mind, or to perform the ordinary offices of friendship.

I believe that there are other ways than Sir Oswald Mosley's for securing the organization of industry, reform of parliament, redistribution of income, and renaissance of national vitality. And

171

I do not particularly desire to advertise my political loyalties by the wearing of a coloured blouse.

These observations would, I think, alone convince me; but there is one other. At present I feel and think as a citizen and an individual; if the Blackshirts were victorious, I should be expected to think only as a woman. 'The part of women in our future organization will be important, but different from that of the men,' wrote Sir Oswald in his latest book, *The Greater Britain, 'we want men who are men and women who are women.'* The italics are his. They are characteristic of a creed which, wherever practised, has resulted in an attempt at sex-segregation.

'It has been suggested that hitherto in our organization too little attention has been paid to the position of women,' says Sir Oswald. 'This is not because we underrate the importance of women in the world, but because our political experiences have led us to the conclusion that the early stages of such organization are a man's job.' Whose experiences? Whose conclusion? Not the women's, I somehow feel – not that young woman's marching down the King's Road.

I agree that there is today a tragic sex war in industry, where women are made involuntary blacklegs; but you won't cure that by putting the men into black shirts. Fascist methods as adopted in Germany by Herr Hitler and advocated in England by Sir Herbert Austin may create temporary employment for men by driving women out of industry; but that is no permanent solution.

Perhaps even least of all do I relish leadership by the type of mind responsible for Sir Oswald's utterances on the middle-aged woman. Speaking of Parliament in that same article, he says, 'The field of women's interests is left clear to the professional spinster politicians' (elsewhere called by him 'elderly spinsters') who used irrelevantly to be described as the "members for No Man's Land". It will not be surprising to those familiar with this distressing type that the interests of the "normal woman" occupy no great place in the attention of Parliament.'

When I remember how certain 'professional spinster politicians' such as Susan Lawrence, Ellen Wilkinson and Margaret Bondfield, how certain middle-aged women of this 'distressing' though not spinster type, such as Lady Astor, Mrs

Wintringham and Lady Noel-Buxton, have worked in Parliament for better education, maternity and child welfare, child protection, school meals and slum clearance, I hesitate to respect Sir Oswald's powers of observation. Nor can I feel great enthusiasm for the quality of culture represented by a gentleman who suffers from that painful complaint of super-sensitiveness which leads certain men to regard women between the ages of – shall we say – 40 and 70 (silver-haired mothers being sacred anyway) – with the disappointed aversion of one who, expecting a good hot meal, finds only the congealing substance of an under-boiled egg left too long in the shell.

I am not at all sure that I am not one of this distressing type myself, or soon shall be; so I somehow feel that black blouses are not the wear for me.

News Chronicle, 4 May 1934

∽

RED FLAGS IN LONDON (see note p. 362)

'If they aren't intending to make trouble, why are they marching?' … 'Shopkeepers along the line of route are advised to board their windows … ' 'Special constables have been drilled to take over traffic duties while the Regular Force are released to maintain order … ' 'I wouldn't go near the Park for fifty quid tomorrow. I got my arm twisted last time. This time they say the coppers are going to have machine guns – like in Austria.' Press rumours, street rumours, committee rumours among those knowledgeable members of the Left who claim to recognize a copper's nark even if disguised as a dustman, and to know the secret thoughts confided by Lords Lloyd and Trenchard to their midnight pillows. If all these could have aroused expectations of terror, surely they would have done so.

But whether because of the reports of the orderly march along the country roads, or because of the rain drizzling mildly from a field-grey sky, or because of the natural irresponsible optimism of English sightseers, the crowds that followed the marchers into the park, and strolled among the peanut vendors and souvenir programme sellers, wore no aspect of witnesses at Revolution. They came with babies in arms, with bicycles, with perambulators; they came in fur coats and running shorts and mackintoshes; one young girl trod the muddy grass with a pale blue ankle-length dance frock below her winter coat.

And they were justified. Never can there have been a more orderly demonstration. Punctually at three o'clock the helmets of mounted police nodded above the crowd; the thin music of drum and fife played the *Internationale* (pronounced 'internationally', because it has to rhyme with 'rally', a trick which gives it a significantly cosmopolitan air); the first crimson banners tossed and swayed from Marble Arch, and the southward march of the Glasgow contingent reached its final stage. From north, south, east and west the serpentine processions wormed their way towards the eight Co-operative coal carts waiting innocuously in the mud. There were ironworkers from Middlesbrough, Tyneside shipbuilders, twenty lads from Lincolnshire, Welsh miners' wives in red berets. There were students barking out quick little marching slogans like American college cries:

> One, two, three, four,
> We are for
> The Working Class!

Or,

> We won't fight for King and Country!
> We want Pollitt! We want Mann!

They had pennants and posters, proclaiming:

> We want bread, not battleships (Portsmouth)
> School feeding – not poison gas (South Wales)
> We want work, not slave camps
> Down with the starvation government

But if their words were fierce, their demeanour was like that of a well-drilled boy-scout jamboree, with comparable smartness and discipline.

It is said that five thousand police were in the Park. If so, they made themselves uncommonly inconspicuous. It is true that near

Marble Arch was a bivouac of sleek horses beside a marquee and steaming camp-kitchen; along the palings squatted rows of rounded blue posteriors, their stiff cloaks sticking above them, like autumn swallows on telegraph lines; little knots of policemen stood about nonchalantly smoking cigarettes with such an air of 'This-is-the-village-club-feast' that one plump lady was heard to observe to a promising specimen of 'Trenchard's Own', 'Quite a nice little holiday for you, isn't it?' As the marchers re-formed and, promptly on time, moved out of the park again, two policemen at least were seen to be muttering the *Internationale* as they tramped beside the singing procession.

In Bermondsey Town Hall the Unity Congress was sitting: 'organized to mobilize the working class for action against the National Government, especially its new Fascist Unemployment Bill, and against the attacks of the employers on trade union standards and conditions'. Congress members wore a scarlet ticket on their coats. On Tuesday I asked one what he thought they had really done. His face lit up. 'It depends what you call "done" ', he said. 'Lenin told us that if one method failed we had to try others. Some of the older men don't realize that. A lot of time was wasted arguing about method. But I'll tell you something. There were fifteen hundred delegates at that congress, and some like me had never been to one before. We are all going back home filled with a new hope. If we had no hope we should commit suicide. What has life for an unemployed fellow like me? But revolutionaries don't commit suicide. We wait for the Day. That is what the Congress has done for us. This may be the beginning of the end.'

I met that young 'revolutionary' in the middle of the Lobby of the House of Commons last Tuesday. He was waiting for his Member of Parliament; Mr MacDonald having refused either to receive a deputation at Downing Street or a petition at the House, individual marchers were sending for their own members (and some privately hoping that they would not come, so as to be able to damn the whole ruling class to their constituents). This particular lad wore a leather jerkin above his khaki shirt; his brown hair curled, and he had a charmingly affable grin. He told me he had spent two nights in Cambridge, where he had had to teach the elements of social economics to a lecturer of Philosophy in Trinity College ('The ignorance of those dons! But kind. I will say that.') He told me that food had been lavished upon them at points along the route, but it was oddly chosen – all bread, cheese, boiled eggs and tinned beef – and in consequence the marchers suffered from pimples and constipation. His contingent had never dropped one marcher, though from others they had fallen out through illness, arrest, or lack of discipline. 'But we picked ours – twenty out of forty-seven. All politically educated, if you know what I mean. The people think we're poor, hungry devils; but we're something better than that!' His eyes flashed. He held his head high. Just then his member's name was called. I said good-bye, and wondered whether I ought to add some appropriate phrase like 'Good luck, Comrade'; but he settled that for me. 'OK, kid', said he, and unintimidated by a pomp he mentally doomed to destruction, he crossed the marble floor to greet the representative of Capitalism ...

Later that evening he was to march in the suburbs with other processions, trying to 'win the working class of London' for the class war. But beyond impressing the general public with an unexpected appearance of discipline and decency, the demonstration had no great reception. Outside the House of Commons all day both uniformed and plain clothes police were on duty in large numbers, but except for the cordon across Downing Street when the deputation called on the Prime Minister, they had little to do. A few more strangers loitered round the Commons entrance. A few more visitors, shabbier than usual, stared at the mural paintings in the outer lobbies. That was all.

The absence of official Labour from all these demonstrations struck as curious those unfamiliar with the more delicate shades of political coloration. They do not understand why Transport House should appear to be far more scared of bright red than of true blue. A Socialist League weekend conference had been arranged for that particular period; one Transport House organizer was speaking in Oxford, another in the West Country. Only at question-time in the House on Tuesday did Labour members with Samuelite Liberals and the ILP rebels stand up for Mr McGovern's motion that the right of the marchers to be heard should be debated on the adjournment. The debate, acrimonious and personal, took place at midnight.

While the individual marchers waited to see their members in the gracious rooms overlooking Embankment Gardens now allotted to their work, Colonel Wedgwood's team of historians were holding a tea party to celebrate their growing history of British Parliament – a fine piece of research undertaken with enthusiasm and resource. While they talked of Simon de Montfort, the Wars of the Roses, and the growth of representative institutions, one peer remarked to a journalist: 'I saw you down below talking to that boy. What do they think they are doing, poor devils? We all know they're hungry. We're all sorry for them. But what can they *do*?' I remembered the boy's phrase: 'It depends on what you call *done*.' But the troubled and friendly peer was no more like the marcher's picture of 'fat capitalists with shooting-boxes in Scotland' (he used those words) than the marcher was like the peer's picture of a poor devil.

... 'In any other country the conditions of the unemployed would have caused rioting', said Sir Herbert Samuel. 'Our citizens behaved with perfect decency and order.' ... 'If we don't listen when they behave like this,' exclaimed one well-to-do woman, summoning her chauffeur, 'next time they come they *will* break our windows!' But the windows have not yet been broken. The red flags in London were carried like civic emblems. The police smoked cigarettes and exchanged repartee in Hyde Park. Can this national friendliness of temper be turned into a political instrument? Can this country avoid the horrors of both insurrection and repression? The answer depends upon how far the explorers of the middle way can find a constructive solution. It is not yet too late.

Time and Tide, 3 March 1934

༄

GENERAL HERTZOG'S NATIVE POLICY

Since the political emancipation of the Cape native in 1853 the relationship between black and white in South Africa has been regulated by an opportunist policy. The South Africa Act of 1909 left the condition in each province unchanged; the Cape native retains his right to be registered as a voter if he owns £75 value in property, or earns £50 a year and can write his name; in Natal a native achieving a high standard of culture may apply for the right to vote, though this is rarely given to more than six out of a population of 900,000; in the Free State and the Transvaal, the native has no vote at all. The moderating influence of the Colonial Office has disappeared with the grant of self-government; owing to the sensitiveness of South African feeling over Dominion Status all attempts at interference are deprecated. As problems have arisen they have been settled without much regard for wider issues. The Land Act of 1915 restricted native powers of purchase in European areas. The Colour Bar Act of 1926 gave power to the Governor to exclude natives from skilled employment in the mines and elsewhere. The Native Affairs Act of 1920, though improving native status in some small points, was deeply opposed by most thinking natives. White opinion is largely divided between a small handful of men really concerned with native interests; the South African Party, dominated by the industrialists of the Rand, who favour the employment of natives even on skilled work because they are cheap; the Nationalist Party, largely controlled by agricultural interests, desiring cheap and docile black labour and by the influence of the Dutch Reformed Church which has laid down the inequality of black and white as part of its doctrine; and the White Labour Party, which concentrates upon the preservation of a high standard of life for white workers, and thus fears undercutting by cheap black labour. The present Pact Government is composed by the union of Nationalists and White Labour, united in their antagonism to the industrialists and by their fear of black competition. Once in power, General Hertzog made up his mind to carry through the first deliberate attempt at a reasoned native policy for South Africa. On 11 May, 1926, speaking on the Colour Bar Bill in the parliament at Cape Town, he declared, 'I say that the time has come when South Africa is no longer to pursue a policy of carrying on from hand to mouth. We have to keep our eyes on the future, and we must lay it down where we stand and where we are going.'

The policy which he has framed is directed towards the

preservation of 'a White South Africa'. Ideally stated, its principles are those which would initiate 'parallel institutions, leaving the European master in his own household', combined with modified territorial segregation. Actually, it has been framed without regard to black opinion, black interests or black liberties. The Colour Bar Bill of 1926 formed the first instalment of the policy. The second stage came with the proposal of four Native Bills, the Native Council Bill, the Coloured Persons Rights Bill, the Representation of Natives in Parliament Bill and the Natives Land Bill. These propose, first, a uniform system of political representation for natives throughout the four provinces. The present annual Native Conference will be transformed into a Union Native Council, mainly elective, with a definite status and some legislative as well as advisory powers. In the Legislative Assembly, the Cape natives will lose their present franchise. In exchange they will be classified together under a communal franchise scheme and be permitted to return two natives; the Transvaal and Natal will likewise have two members each, the Free State one. These members must be European. They may sit and speak and vote upon minor questions. But they may not vote upon questions affecting the basis of native representation itself, nor upon 'questions of confidence' unconnected with the native question. On the other hand, the Coloured people of mixed blood are to be gradually assimilated with the white population. No colour bar shall cut them out from industry. They may keep their political power. With these constituted measures goes the Land Bill which initiates a system of territorial and economic segregation, to be applied gradually. Last session a committee of 19 members of all three parties discussed the four bills without concluding their inquiries. They recommended that at the next session, which is now sitting, a Select Committee might be appointed to continue the inquiries. Meanwhile the evidence heard before the first committee has been published, in a closely printed volume of some 400 pages. It constitutes a most valuable document upon native affairs. Fifty-one witnesses were heard, some representing individuals, some organizations, some black, some white. From the evidence published and from other available information it is evident that the whole bulk of articulate native opinion is opposed to the policy. Territorial segregation is suspect, because in the past almost every change in the land-holding has been a change for the worse. The white landlords in possession refuse to part with land of any value unless they are forced to do so, and the natives think that Hertzog is unlikely to alienate his farmer friends by insisting upon adequate reserves for the natives. The destruction of the Cape native franchise is deplored. The northern natives, said Professor Jabavu, 'feel that if there is any offer made to them which involves the whittling down of the Cape franchise, they are prepared to remain as they are', while the Cape natives regard their possible loss of votes with no more complacency than Englishmen would regard deprivation of their franchise. The proposal to treat all bills as interlocking is profoundly suspect, and black feeling, already embittered by the Colour Bar Act, grows increasingly hostile to the new proposals.

The Native Administration Act which came into force last December must be interpreted in the light of these events. It gives the Governor-General most arbitrary powers over native ownership of land. He may (clause 7) revoke any land grant; he may move tribes from one place to another; he may prohibit meetings or destroy 'anything' which appears likely to lead to hostility between black and white; some of the clauses are taken straight from DORA. The intention of the Act is twofold; it responds to an appeal for active measures against the vigorous native trade union movement which has arisen within the last ten years, and it gives the native administration department power to check any expression of opinion criticizing the new native policy as it arises.

The importance of these Bills to us in England is twofold; we cannot entirely resign our moral responsibility for the natives in this part of the British Commonwealth of Nations, and we still retain responsibility for the natives in land under the Colonial Office. We have reason to believe that the Hertzog policy will find its repercussions further north. Sir Edward Grigg, Governor of Kenya, returning from his recent visit to South Africa, said that he had learnt much from the older country. Mr Amery has recently undergone a carefully edited tour of South Africa. There is a real danger lest the South African native policy, born of prejudice, race interest and opportunism, may become the model for the rest of the world to follow.

Women's International League for Peace and Freedom, News Sheet,
November 1927

❧

BETTER AND BRIGHTER NATIVES

During the past ten days we have been reading about native riots and European police raids in Natal. We have been told that this is an interesting piece of news, which is none of our business. An official from Rhodesia reminded me yesterday, 'At least we colonials don't come to London and tell you here how to deal with your slums and unemployed.' Indeed, they do not; but the men on the spot sometimes forget the curious constitution of this Commonwealth of Nations, which makes the member for Tooting Bec responsible to his constituents for a vote affecting the future of the Kikuyu and Masai. Deputations from Uganda wait on the steps of the Colonial Office in Whitehall; petitions from British Guiana disturb, or properly should disturb, the sleep of citizens at Ilford. The House of Commons has now before it the report of a commission on East Africa, and amendments to a South Rhodesian Land Bill. However much we like to keep ourselves to ourselves, we find that we are willy-nilly our brothers' keepers. And we cannot even ignore events in a self-governing dominion like South Africa, because General Smuts comes over to Oxford, and in the Sheldonian Theatre tells young men and women, who are presumably the statesmen of the future, that 'the new countries to the north' – for which we are in some measure responsible – 'can start with a clean slate. They can learn from the mistakes which we have made in South Africa.' So upon the best authority in the world, we go to school, and read the reports of Reuter's agent from Natal, in order to point the moral for our own colonial tale.

On 14 November, we learn, the police, armed with tear-gas bombs – and according to the *Manchester Guardian*, with machine-guns and bayonets – raided the Durban compounds, accompanied by the Minister of Justice, examined six thousand natives to find defaulters who had not paid poll tax, and made six hundred arrests. Violence, beyond a little display of fisticuffs and the throwing of one gas-bomb, was unnecessary, but the following night 'a warlike atmosphere' was reported in the town. The Minister returned by aeroplane to Pretoria, but on Sunday another raid took place, and seven hundred more arrests were made. Reuter's telegram reports that 'increased support is being given to the Government in the action which it is taking to stem the tide of lawlessness among the natives'. There is much talk of communist agitators. The chief native trade union, the ICU, has been accused of stirring up native trouble, and the Government is bringing forward a new Bill to enable it to deal severely with propagandists. Nor is this an isolated incident. Last June, Natal was the scene of another Durban 'riot', in which over a hundred people were killed or wounded, all but about twenty of these being natives.

Natal, we might imagine, was a particularly dangerous province, full of discontented, politically minded natives, in the hands of unscrupulous agitators, and the Government might be thought to have done no more than its duty in putting down unrest with a strong hand. But the strange thing is that Natal has not in the past been thought of as a storm centre for natives. The mine natives of the Rand, or the industrialized natives of Port Elizabeth and East London, are more probable victims for 'Moscow agitators'. Something curious must have been happening to Natal. If we follow the advice of General Smuts and look more closely into South African affairs, we shall find that something curious has been happening. 'Agitators' rarely arouse passions unless grievances exist, and 'agitators' may agitate on both sides of the colour line.

For the past three years South Africa has been attempting to carry out that reorientation of policy which General Smuts advocates for the new countries further north. The famous Four Native Bills of General Hertzog ideally aim at parallel political institutions combined with modified territorial segregation. The ideal might not have been displeasing to the vast majority of natives; but the launching of the policy has been anything but

Winifred Holtby with Vera Brittain and John c. 1931
(*Courtesy of Shirley Williams*)

Winifred Holtby and Dorothy Clark at a fancy dress dance at Somerville College c. 1921 (*Courtesy of Paul Berry*)

Winifred Holtby on her graduation c. 1921 (*Paul Berry*)

Somerville College, November 1917: Winifred Holtby, far right; Dorothy Clark, front row centre (*Paul Berry*)

'Millinery in Teneriffe' a drawing by Winifred Holtby in a letter to Vera Brittain written from Teneriffe, 19 January 1926 (*Paul Berry*)

Vera Brittain in 1924 (*Shirley Williams*)

Winifred Holtby c. 1932 (*Paul Berry*)

Winifred Holtby and her mother, after Alice Holtby's election as the first woman alderman on East Riding County Council, 18 March 1934

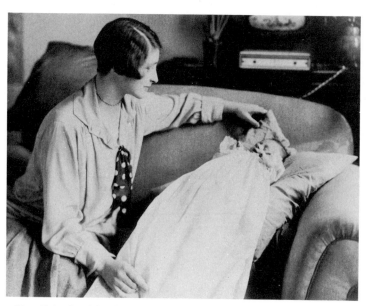

Vera Brittain with John, aged 4 weeks, January 1928 (*Shirley Williams*)

Vera Brittain with George Lansbury, far left, at a Peace Meeting in
Manchester Free Trade Hall, 31 May 1938

Deputation to the Foreign Office organized by the Peace Pledge Union to
suspend Suez mobilization. Left to right: Hugh Brock; A. Fenner
Brockway, MP; Professor Dame Kathleen Lonsdale; Stuart Morris,
Secretary of the Peace Pledge Union; Sybil Morrison; Emrys Hughes, MP;
Vera Brittain; J. Allen Skinner, 15 August 1956

Bernard Shaw, Winifred Holtby and Lady Rhondda at the Malvern Festival, 1935

ideal. Representation on native councils has to be bought by surrender of the Cape Parliamentary franchise, which has been enjoyed since 1853, and which, since the Act of Union, has been regarded by natives in all four provinces as their great political safeguard against exploitation. The new Native Land Bills carry little hope of reversing a policy of land distribution which at present gives one-eighth of the territory in the country to six million natives, and seven-eighths to 1,700,000 Europeans. The attempt to build up parallel economic institutions was begun by the passing of a Colour Bar Act in 1926, designed to keep natives out of skilled industrial employment. The encouragement to natives to return to their traditional discipline, which General Smuts applauded at Oxford, was in South Africa initiated by the Native Administration Act of 1927, which gives such drastic police powers to the Governor-General that one cannot help wondering what is left for the new 'Anti-Agitation Bill' to do. The men who drafted the Bills may have had admirable intentions, but the attitude of their warmest supporters was all too clearly indicated during the election speeches of this spring.

The natives of Natal cannot be blamed if they regard themselves as faced by a government concerned chiefly with preserving South Africa as a white man's country, in which the black man plays a subservient part. They cannot be blamed if they find their own economic position a matter for some anxiety. Durban itself lacks any proper native location. It has native barracks kept up by the profits from selling Kaffir beer; but it has no adequate housing accommodation. It has something of a native unemployment problem. A little over a year ago an attempt to organize native farm workers in a trade union in Natal led to their eviction from the farms on which they worked. The Johannesburg *Star* for 24 September 1928 reported that 'hundreds of native families' had been evicted from European farms; 'everywhere one hears pathetic stories of families wandering about the country in search of places to live in'. They drifted to Durban to seek employment in the newly developing industries there, and it was Mr Justice de Waal, in his official report on the June rioting, who pointed out the lack of accommodation for them in the city.

Natives crowd into the congested areas. They are unemployed

183

or poorly paid, suspicious of the good will of a government that appears to think chiefly of suppressing them, and unhappy about the future. Their first lesson in violence comes from the Europeans. Mr Justice de Waal declared that the June riots would never have occurred if, after an unimportant incident in the morning, Europeans armed with revolvers had not raided the headquarters of the ICU in a high-spirited attempt to pay off old scores against the native trade union.

Motives for native unrest are obvious, and had there been violence, it would not have been surprising. But in fact, the violence both in June and again last week came from the Europeans. We do not in England go armed with bombs and bayonets to collect income tax from defaulters. We cannot be blamed if we, in our turn, suspect a political motive for the police raid.

Natal is the centre of the South African Party, which has hitherto largely opposed the disfranchisement of the Cape natives. It is British rather than Dutch, and mainly critical of General Hertzog's policy. But it is one thing to protest against the disfranchisement of peaceful citizens, and quite another to want to limit the political power of Bolshevists and hooligans. If the white voters of Natal can be persuaded that the natives are lawless and discontented, inflamed by propagandists, and inclined to violence, the support for Hertzog's native police will increase immediately. According to Reuter's laconic message, it has increased already.

What are we to learn from this, we who go to South Africa for our imperial lessons? It might seem as though the policy of segregation can never succeed if it begins with exclusion from opportunity and lack of privilege. Or it might seem as though General Hertzog were making a clumsy if resourceful bid for power while his great opponent is out of the country. Or are we to take comfort from one phrase in the Rhodes Memorial Lecture on Native Policy? 'The new policy of native self-government', said General Smuts – and in South Africa this includes disfranchisement – 'at any rate will provide the natives with plenty of bones to chew at and plenty of matter to wrangle over ... and in that way help to fill their otherwise empty lives with interest.' Are we to conclude that though distressed and frustrated, exploited and attacked, the natives should be grateful to the South African Government, which tries to make them better and brighter, by giving them ample matter for discussion? This might be a new consideration in imperial politics.

Nation and Athenaeum, 23 November 1929

᪐

PROGRESS OR SLAVERY?

Two years ago few fairy stories would have seemed more fantastic than the report that the British settlers of Kenya and Rhodesia were appealing to the Dutch Premier of South Africa for support against the imperial government. But history has taught us that in the face of common danger lion and lamb lie down together, and a situation has arisen in which we may expect to see the European lions and lambs of South and East Africa lying together with remarkable unanimity.

The cause of the trouble was the publication last June of the two British White Papers containing proposals for closer union in East Africa and a memorandum on native policy. The documents themselves, so far as they concern the treatment of the native peoples, reaffirm traditional British policy. Both restate the declaration of 1923 that 'primarily Kenya is an African territory, and His Majesty's Government think it necessary definitely to record their considered opinion that the interests of the African natives must be paramount'. Perhaps 'paramount' was an unfortunate word, since it gives a suggestion of privilege, and all that the African peoples really want or need is equality of status, similar to that given to the black population of Jamaica. Actually, the regulations under which the treatment of blacks differs from that accorded to whites in the papers amount rather to disability than to privilege, though there are several most valuable principles established, such as security of land tenure, equitable taxation, educational advances, and the ultimate desirability of a common electoral roll. These are far in advance of present practice, and though documents alone cannot maintain justice, a clear statement of principle can become a charter of rights.

It is this statement of policy which has united the once antagonistic elements of the 'white aristocracy'. On 8 September the elected members of the Northern Rhodesian legislature published a protest in which they declared that the settlers had honourably fulfilled their trusteeship toward the natives, that 'uninformed or misinformed' interference was resented, and that if the imperial policy was not modified 'those who still desire to remain in this territory will contemplate political relationships under which equality of treatment of whites with natives will be justly maintained'. Friends of the natives will do well to remember that phrase 'equality of treatment'.

South Africa agrees. General Hertzog has received a deputation from Kenya with unfeigned sympathy, and has declared that native policy in Africa is a matter of vital concern to his government. 'In the interest of harmonious imperial relations it is necessary that South Africa's views should be heard and given consideration', and he hopes to have the opportunity of discussing the matter with the imperial government. His Minister of Public Lands, Mr Groebler, goes even farther. Speaking at Pretoria on 17 September he declared: 'We deny that any European nation, England included, has the right to act anywhere in Africa in conflict with our ideals'.

The Convention of Associations in Kenya has sent a deputation, headed by Lord Delamere, to protest against the British policy at the Imperial Conference. The deputation is really unofficial, but Sir Edward Grigg, the retiring Governor, has made no secret of his sympathy with the settlers – 'a very sound, gay, gallant, very misrepresented people, my people' – and it is evident that his voice will be added to the chorus of protest against the policy which conflicts thus with South African ideals.

And what is the South African ideal which arouses such enthusiasm? To be understood it must be remembered in its connection with the old African tradition of slavery and with the belief of the white trekkers from the Cape, who thought of themselves as the Chosen People taking possession of the Promised Land, from which they had the divine mandate to drive Hittite and Hivite, 'to utterly destroy' them, or to make of them hewers of wood and drawers of water forevermore. The doctrine of inequality between blacks and whites has become with their descendants almost a religious principle, and the main intention of South African policy was outlined in Mr Groebler's speech when he said: 'We refuse to consider equality or the forcing of Western European administration on the natives as a solution of the native question. We reserve the right to protect within our own country the future of white posterity. We are convinced that in segregation in all directions we shall find salvation for both races.'

Since General Hertzog now believes in a united front on the African question, we need no longer be debarred by delicacy from discussing exactly what this policy means. Segregation is a vague and pleasant word; but its practical consequences are perfectly definite and utterly unpleasant for the peoples on both sides of the separating barrier. For those on top, it means a fruitless privilege resulting in intellectual stagnation and economic insecurity. For those underneath, it means a form of unacknowledged slavery.

Territorial segregation means a repetition of the enclosures policy seen in England during the sixteenth and nineteenth centuries. All South African statistics concerning native affairs are unreliable, but at present the white population of about 1,500,000 holds about 280,000,000 acres of land, while 4,700,000 natives hold about 20,000,000 acres. Natives are not allowed to buy or hire land, except in certain scheduled areas, without special permission of the Governor-General; thus they not only hold less than a tenth as much land as the whites, though they are four times as numerous, but their land on the whole is poorer. Consequently, each year more and more natives are driven to seek employment in the towns, thus swelling the body of cheap unskilled labour.

Economic segregation is rather different. It consists in compelling the native to work for Europeans while keeping him out of skilled trades and paying him rates amounting to about one-sixth of the standard white wage. Insecurity of land tenure is only one method. There is taxation. The Minister of Justice has just introduced a new bill making any adult male native in the Transvaal liable to a tax of £5 unless he can prove that he has worked for Europeans for at least three months in the year. Though the colour-bar policy inaugurated in 1925 is not yet completely matured, it is proving increasingly useful. On 30

187

August of this year the government published a novel plan for dealing with white unemployment – a serious problem in South Africa – by turning natives out of industry, replacing them by poor whites, and subsidizing the employers for the difference in wages ...

Legal segregation means inequality before the law, so that natives and white men are treated very differently in the courts. The conciliation and labour laws affecting white employment do not apply to the black man, whose labour is controlled by the Masters and Servants Acts and Labour Regulation Acts, which make breaches of contract by black, but not by white, men a penal offence. Daily life and normal movement are rendered almost intolerable by the pass laws. Collective bargaining can hardly escape from becoming 'conspiracy to break the law'. Freedom of speech is curtailed by a savage Sedition Act, and the native lives under the constant menace of arrest for 'crimes' which the state of the law renders almost inevitable. Frequent convictions, however, are a convenience to the white employer, for, according to regulations issued by the Director of Prisons last January, he can hire gangs of 'not less than twenty-five' black convicts to work on his farm at the rate of 1s. 6d. each a day, or 1s. each if food and accommodation are supplied.

As for political segregation, that is to be accomplished by depriving the Cape native of the parliamentary vote which he has exercised since 1853, shutting off the natives from all direct share in the body politic, and establishing instead Native Councils which will have no real legislative authority.

If this system seems bad, it is at least not unique. The treatment of natives in Kenya and Uganda has been mitigated by the authority of the Colonial Office and by the action of a few disinterested civil servants. But the two notable studies of Kenya by Dr Norman Leys and Mr McGregor Ross have shown that in that country at least the imperial principle of 'paramountcy' is anything but an established policy. It seems as though no privileged minority can be trusted to treat with decency a subject class, sex, or race.

The 'United Africa' enthusiasts for a common policy are going to lobby against the British White Papers during the Imperial

Conference. They will bring all possible pressure to bear upon the Joint Parliamentary Committee which is to examine the policy of the government during the autumn. It is high time that the British public realized what is taking place.

Quite apart from any concern for the honour of our imperial government, a concern which can be felt by the opponents as well as the supporters of imperialism, we dare not let the segregationists have their way. Their victory would mean the creation of a pool of cheap and helpless labour, which in these days of floating capital and international combines would be a constant menace to those workers who are trying to maintain a decent standard of living. It would mean protracted stagnation of the African market, which under a progressive policy might develop into one of our best customers. It would mean the embitterment of more than fifty million people, who must inevitably one day learn how to use the weapons which civilization has forged and exact a terrible revenge; for the 'United Front' does not mean real union in Africa, it means permanent and growing division from the native peoples.

We in Great Britain, as well as the South African government, feel a responsibility toward posterity. We must act before the Joint Committee has published its decisions, for we dare not face the consequences of an Africa enslaved.

New Leader, 3 October 1930
(Reprinted in the Nation, New York, 26 November 1930)

THE EVIL GENIUS OF SOUTH AFRICA?

'Rhodes', by Sarah Gertrude Millin (Chatto & Windus)

It seems impossible for people to think calmly about Cecil Rhodes. I have met in Kimberley an elderly man whose house is a museum of Rhodes relics, and who counts his brief opportunity to serve his hero as adequate compensation for a lifetime of disappointing mediocrity. I have read J.G. McDonald's *Rhodes: A*

Life, a tribute glowing with enthusiastic admiration, written by one of the small company present during Rhodes's greatest feat of spell-binding when, in the Matopos Hills, he won over by unaided force of personality the Matabele whom he had seduced, betrayed, exploited, succoured and lost again – the Matabele who gave him when he died, alone of all white men before or since, the royal salute, 'Bayete!' I know that Lord Grey told the chartered shareholders, 'He was in truth the most strenuous lover of his country, the most single-minded and the greatest-hearted man I ever met. During his life he gave all his energies and all his wealth to the service of the Empire, and in his will he bequeathed to the entire Anglo-Saxon world the priceless legacy of an inspiring ideal.' The German ex-Kaiser, after their momentous interview, is said to have repeated – consciously or unconsciously – Napoleon's tribute to Goethe: 'There goes a man.'

And this is the man about whom today other people can find no words bad enough. 'The evil genius of South Africa', Harcourt – to whom Rhodes had opened his heart is one of his many self-revelations – said of him. Olive Schreiner, who had called him 'the only great man and man of genius South Africa possesses', came to see 'below the fascinating surface the worms of falsehood and corruption creeping' and, in spite of a personal sympathy – not reciprocated by Rhodes for her – to speak of 'his master passions of ambition and greed unrestrained by conscience'. One of the few English women intimately acquainted with the language and opinions of the Matabele even told me that the chiefs, who so signally honoured him, suspected Rhodes all the time.

It may be so. As Mrs Millin says: 'The Matabele may well keep the peace. They have little else to keep.' That is what Rhodes and those who made 'his North' left to them. The acknowledgement, in its candour, and in its dramatic staccato brevity, is typical of this exciting and moving biography.

For Mrs Millin is no exception to the rule that people cannot think of Rhodes with calm detachment. Her short sketch of him in her former book, *The South Africans*, showed that she had fallen beneath the spell of the great spell-binder. Her study is no solemn and weighty historical treatise – nothing like Morley's *Gladstone* or Garvin's *Chamberlain*. From its striking prelude – the answer to

Meredith's 'I would crown him and then scourge him with his crown still on him', given in a sharp, poignant picture of the dying man struggling through the ferocious African heat, 'a man might think the worshippings, crownings and scourgings of his world an equal futility, who had given his name to a country and could not get a little air' – until the final passage describing the burial on the Matopos Hills, this is an excited book, written with an effect of speed and drama, and that heightened vividness and tension which comes to the vision of one who is just a little in love.

Yet it is no lazy-witted eulogy. Mrs Millin is an artist and a novelist. The glamour intensifying her sight has not dazzled her brain. She sees Rhodes as a man who made hideous and irretrievable mistakes, mistakes due to gross defects of character, and mistakes which did irreparable harm; yet she does not belittle him. She knows what she is writing.

He exemplified this largeness of spirit, this desire, for good or evil, to go big, which is called greatness and which is the attribute of no nation. For greatness is a sort of genius: a quality, not an accident or an achievement, a gift and not an inheritance. It inhabits a man like poetry or courage.

And again:

For what was Rhodes working now? For his own greater power or the greater power of England? It does not matter. The primary purpose, not merely of an artist but of any man, is to express himself. If the world benefits, good for the world.

Rhodes was an artist and an enthusiast. 'Enthusiasm,' says Mrs Millin, 'is inspiring even when it is selfish' … 'He loved beauty for its own sake. He had the imagination. He had that poignant sense of the appropriate which is taste.' That is well said. The book glitters with shrewd things well said. And behind its vivid movement, as the appendices on sources and chronological tables show, is a background of patient scholarship and record-sifting which only great vitality can recreate into a living picture.

Mrs Millin paints her portrait unforgettably. She makes no final judgment; though she makes many incidental and illuminating judgments on the way – such as her agreement with Spengler that Rhodes, for all his Roman and Elizabethan dreams, was a Teuton in temperament. The final judgment on so ebullient, so brilliant, so fated a man is not possible in isolation. He wished, he said, above all things to serve his country. It is only when we set his figure beside a Nansen or a Schweitzer, men whose genius it was to serve humanity, that we can see his aspiration as at once too great for him and too limited. In one passage Mrs Millin comments upon one of Rhodes's naïve outpourings: 'It reads strangely like the final letters of young men who have gone wrong and found the world too much for them.' Rhodes too early acquired the powers of a man and too late retained the imagination of an adolescent. Never, even after his failure and heroic recovery, was he quite adult; even his cynicism expressed a boy's disillusioned romanticism. Yet the issues he faced demanded the full application of the adult mind. It was his tragedy to die both too soon – and too late.

Time and Tide, 11 March 1933

❧

JAN CHRISTIAAN SMUTS

One morning in the winter of 1926 – winter south of the equator, I mean. It was midsummer in England – I scrambled down a steep, winding, sequestered little path on the lower slopes of Table Mountain. Below me lay parks and gardens, green, diligently watered grass, strange trees with silver leaves like scintillating chain-armour, flaming patches of cannas and watsonias, and, beyond the gardens, Cape Town splashed along the ragged coast like pale foam thrown up from the vivid restless sea. All round me were aromatic scented herbs and bushes, clicking with grasshoppers, like the coastal hills of southern France, and above me the exhilarating, sea-salted, sun-steeped air of one of the loveliest climates in the world. I had just completed a tour through all four provinces of the Union of South Africa. I had seen the sloping vineyards, gracious colonial Dutch architecture, and bare, thorny native reserves of the Cape, the rolling hills, reminiscent of Hungary, that surround the Orange Free State, the silver-mine dumps of the Rand, the teeming locations of the industrial Transvaal, the semi-tropical, moist, rich Indian gardens along the Natal coast. And I had heard conversations in trains, restaurants, cafés where students meet, on the stoeps of private houses, during passionately vehement political meetings, and in those controversies and monologues one man's name had recurred, with love, with loathing, with reverence, with execration. I could not avoid him; wherever I turned, whatever I said, I found that the answer in some way involved his personality. His thought, his actions, his influence, permeated that convulsive, beautiful, violent and sunlit country. I was to meet him for the first time that morning at lunch. I was to hear him speak that day in the House of Assembly on the Flag Bill question which was rending the country and its Dutch and British minority in twain. I was excited.

And as I turned the corner, I came upon a man, stripped to the waist, brown, hard, muscular, playing with a dog who apparently desired to prevent him replacing his shirt after a sun-bathe. The man was laughing, his bright, light eyes shining like the Pied Piper's in Browning's couplet:

And green and blue his sharp eyes twinkled
Like a candle flame where salt is sprinkled.

His shortish stocky figure, trimmed beard, finely shaped head and youthful carriage were vaguely familiar to me. I stood and watched the game with the dog. The two players did not see me. They vanished among the herbs and bushes. But when, in the House of Assembly later that day, I was introduced to my host, General Smuts, I said at once: 'Oh, but of course, I've met you already this morning', and we made friends over the delights of Table Mountain, aromatic bushes and sunbathing. This was the man.

There are few personalities who impress one as great at the first meeting. They offer vitality, quickness, confidence, and an indefinable stimulus to the imagination: Bernard Shaw, Dame Ethel Smyth, Lloyd George, H.G. Wells, General Smuts – these come to my mind immediately, though I can think of others – Beneš of Czechoslovakia, a little, though he is rather too agile and accommodating in manner for that peculiarly formidable yet exhilarating vigour; a biochemical specialist in London, who may one day be as well known as the others, a Jewish trade-union organizer from Palestine … There is something physical, brilliant and spontaneous in their immediate effect; they all have greatness *in posse*, if not all *in esse*. Their quality is as varied as their achievement. And among these, General Smuts leaves as much as any that sense of dancing and inexhaustible vitality, of capacity that is versatile and acute, of resilient power. He is a great man. His imagination sweeps the world. He has said, in his time, as many profound and wise things, as any contemporary statesman. He has shown judgment, courage and prescience. He has achieved superb feats of generalship, statesmanship, and intellectual synthesis. He is a lawyer, a scientist, a soldier, and a statesman. He was an indefatigable general in the nationalist Boer War; an architect of empire in the years succeeding it; he and his friend Botha brought South Africa on to the British side in 1914; he helped to design the Covenant of the League of Nations; he helped, wisely and adroitly, to settle the post-war chaos of Central Europe; he invented the mandate system; he has more recently been largely responsible for keeping his country within the British Commonwealth of Nations, and for achieving the fusion between the Dutch and British sections of the white community, which should, if it ultimately succeeds, weld two factions which, in 1926, when I was in South Africa, were as ferociously hostile as any European racial minorities, into a united nation.

And now he has been to St Andrews University, three years after his rectorial election, and made there a speech upon liberty which has won the acclamation of the English-speaking world. It is such a fine speech that I propose to quote sections from it. They deserve remembrance. I use *The Times* report:

'The individual was basic to any world order that was worth while,' said General Smuts. 'Individual freedom, individual independence of mind, individual participation in the difficult work of government seemed to him essential to all true progress ... ' But that sturdy spirit which demanded the right of participation in the control of the nation 'seemed to be decaying in an atmosphere of lassitude and disillusion. Men and women had suffered until they were abdicating their rights as individuals ... Freedom itself seemed to be in danger.' He continued: 'The issue of freedom, the most fundamental issue of all our civilization, is once more squarely raised by what is happening in the world and cannot be evaded ... Once more the heroic call is coming to our youth.

The fight for human freedom is indeed the supreme issue of the future as it has always been in the past ... Popular self-government and parliaments are disappearing. The guarantees for private rights and civil liberties are going ... Dissident views are not tolerated and are forcibly suppressed. For those who do not choose to fall into line there is the concentration camp, the distant labour camp in the wilds, or on the islands of the sea ... I maintain that such a basis of human government is an anachronism ... The denial of free human rights must in the long run lead to a cataclysm ... Freedom is the most ineradicable craving of human nature. Without it peace, contentment and happiness, even manhood itself, are not possible. ... The vision of freedom, of the liberation of the human spirit from its primeval bondage, is, perhaps, the greatest light which has yet dawned on our human horizon ... Are we going to leave a free field to those who threaten our fundamental human ideals and our proudest heritage from the past? Or are we going to join in the battle – the age-long battle which has been going forward from the dawn of history – for the breaking of our bonds and the enlargement of our free choice and free action? Remembering the great appeal of Pericles which rings through the ages, let us seek our happiness in freedom, and bravely do our part in hastening the coming of the great day of freedom.'

Grandly, superbly, opportunely said, is it not? This soldier-statesman-scientist is an orator as well. The inspiring phrase, the splendid dignity of rhetoric are also his – also part of his characteristic competence in action. But, but, but, but, BUT ... But, as I read, as I imagined that crisp, clear, soldier's voice ringing through the hall, as I myself glowed in response to this challenge to our lethargy and cowardice, I began to remember. And the more clearly I remembered, the more profound grew my excitement at General Smuts' address. For I was thinking of the fascinating, exasperating country whose destiny he, in so large a part, controls. I was imagining the impact of his words if they were repeated to its younger generation. I was remembering the experience which has taught General Smuts what tyranny may mean.

'*Popular self-government and parliaments are disappearing,*' he said. '*The guarantees for private rights and civil liberties are going.*' Quite. Smuts should know. In the Cape Province, till 1931, there was no constitutional distinction between European and non-European citizens in the matter of franchise and property. True, the educational tests and property qualifications for voting were so arranged that only a minority of black men were enfranchised; true, that in Natal only one African was qualified to vote, and that in the Orange Free State and the Transvaal, none but the European minority had any rights of citizenship at all. Still, liberty broadens down from precedent to precedent, we are told. The large freedoms of constitutional privilege were only withheld until Africans had acquired sufficient civilization to use them advantageously. All change, we thought, would be an extension of freedom, at least under men like General Smuts. In 1931 European women were admitted to parliamentary franchise; non-European women were excluded. Today before the country is a Bill, almost certain, as soon as technical formulae are circumvented, to be passed, disenfranchising non-European males as well as females. The Native Conference, supposed to serve as a substitute for other constitutional powers, criticized this and other Government proposals in 1926 and 1927, so has not subsequently been summoned, except in December 1930; its postponements being excused upon the grounds of 'absence of matter for discussion'. 'Absence of matter' meaning, presumably, matter upon which Africans could support their European governors, since the entire structure of African citizenship is under orders of demolition ... 'Dissident views are not tolerated and are forcibly suppressed.' Smuts should know. He himself encouraged the South African Government to pass the Riotous Assemblies Act – an Act which makes 'incitement to ill-feeling between black and white' an offence punishable by banishment. Now where conditions in a country are as they are in South Africa; where a Colour Bar Act shuts out a man from certain skilled employments just because his skin is black; where men, for the same reason, must carry passes when they go out at night, and when they move from place to place; where they can be arrested and sent to prison simply for failing to carry on their persons a tax receipt – merely to speak aloud of the laws and administration precisely as they exist is adequate to 'incite ill-feeling'. The Act has been used to prevent the development of trade unionism, to prohibit political protest, to render inarticulate any form of native criticism; it has been used to enable politicians to say – 'But the natives themselves do not object'.

'For those who do not choose to fall into line there is the concentration camp, the distant labour camp in the wilds, or on the islands of the sea.' Smuts must have been looking unconsciously at his own continent when he framed those eloquent and picturesque phrases. Under the Revised Code of Native Laws in Natal, passed two years ago – not under Smuts' government, it is true, but without his serious opposition – a native can be imprisoned without trial for three months at the request of the Native Commissioners if he can be accused of 'agitation', if he refuses to 'fall into line'. Critics of government, or even of private economic measures, are banished. 'Round-ups' for breaches of the pass-laws reap a fruitful harvest of convicts, whose loan at low hire-prices to private employers conveniently lowers the standard of wages. Educational disabilities (1,100,000 native children receive no education. For the 300,000 who are being educated, £2 3s. 6d. per capita is spent annually by the State, against £25 13s. for the 384,000 European children whose educational opportunities are among the most generous in the world) as well as penal repression, assist in silencing those unprepared to 'fall into line'.

… '*The denial of human rights must in the long run lead to a cataclysm.*' In Natal also, a native woman, under the new code, remains in perpetual minority, to her father or her husband, however civilized, however economically independent, however far removed from tribal tradition and custom she may be. A Select Committee of the Senate recommended a change, since this legal servitude has certain obvious inconveniences; but the political party which Smuts leads saw no reason for demanding that amendment. The vision of freedom, of 'the greatest light which has yet dawned on our human horizon', has not yet gleamed upon South Africa.

Why? Because of a very simple reason. Because, for General Smuts and his contemporaries, the human horizon does not yet extend to coloured races, as, for Fox and his eighteenth-century contemporaries, it did not extend to English women. General Smuts is not a hypocrite, though he may be an over-adroit politician; he is, I believe, quite sincere in his worship of 'our proudest heritage from the past'. He summons youth with a vigorous challenge to 'join in the battle ... for the breaking of our bonds'. It never occurs to him that his St Andrews speech is a call to African youth, that he himself is guilty of incitement to ill-feeling in his outcry against tyranny, that if he had spoken to a congregation of his own countrymen – black mine workers on the Rand, brown Indians in Natal, coloured farmers in the Cape – he would have been guilty, flagrantly and unquestionably guilty, of an offence against the Riotous Assemblies Act, child of his own political imagination. It never occurs to him, because he does not see those black and brown men and women as his countrymen; he does not see them as human beings at all. Nice natives, good dogs, merry, obedient, rather stupid servants, gay singers and players, swift runners, impossible economists, tribal humorists, inheritors of folk-law priceless to anthropologists ... yes. But human beings, no.

These abrupt failures of the imagination are among the most fruitful sources of injustice in the world. They are more common than deliberate sadism, more insidious than fear. Indeed, they breed fear. In Africa the European minority is afraid of the natives because it sees them as something alien, hostile, terrible in potential enmity. To 'preserve white civilization', to keep the race clean, are motives strong enough to bring Dutch and British together in common cause against that half-defined, half-indecent, unmentionable menace. 'Fusion of parties' in South Africa represents partly the stand of white men for their common blood. The Jews to Nazi Germany, the Catholics to the Ku Klux Klan, Negroes to a southern states lynching party, women to eighteenth-century liberals – they are not human; they need not be accorded human privileges. The mind closes against any conception of their own point of view. Of course there are a few white men even in Africa whose imagination is large enough to embrace humanity. A few judges, a few missionaries, a few civil servants, private citizens, the founders of the newly growing co-operative movement, these men and women whom General Smuts certainly, because they are white, acknowledges as human, are prepared '*bravely to do their part in hastening the coming of the great day of freedom*'. The results may be disconcerting to the Rector of St Andrews University.

Time and Tide ('Notes on the Way'), 27 October 1934

✍

'BRING UP YOUR REARS!'

'From Man to Man', by Olive Schreiner
(T. Fisher Unwin)

'If only the powers that shape existence give me the strength to finish this book, I shall not have that agonized feeling over my life that I have had over the last ten years, that I have done nothing of good for any human creature.' Thus Olive Schreiner wrote in 1907 of the novel, begun in 1873, which her death in 1920 left unfinished. The first fourteen chapters have now been published by her husband and we can read for ourselves the book mentioned so often in her letters, which she loved 'a hundred times better than ever I loved *An African Farm*', and which she prophesied would be 'quite different from any other book that was ever written, whether good or bad I can't say'.

We may not, today, find *From Man to Man* as completely different from all other books as its author supposed, but its likeness signifies the measure of our debt to Olive Schreiner. If we are no longer startled into shocked reticence by the frank discussion of sex in human relationships, if the problem of prostitution awakens in us an intelligent indignation instead of a blind panic, if the social theory implied in her watch-word 'Bring up your rears!' no longer cuts across the complacent philosophy of the 'survival of the fittest' which dominated the great and prosperous Victorians, these changes are partly due to the influence of Olive Schreiner. All great thought ultimately destroys the semblance of its own originality. We no longer think differently from our neighbours when we have persuaded them to think like us. It was not because Olive Schreiner thought differently, but because she thought for herself, with a compelling urgency of conviction and a fierce intensity of feeling, that she was, and remains, one of the profoundly original thinkers of modern times.

This posthumous novel is the expression of her maturity, as *The Story of an African Farm* was the expression of her youth. Like many others endowed with spiritual responsibility, Olive Schreiner passed from preoccupation with the individual to preoccupation with society. Since the earlier book, she has broadened her canvas; she has gained in sophistication; her psychology is more subtle – Bonaparte Blenkins and Rebekah's husband are creatures from different worlds – yet the old astonishing vehemence is here, the sweeping grandeur of conception, the extravagant incoherence of form. When she wanted to say something, she said it, even if she had to hold up her narrative for forty pages in order to do so.

Few books could be more personal and more revealing. When *The Story of an African Farm* was published by an unknown 'Ralph Iron' we said, 'This is a wonderful book'. But since then Olive Schreiner has lived and died, and we have recognized her power, as feminist, as political thinker, as literary artist. When we read *From Man to Man* we say instead, 'This was a wonderful woman'.

'The subject of my book', she wrote to Havelock Ellis, 'is prostitution and marriage. It is the story of a prostitute and of a married woman who loves another man and whose husband is sensual and unfaithful.' The story of Bertie, the prostitute, is told with an objective restraint unequalled in her other published work, but when writing of Rebekah, she becomes herself again.

She has left to Rebekah the heritage of her social philosophy. From her consideration of prostitution, she was led to criticize all moral judgments and to the shifting of ethical concern from expediency to truth. She finds the key to this in the unity of creation, revealed by science, which has destroyed irrelevance in a world where we are all members of one another, and where, consequently, no individual can attain to full perfection until his brethren share his opportunities. 'Is it not a paradox covering a mighty truth that not one slave toils under the lash on an Indian plantation, but the freedom of every other man on earth is limited by it? That not one laugh of lust rings out but each man's sexual life is less fair for it? That the full all-rounded human life is impossible to any individual while one man does not share it?

Bring up your rears! Bring up your rears!'

Here, for her, lies the ultimate condition of progress, here the connection between her *Thoughts on South Africa*, her allegories like *The Sunshine Lay*, and *Woman and Labour*. While half humanity, whether of the 'inferior' sex or the 'inferior' race, is deprived of opportunity for development, it endangers the whole progress of civilization; for it is the tragedy of the dispossessed, not only themselves to suffer, but also that they shall imperil the fortunate.

Time and Tide, 15 October 1926

Vera Brittain

'OUR BACKS TO THE WALL'

Nearly ten years ago, on the evening of 21 March 1918, an Army
Sister and I – then a very youthful and ardent VAD – were walking
among the yellow sandhills on the French coast close to Etaples.
Both of us worked on the staff of a large base hospital, celebrated
in those days throughout the British Army, but of which all trace is
now covered by the gorse and scrub that has grown over the old
camps along the main railway line from Boulogne to Paris. The
Sister is now the superintendent of a military hospital in India,
while my own endeavours to combine marriage with the career of
a writer have removed me very far from the nursing world in
which I spent four strenuous years of unintended experience.
Those years have vanished into the past and nothing is left of them
– nothing except the crowded cemetery at Etaples and a host of
memories.

Memories, however, last longer than war, and often longer than
man. I can still recall vividly the queer menace of that evening
among the sandhills; everything was wrapped in an unearthly
stillness, and even the waves breaking upon the shore appeared to
make no sound. A copper glow surrounded the setting sun, which
hung like an angry ball of fire in the midst of a battalion of
thunderous clouds; it reminded us, I remember, of the
superstitions that were rife in the first days of the war, when people
said that they had seen blood upon the sun and moon. We
returned to the camp to learn that the rumours of the morning
were confirmed, and that the great German offensive had begun.

The days that followed are a confused recollection of convoys, ambulances, operations, evacuations to England, and the continuous sounding of the 'fall-in'. The hut of which I then had sole charge had been hitherto used for light medical cases; it was hastily converted into a surgical ward during the night, and I came on duty the next morning to find all the beds occupied, and the floor covered with stretchers, scattered boots, muddy khaki and other hastily removed remnants of field service kit. Ten cases were marked down for immediate operation and a dozen more for x-ray. I remember gazing ruefully at the solitary pair of forceps standing in their jar of methylated spirit which constituted the entire range of my surgical equipment. Fortunately for myself I burst out laughing, and ran to bombard a half-frantic dispensary with the gay feeling that one gets when catastrophe has advanced beyond the utmost limit of human capacity to cope with it.

Day after day some fresh conquest of our adversaries was whispered first with bated breath and then published tentatively abroad. Péronne, Bapaume, Beaumont Hamel and finally Albert itself, fell into German hands; even Armentières, British for so long, had to be evacuated owing to the gas from exploding shells. From the fog of unreliable rumour which always covers the progress of a great retreat came the fear of a permanent break-through, and at Etaples preparations were made for the flight that before long might become necessary for us all. As the battle surged closer, the boom of the guns, a sense rather than a sound, shook the earth by day and night, and when darkness had fallen flashes of light could be seen on the horizon. From nearer at hand the air was filled with a dense and deafening roar; trains with reinforcements thundered all day up the line or lumbered down more slowly with their heavy freight of wounded; motor lorries and ammunition waggons crashed endlessly up the road. Occasionally the wounded – who escaped in anything that would pick them up, from staff cars to cattle trucks – were accompanied by Sisters fleeing from the captured casualty clearing stations; more often they arrived with no attendants at all and with the first field-dressing still unchanged. Only too frequently it was dead men whom the orderlies lifted out of the trains, and many a time the more serious cases had to be cut off the stretchers on which they had lain with their inadequately covered wounds undressed for many hours.

Three weeks of such sights and sounds, of fourteen-hour days without off-duty time and with frequent calls at night, will blunt the edge of the youngest and most adventurous spirit. Weariness of limbs and sickness of soul had engendered the despairing sense that nothing mattered except to end the strain one way or another; victory and defeat seemed to be, after all, very much the same thing. As it happened, this impression was correct; but fortunately for their duties in the last months of the war, it was not until two or three years afterwards that the men and women who took part in it were to learn for good that lesson of disillusion.

On 10 April a few fellow-workers and I stumbled through the long camp to the Sisters' quarters for our midday meal with the certainty that we could not go on – and saw, pinned up on the notice-board, Lord Haig's famous 'order of the day'. Standing there, with our weariness and our hunger strangely diminished, we read the words which put heart into so many whose need of endurance was far greater than ours:

There is no course open to us but to fight it out. Every position must be held to the last man; there must be no retirement. With our backs to the wall and believing in the justice of our cause, each one of us must fight to the end. The safety of our homes and the freedom of mankind depend alike upon the conduct of each one of us at this critical moment.

Most of those who were reading, at any rate among the VADs, belonged to that generation which has grown into womanhood with a scorn of showing its feelings and a reluctance to admit even their existence; but fatigue had made us vulnerable to emotion, and we left the notice-board fired with a tearful and glowing determination. Whatever our private views about war, we were then in the midst of it, and individuals – whether fighters or merely workers – who are faced with the alternatives of resistance and collapse seldom stop to argue the merits of the case until afterwards. No doubt we were all mad, and a noble madness is the most dangerous form of insanity; the fact remains that it was nobility at which we aimed, and nobility that Lord Haig's order enabled us for the time to achieve.

A month later the crisis was over, and I went home on leave. For the best part of six weeks, off-duty hours and walks to Le Touquet had been unattainable; my eyes had seen nothing but the long huts and the stretcher cases on the beds and along the trampled floor. Looking out of the train window as we passed through the woods and glades that surround Hardelot, the green veil flung over the trees and the yellow gleam of daffodils in the grass startled me into amazement, and I almost wept with joy as I realized that, like a thief in the night, the spring had come.

Manchester Guardian, 3 February 1928

❧

'THEIR NAME LIVETH'

Through our cities and towns and villages on Armistice Day, we meet to revive our memories – now slipping further back into an ever dimmer past – of ten, eleven, twelve years ago. In London we file past the grave of the Unknown Warrior and lay wreaths on the Cenotaph. In the larger towns which possess cathedrals or important churches, some part of these has usually been transformed with the War Memorial, and here we gather quietly for the silence, bowing our heads and dipping our flags. But in the smaller towns and villages a hill-side or a village green, along which everybody passes, has often been thought more appropriate than the tiny church for the site of the memorial cross or cenotaph which records the sacrifice that was none the less bitter for having been demanded from a mere handful of obscure individuals.

Perhaps because the soldiers whom they commemorate were for the most part simple men, who died in a simple faith that knew nothing of the economic intrigues and the secret treaties which are the motive power of modern warfare, these village crosses have become hallowed oases endowed with a strangely moving serenity that touches the heart more deeply than the elaborate memorials in the churches. The memories that they inspire, completely dissociated from sect or dogma, somehow seem more personal and poignant.

I passed by one of them only the other day, as I walked over a wooded hill near Pangbourne on a Sunday morning. Devoted hands had just arranged two tall green vases of red and golden autumn flowers on either side of the cross, but a strong breeze was blowing, and one of the vases had fallen over, casting the bright dahlias and daisies untidily down the steps of the little platform. When I had refilled the vase and gathered up and replaced the flowers – an action which seemed more truly a sacrament than any that the church bells ringing in the valley would have demanded of me – I read the brief tale of names on the cross. And as I had expected, and as is the case in ninety-nine out of every hundred of these memorials, the names inscribed were all names of men.

'Where war', wrote Olive Schreiner in *Woman and Labour*, 'has been to preserve life, or land, or freedom, unparasitized and labouring women have in all ages known how to bear an active part, and die.' In the Great War, which they then believed to be waged for freedom, the women of this country knew how to bear an active part; they accepted gladly the strain and the burden and the small rewards, though many of them were throwing off parasitism for the first time. But for the most part they did not die. The war was not fought on their soil, and when they served abroad, the tradition that sets, even in war-time, the exaggerated values of sentiment upon individual female life, protected the majority of them in their own despite against the ravages of aerial bomb and submarine torpedo. They worked, but they also went on living and suffering and remembering; and immortality – as so many of the disabled and the unemployed have since had reason to realize – is the reward only of a life laid down. In wartime it is necessary to die in order that one's name shall live for evermore.

For this reason the large number of war-records that have taken shape during the past eleven years in literature, in painting and in sculpture have in general ignored the active war-work done by the women. There are, of course, exceptions, such as the curiously repellent statue of Nurse Cavell above Trafalgar Square, and the vivid description in *The Well of Loneliness* of women ambulance drivers at the front. I am told that the lovely Edinburgh War Memorial has a window dedicated to the women doctors and nurses and auxiliary corps and land-workers, while records of these activities exist along with the rest in the cloistered peace of the Imperial War Museum. But for the most part war memorials, war paintings and war literature reveal to a later generation only the work and agony of the men, because this was crowned and immortalized by death.

The absence of allusion to women's work in the better-known examples of war literature may perhaps be attributed to the fact that the best-known plays and novels have so far been contributed by men. It is men who therefore predominate in the batch of contemporaneous German war novels which have recently acquired such fame, and men who hold the stage exclusively in the play *Journey's End*, which owes so much of its worldwide triumph to its unpretentious photography. In so far as women have been included in war literature at all, they have appeared chiefly in the rôle of passive sufferer – that rôle which is so poignantly expressed in the beautiful and too little known lines of May Wedderburn Cannan:

> When the Vision dies in the dust of the market-place,
> When the light is dim,
> When you lift up your eyes and cannot behold his face,
> When your heart is far from him,
>
> Know this is your War; in this loneliest hour you ride
> Down the Roads he knew;
> Though he comes no more at night, he will kneel at your side
> For comfort to dwell with you.

One or two of the best-known English war novels have failed to recognize even thus far the wartime heritage of pain which comes through their wifehood or motherhood to the great majority of women. In *Death of a Hero*, for instance, Mr Richard Aldington savagely attacked both these relationships, exploding in a cynical fury of scorn what seemed to him the myth of their sanctity. His two 'heroines', Elizabeth and Fanny, like the mother of his 'hero', George Winterbourne, create the illusion that the normal part played by woman in wartime was that of a luxurious parasite battening upon the sufferings of much-enduring man. The same impression is left by Major Acland's story of the Canadian troops, *All Else is Folly*, which actually takes for its text the words of the misogynist Nietzsche in *Thus Spake Zarathustra*: 'Man shall be trained for war and women for the recreation of the warrior; all else is folly'.

Details of women's activity in wartime exist of course in government blue-books, such as the reports of the Women's Employment Committee and of the War Cabinet Committee on Women in Industry, but records in this form are virtually buried in so far as the man and woman in the street are concerned. They exercise no popular influence, and strike no chord of recollection; they arouse respect and admiration in no one but the patient research-worker. Even the argument that the various Acts which have enfranchised and opened the professions to women are the real memorial to their war-time achievements does not really hold good, for these Acts were the logical consequences of the feminist movement, and though the war hastened them they would in any case have come in time.

The active part played by women in the Great War requires its own poet or novelist or dramatist, who will transform the dry sentences of government reports into living words before the memories of 1914 to 1918 pass into oblivion with the war generation.

Manchester Guardian, 13 November 1929

&

'A POPPY FOR HER COT'

The other day I overheard a curiously significant conversation between my nurse and my two children. Nurse, a buxom, bright-faced young woman of 20, was correcting an adjustable calendar, transposed by the roving fingers of John Edward, who now, by standing on the fender, can just reach the mantelpiece.

'Why, John!' I heard her cheerfully remark. 'It's the first of November! Soon it'll be November the eleventh. Then we'll get John a big, big poppy – and Shirley can have a poppy for her cot!'

'A poppy for her cot!' My mind echoed stupidly the words that had struck so sharply upon my affronted ears. Did this young woman, my outraged memories demanded, so utterly lack imagination that she really proposed to attach that symbol of grim death to the frill of yellow muslin which shielded my baby daughter's innocent head from the colder winds of Heaven?

And then, more reasonably, I remembered that the twelve years which have carried the war generation from its earliest youth into its thirties have bridged for its successors the far wider gulf between childhood and adulthood. My nurse was only 8 when the first Armistice Day fell with such a strange silence upon the deafening clamour of a world at arms; she was only 4 when the tread of hostile armies marching across Europe to destroy one another first sounded in the thrilled ears of our younger selves, boys and girls just home from our years at school. Why, then, should I so resent the fact that she sees in the sale of Flanders poppies merely a rather superior Flag Day? For her the Armistice belongs to those periodic national celebrations which began before her awareness of the world had developed into a conscious realization of its meaning. It has taken its place, with Trafalgar and Waterloo, in the sequence of historical events for which she and her contemporaries were in no way responsible; like Mafeking and Ladysmith for us, it is associated in her mind with ancient songs and long-ago conversations emerging from the dim shadows of early childhood.

And to my children, I reflected, it will not even be this. On my mantelpiece beside the calendar which Nurse so cheerfully adjusted, stands the photograph of a second lieutenant in uniform – a portrait of the children's uncle, my young brother, who has lain these dozen years in his grave on the Asiago Plateau, but who – apart from the fact that every year he seems to grow more curiously juvenile to be my brother – is as real to me as he was in 1914. I realize with a shock that he was killed in action nine years before John Edward was born, and that to my boy and girl he will be but a name, a legend, scarcely distinguishable in their dawning imaginations from Kingsley's fabulous heroes, the sons of the Immortals, who went forth to fight the Titans and monsters, the enemies of gods and men. Each year a poppy is sadly placed in a vase before his photograph; this year a poppy will jubilantly decorate my little daughter's cot. It is all one to nurse and the children.

This tale, however, has a moral, for it shows very clearly that memorial celebrations are not enough. Time has a deceptive habit of blurring our pain while preserving the glamour of our larger-scale tragedies. Our tears and our anguish fade into oblivion, but the thrill of catastrophic events, the odd brightness of happy moments shining through the storm-clouds of disaster, keep the same peculiar vividness that they wore in the yesterday to which they belong. And Nature herself conspires with time to cheat our recollections; grass has grown over the shell-holes at Ypres, and the cultivated meadows of industrious peasants have replaced the hut-scarred fields at Etaples and Camiers where once I nursed the wounded in the great retreat of 1918.

By what means shall we recall to life our grief and our terror, in order that posterity may recognize them for what they were? It cannot be, at best, an easy task, for nothing is more profoundly true than the fact that an individual usually differs far more from his or her self of fifteen years ago than from any contemporary. We have done so many things since the war, learnt so much in a world of which the artificial conditions of wartime kept us ignorant so much longer than is normal for young men and women. We have worked so hard, some of us almost frantically, to retrieve those lost years, have flung ourselves into causes, founded families, fought for careers, until the war has come to appear to us as an event that happened long ago in the lifetime of somebody else.

Though a mass of literature has already grown up around the war, it is still – despite the fact that the immense civilian armies were more articulate than actual fighters have ever been before – inadequate to save from self-destruction a new generation which is eager, as all new generations are, to despise its elders and disregard their warnings.

The decline of enthusiasm for pacifist movements, the growing strength of aggressive nationalism, the setting up of dictators in one after another of the states of Europe – all these testify to the failure of our ceremonies, our war-books, our peace propaganda as yet to bring about that great reformation which they set out to achieve in the hearts of men. How to preserve the memory of our suffering in such a way that our successors may understand it and refrain from the temptations offered by glamour and glory – that is the problem which we, the war generation, have still to solve before the darkness covers us.

Manchester Guardian, 11 November 1930

WHILE WE REMEMBER

Once more as Armistice Day comes round – so swiftly, it seems, to those of us who remember as though it were yesterday the startling sound of victorious guns rolling up the river from Westminster – the usual protests against the perpetuation of the ceremony find their way into the press. The Derbyshire vicar who has refused to hold a special service in his parish church is by no means the only exponent of the view that Armistice Day is a dying institution.

This attitude towards the war and its aftermath, like novels of escape, and sweepstakes, and popular interest in society romances, appears to be one more example of the flight from reality which Mr Wyndham Lewis has called 'the supreme immorality of the desire to forget'. It is not a stimulating or a hopeful world which the determined realist faces today, and for those who decide that modern life is too uncomfortable to be honestly faced at all, Armistice Day with its universal poppies and its garlanded war-memorials is full of inconvenient reminders.

Many of us are now drifting into an apathetic indifference which those who cannot remember the war have perhaps never drifted out of – an indifference which ignores the fact that apparently remote political causes have intimate personal effects, and refuses to acknowledge that, in a shrinking world of economically interdependent nations, there is no such thing as complete private irresponsibility for public catastrophe. 'They think Hitler doesn't matter to them so long as there's plenty of dry soap in the house', a very intelligent north country woman once ruefully remarked to me of her feminine neighbours. If most of us, from the very young to the very old, had not adopted that same attitude twenty years ago, the Great War would probably never have happened, for the peoples would not have permitted their governments to wage it.

On the night of 4 August 1914, I remember standing in the confused darkness of a Buxton street, waiting with a crowd of bewildered men and women for the reply that never came to the British ultimatum to Germany. To me and my contemporaries, with our hitherto unshaken confidence in the benignity of fate, war was something remote, unimaginable, its monstrous destructions and distresses safely shut up, like the Black Death and the Great Fire, between the covers of history books. In spite of the efforts of an unusually progressive headmistress, at the school that I had just left, to interest us in the larger implications of political crises, 'current events' had remained for us unimportant precisely because they were national; they represented something that must be followed in the newspapers but would never, conceivably, have to be lived. What really mattered were not those public affairs but the absorbing incidents of our own private lives – and now, suddenly, on that summer evening, the one had relentlessly impinged upon the other, and public events and private lives had become inseparable.

For four calamitous years, with every newspaper, with every ominous telegram, with every startling ring of the telephone bell, that inescapable identity of man and the state in the modern world was forced upon our reluctant consciousness. After the war, some of us remembered that stern lesson in social responsibility for five years, some for ten. Today a few, but only a few, remember it still. Most of us, apparently, do not even trouble to pass on our knowledge to our young successors.

How many schools, in this fourteenth post-war year, have yet begun to teach their pupils that political crises affect domestic conditions? How many give lessons in current events at all? Only a few days ago a correspondence, started by a 'Worried Father' who protested that his daughter knew nothing of the world she lived in, raged in the columns of a daily paper on this very subject, and though a few girls acquitted their schools of negligence, the greater number complained that no effort had been made to keep them in touch with contemporary history. Some of them seemed blankly unaware that their elders were still dealing – or rather, failing miserably to deal – with the results of that bygone catastrophe which many people now feel that they need not remember.

Eight years ago, after making a tour of the occupied areas of Germany – the Ruhr, the Rhineland, the Saar Valley – I first began to suspect that my generation would not be able to contribute very much to the rebuilding of civilization, for the simple reason that the results of the war would last longer than ourselves. Today I know – as authoritative economists such as Sir Arthur Salter and

212

Mr G.D.H. Cole are continually making clear to those who trouble to read them – that a heavy burden of reconstruction will lie upon the shoulders of our children; and yet, it seems, we are keeping secret from them the alien kingdom of our memories, and failing to endow them, when their day comes, with a greater power to control political and economic forces than is possible for a bankrupt and shattered generation.

For this reason I hope that we shall not cease to commemorate the Armistice; it is one of the few simple, comprehensible institutions which periodically remind us that between public events and private histories lies a close and profound relationship which we dare not forget.

Manchester Guardian, 11 November 1932

✍

ILLUSION ON THE SOMME

One recent summer's day in France – a day which vividly recalled to me the little war that you've probably forgotten, since it happened so very long ago – I drove out of Amiens towards the Somme battlefields with two companions. One of these was a writer of satires on contemporary life; the other chanced, most appropriately, to be a book – the *Cry Havoc!* of Beverley Nichols.

At the hour when we left the street beside the once-threatened cathedral, where the specimen collection of war memorials and the still shattered windows smashed in the German offensive of 1918 preserve the war for our ex-allies as an event of only yesterday, the majority of worthy citizens across the Channel were still enjoying their London newspapers. And some of them that morning were doubtless edified to learn that 'there are moments in the history of a nation' (such as 4 August 1914) 'when decisions are reached by instinct rather than by calculation and reasoning.'

In my early youth I was often told that women were an inferior species because they based their actions on instinct instead of upon reason. But apparently this quality, so deplorable in the case of females, becomes admirable – for reasons which are not quite clear to me – as soon as it characterizes a whole people; for a little further down in the column, the leader-writer concluded that 'the nation ... has never had cause to repent its resolution'.

Except in the most accessible French towns, the larger London newspapers are not available on the day of publication, so I had not this inspiring thought to console me as I stood on Thiepval ridge beneath the arch of the great memorial to the missing of the Somme, and looked across the now verdant slopes of the River Ancre to the reconstructed village of Beaumont Hamel.

It was a perfect summer day; all over the undulating miles of the Somme valley, rolling away into the blue-grey distance which hid the spires of Amiens, the French peasants were gathering the harvest. 'No cause to repent' – since the blood which once watered those fields and the flesh that manured them have apparently created a richer dust for the satisfaction of the spring sowers. I wonder whether the mothers and wives and sisters and sweethearts of the 73,367 undiscovered or unidentified men whose names are inscribed on the Thiepval memorial would accept that statement? And whether we, to whom all but one or two of them were strangers, have no reason to regret that they are not with us, to raise the standard of our literature, our art, our science, our struggling, floundering politics?

Is there, finally, no cause for repentance in the manner of their deaths – those agonizing mutilations, those grotesque defacements which left nothing but a shattered arm, an isolated leg, the obscene remnants of a detached human skull, to indicate that here was one of those young men who composed what Mr Hugh Dalton, in a House of Commons speech quoted by Beverley Nichols, described as 'the morning glory that was the flower of Anzac, the youth of Australia and New Zealand, yes, and the youth of our own country'? That horror of utter, humiliating annihilation cannot be concealed even by the lofty inscription carved so gracefully upon the memorial:

Here are recorded names of officers and men of the British Armies who fell on the Somme Battlefields, July, 1915, to February, 1918, but to whom the fortune of War denied the known and honoured burial given to their comrades in death.

Grave and beautiful words, you say, which bring tears to the eyes and a sob to the throat? Yes, no doubt – but let's have the truth. They are all a cheating and a camouflage, these noble memorials, with their mown, scented lawns, these peaceful cemeteries filled with red roses and purple pansies, these harvest fields which help to create the illusion that war is a glorious thing because so much of its aftermath can be rendered lovely and dignified. They do not compensate the young men for the lives that they laid down, and they do not recompense you and me for having to go through the long years without them.

I am glad that I carried Beverley Nichols' book with me through Hédauville and Thiepval, and to Albert, with its shining rebuilt basilica, and to La Boiselle, where the homely hens peck on the edges of the mine-craters, and to Pozières, with its Australian monument, and to Bapaume, with its modern, labour-saving houses, and to Péronne, which now flourishes exceedingly as the post-war godchild of Blackburn. I am glad because his book assisted me to remain undeluded by those beautiful memorial acres, for it reminded me that the Somme battle need never have been fought at all. 'Germany', he states, 'would have capitulated in 1915, its ironmasters have since admitted, if Briey had been bombarded'. For Briey, so Mr Nichols tells us, was the region which furnished the material for the guns that slaughtered the French and British troops, and through the influence of the great metallurgical industry it remained immune from Allied attack all through the war.

This sinister jewel of information brings me, along with the author of *Cry Havoc!* to another theme which may, if we reflect upon it, give all of us sufficient cause for repentance before we are done. If Beverley Nichols and his instructors – the expert contributors to *What Would be the Character of a New War?* and the writers of that admirable UDC pamphlet, 'The Secret International' – are not deceiving us, there will be no dignified memorials after the next war to end war, and no one to put them up. In that war we shall all be the missing – you and I and editorial leader-writers and our small sons and daughters who now play their games with such happy confidence in the world that politicians and generals and armament manufacturers have made for them. Far more expeditiously than the missing of the Somme we shall be reduced by air attacks and gas shells to putrescent heaps of rotting flesh and poisoned blood and disintegrating bones.

But such a remote contingency, you say – you who live so comfortably in King's Lynn or Truro or Cheltenham. Let me assure you that these things are not nightmares but strong probabilities, and once war breaks out again they will turn into certainties. If you don't believe me, read Beverley Nichols – or, if you have a scientific turn of mind, tackle *What Would be the Character of a New War?* itself. And if these still fail to convince you, take a car from Amiens on your next holiday and visit Aveluy Wood.

Comparatively few gas shells were used in the last war, but where they fell Nature has alone been unable to repair the hideous wrongs wrought upon her hills and fields. Aveluy Wood is one of the 'beauty spots' in which they were used, and in the midst of it are treeless spaces where the chemically changed earth has turned rust-red. Stand, as I did, upon the road from Amiens to Albert, and look at those acres where, even in the elementary days of gas, resistant Nature was so transformed that 15 years afterwards she still preserves the illusion of spilt blood. And I don't think, even if you do live in Cheltenham or Harrogate, that you'll feel altogether happy about that next war.

New Clarion, 30 September 1933

જ

CAN THE WOMEN OF THE WORLD STOP WAR?

The world today is threatened by the gravest danger that has confronted it since 1914. During the past eventful twelve months there have been international crises in every part of this earth – in Geneva, in Germany, in Spain, in Russia and in the Far East. Unless humanity makes a mightier effort to save itself than it has yet achieved, the civilization that we know may well go the way of Greece and Rome, and mankind be plunged into a new Dark Age.

At such a time of possible catastrophe the part which women

might play in the prevention of war becomes a question of special urgency. Men have controlled the world for centuries, yet their civilized ideals are still at the mercy of their primitive impulses. Women, however, represent a new element in politics. In many countries they are still powerless, but most civilized nations have now granted them a large measure of political influence.

Can they, and will they, use this influence to prevent a repetition of that organized slaughter which between 1914 and 1918 destroyed the fine flower of a whole generation?

The other day, while preparing an address on 'How War Affects Women', I reread part of Olive Schreiner's famous book, *Woman and Labour*, published in 1911. And in the chapter on 'Woman and War' – written, appropriately enough, only three years before the Great War broke out, and only seven before the vote in England was granted to women over 30 – I came across these words:

That day, when the woman takes her place beside the man in the governance and arrangement of external affairs of her race, will also be that day that heralds the death of war as a means of arranging human differences.

Today, when the largest and most influential section of English women has had the vote for over fifteen years, can we say that Olive Schreiner's prophecy shows signs of fulfilment? It is true that woman's place in politics is hardly as yet, an equal place 'beside the man'. But it is also, I fear, too true that women have not yet exercised that strong influence on behalf of peace in which Olive Schreiner believed with eager confidence.

A few organized women, such as the members of the Women's International League, are working nobly and continuously. One or two women writers – Miss Storm Jameson, for instance, whose brilliant *No Time Like the Present* was one of the outstanding books of 1933 – constantly urge upon their readers the waste and futility of war.

But a terrible, inert mass of lethargic womanhood still does nothing, and apparently cares nothing. It does not realize that a civilization in which military values prevail is always hostile to women's interests, and that our enormous expenditure upon armaments is largely responsible for the fact that women, as a sex, are still so poorly endowed and so badly equipped. Because we, as a nation, spend our money upon guns and battleships, the great majority of women have to live in wretched, inconvenient houses, and manage with old-fashioned, second-rate tools. Because English statesmen are still dominated by military ideals, many mothers who might be saved continue to die in childbirth.

Let me give you one or two examples of these lunatic values. Do you know that 20,000 new houses, of the type with low rents which are so badly needed, could be built for the cost of one armed cruiser? Do you realize that our preliminary bombardments at Arras, Messines and Passchendaele during the war cost this country fifty-two million pounds, but that a National Maternity Service would only mean a yearly expenditure of two-and-three-quarter millions? For the money, therefore, which we spent upon those three destructive bombardments we could have had a National Maternity Service, with all that it would have meant in the reduction of maternal mortality, for nearly twenty years!

When I think of such facts as these, I am not so much dismayed that women have failed to put an end to war, as astounded that so few of them have even tried to do so. Because women produce children, life and the means of living matter to them in a way that these things can never matter to men. Yet too many wives and mothers make a virtue of taking no interest in 'politics', although it is only by political methods that a new and yet vaster annihilation of human life can be prevented.

The woman who today restricts her interest to her own domestic affairs and refuses to accept what Sir Norman Angell has called 'the moral obligation to be intelligent', is guilty of gross irresponsible selfishness towards her children and society. It is useless to have an ideal nursery if you do nothing to prevent that nursery from being blown to bits within the next few years.

I believe that the women of the world could stop war if they ceased to be completely absorbed in themselves and their homes and their children, and began to realize that their duty to mankind extends beyond their own little doorstep.

I sometimes feel that what the women's peace campaign really needs is the sudden uprising of a movement as swift and dramatic as that of the militant suffragists, which would adopt expedients similar to theirs, such as the refusal to pay income tax for war purposes, or the interruption of military pageants and tattoos with protests still more vehement than those already attempted by Dr Maude Royden and her supporters. But a movement of this kind requires a leader at least as gifted and inspired as Mrs Pankhurst, and though such leaders have a habit of appearing at the psychological moment, I believe that, even without a guide of this type, women could exercise a decisive influence for peace if they adopted the right methods on a large enough scale.

The first essentials are awareness and organization. To study the influence of public events upon private lives, to follow the course of international affairs with enough intelligence to understand what type of men and women our representatives should be and how we can ensure their choice – these are duties from which no domestic preoccupations can now excuse us. And we can best employ such knowledge and the power that it brings by giving our support to peace organizations, which exist in sufficient variety to represent all shades of opinion, from the right-wing League of Nations Union to the Anti-War Movement on the extreme left. We can use these, as well as the ordinary machinery of politics, to demand the expenditure of the nation's money upon the means of life instead of the instruments of death.

In addition we can take, as individuals, certain drastic steps which would have a compelling effect if universally adopted. We can refuse, for instance, to send our sons to schools which run an Officers' Training Corps, and we can ostracize any acquaintances known to have shares in armament firms or to deal with such firms on a business basis. Society has always condemned the thief and the forger, but these are less anti-social than the man or woman who grows rich from the murder and mutilation of humanity. Our country's policy would soon change if no advocate of increased armaments could get a woman to vote for him or invite him to her house.

I refuse to believe that women, who produce life, will permit mankind resignedly to accept death from the diabolical instruments of its own invention. Since men throughout their centuries of authority have not succeeded in extending the reign of law to international relationships, it is our task today to explore every method by which the heroism and resourcefulness that respond so swiftly and tragically to war can be dedicated instead to the service of peace and of life.

Modern Woman, February 1934

❧

WHY NOT A REAL PEACE CRUSADE?

A few years ago, at a No More War Conference, I heard Mr Wickham Steed complain that the trouble about peace was that it had no news value.

I have frequently reflected upon these words, for the reason why peace has no news value is that too often, owing to the way in which its cause is presented, it makes no appeal to the imagination, and has, therefore, no glamour.

In a recently published book called *Testament of Youth* – a book which I wrote as a vehement protest against war, and a passionate plea for peace – I endeavoured to face up to this difficulty. I believe it to be the greatest difficulty confronting the peace-worker today, for it is rooted, not in conditions which, however menacing, are temporary, such as the policy of armament firms or the present chaotic state of Europe, but in the deepest and finest qualities of human nature.

The problem, in my book, was stated thus:

It is, I think, this glamour, this magic, this incomparable keying up of the spirit in a time of mortal conflict, which constitute the pacifist's real problem – a problem still incompletely imagined, and still quite unsolved. The causes of war are always falsely represented; its honour is dishonest and its glory meretricious, but the challenge to spiritual endurance, the intense sharpening of all the senses, the vitalizing consciousness of common peril for a common end, remain to allure those boys and girls who have just reached the age when love and friendship and adventure call more persistently than at any later time. The glamour may be the mere delirium of fever, which, as soon as war is over, dies out and shows itself for the will-o'-the-wisp that it is, but while it lasts, no emotion known to man seems as yet to have quite the compelling power of this enlarged vitality.

I should have thought that the meaning of this passage was clear enough, but one or two of my critics have chosen to interpret it as an apology for war, or an endeavour to vindicate those who fight. This, of course, is absurd. The men who fell in the Great War require no vindication from me or anyone else; their reasons for going may have been mistaken, but their motives, in most cases, were beyond criticism. I should like, therefore, to take this opportunity of stating that I am as convinced an opponent of war, and as determined a protagonist of peace, as I have ever been since 1919. No men or women in their senses can today be otherwise.

But it seems to me not only useless, but criminally stupid, to work for peace without intelligently examining the chief forces that threaten it. Our difficulties are not minimized, but increased, by the fact that all too often it is not the black but the white angels which 'fight so naïvely on the side of destruction'.

Fortunately – and herein lies the possibility of salvation – it is not war alone which heightens consciousness, vitalizes the senses, and keys up the spirit. All intense emotion does that, from first love to ultimate sacrifice. The trouble with war is merely that it performs this function for lethargic humanity on a larger scale than anything else.

The heroic ecstasy which illuminates war is found throughout history in fields quite other than those of battle. It obviously inspired the great discoverers of the sixteenth century; it sent the famous explorers of the nineteenth, such as Livingstone and Stanley, into darkest Africa; it must have fired Sir Ronald Ross in his search for the source of malaria, and Lord Lister in his discovery of the secret of modern surgery. The same spirit illumined the men who went with Scott and Shackleton in quest of the North or South Pole; it has nerved the climbers of Everest, and the men and women who have flown the Atlantic.

How can we get this spirit of adventure into the peace movement? Too many League of Nations Union secretaries, conscientiously toiling in isolation, imagine that the world can be saved by secretarial work. Such work is certainly an essential part of the background of every great movement, but no cause will ever succeed by that alone. I suggest that, at least by way of beginning, a real uniformed peace crusade might be organized on the largest possible scale. It would resemble no peace crusade yet undertaken, for its mainspring would be, not speeches and pamphlets, but action of the most spectacular kind.

Amongst its organizers would be several advertising experts who have studied the psychology of human response to every kind of appeal, and who would know how to invent slogans to arrest popular attention. Every type of device from banners to sky-writing would be employed to circulate these slogans. Methods would be adopted for calling processions into being at very short notice, to protest actively whenever rumours of war threatened to destroy peace, or to celebrate whenever a measure of disarmament was passed, or some event of importance occurred in Geneva. Every constructive form of social service – such as fire-drill, life-saving, first aid and emergency nursing – would be learnt and practised by the crusaders as they are by members of the Scouts and Guides.

Money? Well, it would be needed, of course, but money is apt to flow in whenever a movement is dramatically presented as a life-or-death issue. Organizers? They should be forthcoming quickly enough, as they have been for Fascism, if peace were associated with action and initiative instead of being identified with perpetual pamphlets and the dreary droning of tired voices in somnolent lecture halls.

Have we who are members of the League of Nations Union grown too cautious and middle-aged for such an adventure? I cannot believe it, for it is only by some great adventure that the cause of peace will be saved.

Pamphlet 'The Lighter Side of Peacemaking' published by
Quarterly News, 1934

∽

NO COMPROMISE WITH WAR

Nothing is more gratifying to human nature than a supply of sound moral reasons for doing exactly what it wants to do. The nobler the alleged motives can be made to appear, the more thoroughly do they conceal that pursuit of self-interest in which mankind, especially of the British variety, has a peculiar distaste for acknowledging itself to be engaged.

In England we are always completely innocent of aggressive intentions. When we decide, with expressions of profound reluctance, to embark upon a heavy armaments programme, it is never in order to outpace an ambitious neighbour, nor even to hold those vast possessions which we acquired so comfortably when there was no League of Nations or organized pacifist opinion to interfere in our military adventures. With impeccable altruism we build tanks and bombing aeroplanes to defend the cause of peace. Our new programme, in the unimpeachable words of a recent *Times* leader, is designed 'to use the strength of this country to promote a more reasonable temper in the world'. How natural that our rulers should be hurt and surprised when less philanthropic governments misunderstand their pacific motives and credit them with quite other and preposterous intentions!

In 1920, when the League of Nations held its first assembly, many of us pinned our war-tattered hopes to the brave new banner of collective security. Believing that the gradual strengthening of an international authority would make progressive disarmament possible, we overlooked the incurable tendency of every state to view its conduct in a favourable and forgiving light never vouchsafed to the behaviour of others. Or if indeed we did realize the ingenuity with which mankind is liable to camouflage its most questionable actions, we believed that the terrible lessons of the war would compel the leaders of the suffering peoples to face honestly the alternative between annihilation and a new conception of international morality.

True, a flight from hypocrisy had not always been the consequence of previous wars. We recalled, for instance, the Holy Alliance of 1815, that grandiose experiment in international amity which Metternich scorned as 'mere verbiage', Castlereagh repudiated as 'a piece of sublime mysticism and nonsense', and Canning (in language reminiscent of present-day armament magnates) finally dismissed as 'a beautiful phantom which England cannot pursue'. Forced upon his fellow-rulers by Emperor Alexander I of Russia – the President Wilson of the Vienna Congress – its first article has a sound disconcertingly familiar to those accustomed to the public pronouncements of contemporary European statesmen:

The three contracting monarchs [of Austria, Prussia and Russia] will remain united by the bonds of a true and indissoluble fraternity, and considering each other as fellow-countrymen, they will on all occasions and in all places lend each other aid and assistance: and regarding themselves towards their subjects and armies as fathers of families, they will lead them in the same spirit of fraternity with which they are animated, to protect Religion, Peace and Justice.

Even by 1822, the year of the Verona Congress, Europe, in the words of a historian of that period, had already 'moved away' from this particular brand of collective security. But after all (so we argued in the confident nineteen-twenties), the Holy Alliance was made by monarchs, not by the elected statesmen of democratic countries. The Covenant of the League rang more modestly in our ears. It had less to say about religion, peace and justice, yet it proposed methods of reaching these desirable objectives – 'by the acceptance of obligations not to resort to war, by the prescription of open, just and honourable relations between nations … ' Yet, in the end, the chief difference between the aftermath of 1920 and that of 1815 lies in the fact that it has taken the post-war world sixteen years, instead of seven, to learn that 'open, just and honourable relations between nations' are as difficult to maintain as religion, peace and justice themselves.

So great have been the obstacles in the way of this noble ideal, that today we find collective security identified with a particular alliance of the so-called 'democratic' powers against the dictators. No amount of pious talk about a 'Franco-Soviet Pact supported by Great Britain to defend collective security through the League of Nations' can disguise the fact that this gilded angel of internationalism is nothing more than the reincarnation of the Triple Entente which made the Great War inevitable by dividing Europe into two hostile camps.

The past half-decade has proved with disillusioning clarity that resistance to war-making by a superior aggregation of war-making forces merely results in entangling the machinery of peace with the machinery for war – which is better organized, more technically efficient, and directed by highly trained intelligences unimpeded by scruples. The precedents set up by Manchuria and Abyssinia have already demonstrated to would-be war-mongers that an aggressor will always get away with the spoil while the representatives of law and order are busily engaged in letting each other down.

Armaments, as Dr L.P. Jacks recently pointed out, 'are, of all the possessions of a sovereign state, the least susceptible of being pooled for any common purpose, since this would inevitably limit the sovereignty they are intended to maintain'. As for sanctions, these complicated expedients appear in a different light the moment that a nation ceases to be the guardian of virtue applying them, and becomes the object of their infliction. Needless to remark, Great Britain could hardly imagine'herself in any less dignified role than that of avenging champion of peace, but her attitude towards sanctions would undoubtedly undergo a sea-change if they were exercised, let us say, against her right to bomb the native inhabitants of 'outlying territories'.

An article in the April number of *Headway* by the Secretary of the League of Nations Union illustrates the tragic fashion in which integrity is gradually lost by those peace-makers who endeavour to compromise with war. During the years immediately following the Armistice, many whole-hearted pacifists supported the League of Nations Union because of its magnificent and successful endeavours to create a peace-minded people. More recently the leaders of this organization have changed, by almost imperceptible stages, into sorry apologists for the new militarism. When a prominent Union official can write that 'the task of creating and maintaining justice ... is more far-reaching and will loom larger ... than the negative business of preventing war', it is clear that, by such advocates, the cause of peace is already lost. It was in the name of 'justice' that the victorious Allies perpetrated the criminal blunder of Versailles – the bill for which is now being presented to them by Fascism. Those who exercise coercion and call it justice are liable to have such bills presented to them till the end of time.

Modern pacifists are no longer impressed by the argument that 'preponderance of power' must enable 'the forces available for preserving law and order' to 'remain overwhelmingly greater than those of any likely aggressor'. For some of us who recently took part in the BBC programme, 'Scrapbook for 1912', this contention bears an uncomfortable family likeness to certain words used at the Lord Mayor's Banquet of that year by Mr Winston Churchill: 'The relations between the two countries' (England and Germany) 'have steadily improved during the year. They have steadily improved side by side with every evidence of our determination to maintain our naval supremacy. And the best way to make these relations thoroughly healthy and comfortable is to go right on and put an end to this naval rivalry by proving that we cannot be overtaken.' The fact that the guardian of law and order was then (in British eyes) the British navy backed up by a grand alliance called the Triple Entente, whereas it is today the British navy and air-force backed up by another grand alliance called the League of Nations, makes little difference to the certainty that explosive weapons, whatever the name in which they are collected, are equally liable to go off if a match is flung into the powder magazine.

For this reason the statement in *Headway* seems to me to embody not a peace policy but a war policy. Certainly it is a war policy for which the most edifying reasons are given, but this is a common characteristic of all war policies now that Field-Marshal Propaganda has become chief of staff. Not a single recruit would consent to die, let alone kill, for his country if the causes of any modern war were frankly stated. Nowadays, therefore, no nation fights any war but a righteous war, or piles up armaments for any reason but that of 'defence'. If the advocates of collective security intend to circulate this type of casuistry, the sooner they shut down and leave their job to the recruiting sergeant, the better for the honesty of mankind.

From the standpoint of the genuine pacifist, collective security was bound to fail just because it always has involved this compromise with militarism which is the final disloyalty to the peace ideal. For its acceptance it has been obliged to depend in peace-time, upon exactly the type of specious argument which is used to encourage enlistment in war.

'Just *this* war because it is quite different from all other wars. It is waged against militarism (or Kaiserism, or Fascism, or Communism) and is therefore a war in defence of peace and righteousness. Only help us to win this, and the world will never have to fight another.'

So, in each successive crisis, the advocate of peace has been obliged to reconsider just what degree of war his conscience will permit. In the attempt to satisfy that conscience he has been presented with one ingenious justification after another – until recent disasters have shown him unmistakably that war-mongering will never be restrained by a policy of coercive alliances.

We shall keep, I hope, the League idea and the League organization, for, apart from its valuable service of teaching the nations to co-operate in humanitarian causes, the Geneva machinery might work in a community of nations each of which had delegated a part of its national sovereignty to an international body in response to a general programme of disarmament. It cannot work while states still dominated by balance-of-power doctrines are prepared to use its institutions as a camouflage for nationalist policies directed towards the maintenance of individual sovereignty.

So persistently have recent governments closed their eyes to the more disquieting lessons which experience teaches, that it now appears more feasible to persuade a majority of the populations in each country to repudiate war, than to get a majority of governments to agree upon any policy which involves abandoning their determination to be the supreme arbiters of their fate. This is not because no precedents exist for conciliation and commonsense on the part of statesmen. Monroe and Castlereagh took a considerable risk when in 1817, two years after an inconclusive treaty following a bitter war between the United States and Great Britain, they negotiated the Rush-Bagot agreement which for one hundred and twenty years has maintained peace along the three thousand miles of Canadian–American frontier. In 1860 Gladstone and Cobden, by arranging with Napoleon III that exemplary act of goodwill and commonsense known as the Cobden Treaty, bound up the commercial interests of England and France with the establishment of mutual friendship between those long-hostile powers. But present-day statesmen appear to resemble not Monroe or Gladstone so much as the restored Bourbons, who after the Napoleonic Wars, so historians tell us, 'had learnt nothing and forgotten nothing'. Our politicians exceed even this limit of ineptitude, for they have learnt nothing and forgotten everything.

The past five years have proved beyond doubt that peace can only be attained by constructive peace proposals, and security by a fearless abandonment of the ancient and time-dishonoured game of power-politics. If this involves the break-up of imperialism, we could not see our Empire disrupt in a better cause. If it means a simpler, quieter, less arrogant way of life, at least it will be life instead of death.

No pacifist denies that a policy of disarmament has its risks in a world distraught by passions, grievances and ambitions, but all history shows that the willingness to take risks is an essential quality of distinguished statesmanship. Conciliation may fail, but it has an even chance of success. Rearmament, whether undertaken in the name of the League or of naked nationalism, can lead us nowhere but the edge of the abyss.

World Review of Reviews, May 1937

ى

ON THE SPANISH CIVIL WAR

As an uncompromising pacifist, I hold war to be a crime against humanity, whoever fights it and against whomever it is fought. I detest Fascism and all that it stands for, but I do not believe that we shall destroy it by fighting it. And I do not feel that we serve either the Spanish people or the cause of civilization by continuing to make Spain the battleground for a new series of wars of religion.

Contribution to 'Authors Take Sides on the Spanish War', pamphlet published by the Left Review, December 1937

ى

PACIFISM AFTER MUNICH

To English pacifists the recent crisis represents the clearest possible example of historical retribution for the crimes and blunders of statesmanship during the past twenty years. Though Germany is now the undoubted cause of the present political neurosis, we regard her as only one amongst many powers who are mutually to blame.

Arriving in America just after the tension was over, I was astonished by the violence of anti-German feeling amongst many peace workers of long standing, for in England – except in terms of extremists who belong to the Left Book Club and the Communist Party – it is not felt with comparable vehemence. In Whitehall, during the worst days of the crisis, pro-war demonstrations were confined to the same small, unrepresentative group. The ordinary men and women who went down on their knees in prayer on the pavements round Downing Street when Chamberlain's first visit to Germany was announced, raised no cry of 'Down with Hitler!' comparable to the 'Down with the Kaiser!' shouts of 1914. That test of popular feeling, the cinematograph news reel, produces fewer English than American hisses when Hitler appears on the screen, though it will be British heads on which the bombs will drop if war comes.

The explanation does not lie entirely in British fatalism and our national capacity for resignation. It is due to a largely, unconscious acceptance of the pacifist view that Hitler is not a paranoiac, a 'mad dog', or one of those fortuitous phenomena known to insurance companies as 'acts of God', but is the inevitable product of a situation for which the victors of the Great War are all responsible. Long before Hitler created modern Germany, post-war Germany had created Hitler. The product of Clemenceau and Lloyd George at the so-called 'Peace Conference', and of Sir John Simon at the strangely named 'Disarmament Conference', he is now presenting them with the bill for Versailles. Though Germany is the immediate cause of the recent crisis, I feel that English and American peace-lovers should hesitate before the temptation to fix 'war guilt' upon a nation and an individual with a short-sighted bitterness only comparable to that of 1918.

Let us admit – and British pacifists are the first to do so – that the Munich settlement is an inglorious peace, purchased at the expense of a small power whose sacrifices left her greater neighbours free to make none. But given the context of a rapidly deteriorating situation due to twenty years of mismanagement, we who believe that any kind of peace is better than any variety of modern war, feel that Chamberlain did the best that was possible at the given moment.

Opinion in the United States, dominated as it is by that tendency to divide into black and white, characteristic of a vital people with a passion for justice, appears to assume that an honourable settlement could somehow have been made at a reasonable price. In 1933 such a settlement might have been possible; even in 1936 it was still not too late. But by 1938 the time had gone by. England was faced, not with the alternative between good and evil, but with the alternative between one evil and another. Chamberlain, as some of us believe, rightly chose the lesser, for a European war would have had three immediate consequences which no pacifist – and indeed no man of good will whatever his opinions – could regard with any sentiment but horror.

In the first place Czechoslovakia, the scene of the opening campaign, would have suffered immediate annihilation. Today, despite her losses, she has something left – the nucleus of a state even now larger than Belgium or Switzerland, which may still take advantage of the infinite possibilities of change and restitution that exist in a world where most countries are still at peace.

Secondly, in all the fascist countries, war would undoubtedly have been followed by a massacre of the Jews on a scale to which the past and present Jewish persecutions, bitter as they are, bear no comparison.

Thirdly, the warring democracies, in order to counter their fascist adversaries with any hope of success, would have been obliged to undergo a rapidly increasing fascization, leading to restraints on liberty far beyond the restrictions likely to be imposed in peace-time by the mild variety of fascism which some prophets predict in England as the consequence of Chamberlain's 'bargain' with Hitler.

Within a few weeks everything for which the war was fought would have been lost, but the war itself would have remained to be fought to the death. The juggernaut machine, as in 1914 to 1918, would again have taken control of the men who nominally directed it, until civilization itself became the last and greatest casualty.

Faced with such a prospect, Chamberlain preferred the uneasy truce which now confronts us. It is the task of the pacifist movement, in England and elsewhere, to contribute to the limit of its powers to the transformation of that truce into a more permanent peace. The educational function before it involves the presentation of two theses to the public mind. First, if peace is to endure, the great powers must be prepared to make their own sacrifices instead of exacting them from smaller and weaker neighbours. The British Government, for example, will contribute nothing to any permanent settlement unless it is prepared to regard colonial possessions and British economic policy as open to drastic revision.

In the second place, a public unhappily divided in its views between the respective merits of punitive action and conciliation, should be reminded by pacifists that the present tragic situation is the direct consequence of attempts to humiliate a proud and industrious people, and that a similar catastrophic 'remedy' could only raise similar terrible problems for our children to solve. Neither a nation nor a political philosophy can be permanently suppressed by resort to arms; like indestructible phoenixes, they rise again from the ashes of defeat, wearing new names with each reincarnation. Quite obviously a threat of force may keep the peace at a given moment, but equally obviously it offers no final solution for the harsh dilemmas of this world.

Our one real hope, in the respite now given us, lies in the demand for a sincere and comprehensive peace conference to settle outstanding political, economic and territorial grievances before war breaks out. We English pacifists therefore believe that we should continue to press for it even though the immediate future appears unfavourable and the attitude of the totalitarian states remains uncertain. We hope that American pacifists will help us by urging that the initiative be taken by that most powerful of all 'neutrals', their own President, despite the real difficulties presented by divided official counsels and a large scale rearmament program.

In thus urging conciliation rather than 'discipline' in spite of all the portents, we know that we are choosing a policy beset with problems and fraught with peril. But we believe this chance to represent the only path to a tolerable future. The sole alternative is an ever-darkening night of hatred, suspicion and fear, until death and destruction descend upon the treasure-house of civilization which mankind has constructed through long aeons of conflict and pain.

Fellowship (US), November 1938

LIFT UP YOUR HEARTS!

For the second time within a generation, worldwide calamity has descended upon us. Those few who refused to believe that mankind could require another lesson see their confidence in ultimate human sanity destroyed.

Some who have written and spoken and struggled for twenty years because the First World War took 'our youth, our joys, our all we had', may well feel that their efforts have been futile, their lives lived in vain.

We may weep for ourselves as individuals. Not one of us now is free from peril. As husbands, as wives, as parents, as children, we must bear the intolerable burden of unceasing apprehension, not only for those on the battlefield, but for one another. At any moment we who belong to Class 1914 may lose in one shattering blow the second little world of personal hope and love and trust and tenderness which we have built up on the ruins of the first. Yes, we may weep for ourselves. But for the pacifism which is our faith we need not weep.

Nothing can prove more surely than the past few days, weeks and years of history, that never, now, will mankind live in peace and security until the policy for which we stand is nationally accepted and carried out. Sorrowfully we perceive the realization of all our prophecies. Provocation has led to provocation, force to more force. War preparations have caused the explosion that we all foresaw. Far from armaments giving us 'security', they have brought us to a peril compared with which the disarmament that we advocated was a negligible risk.

The worldwide dismay which has greeted this cataclysm, the absence of marching songs and flag-waving and boastful jubilation, themselves indicate how near the common people of all nations were coming to the acceptance of our pacifist creed. Civilian casualties will be many in this conflict, and those who have led the peace movement cannot all hope to see its post-war rebirth. But so long as the breath is in us, we can go on working with the certainty that what we stand for will one day triumph.

Why, then, for the moment, has our policy failed? There are two answers, I think. One is – and always is – that we have none of us done quite enough. We lose confidence too soon, or we are too easily satisfied.

We cannot, we say constantly, be all Dick Sheppards. Perhaps not; but more of us, I suspect, would approach his stature if we all worked as he worked, loved humanity as he loved it, and took the trouble that he took over the humblest individual.

But we have also failed temporarily because our policy is a difficult policy requiring an abandonment of preconceptions too revolutionary for our intelligences, a measure of sacrifice too severe for our small hearts.

Great qualities, such as consistent pacifism requires, are slow growers in both individuals and nations. It is easy to put the blame on others, to hate, to fight, to see our opponents as evil incarnate; those are the natural tendencies of human nature. Constructive peace-making requires a measure of faith and resolution which only sincere and deliberate cultivation can render strong enough to confront the follies with which we destroy ourselves. Above all, it needs an endowment of wise foresight and impersonal imagination which does not always come naturally even to sincere peace-lovers, who sometimes overlook 'the moral obligation to be intelligent'.

On 30 August, when the international tension was reaching its climax, I received an anonymous letter from a correspondent in Scotland. I do not apologize for quoting it, for it explains why the noblest endeavours of the human spirit suffer periods of setback, and why those who work to liberate humanity from itself occasionally feel as though they had spent an eternity in beating their heads against a stone wall.

Dear Miss Brittain,

Can you not do something before it is too late. Is there *nothing* that women ... who remember last time can do except sit down, and calmly wait for the slaughter to begin? I am not a member of the Peace Pledge Union, nor of anything else, I am only a mother of a 21-year-old boy. Could not a million women make their voices heard somewhere in Britain and Europe? Your *Testament of Youth* made a lasting impression on me, and now I wish I hadn't read it, as my thoughts on mustard gas and my dreams at night are a nightmare. No, I am not hysterical or afraid of war as it used to be, but *this* is not war, but what can one woman do? ...

My correspondent asks me to *do* something – but she admits that she herself has done nothing whatever. She is 'not a member of the Peace Pledge Union or anything else' – but she wants those of us who are to save her now. She wants a million women to raise their voices against war, as though their collection and organization were the work of a moment. Apparently – since she did not help – she is unaware that the National Peace Council recently spent six months in collecting one a a half million signatures in favour of a new international Peace Conference.

Moreover, when my correspondent read *Testament of Youth* six years ago, the description of my patients who died of mustard gas in 1917 did not move her sufficiently to stir her to action. It is only now, when the dread poison threatens herself and her son, that her thoughts become nightmares.

She was not afraid of 'war as it used to be', for women had a grand time in all previous wars. Even in the war of 1914, the numbers who actually ran risks from shells, bombs and submarines was very small indeed. The majority got a tremendous thrill out of the feeling that fine young men were dying for them, and almost as great a kick from handing white feathers to the ones who weren't.

But now that women are faced with the possibility of dying themselves, war has ceased to be quite such fun. Even white feathers lose their glamour when the front line shifts from trenches comfortably distant in Flanders to one's own doorstep.

My correspondent is a proof that war will certainly be destroyed sooner or later by the fact that its horrors have ceased to be vicarious. But I hope and believe that there are enough men and women with imagination, compassion, energy and initiative to put an end to it without waiting for the negative operation of universal fear. If we want peace we must *work for it ourselves*, and not turn to others to save us. Let those who are prepared to work for it join the Peace Pledge Union and *begin now*.

We have, all of us, certain important things to remember. First and foremost, our task is to hasten the coming of peace and to set our faces against all that delays it – the surging tide of hatred, the rising flood of mendacity. Let us look carefully for the truth, and when we have found it, let us tell it lucidly and without provocation.

One truth is already being overlaid in speeches and articles because, as in all wars, we have created a devil to fight. We are not really at war because Herr Hitler is a terrorist dictator without mercy. We are at war because our treatment of Germany and the rational leaders whom she elected from 1919 onwards provoked her into choosing a terrorist dictator as a last resort.

Let us remember and repent of the wrong that England has done; but let us remember that she has done great and wise and merciful things too, and will do them again if we, her people, are determined that she shall. Finally, let us never forget that she is our country; and let us seek, by means of thought and love and pity which inflict no suffering, to mitigate the burden laid upon her and her citizens of whom we are part.

Again and again, during the holiday weeks spent this summer with my children in the New Forest, I have walked through the green glades and watched the heather deepen from mauve to purple, reflecting that for all her destructive follies which have once more helped to plunge the world in sorrow, I desire no other country than this.

Let us remember that she is ours no less because we are ready to die for her without seeking to kill. Our love for her is increased rather than mitigated because we wish to see her yield her domination, not to superior force, but to the noble ideal of a community of free and equal nations which we must strive to keep alight in the dark period that lies before us.

Amid the tide of hatred which threatens to engulf even this continent of disillusioned fighters, we who care for peace must make it our constant task to save the purity of that ideal from self-seekers who would interpret it to serve their own ends, and insist that those whom we call our enemies have an equal right to belong to it with ourselves. Whatever we may suffer at their hands, let us remember that they are suffering similarly at ours, and that we and they now belong alike to the company of those that mourn.

We of the pacifist movement are here not to destroy but to fulfil. Our watchword is not recrimination but compassion. More than ever before – more than it is capable today of realizing – our country will need us and our message. *Sursum corda*. Let us keep our heads and lift up our hearts!

Peace News, 8 September 1939

WHY I OPPOSE ECONOMIC BLOCKADE

Since the war began, the phrase 'economic blockade' has been hopefully cherished by many of this country's better-nourished inhabitants. Round it circulates much of the wishful thinking which at present afflicts our nation.

Some of my acquaintances – kindly, well-meaning people who would hesitate to kill a fly and could certainly draw the line at running over a dog – talk with glib optimism about the effectiveness of 'our blockade'. 'After all,' they assure each other, 'we've got command of the seas. We'll soon starve Germany into submission!'

What exactly does that mean in terms of social misery and individual suffering?

I have never forgotten an evening in 1924, when I spoke about the League of Nations in halting German to a group of tolerant, friendly razor-makers from a factory at Solingen, near Cologne.

My host, the local pastor, was the father of three thin but riotous little sons, whose care, added to a constant battle with stringent economy, had so exhausted his gentle wife that her patient, beautiful face haunts me still. Before the meeting, the pastor showed me the photograph of their eldest child, a small fair-haired girl. 'We lost her,' he told me with tears in his eyes. 'She was delicate, and we could not get milk for her during the blockade.'

Only recently, a correspondent confirmed my own recollections of Central Europe during those nightmare years which will soon repeat themselves in thousands of German homes. 'What I saw,' she writes, 'in Germany soon after the last war when, as a member of the Society of Friends, I went there to help with the feeding of the children, has lain like a heavy burden on my mind ever since.'

Another post-war visitor to Germany has told me how, in 1921, he observed Austrian children, their bones soft as paper, lying like limp rag dolls in the parks of Vienna. By 1924 this pitiful suffering had been tidied out of the streets, but the slums and hospitals of German cities were still filled with children of all ages suffering from rickets and tuberculosis. And now we, who have made such proud progress during the past twenty years in the feeding and care of our young, are preparing to rejoice that German children will suffer once more.

The policy of blockade, though less gruesome than air raids, is more malevolent because its effects continue. Long after states have ceased to quarrel, the consequences of their disputes are visible in the impaired development, the depleted vitality, sometimes even the living death, of their weakest and most vulnerable citizens. There are always rations for statesmen and soldiers. However poor the quality, labourers, artisans, clerical workers both male and female, have also their portion reserved. Those who suffer most in economic warfare are pregnant women, nursing mothers, babies and small children.

Nobody values more deeply than myself the privilege of free speech and a free press. These democratic rights are the basis of my personal life and my professional career. But, as a mother, I regard even these as too dearly bought at the cost of a nation's children.

Daily Herald, 15 November 1936

↶

'NO PITY! NO MERCY!'

Let everyone, then, who thinks with pain on all these great evils, so horrible, so ruthless, aacknowledge this is misery. And if anyone either endures or thinks of them without mental pain, this is a more miserable plight still, for he thinks himself happy because he has lost human feeling.

St Augustine, *The City of God*

Dear Reader,

While travelling to a lecture on Sunday 6 June, I happened to read the leading article in the *Sunday Express*. It was entitled 'NO PITY! NO MERCY!' If you too saw it, you will probably remember the following paragraphs:

Three years ago we stood alone ... Now we attack, and the beast – apparently very strong, formidable and ferocious, yet possibly nearer the point of cracking than we think – is caged.

237

If we are to succeed we must not harbour cant and humbug. Voices are already heard, crying that mercy must temper justice, that vengeance belongs alone to God, not to His instruments, that bombs on women and children are wicked, that the destruction of dams and the release of floods is not clean warfare, that we must not sink to the level of the Germans ... As the doom of Germany becomes more certain the voices may grow louder. They may well have a sinister inspiration. The sincere and well-meaning voices are probably encouraged by the sound of the voices made in Germany ...

All these sentimental appeals are bunkum and hypocrisy in effect, whether they come from a familiar prelate or some unsuspected quisling ... We must show no mercy till the deed is done. If we do we shall be traitors to humanity.

I am obviously one of the voices selected for condemnation by the *Sunday Express*. Mine is only a small voice. But if I were the only voice left in England to say it, and were to be shot tomorrow for saying it, I should still maintain that by every civilized standard, Christian or otherwise, it is brutal and wicked to attempt to win a war by burning and starving to death the young and helpless, and by letting loose overwhelming floods upon unsuspecting mothers and their innocent children in the small crowded homesteads of an industrial area. And judging by the conversations that I hear in trains and shops, I believe that the great majority of England's population agree with me, though most of them dare not say so.

Twenty-five years ago, in the spring of 1918, I was nursing in a military hospital at Etaples. At that time the main line to Paris had been protected from air attack for nearly four years by the long chain of army hospitals dividing the road and the railway between Etaples and Camiers. For several weeks during that spring, it was reported to the nurses that German reconnaissance planes had been over the camp dropping leaflets: 'Move your railway line or move your hospitals!' Needless to say, nothing was done – not even when a small preliminary raid on Etaples village put the bridge over the River Canche out of action for twelve hours. Finally the Germans came over, bombed the line, and killed a number of nurses and patients in the adjacent hospitals. From England went up a howl of indignation which drowned whatever apologetic mention might have been made about the warning leaflets. They had been dropped none the less, as we knew who were there. Could not our rulers who pride themselves on their superiority to German brutality have done at least as much for the women and their children in the Ruhr valleys, before they were swept away with no chance of escape when the dams were broken?

I need hardly explain to you, I think, that I am not a 'quisling'. I do not know, and never have known, a single member of the Nazi Party. I listen neither to Lord Haw-Haw nor to the BBC, and I take my views even less, if that were possible, from Dr Goebbels than from the *Sunday Express*. I only know that if I were one of the airmen who broke the dams, I should be haunted by the thought of those drowned floating faces for the rest of my life. In the *News Chronicle* of 11 June, an eyewitness quoted by Stockholm reports the scenes in the graveyards where the German people buried their families, as 'indescribable'. But it is not, I know, with the young pilots, but with those who give them their orders, that responsibility really lies. One can only pray that God's mercy may be with them, and with all other war-makers to whom, in varying degrees, belated realization will come. As I sit here writing above the Thames in our much-blitzed borough, I know that, whether I live to see it or not, the time will arrive when a flood-tide of reaction against hate will sweep the present false standards away, and horrify the men and women who temporarily subscribed to them.

In that day not honour but execration will be the portion of those who adopted from the Nazi leaders the standards of unrestricted cruelty against which they profess to be fighting. After all, people sometimes say to me, the Germans began it. Why always blame the British? My reply is that I am not responsible for cruel deeds done by the Nazis in the name of the Germans, and much as I deplore them I cannot prevent them. But so long as the breath is in me I shall protest against abominations done by my government in the name of the British, of whom I am one. The mercilessness of others does not release us from the obligation to control ourselves.

Looking round for a congenial explanation of such 'sentimentalists' as myself, the *Sunday Express* suggests that we are moved by 'sinister inspiration', 'encouraged by the sound of the voices made in Germany'. Does this editorial writer really dare to imply that the Gospels are of German origin, or the Epistles of Paul, or such masterpieces of meekness and truth as Bunyan's *Pilgrim's Progress*? Have we reached a stage at which our editors are so frightened of the eternal verities and their implications, that the only escape from them is a dishonest attempt to identify with German propaganda? It is not my voice, but the voice of the *Sunday Express*, which carries a sound reminiscent of those German and Italian teachers whose work laid the foundations of the Nazi philosophy. 'It is better', wrote Machiavelli in *Arte della Guerra*, 'to conquer an enemy by hunger than by fighting, in which last victory fortune has more share than virtue or courage.' And it was Heinrich von Treitschke, the German historian, who wrote: 'We live in a warlike age; the over-sentimental philanthropic fashion of judging things has passed into the background ... The greatness of war is just what at first sight seems to be its horror – that for the sake of their country men will overcome the natural feelings of humanity.'

I am proud to be one of those voices derided by the *Sunday Express* – and by Treitschke. I take courage from the echoes of other and greater voices which have spoken throughout history in the accents of pity, mercy, toleration, and love. Listen to some of them and take courage yourself. 'The man of noble mind seeks to achieve the good in others and not their evil', said Confucius. 'The little-minded man is the reverse of this ... ' 'When men speak evil of ye', said Buddha, 'thus must ye train yourselves: "Our heart shall be unwavering, no evil word will we send forth, but compassionate of others' welfare will we abide, of kindly heart without resentment" ... ' 'Blessed are the merciful, for they shall obtain mercy', said Jesus Christ. 'Blessed are ye, when men shall revile you and persecute you, and shall say all manner of evil against you falsely, for my sake ... ' 'Be ye kind one to another, tender-hearted,' wrote Paul to the Ephesians, 'forgiving one another, even as God for Christ's sake hath forgiven you.'

Britain, as we are so often reminded, is still a democratic country. You and I and the rest of our fellow nationals are free, as the *Sunday Express* editorial writer urges, to bomb, burn, drown and starve our enemies (and sometimes, in the attempt, our friends as well) without that compunction or those misgivings which distinguish the human being from the beast of prey. But let us make no mistake about whose company we join when we do these things – or whose we repudiate.

Yours very sincerely,
  Vera Brittain

'Letter to Peace-Lovers', No. 111, 17 June 1943
Reprinted in Forward, 26 June 1943

∽

PUNISHMENT OF A CONSCIENTIOUS OBJECTOR

Under the heading 'Six Months for C.O.' in your issue of 16 September, which I have only just seen, it was reported that Howard Whitten, joint organizing Secretary of the Food Relief Campaign of the Peace Pledge Union, was at Clerkenwell sentenced to six months' imprisonment for failing, as an opponent of conscription, to comply with a condition of his registration as a conscientious objector.

As Chairman of the Food Relief Campaign I was present at this hearing. Your summary of the case correctly records that the same magistrate had previously sentenced the same conscientious objector to two months' imprisonment on a similar summons in April. You do not, however, mention that the magistrate, in sentencing Mr Whitten for the second time, informed him that if he came back to the same Court on the same charge, he would probably get a still longer sentence.

What is the social value of thus threatening a young man who is unlikely to change his convictions however severe his punishment? These recurrent sentences have an uncomfortable resemblance to official vengeance on those who hold a minority point of view. Even if it were possible to break the spirit of a conscientious objector, which is usually difficult, would a man who was induced to violate his conscience by such methods be of any real value to society? And is not this type of 'cat and mouse' treatment precisely the kind of victimization which the Prime Minister himself has condemned as unworthy of our democracy?

Letter to the Editor: Manchester Guardian, 22 September 1943

✍

POLITICAL SCHIZOPHRENIA

Within recent years, those who follow the accounts of murder trials and other criminal cases have become familiar with a psychological abnormality known as 'schizophrenia'. This technical expression means 'divided mind', and those who suffer from it are directed, as it were, by two distinct personalities, the one normal and benevolent, the other sometimes eccentric and malevolent. In literature the classic instance of this phenomenon is the story of Dr Jekyll and Mr Hyde.

Unfortunately schizophrenia – or some affliction which closely resembles it – is not confined to men and women who appear in the law courts. We should live in a happier world today if a larger number of our political, religious, and intellectual leaders regarded consistency (a word which sometimes seems to be interchangeable with integrity) as not only attainable, but desirable.

The other day a few friends and I were discussing the problem of bombed and blockaded Europe with a kindly and cultured man well known in public life. In the course of conversation this distinguished man earnestly explained to us that the war leaders responsible for raiding and starving the Continent were humane men who disliked their jobs and in some cases would even have preferred to be on the side of their critics. They hated being cruel in order to be kind, but felt it to be their duty to help the war effort by assuming these grim obligations.

Our informant genuinely accepted this view. He was really sorry for the men whose political positions made them responsible for the death and suffering of millions. We were left with the impression that their method of making war hurt them at least as much as it hurt the hungry and mutilated children of Europe. They had, it seemed, overlooked the fact that for men and women anxious to assist in a war effort which they believe unavoidable

242

without themselves causing injury to their fellows, there are still any number of jobs to be had.

Undoubtedly, in these days of depleted civil defence and fire services, a capable elderly man could find work as an air raid warden in the East End of London, or in helping with the evacuation and billeting of bombed-out families, where his administrative experience would be of value. Or, if he preferred the country, where he could occasionally slip away to the local golf links and imagine himself back in a normal weekend, there are numbers of farmers already beginning to look ahead to the summer and wonder how the harvest is to be gathered in. Or again, when the noisily publicized Second Front really gets going, there will be so many hospital jobs waiting to be filled that a man capable of carrying a stretcher or acting as ward-orderly need look no further than his own locality.

Of course these humble duties don't bring the same prestige or financial advantages as a ministerial salary, or carry pensions like the positions of civil servants. But when people expect salaries, pensions and prestige in addition to helping the war effort without losing their reputations for personal humanity, they can hardly avoid finding the moral situation a little complicated.

It is unreasonable of me, no doubt, but I must confess to remaining unconvinced by the 'humanity' of these politicians who are devoted husbands, kindly fathers, and reliable friends, yet who initiate or endorse policies which mean the starvation and mutilation of other people's wives and children in other countries. The blunt gangsterism of Mr Churchill's 'What we have, we hold', or of Brendan Bracken's 'bomb, burn and ruthlessly destroy', seems to my naïve and doubtless politically uneducated mind to be preferable to this form of apologetic hypocrisy.

The 'humane' dealers of death to Europe remind me of the Empress Maria Theresa of Austria, and her part in one of the three Partitions of Poland. 'The more she wept', the historians tell us, 'the more territory she demanded.' These men who cherish their benevolent reputations are either suffering from that form of schizophrenia which in less exalted circles is apt to land its victims in a criminal lunatic asylum, or they are deliberately committing the sin against the Holy Ghost. For this sin is to know what good is, yet deliberately to do evil – and, in nine cases out of ten, to seek to justify that evil in plausible terms which allege the existence of some common denominator between bombing and/or blockade, and Christian teaching.

The man who understands the meaning of truth, charity, compassion and forgiveness, and endeavours to practise these virtues in his private life, yet in his public policy deliberately sacrifices them to a totally different set of moral values known as 'working for victory', is committing that blasphemy of which Jesus said: 'It shall not be forgiven him, neither in this world, neither in the world to come.'

We shall begin to see a better international world, and the end of war with its ruthless cruelty practised at the expense of the innocent and helpless, when responsible, well-paid, highly-respected politicians have the courage to resign, lose their salaries and suffer criticism, rather than carry out policies which offend against their sense of private virtue. The divided mind – the mind which accepts one set of values at home, and another quite different set in public life – is the mind which lies at the root of war and all social evil.

Peace News, 5 May 1944

HUMANIZING WAR?

In his comments on my booklet, *Seed of Chaos*, George Orwell seems to assume that if pacifists do not succeed in preventing a war, they must throw up the sponge and acquiesce in any excesses which war-makers choose to initiate. This alone can explain his strange supposition that, because I protest against 'saturation' bombing, I am 'willing and anxious' to win the war by 'legitimate' methods.

It is true that when war comes the pacifist has admittedly failed for the time being in his main purpose, but that does not exonerate him from any attempt to mitigate war's worst excesses. On the contrary, his very failure to prevent war makes its excesses his direct responsibility, which he would be 'dodging' indeed if he were to sit back self-righteously excusing himself from the difficult endeavour to restrain the growth of barbarousness in his own community.

If Mr Orwell had read my book with any care, he would have realized that the death of civilians is not my main concern, though direct attack on civilians does constitute an abandonment of the standard laid down for international conduct by international law. My chief concern is with the moral deterioration to which a nation condemns itself by the unrestrained infliction of cruelty; and with the setback to European civilization which obliteration bombing must cause in addition to blockade and invasion. The century which followed the Thirty Years' War showed that there are degrees of chaos and privation which civilized values cannot survive.

Mr Orwell's statement that 'all talk of "humanizing" war is sheer humbug' is simply unhistorical. Prof. A.L. Goodhart (*What Acts of War Are Justifiable?* pp.4-6) describes the improvement in international morality owing to the reaction initiated by Grotius against the horrors of the Thirty Years' War, and continues: 'Further progress was made during the eighteenth century with the result that the unrestrained cruelty of former times was in large part absent from the Napoleonic Wars.' Even in this war there are depths to which the combatants have not yet descended – such as a general massacre of all prisoners, bacteriological warfare, and the use of poison gas. Though gas, as Mr Orwell alleges, may be ineffective in a war of movement, certain American voices have already suggested its use against the Japanese invaders of Pacific islands. The fact that these voices have not been heeded means that the USA has not yet abandoned itself to the advocates of unrestrained cruelty – of whom, somewhat oddly, George Orwell appears to be one.

Letter to the Editor: Tribune, 23 June 1944

ᔥ

AFTER THE CEASE FIRE

The second European war of our lifetime has ended at last – in cheers, flags and floodlights for Britain, in grief, humiliation and chaos for Germany. Amid the first onrush of conflicting emotions which threatened to overwhelm the stunned and weary mind, it was difficult, particularly for Londoners, to feel anything more constructive than relief, and gratitude for the palpable night silence which has succeeded the explosive terrors of five perilous years. Yet our survival will have no meaning unless it is accompanied by a resolute facing of the problems left in the track of the storm, and a determination to dedicate the lives given back to us to the service of peace and the cause of God's Kingdom. A second chance to rebuild a shattered society is clearly being offered to the erring, disobedient race of men, and especially, perhaps, to the people of Britain, who has been left by the war too weak to dominate the international scene, yet strong enough, if she so chooses, to give a moral lead to mankind. If we fail to use that chance rightly, we dare not count on the hope of a third.

In many countries of three continents, the once fair surface of the earth has been made hideous by ruined cities, blasted homes, fields formerly fertile destroyed by fire and flood. In Europe we are confronted with a scene of havoc and anguish such as the most hideous devastations in all history have never equalled. It is difficult to believe that any of the possible alternatives to war which might have been arranged in the nineteen-thirties, or any of the negotiations short of unconditional surrender which were so scornfully rejected as soon as the Allies became certain of victory, would have brought one-tenth of the spiritual, mental and physical torture which has come to so many millions.

But the opportunity to stay the flood of death has gone by; it is with the after-effects of that tidal wave that we are now concerned. In our own country and every other, we face an uncounted multitude of exhausted men and women, cynical and disillusioned, yet weary to death of hatred even while, incited by cinema and radio, they continue to hate. Like the parched wanderers who seek the mercy of water in a desert, they long for some message of help and hope which will reinforce their lost confidence in humanity, and enable them to believe that mankind is basically good rather than evil.

At such a moment it is vital for pacifists – who have stood aside from the national conflict and can claim no share in the military victory – to hold fast to the faith of Abraham, 'who against hope believed in hope'. After more than five years in which our chief service has been to stand fast and wait, the call comes clearly to us to use the perception which arises from detachment on behalf of the myriad victims of bewilderment and despair. For mankind's ability to take its second chance depends on the extent to which it is possible to increase that power of vision whereby men and women learn to understand what is really happening to themselves and others, and to estimate the significance of experience. This growth of awareness is the first stage of that moral insight which accepts what Victor Gollancz, in a threepenny booklet entitled *What Buchenwald Really Means*, calls 'the doctrine of political responsibility – of the direct responsibility of every human being for what happens to other human beings throughout the world'.

I urge every pacifist – and every non-pacifist – to read this remarkable and timely pamphlet, which proves (to my mind conclusively) that British civilians, free amid their democratic institutions to question, examine and protest both before and during the war, were more to blame for the continued obscene horrors of the concentration camps than the German civilians whom years of fascist suppression had terrorized into acquiescence. It is another of those deeply moving endeavours 'to hold a hand uplifted over hate' in which the Christian Churches appear to have left the main initiative to a non-Christian member of that Jewish race which the Nazis have destroyed in its millions.

In *The Meaning of History*, Nicolas Berdyaev wrote that 'it is only the experience of historical failure itself that has proved fruitful, in the sense that the consciousness of humanity has thereby been increased.' Certainly it is true that periods of historical failure such as the present lead, as epochs of complacent prosperity seldom lead, to desperate soul-searchings and the asking of fundamental questions. It is the task of pacifists to evoke those questions and try to supply the answers.

Recently a delegate at the Annual General Meeting of the Peace Pledge Union, after a report on 'Study', protested that the movement spent too much time in studying. 'What we need', said the speaker, 'is more action'. My mind went back to an article in which Winifred Holtby, describing the political vicissitudes of Sir Oswald Mosley many years ago, gravely assured her readers that 'even a somersault is action'. I believe that there are occasions which summon us all to action, both direct and indirect; but action is valueless unless it is, in the fullest sense, *conscious* action, based upon a knowledge of history and a clear perception of the direction in which we intend to move.

The task of enlarging consciousness should surely begin with an attempt to perceive, and then, so far as we are able, to show to others the true character of this age. Many students of history have recently told us that we are living at the end of that historical epoch which began with the Renaissance and the Reformation. Within less than a lifetime, vast revolutionary changes have brought tumbling about our heads the apparently secure world in which those over 35 were born. Because these changes were beyond the comprehension of the great majority, it has been easy for the expert propaganda of two great wars to deceive the public about the true nature of their deep underlying causes. In this island an anxious and bewildered people have been taught to believe that a simple method of restoring the old happy conditions could be found, and that the lost comfort and security would re-emerge from the destruction of 'German militarism'.

But German militarism, though real enough, is in the total perspective of history only a relatively small aspect of a much larger problem. We cannot understand it, and find a cure for it or any other form of militarism, without at least some comprehension of that larger problem of which it is a part.

What are the underlying causes of the revolutionary situation which has produced two world wars, bringing agonizing death and immeasurable suffering to countless millions? Chronologically, and also perhaps from the standpoint of urgency, the first is the centuries-long growth of nationalism – not German nationalism, which was a late example of the deadly phenomenon, but the nationalism of those early-established maritime powers of which Britain and France were among the first. The beginning of this process coincided with the Reformation, which accelerated it by bringing into being those State churches whose priests preferred the religion of nationalism to the Gospel of Christ.

Some theologians would even trace the causes of total war as far back as the Dictate of Constantine, which first undermined by compromise the spiritual power of the ecclesiastical authority that for twelve more centuries kept Europe united. From nationalism sprang the competitive imperialism which, by the beginning of the First World War, had given to Britain and France the combined possession of sixteen million square miles of territory. Not, in the first instance, from national aggressiveness, but from the inequitable division of the earth's surface with the concurrent privileges of possession, arose the frantic cry for 'Lebensraum' of the Have-not Powers.

But though it is the control of rampant and predatory nationalism which has chiefly exercised the minds of the delegates at San Francisco, the problem of our time is not to be explained in terms of nationalism alone. We must look also to the failure of the economic system known as capitalism to give security and a decent life to the common man; a failure which both German Nazism and Russian Communism have tried in their similar yet distinct fashions to remedy, with the consequent enormous upheavals that most of us have seen. Finally, with a careful eye upon the future researches of the young would-be scientists among our sons and daughters, we must face the fact that the amazing scientific achievements of the past two centuries have outpaced the moral power of their inventors to direct and control them. Today, because twice over Juggernaut has run away with his charioteer, we see a continent which was the inspiration of cultural progress reduced to squalor by the misuse of explosives. It is as though man, like an irresponsible child, discovered a deadly toy before his mental and spiritual maturity had taught him to refrain from playing with it. Part of our task is to develop that maturity by diverting the scientific energy which has found expression in the invention of ever more deadly weapons to the study of our perverse and degenerate selves, who perceive the way of life, yet deliberately choose the road to sin and death.

At this moment, as never before in history, it has become clear that no peace, whether manufactured at San Francisco or elsewhere, will endure unless it leads at long last to the reversal of these catastrophic historical processes. It will merely join the collection of treaties, alliances and covenants which lie on the gigantic scrap-heap of political good intentions unless, beyond their immediate concessions to 'realism', its makers look to the renaissance of Christianity; the delegation of national sovereignty to an international authority; the building of a new economic system in which man ranks as an individual and not as a pawn; and the development of moral and spiritual responsibility to a higher level than technical skill.

We should be wishful thinkers indeed if we imagined that more than a tiny minority of the statesmen at San Francisco have been preoccupied with the ultimate attainment of these ideal ends. But we should fail in the faith and courage now needed above all other qualities by our cynical and fatigued generation if we did not constantly proclaim that in the growing consciousness of these historic truths lies the only realistic route to salvation.

There is a genuine danger that, in the present mood of world-wide pessimism, the political leaders of the nations may underrate man's capacity in peace, as so recently in war, to achieve gigantic aims which at the outset appear impossible of realization. It is for us who have watched and waited to persuade them that more, not less, should be asked of the fortitude which endured from the beaches of Dunkirk to the sober rejoicings of VE Day, and to remind ourselves that in the last resort the redemption of mankind from war depends upon the spiritual and moral quality of men and women.

Based on a speech made at the 1945 Annual General Meeting of the PPU:
Christian Pacifist, June 1945

◈

MASSACRE BOMBING – THE AFTERMATH

And much it grieved my heart to think
What Man has made of Man.

Wordsworth, 'Lines Written in Early Spring'

Shortly before the war ended in Europe I was in a cinema at Southampton – one of the worst wrecked of Britain's smaller cities – when a picture of the nightmare ruins of Hanover appeared on the screen. Even from that damage-accustomed audience, an immediate gasp of horror went up. A few days later came pictures of the Nazi concentration camps, and the numbed minds of the much-bombed British were diverted from one atrocity to another.

One of the many large uncertainties concerning which a strange silence has prevailed since VE Day is that of the long-range effects of obliteration bombing in Germany. There was a period when the European war was approaching its conclusion in which correspondents representing newspapers of many types and outlooks freely expressed their dismay at the amount of bomb damage they found and at the effect of mass bombing upon the social and moral life of German civilians. Since national memories are short, especially when the barbarities inflicted originate at home, I append a selection of comments from that time, taken at random from a large collection of press clippings.

When the sun grows cold and the last cities on a crumbling earth are dying ruins, I suppose that the surviving remnants of human life will live as they live today in the bowels of Cologne. (S.L. Solon, *News Chronicle* war correspondent, 14 March 1945)

This is a picture of München-Gladbach ... Thousands of people are still living in cellars under rubble or in huge 'bunkers'. Conditions in these are indescribable. (*Daily Dispatch*, 15 March 1945)

Duisberg ... has had the life drained out of it ... You wonder how the civilians existed in a city which has had no water, light or drainage for six months. (Ronald Walker, *News Chronicle*, 31 March 1945)

I could not recognize much in the old city, for all its picturesqueness has been bombed to fragments. It is as though some giant has crashed his foot down ... Nuremberg has been wiped from the face of the earth. (Anne Matheson, *Evening Standard*, 4 May 1945)

This is no longer a city. It is a desert of dreadful destruction ... I was sick with horror and frightened. (Clifford Webb, *Daily Herald* special correspondent in Berlin, 11 May 1945)

One of the most grim and graphic descriptions of massacre bombing was published by the United States forces' newspaper, *Stars and Stripes*, 5 May 1945, in relation to the Allied raid on Dresden on 13-14 February:

Nine British POWs were working in Dresden during the raid and said the horror and devastation caused by the Anglo-American 14-hour raid was beyond human comprehension unless one could see for himself. One British sergeant said, 'Reports from Dresden police that 300,000 died as a result of the bombing didn't include deaths among 1,000,000 evacuees from the Breslau area trying to escape from the Russians. There were no records of them. After seeing the results of the bombings, I believe their figures are correct. They had to pitch-fork shrivelled bodies onto trucks and wagons and cart them to shallow graves on the outskirts of the city. But after two weeks of work the job became too much to cope with and they found other means to gather up the dead. They burned bodies in a great heap in the centre of the city, but the most effective way, for sanitary reasons, was to take flame-throwers and burn the dead as they lay in the ruins.

In the *Observer* for 8 April, its war correspondent, George Orwell (who last year adversely reviewed my booklet, *Seed of Chaos*), commented from Germany as follows:

The people of Britain have never felt easy about the bombing of civilians ... but what they still have not grasped – thanks to their own comparative immunity – is the frightful destructiveness of modern war and the long period of impoverishment that now lies ahead of the world as a whole. To walk through the ruined cities of Germany is to feel an actual doubt about the continuity of civilization.

Since those words were written the western Allies appear to have made little effort to reconstruct and continue the civilization of Europe, nor is there much evidence that they are planning to do so. Their attention has been distracted by other matters. The United States suffered the great convulsion, foreseen only by a well-informed few, of the death of one President and the succession of another. This domestic upheaval was quickly followed by the San Francisco conference, which transferred the gaze of foreign policy specialists from Europe to the Pacific coast. Before this, in both the USA and Britain, had come the publicity about the Nazi concentration camps – abominations to which attention had been strenuously drawn as far back as 1933 by such students of Europe as the publisher, Victor Gollancz, in *The Brown Book of the Hitler Terror* and other publications. Whether the sudden outbreak of Anglo-American horror at the discoveries in the camps was a fortunate coincidence for the organizers of mass bombing, or whether it was deliberately 'played up' by radio, newsreel and press to divert public interest from the ruined Germany by which soldiers as well as newspapermen were so deeply perturbed, time alone with reveal.

Shortly afterwards came VE Day, when here in Britain the none-too-vivid imaginative consciousness of German devastation was lost in an outbreak of adulation for Mr Churchill, and the comments of captured Nazi generals – whose word would never have been believed had their verdict been unfavourable to Allied policy – indicated that obliteration bombing had been a main cause of German defeat. (According to the *Evening Standard*, Field-Marshal Kesselring carefully distinguished between 'Allied strategic bombing behind the German lines' and 'terror raids against the German civilian population', adding in relation to the latter: 'I say this with regret, as I was once an air force commander'.) Such judgments increased the self-congratulations of the Bomber Command, and Sir Arthur Harris was decorated for his share in the glorious victory purchased with the blood of mothers and children.

Shortly afterwards, Britain found herself in the throes of a general election, and for a few frantic weeks the future of civilization was subordinated – at any rate by the Beaverbrook press – to a rampageous argument concerning the constitutional relationship between Clement Attlee and Professor H.J. Laski.

Finally, of course, there is the war with Japan – a war which most Britons still feel to be remote from them, and in which they tend to take less interest than Americans. The International Red Cross, whose reckoning is probably conservative, estimated that 200,000 actually perished in the raid on Dresden. Those who are tempted to gloat over press accounts of 'record' raids on Japan, with its crowded cities of flimsy inflammable houses, would do well to remember *Stars and Stripes'* description of the Dresden holocaust. There are some who excuse the massacre bombing of the Japanese by saying that pagan Japan does not attach the same value to human life as ourselves. Is that a reason for abandoning our own Christian standards?

Can we tell, as yet, what the long-range results of massacre bombing are likely to be? Amid the confusion, suppression and contradictions of evidence, there are still two distinct methods of approach to this question. We can regard it from the religious, moral and social standpoint; or we can consider it solely from the narrow utilitarian angle (euphemistically described as 'patriotic') of its efficiency as a method of winning the war and establishing that peace, security and ultimate prosperity for the sake of which the war was presumably fought.

For those who place the welfare of mankind before the self-seeking and temporary interests of nations, there can be no question that the ruthless mass bombing of congested cities is as great a threat to the integrity of the human spirit as anything which has yet occurred on this planet. It is not merely that such bombing reduces human beings to a condition of subhuman terror, deprives them of homes, families, possessions, food, medical care and the means of cleanliness, and finally degrades them to a primitive animal-like existence in which the most elementary social and moral standards become impossible. The true and terrible significance of obliteration bombing, like the mass extermination of the Jews by the Nazis, lies in its utter denial of any sacredness in human life. Its only sanction is that 'reason of state' which ignores the right of men, women and children to go on living if their survival slackens the speed of the mechanistic juggernaut to which modern nations at war have harnessed their will. By denying the divine spark in man, it denies the God in whose image he is made. From the standpoint of Christianity – renamed 'sentimentality' in the debased language of war propaganda – there is no military or political advantage which can justify this fundamental blasphemy.

But even from the standpoint of the 'national interest', the efficacy of massacre bombing is by no means established. Doubts and questionings regarding the amount of blood and treasure expended by those who have carried out this policy have naturally not been broadcast by a government-controlled press, but from time to time they have nevertheless appeared. Here, for example, is an extract from an article entitled 'Bombing: Has It Paid?' by Air Commodore A. W. Glenny, MC, DFC, which appeared in the British weekly magazine *John Bull* for 17 March 1945:

Sir Arthur Harris, AOC-in-chief of the command, claimed, in June 1942, that 1,000 bombers a night over Germany would end the war by the autumn. We now see the war being ended in traditional style by land forces. Our textbooks never claimed that bombing alone could win victory. But we all believed it could, as near as made no matter – though the only experimental evidence was the bombing in the last war and our air action against tribesmen in Africa and Asia. We were satisfied that the moral effect of bombing would be tremendous. As for the material effect, we were less sure. What would the destructive power of the big bombs be? Figures now available suggest that during recent operations one ton of bombs was needed to destroy one built-up acre; and that it took one ton of bombs to kill one person.

More recently, a paragraph by the *News Chronicle* war correspondent, S.L. Solon, recorded on 29 June the surprising fact that, 'despite bombing, German armaments production in 1944 was higher than in any previous war year ... At no time until the end was there a collapse of German war production or, over a long period, any serious deficiency in meeting the army's requirements.'

Those who suffered were, and are, the old, the young and the helpless – and especially the inhabitants of prisons and concentration camps as bombing steadily destroyed the transport and communications on which they had depended for their meagre supplies. Today, when all Europe is crying out for raw materials and the products of industry, the great coal mines and industries of the Ruhr remain submerged in an abomination of desolation.

Not, probably, until next winter will the full price of massacre bombing come home to half-starved, half-frozen Europeans. It made no undeniable contribution to military victory, and it relegated men, for whose salvation Christ died, to the level of hunted and outraged beasts. It has postponed to a degree not yet calculable the true dawn of peace and reconstruction, which arises, and can only arise, from international security, confidence and hope.

Christian Century (US), 1 August 1945

IT CAN BE PEACE

The realization that peace, like freedom, is indivisible has been one of the great discoveries of the twentieth century.

In the nineteenth century peace was relegated to one watertight compartment, and different varieties of freedom to several others. Liberal and progressive people fought for Catholic emancipation at the beginning of the century, and woman suffrage at the end. Peace was a political concept, having little to do with freedom; it was the subject of conferences called by Czar Nicholas I at The Hague in 1889 and 1907.

Far away in South Africa, a lone voice spoke as early as 1883 on the indivisibility of all progress. In that year Olive Schreiner published *The Story of an African Farm*, aflame with the fiery vision of the young woman who saw a 'new deal' for all women ending the double standard of morality.

A later book, *Trooper Peter Halket of Mashonaland*, published in 1897, linked the causes of feminism and racial equality. In 1911, *Woman and Labour* emphasized that the woman's cause was also the cause of peace.

That day, the author prophesied, when the woman took her place beside the man in the government of human affairs would herald the end of war as a means of settling human differences.

This prophecy has still not been fulfilled, for woman has not yet 'taken her place' beside man in policy-making except as a very small minority. But Olive Schreiner was right in believing that woman's values were normally, because biologically, creative and constructive; the woman who shouts for war is hypnotized by propaganda into denying her nature as woman.

And many people who have never heard of Olive Schreiner understand today that you cannot have equality for women while exploiting the world's workers, or expect peace if not only workers, both men and women, but non-white races are denied human rights.

'Peace', wrote Spinoza, 'is not the performance of an act, but a virtue born from strength of soul.' In spite – and perhaps indeed because – of this century's many disasters we are nearer to that strength of soul today than ever before in the history of mankind.

Even the United States – one of the two most belligerent powers in the present world – realized that Marshall Aid was something more than a bribe to stricken countries to join the fight against Communism; it was a means of helping to mitigate conditions which gave Communism its point and purpose.

Notwithstanding its present mood, America has a better record for its treatment of women and white workers than any other country. Today its northern Negroes also receive a fair deal, and even in the South the interracial tension, heritage of the Civil War, is gradually diminishing.

But what of the other belligerent power – the USSR, now mourning its great dictator? Does the phrase 'It can be peace' make sense even though Malenkov, feeling his way cautiously in a new situation, talks peace to his cold-war opponents?

Since peace and freedom are indivisible, we know that the USSR has contributed to the cause of peace, whether intentionally or otherwise.

By giving her workers a status and transforming her women from submissive animal-like peasants to self-respecting citizens, Russia has begun to eliminate the personal frustration and bitterness which is the source of war in the hearts of men, and eventually seeks compensation in political aggressiveness.

From a psychologist's angle the wars of this century were anachronisms before they occurred – their makers sought a means of 'settlement' which in the eyes of all who understood human nature was outdated and self-defeating. Because the man in the street so often perceives this more keenly than his leaders, we have seen the division between the policies of statesmen and the wishes of the people, which was a mere fissure in the First World War, become a yawning ravine in the Second.

It can be peace because so many countries, in spite of themselves and sometimes without even realizing it, have already begun to eliminate the basic causes of war.

Peace News, 27 March 1953

⌁

CHRISTIANITY OR EXTINCTION?

On 6 August 1945 the first atomic bomb fell on Hiroshima. With its invention mankind was believed to have crossed a terrible Rubicon between 'manageable' war fought with conventional weapons, and the growing threat of unlimited destruction.

Actually, in the history of bombing during the past fifteen years, two separate developments have occurred. The increasing misuse of power is merely the logical consequence of the moral decline which followed the change of Allied policy from 'precision' to 'area' bombing in March 1942.

Not the scientific discoveries which made possible the creation of the atomic bomb, but the decision to use it, has brought humanity to the brink of the dark Avernus where friend and foe alike lose their identity. That decision was rendered easier by previous decisions, less alarming in their consequences, but morally no different. Civilization's Rubicon was crossed when the indiscriminate destruction of persons living within a specified area became a recognized feature of military policy.

Twelve years have passed since that policy began. Today the saner sections of society abominate the activities of 'back-room boys', but have forgotten 'Bomber Harris' and his Allied counterparts, and the governments which encouraged them to destroy Cologne and Dresden.

At the beginning of the 1939 war, British statesmen and strategists scrupulously refrained from attacking targets other than 'military objectives'. In January 1940 Mr Winston Churchill, then First Lord of the Admiralty, described the bombing of enemy civilians as a 'new and odious form of attack', and refused to listen to the popular clamour which insisted that RAF planes should cease to drop leaflets by night and load up with 'beautiful bombs'. Three and a half years later (21 September 1943) he told the House of Commons, as Prime Minister: 'There are ... no lengths in violence to which we will not go to destroy Nazi tyranny'.

We should not regard the slaughter of a man who wears uniform as any better justified than that of a road-sweeper in his dungarees; soldier and civilian alike are repositories of the life which God gave and no man has the right to take. But so long as a distinction between combatants and non-combatants persisted, governments and their servants remained committed to a recognition of human rights and the unique quality of human individuals. The hydrogen bomb 'lay in the logic of history' as soon as this distinction gave way to a policy of massacre bombing, which treated soldiers and civilians, men and women, young and old, the active and the sick, as an anonymous group of 'casualties' whose destruction represented a military achievement.

The moral consequences of the new policy were instantaneous. Press and BBC alike hailed as triumphs of Allied strategy the obliteration by bombs of such areas as the anti-Hitler working-class suburbs of Hamburg, and the breach of the Eder and Möhne dams which drowned hundreds of mothers and children in their homes. The cultural treasures of the ages – Cologne's museums, Münster's Cathedral, the Römer at Frankfort, Nuremburg, Monte Cassino – became less important in the eyes of the war-leaders than a temporary national advantage. The few isolated voices (from the pacifist movement, the Quaker community, and occasionally from pulpits) which protested that human life was sacred, and the expression of the human spirit in art and architecture more important than ephemeral advantage in a battle, either went unheeded or were publicized as the voices of traitors.

Such protests were none the less maintained on a small scale throughout the war, in Britain by the Bombing Restriction Committee founded by Corder Catchpool, and in the United States by the Fellowship of Reconciliation and the Society of Friends. In March 1944, when the New York Fellowship published a pamphlet entitled *Massacre By Bombing*, they and the author inspired a chorus of vilification in over 200 American newspapers. The Catholic press and Dr Felix Morley's courageous weekly, *Human Events*, almost alone insisted that the inconvenient critics of bombing represented, not treachery, but the challenge of the Christian conscience to spiritual bankruptcy.

After the war, when lives and treasures had vanished beyond recovery, obliteration bombing and its protagonists were discredited on strategic grounds. Aerial massacre had strengthened rather than weakened enemy resistance; it had reinforced the unconditional surrender policy of the 'bitter enders' who spurned the sanity of a negotiated peace; and it had resulted in large-scale civilian damage while leaving many military and industrial objectives unimpaired. Post-war visitors to the Rhineland and Ruhr found that every destroyed school, hospital and hotel had created a headache for some harassed British official.

It is, however, significant that military and not moral reasons were responsible for the condemnation of 'area' bombing. The moral corruption which it had brought widened and deepened, and at last has borne fruit in the dangerous experiments by the Americans in the Pacific and the Russians in Siberia. These experiments have shocked mankind into an unwilling recognition that the small, much-abused wartime group which opposed 'obliteration' were on the side not only of Christian values but of human survival. The latter is now belatedly perceived to depend upon the former, however officially described.

The choice between Christianity and extinction confronts us. Can we learn our lesson at the eleventh hour, and pass from the shadow of doom to our Easter Day?

Peace News, 30 April 1954

∽

CHANGES IN THE PEACE MOVEMENT

In 1933, when I published *Testament of Youth*, the present emphatic division between pacifists and other workers for peace hardly existed. Throughout the 600 pages of that long book – an implicit plea for peace based on tragic human experience – I used the word 'pacifist' only once.

During the twenties and early thirties, the pacifist and non-pacifist seekers after a society united through reconciliation did not exhaust their time and energies in conflict with one another, for there were then real and formidable opponents – the genuine war-mongers, immortalized by David Low in 'Colonel Blimp' who believed in crude force and 'my country right or wrong'. Though differences of principle were recognized within the peace movement, they did not prevent those who would not accept war in any circumstances from co-operating amicably with others unable to go so far. Thus, it was possible for such out-and-out pacifists as Mrs H.M. Swanwick to appear on League of Nations Union platforms, and even, during the first Labour Government, to attend the League of Nations Assembly at Geneva as an official substitute-delegate.

As the Second World War approached – the last global war which men would be able to fight without extinguishing the human race – the latent differences between would-be peace-makers inevitably hardened. Soon, it was clear, individuals would have to decide whether they would fight in the last resort, or dissociate themselves, members of an unpopular and suspect minority, from the 'war effort', and work for the return of peace. The distinction between these groups was further emphasized when Dick Sheppard founded the Peace Pledge Union with its categorical undertaking – a vital form of witness at that time.

During the war itself, it is not surprising that the gulf between the pacifist and non-pacifist sections of the peace movement became very wide even when (as often happened) they were in full agreement about their objectives. Both groups uncompromisingly opposed the starvation of Europe's children by the blockade and the massacre bombings of helpless German and Italian civilians, yet even Dr Bell, the good Bishop of Chichester, so much respected by all peace-makers, would not accept pacifists on his committees, and found it difficult to use pamphlets by pacifists even though he agreed with every word they wrote.

When the war ended it might well have been expected that the gulf would narrow again (as it habitually narrows between wartime fighters and their ex-enemies), and that all categories of peace-workers would join hands in the urgent attempt to save their society from the new threat of destruction by nuclear weapons. Unhappily, international Communism chose that moment to wave a banner called 'Peace', which thenceforth became a dirty word. The term 'pacifist', though still deeply discredited in the eyes of the Establishment, at least distinguished those groups for whom peace was their final purpose from the political organizations which treated it as a useful means to a totally different end.

Thus, by the nineteen-fifties the distinction between 'peace' and 'pacifism' remained sharp, but as the implications of A-bombs and H-bombs came to be better understood, a new phase developed within the peace movement. It was now evident that the individual renunciation of war, though still as morally significant as the Friends' Peace Testimony, could no longer exercise any political pressure. A million people saying 'No war', whatever their educational value, would be totally ineffective against one Cabinet Minister who had decided to use the H-bomb.

Something more than a moral example was now needed, and it soon appeared in the shape of groups training themselves to oppose modern warfare with non-violent forms of direct action. For their precedents these groups looked back, not to the useful educative campaigns between the wars, but to Gandhi's civil disobedience movement in India, and to such varieties of non-violent resistance as the Norwegians used against the Nazis between 1940 and 1945.

The Campaign for Nuclear Disarmament, with its direct action section, was founded and won many recruits; unlike the older peace societies it attracted particularly the younger generation. New names, such as Swaffham and Aldermaston, captured the headlines, and the example of the modern tactics with which they were associated spread across other parts of the world where similar experiments were already beginning. From America came stories of the *Golden Rule* and the *Phoenix* boldly voyaging towards the Pacific testing areas; from Germany and Japan (as also from Britain and the USA) followed accounts of prolonged mass marches, continuous pickets, sit-down protests, and attempts to enter nuclear reseach stations. This new type of non-violent direct action not only commanded publicity, but affected political parties. Its most spectacular climax up to date was the 1960 Aldermaston March, which was followed (surely not as a coincidence) by the Scarborough Labour Party Conference which refused to accept the Executive's policy on 'defence'.

Amid the enthusiasms generated by these successful modern onslaughts against actual war-making, the distinction between pacifists and non-pacifists again wore thin, and might well have disappeared in practice but for a determined endeavour to keep it alive. The Campaign for Nuclear Disarmament, it has been said, is 'not really pacifist', the kind of disarmament it demands is to be deplored because it is 'not total'. Beneath these criticisms lies the implication that a nation, or group of nations, which had made the tremendous moral decision to abandon the most lethal types of present-day weapons would thereafter immediately go back to using the older, less effective kinds.

To all who look realistically at the picture of the world today, it is surely becoming clear that international peace will not come through peace organizations of any particular brand, though these can most valuably help to create the best climate for its eventual arrival. It will come, and is coming, because the major powers realize that they cannot make war and survive; that, therefore, war is not to their interest; and that such aggression-slanted organizations as the American Pentagon are blinkered and obsolete institutions which must ultimately be replaced.

The most that can be done by the peace movement today, in addition to its educational job of changing the atmosphere and the hearts of war-makers with it, is to hold before mankind the vision of a society which does not yet exist, but could be lived; a realizable Utopia dominated by charity, humility and compassion, whose citizens accept the Sermon on the Mount as their creed not only of belief but of behaviour. I have described the presentation of such a society as 'the most' that peacemakers can do, but it would be an incomparable service to the welfare of mankind if they really did it.

At present the peace movement is nowhere near the accomplishment or even the conception of this pattern, and never will be until it renounces, not war in the abstract, but its own internal conflicts. Only when these are eliminated can it work in unity for the Kingdom of God on earth, based on the Christian teaching which some do not accept, but which nearly all acknowledge to contain the highest standards of conduct as yet laid down for human guidance.

I suggest that a useful first step might be for all concerned to rethink the implications of the word 'pacifism'. Too often, in recent years, there has been in its use an undertone of spiritual pride, as though its eight letters in themselves contained the secret of salvation. Hence, it has become a divisive word, tending to weaken what should be a united witness against the real enemies of our society. Brother no longer clasps the hand of brother, but says in effect: 'Agree with my point of view, or we part company'. Instead of creating friendship and reconciliation, the term itself, with its present emphasis on differences of opinion, tends to bring a new form of psychological warfare into the peace movement.

Jesus said, 'Blessed are the peacemakers'. That great Beatitude has survived the political changes of centuries and the vicissitudes of translation. Why should we seek to improve upon His actual words? The sooner we return to their use and recover their redemptive influence, the better for us all.

Reconciliation, March 1961

&

THE COMMITTEE OF 100

Lord Coleraine's disparaging comments on The Committee of 100 in your issue this morning recall the criticisms of the Suffragette movement that I read in my schooldays. Mrs Pankhurst, the reviled leader of the 'screaming sisterhood', ended up with a statue in Westminster and Lord Russell will doubtless do the same.

The sacrificial fervour of great idealistic crusades begins to capture public imagination and achieve its ends when it takes an active and 'dangerous' form. Not only the Suffragette movement, but Mahatma Gandhi's civil disobedience campaign in India, bear witness to this uncomfortable historic fact.

Letter to the Editor: The Times, 19 September 1961

PART FOUR

A Writer's Life

Winifred Holtby

'MOTHER KNOWS BEST'

I could write before I could read with comfort, and before I could write, I told stories. At the ages of three and four I was as an implacable a narrator of impossibilities as the Ancient Mariner. I used to plant myself on a four-legged wooden stool in the middle of the cold stone floor of the dairy on my father's farm, and there, a book on my knee probably held upside down, I would 'read' immense and interminable narratives to the amiable cook who scrubbed the shelves. I remember one novel recited in this fashion. It was called *Minnie's Berk*. The book from which I pretended to read it was Nat Gould's *Magpie Jacket*, a favourite, because of the picture of a racehorse on the cover. What a 'Berk' was, nobody knew but I. It was a portmanteau word, invented from two which I had recently acquired – 'beck', the shallow stream that stagnated rather than ran through our village, and 'murky', which meant something dark, sinister and forbidding. Into that Berk Minnie was destined to fall. But the story had as many twists and turns as our village stream, and the cook had finished scrubbing the shelves, the bowls of milk, the panchion of home-made loaves, the saucer cheesecakes and pasties and jam jars were put away, and I had fled to seek an audience in the stable yard, long before Minnie reached her hideous destination.

My next effort was editorial. Until I was about seven, my sister and I shared a governess with the daughters of the vicar from a village three miles away. Somebody – I am not sure if it was I – proposed that we should start a magazine. We did – in a half-finished exercise book. We each wrote our own contributions

267

in turn and praised each other's efforts, until the vicar's younger daughter composed a poem in which occurred the couplet:

> The herds
> Of pretty birds.

I have not the least recollection of the title of the magazine or the offending poem, nor have I now the slightest notion why so innocuous a phrase should move me to a fury of derision; but I can to this day remember my small friend's uneven childish printing on the ruled page of the book, and my merciless contempt as I danced round the schoolroom table chanting, in an ecstasy of disdain: 'The *herds* of pretty *birds*.'

Like other tactless criticisms, that broke our paper. We tried no more collaborations with the vicar's daughters.

At that time I was writing verse myself. Yards of it. Miles of it. What I was too idle to set down, I recited to my bored but tolerant sister. My mother encouraged me. In all emotional or domestic crises I was accustomed to console or exhort or admonish her with appropriately pious or didactic verses written on scraps of paper and handed solemnly to her, or laid upon her desk. Far from exposing these to the superior amusement of my elders, she treasured them carefully, and finally decided to exhibit them to a public wider than her appreciative self.

In 1911, when I was thirteen and had been for two years at a boarding school in Scarborough, I accompanied the matron one day just before the Christmas holidays into a stationer's shop in the Ramsgate Road to make some purchases. And there, beside the counter on a special stand, I saw a quantity of pretty little pink and pale green gift books, bound in paper and tied with purple ribbon, entitled: '*My Garden and Other Poems* by Winifred Holtby.'

I felt – well, what would you have felt? I paid my sixpence – borrowed from the matron, who also, properly astonished, bought a copy. I returned to school – on air? No, in the air, a creature transformed (and doubtless most unpleasant). I might be plain, I might be bad at hockey, I might be delicate, tiresome, naughty and unpopular; but I had done something now that no girl in the school, no girl of my acquaintance (except a horrid little prig whose photograph I had once seen and hated in the *Girls'*

Realm) had ever done before. I had published a book.

And what a book! The publication had been arranged (for a sum down, I imagine, though I have never asked) with a local firm. My mother's intention was, I think, to present me with a copy for Christmas; but the ways of publishers are not those of mothers. Commerce frustrated her. But what cared I for her intention? I have known since then countless moments of pleasure, several of rapture and a few of pride, but as I walked back to school with my first published work, I knew so dazzling an ecstasy of achievement that nothing experienced since has even approached it.

I still cherish one copy of those verses. The cover has gone; the pages are dog-eared; but the quality of the verse remains unaltered. I regret to confess it; that quality is execrable – priggish, derivative, nauseatingly insincere. I was, between the ages of 7 and 21, a creature of completely uncritical piety and sentimental convention. One of the earliest efforts runs thus:

> *Only*
> Only a rose-bud
> Tender and soft,
> Dropped from a rose tree,
> Waving aloft.
>
> Only a kind thought
> Spoken by love,
> Dropped like the rose-bud
> From Heaven above.
>
> But the wee rose-bud
> Once pleasure gave;
> The kind thought's remembered
> Unto the grave.

The last effusion, entitled 'Question and Answer', begins:

> Oh, how long is the path and how weary the struggle!
>   The road is so rough and so steep.
> Oh, how far must I climb, and how long must I suffer
>   Before I can lay me to sleep?

Its first part ends with the inquiry:

Oh, why should I suffer? Oh, why should I struggle,
  When fame is a-calling to me?
Oh, why should I toil in the murk of the city
  When I hear the grand roar of the sea?

I had at that time seen two cities only, Hull and London. I adored them both. But I suppose that toiling in urban murk had been presented to my imagination as an alternative to fame and freedom, and convention as usual overcame sincerity.

The most ambitious attempt in the volume was a fragment from an immense blank verse poem which I began to compose when, at the age of 11, I smuggled a stable lantern into a boxroom which opened from the nursery landing and retreated there, preferably at night, sucking a pencil over half-filled account books, glancing with delicious terror into the shadowy corners, where, among the piled boxes, trunks, curtains, chests, bedsteads and lumber, every kind of horror might lurk, then scribbling with a sense of terrified urgency pages and pages and pages of theological speculation. The fragment chosen by my mother and the puzzled schoolmaster begins thus:

Why should we mortals, rulers of this world,
Bow down ourselves to One who went before
And is long dead – One Who has passed before,
Whom we have never seen, nor e'er can see
Till the last trump shall sound, proclaiming all
At end? Both land and sea, and beasts and men,
All mortals to be ended, and the world,
And all the universe one bare blank space,
Devoid of light, of life, of everything
Save His own presence, making all things day;
And life and love perpetually there,
The end of all things, save of Him Himself.

To my embarrassment they had given this effusion the title 'In Milton's Footsteps'. I cannot now remember whether my blushes were caused by resentment at the implications of imitativeness, or by my dawning awareness of ineptitude; but I do know that this seriously annoyed me.

All through my school days I continued intermittently to write verses. Some have been preserved in school magazines. Their quality did not improve conspicuously. But I was also experimenting with another form of expression – the form which throughout my life has most fascinated me, given me most pleasure, and brought no single vestige of success. I was writing plays.

Every Christmas holidays, my sister, a friend called Sybil and I used to compose and perform plays. These also were joint productions. Sybil, a clever child, later to gain an Oxford First and become for a short period a don at St Hugh's, preferred humour. She added most of the jokes. My pretty and gentle sister preferred dressing up and love scenes. I liked Drama. We did not write down the plays; we discussed and rehearsed them, composing the dialogue as we went along. To experienced charade-players, this method presented small difficulty.

We acted the plays in the front kitchen. This was an admirable place for amateur theatricals. Built in the days when the farm hands 'lived in', it was a long, bare room, with three doors opening off one end, and a fourth near the fireplace. Of the three end doors, two opened into cupboards, the third on to stairs leading up to the maid's bedroom and the boxroom which had been my study and which now became a green room. Sides of bacon, hams in muslin bags, and Christmas puddings hung on hooks from the white-washed ceiling. On these hooks we fixed our curtains; in the cupboards we kept our 'properties' and changes of scenery; up the stairs we fled to transform ourselves into the multitudinous characters we chose to play.

The first two plays, *The Highwayman's Curse* and *Grizelda's Vow*, contained nothing more alarming to parental solicitude than a few murders, duels and the like, and one superb suicide when Grizelda (having accomplished her vow to murder her father's enemy) leapt from the kitchen window and flung a croquet ball on the stones below to represent her skull cracking. So, for the third play, my mother thought we might have a more exciting audience than the couple of maids and perhaps an aunt or two, who had applauded our other dramas. Perhaps she had watched with only drowsy attention, for she was a busy woman, and did not guess the macabre possibilities lurking in childish minds. Optimistically she invited the children from two or three neighbouring families and a few local adults to watch the play, and to a supper afterwards.

Spurred by the prospect, we rose to the occasion. This time I wrote a play and we laboriously learned it. It was called *A Living Lie*.

It ran for four long acts and contained, among its milder amenities, one elopement, a strong scene of adultery, a case of leprosy, two murders and a suicide. The 'Lie' was lived by a lady who contracted leprosy under most shady circumstances and murdered the doctor – who was also her lover – and her husband, to avoid deportation to Robben Island, before she stabbed herself across her lover's body.

Before the second act was over, one mother removed her family from the 'theatre'. Before the third, the audience was uneasy. After the lurid curtain, there was little applause. Next year my mother insisted that we should perform only a nice little comedy from French's acting edition – *Two Sharps and a Flat*. Who wanted comedy? I was only consoled by a promise to play the heroine in one of my mother's best evening dresses, and to have an adult male friend, an experienced amateur to whom I was greatly attached, to 'make me up'. But after *A Living Lie*, other people's silly jokes left me cold and I was totally at variance with those adult advisers who repeated to me the unconvincing platitude: 'Mother knows best'.

However, during my last year at school, in 1915, I wrote a drama called *Espionage* (a gross imitation of *Diplomacy*), and produced it with the entire Girl Guide Company in aid of the Red Cross. Out of a passion for originality and revolt against mob-emotion, I made my spy a beautiful but venal American and my German suspect guiltless.

But before this, I had blossomed again into print with my first two journalistic efforts. One was a description of the bombardment of Scarborough, in which one of our school buildings was wrecked. This was extracted by my mother from a letter which I had written to the head girl of the school, who happened to be absent, copied and sent to a paper which not only printed it, but arranged for Australian syndication. The bombardment was a 'hot topical'. The second was a passionate letter to the editor of a local paper against the British use of poison gas. Both were intensely high-minded, rhetorical and ingenuous, but my mother had prints taken of the bombardment article and we sold them at threepence each for the Red Cross and made quite a little sum.

So when, three weeks after my eighteenth birthday, I left school and went to London to train as a probationer nurse in a civilian nursing home, I had seen my poems published in a book, my article and letter in a paper, and my plays produced, in some sort of fashion, on a stage. But from 1915 to 1919 I never even attempted further publication. During the eight months after the Armistice, while I was still in France, I wrote a series of sketches about the WAAC camp where I was stationed, but I had begun to exercise for the first time a certain measure of self-criticism; I knew my work to be sentimental, diffuse, impossible. When I returned from France to Oxford, the tutors who read my essays confirmed my opinion.

I am one of the very few women I know who went to Oxford because my mother wished it, rather than from any very strong personal impetus or scholastic pressure or family tradition. Moreover, when I went there, I was docile. When my immensely long, muddled and emotional history essays were condemned, I accepted the condemnation. It was, I recognized, just. But I set myself with diligence and distress to remedy my shortcomings. I was told that an essay should have a beginning, a middle and an end; that its argument should be capable of division into points, one, two, three, four and five; that these points should be stated briefly, lucidly and without undue decoration. Term by term I set myself to produce from my fuddled, nebulous and fragmentary impressions of the past, something more neatly and concisely designed to satisfy my tutors. I thought I was learning how to get a first and please my mother and my tutors. I did neither. What I was learning was how to earn my living as a journalist and please myself.

I left Oxford with a laborious but undistinguished Second in History, three or four lugubrious verses printed in university magazines, and one ephemeral literary achievement, the joint authorship of a wild farce performed as 'going down play' at

Somerville, called *Bolshevism in Bagdad*. As a mixed skit on *Chu Chin Chow*, *Antony and Cleopatra*, and university politics, it had moments.

But I already had another manuscript in preparation. One day at a coaching on economic history, A.L. Smith, the late Master of Balliol, had directed our attention to the ruthlessness of economic processes, new phases driving out old; the good of yesterday becoming the evil of today; the past making way for the future. And watching his wise old face (for he was then over seventy, dwindled and a little shrunken, though brilliantly alive), I suddenly realized as though in a flash of revelation – Yes, that's it; that's true; that's what happened.

For my father had left the farm which I had loved, and sold it while I was still in the army, and retired to a provincial suburb because he felt unable to cope with the problems of post-war conditions. He was delicate; he was growing elderly; he had never learned how to deal with the new phenomena of government inspection, statutory laws, wage boards and trade unions. He had retired; and part of my heart, I thought, was broken.

But when I listened to A.L. Smith, that breach was mended. I went back to my room and began at once to make notes for the novel I determined to write about it, to instruct myself in the reason for that change which had previously seemed to me an unmitigated tragedy. I forced myself to read histories of agriculture, of trade unionism, of socialism. I tried to set the drama of rural Yorkshire as I knew it, as it had filled my whole horizon until the war destroyed a small and settled world, against the background of historical change and progress, and gradually, reading and thinking, I comforted myself, and invented a story of a young woman (29 I made her, and, God forgive me, thought her middle-aged!) married to a much older farmer, and confronted by circumstances similar to those which proved too much for my frail and gentle father. Two years later, after many vicissitudes, the story was published under the title of *Anderby Wold* by the Bodley Head.

Meanwhile, I had been trying my hand at other, more remunerative businesses. I taught in schools, I lectured, I was part-time secretary to a Member of Parliament. I wrote articles, a few, a very few, of which would be accepted. But I kept trying to remember the instructions of my tutors at Oxford – that an essay has a beginning, a middle and an end; and that its argument must be capable of clear, lucid statement under headings that could be numbered one, two and three.

So one day, when I was working in Bethnal Green as secretary to Sir Percy Harris, MP, and as a member of a group of after-care committees for school children, I planned a series of articles on the 'human side' of the LCC educational machine, and sent them to Lady Rhondda at *Time and Tide*. She had previously rejected several of my manuscripts, but I had read her paper avidly since its first appearance, and was hardened to rejections. This time she did not return the manuscript. She invited me to lunch at her Chelsea flat.

The first thing I noticed when I reached her presence was that, in spite of the fact that I felt almost morbidly shy, I could not stop talking; the second was that there was lobster for lunch. I have the stomach of an ostrich; I flourished on Army rations; I had been a pantry-pilferer since youth, eating once, I remember, even an accidental mixture of treacle and potted turkey with relish; but lobster I could not manage. Still, there it was. There was the first editor who had ever shown a sign of taking my work seriously, and there was the lobster, rich, pink, formidable on lettuce leaves. I had a feeling that if I rejected her lobster, she had a right to reject my articles. I ate what was set before me. When offered more, I took more. I endured throughout the interview. I departed no sooner than was seemly. And then I fled to Sloane Square station, where I was very, very sick. But *Time and Tide* took the articles; Lady Rhondda soon appointed me as a regular note and leader writer, first on educational, then on general political subjects. She took in hand the correction of my style, making me write and rewrite my notes until they were at least readable and comprehensible. Four years later, I became a director of the paper.

As I look back it seems that I have been led, pushed and prodded into authorship. In my betters, genius has burned, an indomitable flame, in spite of the threatening winds of opposition. I was never opposed; I was grossly, undeservedly, and with astonishing optimism, encouraged from the outset, by my mother, my schoolteachers, my Oxford tutors and my editors. The only form of composition which I chose for myself, insisted upon producing, and performed against odds, was that of writing plays. Is it wholly irrelevant that this is the only kind in which I have had no success whatever? I still write plays; I still send them to producers; they are still rejected. Is it true, can it be true – that detested formula repeated to my incredulous youth: 'Mother knows best'?

Lovat Dickson's Magazine, December 1934

∽

IN PRAISE OF TRAINS

I do not agree with Kipling that 'he travels fastest who travels alone'. The railway engine has always impressed me by the indifference with which it hauls ten or two hundred people. But the single traveller certainly tastes best the sweets of travel. It is he who can relax his social nerves and rest from that continual adjustment of personality to the taste, needs, wills, and habits of his neighbours which all life in company demands. An hotel is too distracting, a ship too convivial, a hermitage too solitary for complete refreshment. Only in a train can we be present with our neighbours in body but not in spirit, can we taste that undisturbing intimacy whereby we sleep in the same compartment, eat from the same table, and contemplate through a whole day each other's faces and yet exchange no word.

The journey must be long enough to permit an orderly routine of breakfast, lunch, and dinner, of sleep and wakefulness, of leisurely occupation and monotonous tranquillity. For the traveller need never be bored. If studious, he may read; if sociable, talk; if greedy, eat; if idle, sleep. But he who reads must show nice taste in literature. Daily papers, though common, are uncomfortable. Their flapping pages, their tendency to blow into other people's eyes, their squalid habit when abandoned, and their disquieting connection with the world outside, all unfit them for train reading. Romance, detective stories, and adventure are too absorbing. I missed my first sight of the Danube through total immersion in John Buchan. Politics are too controversial, travel too stimulating, poetry too precious. The perfect train book must interest without exciting; it must be easy to hold; it must demand no great physical nor mental effort; it must permit the eye to wander from the printed page to the flying landscape and back to the page again with added pleasure. 'De gustibus', of course, there is no arguing; but for myself I choose Jane Austen, William James, St Augustine, Stella Benson, and *Home Chat*. The Bible would be excellent, if one could read it in a yellow cover, without feeling self-conscious.

But food for the mind is insufficient. When travelling, man cannot live by print alone. There are no circumstances in which the choice and consumption of food are so agreeable as in a train. Perhaps it is the accompaniment of the flying scenery that gives the food its sauce. For the landscape from the carriage windows is an uncovenanted mercy. We do not take a ticket from King's Cross in order to enjoy the grey-green fields falling away from the smooth line in Lincolnshire, but because we want to reach Hull. We travel through France to reach Marseilles, not to watch the acacias and sycamores, the plane trees and beeches throwing off the morning mist and shaking their young leaves in golden light. We do not cross Germany for its bleak, bracing plains, Hungary for its scattered villages, nor Cape Province for the Karoo. We always ask 'What time does the train get there?' never 'What shall we see on the way?', as though Stevenson lied when he said that to travel hopefully is better than to arrive.

The true poet of the train will come, I think, from Africa. Here travelling in trains is the best on earth, by which I mean, of course, the best I know. For since a flood in Mesopotamia became a deluge drowning the whole world, human egotism has limited the earth within the compass of a man's experience.

English trains are cleaner, German trains more punctual, French trains faster, Italian trains are more convivial, and Hungarian trains more unexpected. For anything that I know, Chinese trains may be wilder, Brazilian trains more commodious, and those of New Zealand better organized; but still I think that South African trains are best.

Their virtue is compounded of many excellences. They are

cheap; here the second-class traveller may sleep in a real bed for three shillings. They are friendly. I have never known officials so confiding. One forms here friendships fleeting but complete. I have met an engine-driver's father in the Western Province, an inspector from the Free State, a ticket collector in the Transvaal, and a waiter in Natal whom I count my friends for life. So personal are the trains that the names of the chef and head waiter are printed on the menus. For people matter here.

There was a train in the Cape which one could hire complete with stokers, engine-driver, guard, and all for two pounds a day, and go with it off into the forest, cosy and private, to chase pigs or gather flowers or picnic in its shadow.

'Yes, we can understand this love for Natal or the Drakensberg or Sabie Game reserve or the Garden route,' my friends say, 'but you can't maintain that travelling through the Karoo in February has attractions.' Perhaps the Karoo most of all, when the day comes up hot and hot, and the traveller has to fold a rug between his nether person and the scorching leather cushions. Like the breath of a dragon the fiery wind catches the corridors. Through the open window it comes like air from an oven. And then for the first time the traveller newly arrived from England knows the wisdom of Stephen Hawes:

> After the day there cometh the dark night,
> For though the day be never so long,
> At last the bells ringeth to Evensong.

I believe that there is actually a moment at noon when the sun, having done its worst, begins to give way; when the prickly pears grow their first fringe of shadow on the eastern side, and the long day turns and looks towards the cool of the evening.

Then, if ever there is rest after weariness, refreshment after drought, peace after turmoil, comes the pale twilight from behind the hills. And such a royal sunset flames above the black heads of the kopjes that they must bow abashed, trailing their heavy shadows. And the sweet chill of the wind blows down the corridor on to the hot temples of the traveller, as beneath the first faint points of stars the darkness stretches over the Karoo.

Manchester Guardian, 12 August 1926

THE PERSONAL PRONOUN

The other day my business took me into the office of a certain socialist editor whom I did not know very well. The circumstances of our meeting had not been wholly fortunate, and at first our conversation went haltingly. But as discussion proceeded and we both became really interested in our subject the editor lost his constraint. He pulled out his pipe, lounged with his feet on a chair, and began to call me 'brother'.

At first the unexpected title amused me and almost disconcerted me. Then, as I realized its implication, I became unusually pleased. For we had grown so much absorbed in the business before us that my new acquaintance had lost all sense of my identity. I was no longer a rather troublesome young woman who might or might not be of use to the particular cause which he was sponsoring – with probability on the side of the 'might not' – I was 'brother', an impersonal creature, sharing for the moment his interests and expectations, drawn into that comradeship of 'Those who want to get something done', who are like the angels in heaven, without sex or nationality.

It occurs to me that at certain periods of that absorption in a piece of work which is one of the most agreeable of all human experiences the personal pronoun fades out of our vocabulary. To the really busy man or woman sex for a time becomes just gender, masculine, feminine, or neuter. And after a certain point of interest has been reached even gender loses its significance. He, she, or it, brother, sister, it matters very little. We have become for the moment agents of a driving power far more important than our individual idiosyncrasies. And, if we are to believe Bernard Shaw, 'this is the true joy of life, the being used for a purpose recognized by yourself as a mighty one; the being thoroughly worn out before you are thrown on the scrapheap.'

The abolition of sex would not be desirable even if it were possible; but I have sometimes wondered whether the abolition of gender might not be convenient. In a society where occupation and character is no longer finally determined by sex, what does it matter whether you address an editor or lawyer as 'Dear sir', or 'Dear madam'? The dairy worker may with equal efficiency and probability be either he or she. The gardener, the spinner, the stenographer, the lecturer are in their work without sex differentiation, yet continually the little personal pronoun obtrudes itself, demanding recognition for their forgotten sex.

There is a certain woman secretary to an influential political society who always signs her letters with her plain initial. To call herself Dorothy or Phyllis, or whatever her Christian name happens to be, would emphasize the part of herself which, in that particular work, happens to be quite irrelevant. It does not matter when she is drafting memoranda, or writing minutes, or addressing letters whether for that purpose she is man or woman. In her own personal life she may happen to be very much woman. In this particular case she is pretty, attractive, feminine, and happily engaged to be married to a man who loves her for these and for other qualities. But such facts do not modify her opinion about legislation; they do not affect her memoranda on (shall we say?) the Geneva Protocol or the taxation of land values. Directly she enters her businesslike office and begins to open her morning's correspondence she is neither sir nor madam. She has become 'brother'.

I am not a philologist, and I do not know how far a modification of our grammar is either possible or desirable. If we lived in France or Germany, where even knives and pillow-cases have their gender, the case might be grammatically more complex but socially much easier. But we live in England, where our language recognizes only three sorts of creatures – he and she and it. Tables and stones and mountains share one gender, but men and women are irrevocably divided. Save for the awkward 'one' who occasionally performs actions, the neutral 'we', or the unintimate 'they', when acting alone the human being must be he or she, man or woman, sir or madam, inescapably, perpetually.

We try to evade it. Some papers run by women insist that the sex of their editor is irrelevant and demand that she should be addressed in published letters as 'Dear sir'. It is a justifiable demand, but it is none the less quite artificial. Fond friends confronted by the embarrassing apparition of a new baby endeavour sometimes to compromise by saying 'It', to the indignation of the proud parent. Letters from strangers signed only with initials cause nerve-wracking hesitations, and usually end in a reply being sent to —— , Esq., whereupon they become a source of indignation or amusement to the recipient.

It would seem that for business purposes and the workaday world we need a new personal pronoun, personal but without gender, neutral but not neuter, something more definite than 'one' and less distant than the German *mann*. We want a pronoun, neither he nor she, which will refer equally well to an office-girl or office-boy; to a man or a woman who comes to milk the cows; to a male or female shop-assistant. We need also a noun; but 'comrade', 'colleague', 'friend' all imply stages of intimacy too particular for ordinary purposes. We want a form of address courteous yet sexless, a neutral but not a neuter form of sir and madam. Sadam and mir would not do. We must devise something better. I make no suggestions. Every attempt in my own mind slays itself. But I feel sure that here is a fruitful occupation for philologists.

We do not want the complete destruction of the present forms of pronoun. In our private life there is plenty of room for he and she. Sometimes the mighty purpose in Shaw's definition of joy may be a valiant love between a man and woman. Every human being has some kind of sex life, whether less or greater than other experiences. But this side of life is different from the world of offices and factories. It does not belong to the business of production and education and government in which so many of both men and women are involved. There are today more women than men in the professions. Why should they be labelled continually as 'madam'?

The real problem of the professions and the industries, the arts and government services, is to find the best person for the best work. It does not matter whether that person is masculine or feminine. It matters very much that he (she) should not be neuter. Philologists to the rescue! Find us an alternative, human but quite neutral, and half the difficulty about women in the world of business will have vanished.

Manchester Guardian, 24 February 1928

IS FAMILY LIFE A HANDICAP?

Shall we abolish the family? Does family life handicap us in our quest for personal success? I suppose these questions have been asked ever since primitive man stood on the rocks above his celebrated cave, looking at his children and their mother, and wondering whether he would get on better in the world if he rolled down a boulder on to the lot of them, ate their portions of the fresh-killed rabbit, and went along his road unhindered by their company.

'He travels fastest who travels alone', said Kipling. How true is this of all of us? Everywhere today we hear of a revolt against family life. How far is that a necessary prelude to realized ambition?

The most obvious and most irritating answer to such questions, of course, is 'It depends' – it depends on the family, on the individual, and on the particular ambition which the individual follows. If a young man in the diplomatic service marries a lovely, tactful, capable wife, with great talents as a hostess, and if he becomes an ambassador largely on the strength of her ability, it is clear that his family life has aided his career. But if the said wife happens also to be a biologist, and her activities as a hostess prevent her from working in the laboratory, it is equally clear that the same family life destroys her success outside the home.

If a proud father devotes all his energies to helping his daughter to become a tennis champion, his family life may limit his own professional achievement as a lawyer, an undertaker, or a farmer, but it gives the girl a chance to beat Miss Helen Wills at Wimbledon. One man's meat is another man's poison.

What Samuel Butler and Sir Edmund Gosse told us about the home life of their youth would have been enough to make all bright young Englishmen rise up and smother their fathers, if it had not been for the fact that so many know that their own particular fathers have been their greatest friends.

The truth of the matter is that some of us are helped in our external work by family life, and that some are not. Some people are born to be good 'family mixers', some not. There is no virtue in it, one way or the other. Some of the greatest saints and benefactors and artists and reformers have been hopeless family men.

Family life is a convenience, not a sacrament. Its danger lies in our idealization of it. So long as we regard it as something sacred, and those who prefer to abandon it as somehow sinful, so long will it handicap us all by placing unnecessary restrictions and compunctions and responsibilities upon us.

Family life is no handicap to those who really enjoy it; and nobody else ought to be forced to lead it. Unhappy domestic life is always a handicap, because it exhausts nervous energy that could be better employed otherwise.

We have become so dazzled by the halo that tradition has placed around the family, that often we cannot see what it is really like at all. It happens that the family, whether it consists of a husband and wife alone, or of parents and children, with maids, nurses, aunts, canaries and all other appurtenances thereof, implies a very small and intimate community, where everybody knows a great deal about everybody else, and where success depends on a rule of give-and-take. If, therefore, any individual finds himself in a situation where he cannot give, he has no right to take, and had better get out of it.

Some artists have no right to live in families; almost no saints, explorers, monomaniacs, drunkards, or misanthropes have any right to live in families. Let them go into monasteries, or steam yachts, or Furnished Chambers for Single Gentlemen. As husbands, wives, parents or children they will be failures, and their failure will handicap them in their proper work.

Family life generally involves a mixture of ages. This introduces the element of responsibility and protection into the home. It may be a good thing. The teacher, the doctor, the administrator, the organizer of a large office, is probably far better at any job involving the management of human beings because he or she has been practising on the family. Moreover, the background of family life may give to the holders of non-human jobs just that enrichment of emotional experience which they need to balance their personal development. On the other hand, it may not.

The necessity to provide for a young family may force a father deliberately to wreck his career as an inventor. I know of one brilliant young woman who threw up a peculiarly promising political career because she felt financially responsible for her mother and younger brother. Financial family obligations may be an overwhelming hindrance to professional success, and when local regulations or national laws add to natural difficulties unnatural regulations, demanding the dismissal of married women from paid employment, they turn family life from a difficulty into a disaster.

Family responsibility may hinder the protectors, but that is nothing to the damage it often does to the protected. The first manifestation of human enterprise in a boy or girl often comes only when they leave home. Nothing can be more ruinous to a man or woman than living with over-conscientious parents. 'Good' mothers of the unintelligent, obstinate variety have probably crippled as human beings more sons and daughters than all the wars in history. The best thing that most young people can do with their families is to leave them. They will probably only thus learn to appreciate them.

And husbands and wives? Does marriage really bind them in a prison, curtail adventure and burden them in the race for success? It all depends. There seem to be some people who cannot live without perpetual emotional stimulus from personal relationships. They need variety. The prospect of seeing the same face over the breakfast bacon every morning for 50 years paralyses them. Obviously for such men and women monogamous marriage is a handicap.

There are others who find their emotional stimulus in other passions – the passion for building bridges, or writing poems, or opening new branches of a cash chemist's business, or playing the violin, or piloting Bills through Parliament. Such people take their adventures outside the family; they like to feel that they have one set of quiet, orderly relationships, one emotional security, one certain rest, and to them family life is the ideal basis for external activity.

Of course, the family into which we were born may not be the best one in which to live. The pious fatalism of most English men and women when confronted by an ill-assorted family is one of the marvels of the universe. We do not rest content with the clothes that Nature gave us, or the houses, or the tools, or the professional colleagues. We choose our clerks and foreman and parlourmaids most carefully. Why not our families? There is no mystic and unperishable reason why persons akin by blood should share the same family life. Probably just because of their kinship they are the very last people who ought to live together.

Blood, we are told, is thicker than water. But does this interesting physiological fact prove that young men and women after adolescence should live with their parents? It does not.

The only safe rule about families is that there is no rule. The only real handicap from family life comes when we prolong it after it has become a handicap. Let each man and woman lead the kind of life which is most suitable to their own requirements, and let us stop this stupid attempt to acquire merit by martyrizing ourselves to an ideal of 'Family Life' which has no true value apart from its convenience.

Evening Standard, 2 November 1929

∾

CAVALCADE

After a performance of *Cavalcade* I stood on the steps of the Tivoli, listening to those snatches of conversation which were one of the most interesting parts of the entertainment between the acts of the stage version. As before, the younger people seemed a little puzzled by the whole affair, and, not least, by the emotion of their elders. 'It's got the atmosphere,' said a hard-bitten man in the late forties. 'Aye. It was like that.' 'My dear, horror after horror, wasn't it?' giggled a pretty young thing of 18 or so, in a pert little veiled hat. 'Surely piled on a bit thick?' asked her friend with chestnut corkscrew curls. And had I not been trained by long habit never to speak to strangers, I could have replied, 'But, my dear child, that is just what a big war does seem like to some of the people who lived through it – all the accumulated vengeance of world history, horror upon horror, descending upon the heads of just such pretty, innocuous, unsuspecting little creatures as yourself.' But, of course, I did nothing except powder my reddened nose and watch with sympathetic amusement the similar furtive repairs to mottled complexions made by most of the women over 30, who, like myself, can sit unmoved through tragedy and even face with comparative calmness the disasters of daily life, but who are moved intolerably by the tapping of feet to a half-forgotten melody, the picture of a troop-train leaving Victoria Station, or the gesture of a hand waving farewell beyond a barrier. And I congratulated Noel Coward, Reginald Berkeley and the Fox Film Company for so successfully exploiting those memories that now, after so many years, release the tears we could not shed when they were part of our lives – not shadows on a screen.

But, to counterbalance this inevitably effective exploitation of personal sentiment, the Tivoli offers the most rich and gorgeous nourishment for our instincts of irony and amusement. As we left the place, attendants thrust into our hands copies of a leaflet called *The London Pictorial*, in which we read that *Cavalcade* is 'the most inspired production of any age'. At other times we might, thinking of certain rumoured productions at Athens, in Elizabethan London, Bayreuth, or even Oberammergau, have been a trifle staggered by this flat statement. But after the goings-on inside the Tivoli, we were hardened to anything. For, as an integral part of the entertainment, before *Cavalcade* begins, we were shown one of those 'educational' films whose educative qualities sometimes take our breath away. It is called *Round the Empire*, and is accompanied by a lecture from a gentleman whose suave, complacent voice – the quintessence of post-BBC patronage – positively screams for caricature by John Tilley. He opens by announcing that he will take us on a tour round the Empire inhabited by so many diverse peoples 'all cherishing the same ideals'. With a few scattered thoughts of French-Canadian separatists, de Valera republicans, Indian Congress pickets, New Zealand loyalists, Transvaal nationalists and the Kavirondo Taxpayers' Association, to say nothing about the unanimous (?) agreements of Ottawa, I sat back prepared to enjoy myself. And this was the next remark that stirred me; 'which the world's greatest dramatist, Noel Coward, has so brilliantly portrayed in his epic drama *Cavalcade*'. Now I took my notes in the dark, and I won't swear before God that the lecturer did not say 'the world's greatest living dramatist' – though after *The London Pictorial*, I doubt it; but even so, that, I feel, should make Bernard Shaw, Pirandello, Sean O'Casey, Yeats and a few other inconsiderable triflers with the theatre sit up and take notice.

Those little shocks, however, were mild compared with what followed. We were shown Canada. The chief point of interest about Canada, apparently, is that the policemen resemble their English prototypes – a comforting thought, perhaps, when we think of a few of the little activities along the frontier. I recommend it for the greater ease of readers disconcerted by *Limey*, that strange account by James Spenser of what happens to gentlemen of easy conscience and British birth who cross that frontier into the United States without the sanction of an orderly passport. Then Australia – distinguished, of course, by Sydney Bridge, with a coy side-glance at pretty girls, and a complacent survey of the Air Force. New Zealand has scenery and Maoris, actually Maoris, 'now living peacefully under the flag' and bathing in hot springs. Note the Maoris well. We shall not look upon their like again. For India recognizes only the British and Natives – native police, a fine body of men, for whom our gratitude is invited as a tribute to their self-sacrifice during the Great War. Not a word, naturally, about more recent lathi-beatings and so on. Viceregal ceremonies, garden parties with Princes, and the fortifications of the Khyber Pass present a fine substitute for the courts of Meerut, the slums of Calcutta, the jute factories and barren villages.

But the masterpiece comes with Africa. 'Africa is, even now,' continues that cultured voice regretfully, 'predominantly native.' How sad! Just think of that, after all these years of British rule. In Australia and Canada our virile race succeeded admirably in reducing Red Indians or aborigines to quite insignificant proportions, but the tiresome Africans continue to increase and multiply. I could not help remembering a similar regret expressed by a gentleman called Elliot, a Natal farmer, who in 1927 was giving evidence before the Select Committee on the Four Native Bills at Cape Town. 'You ask whether it is my idea that things will have to be decided by force', he replied to a rather startled question from the Commissioners, 'and that if we want to hold our own we must exterminate these people (the Africans). I think that it will either be that, or I do not know what it is going to be.' Kenya followed, to which 'prosperity has come since it has been under British control' – an observation likely to surprise those settlers now petitioning against the payment of income-tax. Finally, after a glimpse of Gibraltar, we were shown the Royal Navy, 'the symbol, not only of power and majesty, but of universal freedom and justice'. Well, well, well, well. I wonder how many of our foreign friends, attracted to the Strand by the 'Come to England' movement, were present at the Tivoli to ask, 'Oh yeah?'

But after that really splendid vision of battleships steaming off against a sunset to the tune of *Rule Britannia* and the enraptured applause of Britons, came *Cavalcade* itself, with its interesting sidelights upon the behaviour of English natives. There are, apparently, two kinds of Englishmen – the Dignified Gentlepeople, whose partings and deaths and sorrows are tragic – and the natives below stairs – cooks and mothers-in-law and housemaids and the like – whose goings-on are invariably comic. When Diana Wynyard as Jane Marryot said 'Goodbye' to Clive Brook, her gallant and loving husband, we bit our lips and blinked our eyes in sympathy. When Una O'Connor as Ellen Bridges said 'Goodbye' to her equally gallant and loving husband, Alfred, we giggled in appreciative amusement, because low life in kitchens is, of course, always comic, and the scenes in the East End, with the Graingers and Bridges – though their content is no less poignant than the scenes in the Marryot's drawing-room – are, naturally, farcical in tone.

To do justice to 'the world's greatest dramatist', Noel Coward, I must say that his notion that the poor are always funny was shared by his humbler predecessor, Shakespeare. And his equally odd idea that only in the past did our country know 'dignity and greatness and peace' finds honourable precedents in almost all the great mediaeval thinkers except Dante. Personally, I do not really think that the Edwardian era had quite so many advantages as he believes over our present one. Nor do I think that the Cowardesque glimpses of night-club life, homosexual fondlings and twentieth-century blues with which the film ends, present an entirely adequate picture of a society which, after all, contains smallholdings and health clinics, nursery schools and growing universities, village institutes and the Workers' Travel Association, hiking parties and bouncing gymnasium classes at the Polytechnic, busy little families planning suburban gardens, and secretaries of hundreds of inconspicuous organizations working conscientiously for the future without hope of gain. On the whole, I thought, as I walked down the Strand in the fine March rain, a more emotionally riotous and intellectually preposterous entertainment I have rarely seen. By far the sanest comment upon the political ideas of Mr-Noel-Coward-plus-Reginald-Berkeley-plus-Hollywood is the absurd and delicious Silly Symphony of naval warfare and Father Neptune which, quite appropriately, precedes both Empire Tour and *Cavalcade*.

Time and Tide, 11 March 1933

♪

SO THIS IS GENIUS

'Dostoyevsky's Letters to His Wife,'
translated by Elizabeth Hill: Introduction by
Prince Mirsky (Constable)

The publication of this volume constitutes a severe trial for the faithful. Those who hold Dostoyevsky to be one of the world's greatest novelists, a man of deep and tragic perception, a doctor of souls gifted with a sombre intensity of spiritual insight, must read with anguish these long, rambling, egotistic, and quite appallingly unpleasant letters.

Let us face the worst of it. Dostoyevsky was an invalid. He was an epileptic, neurotic, hysterical, afflicted with an infection of the lungs. He suffered from the gambler's mania, coupled with the gambler's gift of self-deception. He was engaged in a continual struggle against ill-health, poverty and the effects of his own social maladjustment. In spite of these eugenic drawbacks he married twice, had children by both his wives, and between his marriages conducted his most passionate love-affair. These letters are addressed to his second wife, a quiet, devoted, self-effacing woman who had been his secretary. They were written during his absences from her: on business in Moscow or St Petersburg, in the health resort of Staraya, Russia, in quest of health, or from the gaming-tables at Ems. As a record of whining self-commiseration, exasperating fussiness, egotistic preoccupation with details of health and diet, and nauseating eroticism, I have never read their equal. The earlier letters, written when Dostoyevsky went from Ems to Wiesbaden, from Hamburg to Bains Saxon, gambling away at each town the money scraped together by his wife to pay for his return, pouring forth pages of effusive endearments, abject protests, and cringing self-abasement, are almost too painful to read. The degradation of the human spirit could hardly sink lower. Yet I am not sure that the medical details of the central letters are not more tedious. Dostoyevsky seems incapable of taking a liver pill without devoting pages to its physical and psychological effects; nor am I sure whether the last letters about his triumph in Moscow at the time of the Pushkin celebrations are not the most unattractive of all, in their naïve yet petulant complacency. As a commentary upon married love and the home life of genius, the whole collection deserves an ironic immortality.

There are two possible responses to such self-revelation. We may deplore this unattractive vision of genius *en pantoufles*. We may avert in horror our noses from the dunghill on which his talent bloomed, or we may turn again in astonished admiration to *The Brothers Karamazov* and *The Idiot*, and *Crime and Punishment*. For the cringing neurotic whose 'seductive dreams' seem so singularly unattractive, was the master of the most passionate, delicate and pitiful moods of human love. The gambler who summoned a fleeting smile because the black beetles could 'smell money coming from the Karamazovs', made of those same Karamazovs an immortal offering at the altar to human goodness; and the tedious hypochondriac who never spared his wife jot nor tittle of the less fanciable evidences of his physical ailments, used this passion for reiterated detail to glorious artistic effect in *Crime and Punishment*.

Why are we so childish as to assume that loveliness must come from lovely things, and that psychological weakness is incompatible with artistic and spiritual strength? Human nature is complex, not simple. The flower Safety grows on the nettle Danger. Once in South Africa I saw behind the foul craziness of a native hovel a heap of filthy manure and rotting rags, out of which grew in dazzling brilliance five immense and quite perfect arum lilies. Which is a parable; which is also relevant consideration for the eugenists who urge the sterilization of the unfit. Which is my final but wondering reflection upon Dostoyevsky's letters to his wife.

Time and Tide, 14 February 1930

ↄ

AN EXPLORER'S RECORD

'The Waves' by Virginia Woolf (Hogarth Press)

The extension of reality, which the artist seeks, does not lie only in the external show of things. We have harboured for some two hundred years the notion that a novelist's business is with the words, actions and conscious thoughts of men and women, especially as these concern their personal relationships with each other. Character, we have said, is the novelist's business, and character is a matter of behaviour at a battle or a tea-party; love is his business, and love is the emotional prelude to marriage, death by a 'decline', or sexual satisfaction, according to the period in which the novel was written. A novelist's scope was wide if, like Tolstoy, he covered immense geographical and social areas; it was deep if, like Dostoyevsky, he descended into the hell of guilt and madness and rose again to the heaven of ecstasy.

But there have always been dissentients. Straying from the beaten track of external appearance, Sterne wandered among the irrelevances of a wayward imagination; Proust dived deep into the echoing caves of memory and sentiment; Dorothy Richardson tracked the more delicate filaments of sensation; and, in a series of novels which are among the most remarkable of our time, Virginia Woolf has been pursuing the reality of experience, of character, of understanding, which lies just beyond the highways of conscious thought and action. She has extended the scope of the novel, not by introducing an immense pageantry of types, like the characters of Dickens, not in seeking the battlefields and throne-rooms of Tolstoy or Thackeray, nor in scaling the centuries, like Naomi Mitchison and Flaubert. Her most adventurous novels are those which have stayed closest at home, dealing, so far as their surface story is concerned, with a very small group of cultured middle-class men and women living in contemporary England. Yet in *Jacob's Room*, *Mrs Dalloway*, *To the Lighthouse* and her new novel *The Waves*, she has not only conducted a sequence of experiments in the novel form; she has explored further and further into the regions of human experience lying outside our bright, busy world of deliberate speech and action.

The regions which she has opened up are still uncharted and largely unexplored. That terrific pioneer, Freud, leapt across them with such a banging of drums and flashing of high explosives that the tumult of his progress has not yet died down, and it is still difficult to see, without distortion, the wildly waving trees and broken jungle beside his crashing trail, as we follow him, menaced by those enormous bogies, the Ego and the Id. Mrs Woolf has entered, stepping delicately yet boldly, her courage fortified by her invincible confidence in the intellect, in the importance of truth, and in the Socratic method of inquiry. Armed by her reverence for reason, she has ventured into those labyrinthine wildernesses where the law of reason does not run, and, keeping her eyes open, her judgment clear, and her poet's vision unimpeded, has seen so much that she is still unable to convey to us the full measure of her extended knowledge. But she is looking, we feel, as deeply into the human heart, and illuminating its processes as brightly, as any living novelist.

The Waves is the report of her most daring journey. It is written in that orchestral-soliloquy form which she devised in her earlier sketches, *Monday or Tuesday*, and developed further in *Mrs Dalloway* and *To the Lighthouse*. There is nothing in the novel but these alternating soliloquies, taking place in the subconscious rather than the conscious minds of the six characters, Bernard, Neville, Louis, Susan, Jinny and Rhoda. These, her usual cultured middle-class men and women, she follows from childhood, through adolescence to maturity. They are bound together by association, and by love for one man, seen only through their eyes, and their story is finally summed up by Bernard, the novelist, when, as an old man, he sits in a restaurant thinking of his friends. The story is accompanied by a series of pictures of the sea, at morning, noon and evening, to symbolize the stages of human growth, and just as the range of thought in the soliloquies keeps, most of the time, below the surface of consciousness, so does Mrs Woolf give us the sense of seeing her characters and pictures through transparent water. The sea-symbols which appear in all her work, here impregnate the story; the surge and stir of the sea move in her lovely prose. She has used the instruments of the poet and the musician; rhythm, balance, metaphor, and repeated design are woven in and in upon her complex themes.

Her character studies are as individual and incisive as any she has drawn. Neville, who seeks one absolute beauty, Louis, forced on by his inferiority-complex to the acquisition of wealth, Rhoda and her fears, Susan and her passions, are vividly recognizable twentieth-century people.

The realm of impulse, memory, emotion, logic and desire which she reveals is one in which the complete human personality is seen, built up from exquisitely small details. Again she shows, as in her pictures of the Ramsay children in *To the Lighthouse*, how youth and age are bound together by the influence of past events. All life is a *recherche du temps perdu*. Rhoda, as a child at school, longs 'to gather flowers and present them – Oh to whom?' When she is a woman, and Percival whom she loved is dead, she buys violets in Oxford Street and scatters them on the Thames at Greenwich in his memory. Neville's mind is haunted in moments of grief by the tale he heard the cook tell of a man with his throat cut, when, as a small boy, he stood on the stairs and watched her pushing the oven dampers. Nothing is lost; nothing perishes; each smallest moment of life is immortal while we live, and while those live whom we have influenced. The brass hoop still glitters on the cupboard; the ladies still sit between long windows; the children scamper still between the trees. But out of this subtle and complex confusion is born a spirit of triumph and defiance. Bernard as an old man sinks momentarily into the lethargy of despair; but that passes. The book ends, not with collapse into the trough of the waves, but on its crest, and even the coming of death is a new adventure, to be greeted 'unvanquished and unyielding'.

The novel is no easier to read than Wordsworth's *Prelude* seemed when it first appeared, no easier than the music of *Parsifal*. But its qualities of beauty and profundity lift it into the circle of those works of art which, by enlarging our knowledge of the processses of our own hearts and minds, extend reality for us, and dignify the human race by adding a cubit to its stature.

Time and Tide, 10 October 1931

❧

HOW TO ENJOY BAD HEALTH

A fortnight after I had left my sheltered and disciplined girls' boarding school, I found myself in the starched apron, collars, cuffs, belt, cap, and other preposterous impedimenta of a probationer nurse in a London nursing-home. For a year I polished sterilizers, made beds, cleaned washstands, helped to bed-bath patients, handed swabs in the operating theatre, and endeavoured in sundry other less orthodox ways to earn the £18 a year 'uniform money' which was my due. For another year in the WAAC as a hostel forewoman I nursed influenza, administered number nines, rubbed sore throats, bandaged scalds and cuts, and took suspected temperatures. Since then I have performed the usual feats of home nursing demanded from any woman who has learnt to know an ear-syringe from a thermometer. And for nine months of last year I was more or less of an invalid myself.

I mention these qualifications just in case anyone should think that I do not know what I am talking about when I say that the phrase 'to enjoy bad health' is not an ironic paradox; it is a practical human experience. There is no reason why one should be less happy when one is ill than when one is well. It is all a question of the right technique. And having studied that technique from both sides of the draw-sheet, so to speak, I am infinitely distressed when I see people painfully enduring nice neat little illnesses, perfectly adapted by circumstances for enjoyment, without the slightest idea of how to make the best of them. It is such waste. And, life being what it is, it seems a pity to waste any chances of enjoyment.

Of course there are certain conditions that should be observed. It is the neglect of these which has given illness its bad name.

First of all, the disease must have good, honest, physical symptoms. I am sorry to blight your hopes, ladies and gentlemen; but neurasthenia won't do. Hypochondriasis won't do. A nervous breakdown, or whatever you choose to call it, is of no use to anyone. Its disadvantages are multiple. They are both positive and negative. Positively, neurasthenia by its own nature makes its victim miserable. I never yet heard of a breakdown into happiness. It is part of the disease that one should feel as ill as possible – in fact, more so. There is sometimes a queer masochistic pleasure in an acute accountable physical pain; there is absolutely none in a pain that is not really there. And it hurts just as much. Break your leg, strain your hearts, inflame your appendices as much as you like. But, whatever you do, if you want to enjoy your illness, keep your nerves clear.

As for the negative disadvantages of neurasthenia, they are equally distressing. Owing to the poverty of human imagination, sympathy for its sufferers is far more difficult to secure; and there is nothing in the world more disheartening than to be told, as you drag your aching limbs from a bed to which the household refuses to carry any more invalid trays, 'Why, come along, old thing. Pull yourself together. You can't expect any sympathy from *me*, you know. There's nothing really wrong with you. Remember what the doctor said. It's all nerves.' Quite. But, nerves or no nerves, it is enough, and a little too much.

For the same reason, I advise avoidance of all kindred illnesses – neuritis, shingles, sick headaches and the like. They are usually accompanied by a nervous condition that leaves one little able to bear them; they are painful; and they are not dangerous.

Now it is an interesting, if perhaps not wholly creditable, phenomenon of psychology that the more precarious life seems, the sweeter it becomes both to ourselves and to other people. That is why the wisest principle for those choosing an illness is 'the maximum of danger with the minimum of discomfort'.

During my childhood a fashion flourished among middle-class households, encouraged doubtless by venerable Associates of the Royal Academy, for a species of mural decoration known as the 'problem picture'. The chief problem suggested by most of these to the domestic mind was, 'Will it cover the stain on the spare bedroom wallpaper?' And indeed, many a time, after arrival at a strange house, have I glanced up from washing my hands in a monstrously heavy china basin decorated with gilt roses and magenta swans, and found myself staring at dolefully dramatic representations of *The Fallen Idol*, *The Doctor*, or *The Sentence of Death*. Particularly *The Sentence of Death* ... It was a favourite guest-room splasher among my relatives; and when, during my nursing-home period, I heard that a distinguished gynaecologist had served – somewhat unsuitably perhaps – as the model for the specialist passing sentence of death upon a middle-aged gentleman (surely it should have been his wife?), I became so excited that, when pouring out water in which he was to wash his egregious fingers, I nearly scalded them to the bone out of sheer reverence.

Still, it was a pretty dismal picture, not because the incident itself was tragic so much, as because it was conceived tragically. Actually, for a number of people, the experience which the middle-aged gentleman found so devastating may be far more like a sentence of life than a sentence of death. For very few men and women over 30 have learned how to preserve their sense of ecstasy. They hardly know that life is good until they are specifically warned that it is fleeting. They hardly see the sun unless they fear to look upon it for the last time. That perhaps is why nearly all our literature of joy in physical life has been written by invalids such as Keats and D.H. Lawrence. In any case there is something intensely dramatic and stimulating in the moment when the unfamiliar specialist, in his frock-coat, hums and haws at the solemn mahogany desk, and says, 'Well, perhaps it's not so much a question of getting better, as of adjusting. If we can help you to adjust ... Of course, I don't say it isn't possible ... ahem, ahem ... '

One young woman of my acquaintance was so highly stimulated by an interview in which a specialist told her – erroneously – that she was unlikely to recover from the disease afflicting her, that she went straight from his consulting-rooms to telephone to an unknown hero of her youth, inviting herself to tea. She was a shy creature, and nothing but the prospect of her imminent demise could have stirred her to such audacity. Afterwards she explained that she would have considered it a definite stain upon her courage had she let herself die without having met him. It happened that he was in; he came to the telephone; he knew her name slightly. Surprised but benevolent, he invited her to tea. They sat and talked tête-à-tête for two hours. He lived up completely to her notion of him, and she had never enjoyed herself more in her life. After that, it was a mere anticlimax to be told a week later that the first diagnosis was wrong and that she might live to a good old age. 'But the point is that if I hadn't thought I might fall dead tomorrow,' she said, 'I should never have had my tea-party.'

The hymns that warn us of *days and moments swiftly flying* or tell us that *brief life is here our portion* do their best; but they can never match the authentic thrill of the specialist's voice when it singles out, not the whole human race as doomed to mortality, but the small exclusive intimate unit who is you or me. Then, and then alone, all lovely things become lovelier, since we may lose them, and all intolerable things more tolerable, since we may be doing them for the last time.

So select, if possible, an illness severe enough to heighten the tension of existence, and to lend dignity to your tentative efforts to keep alive, remembering also that a spice of danger increases your importance in the eyes of the healthy. You cannot possibly be ill without being a nuisance to somebody, and friends and relatives are more likely to bear that nuisance with generosity if moved by the prospect of losing you altogether. They will cut the toast thinner and take the skin off the hot milk more readily if feeling that next year, perhaps, you will not be there to worry them.

But with the maximum of danger must go the minimum of pain. Occasional pain is not completely undesirable. There is something almost satisfactory about a strenuous animal anguish which is short as well as sharp, and the peace which comes when it has passed is notably inimitable. But long, nagging, haunting pain, that wakes you up in the darkness night after night, pain that alienates you from the normal world of the healthy, has inadequate compensations, and is to be avoided.

Now, having chosen your illness, the next thing is to accept it. Do not be resigned. That is a poor, weak, whining attitude beside the sturdy vigour of acceptance. And to worry is futile. 'I'm ill', you say to yourself. 'I'm going to be ill for several months. That means I shan't be able to earn any money. I shan't be able to pay the instalments on the dining-room furniture. I shan't be able to meet the doctor's bill. I shan't be able to look after the children. Oh! Oh! Oh!' And if these reflections lead you to fight your illness, to chafe against it, and refuse the beef tea the doctor ordered, there's going to be trouble. You won't enjoy yourself, and your husband (father, wife, mother, friends or family in general) won't enjoy it. And ten to one you'll get worse rather than better, and all the catastrophes that you foresee will come to pass.

No. The thing to tell yourself is, 'If I'm ill, I'm ill. And either I shall die or I shall get better, or I shall remain an invalid for life. If I can't earn money we must live on our capital; and if we have no capital, we must live on our relatives, or the State. The dining-room furniture must go – in a plain or fancy van, as the case may be – and good riddance. What are kitchen tables for, anyway? The doctor will have to sing for his supper, and, as for the children, well, where's Aunt Lottie? Where's Cousin Mary? What are aunts and cousins for, anyway? If I were dead, they'd have to manage without me.' And they would too. It is tiresome and a little humiliating to find how dispensable we all are.

So there you are – ill, and resigned to it. Wherever possible I should suggest that the next wise step is to get away from home. Go and be nursed where people are paid to look after you, and have proper off-duty times, so that you will not constantly be torn between your desires and your conscience. At home, where all attendance is gratis and amateur, you may, if you are that kind of person, lie for hours with a cold hot-water bottle like a dead fish rather than ask someone to boil a kettle. The kinder you are by nature, the more inclined to 'put up with things' and 'make do' rather than 'give trouble', the more important it is to go away.

But if you cannot, if circumstances are such that neither

hospital, nursing-home nor infirmary can hold you, you must be very clever. Be grateful. Stifle the invalid's natural irritation, and forget that the arrowroot was too thick, and the mattress badly turned. Remember that at the best you are a nuisance, that everyone has to pay for service somehow, and that, in spite of all that has been said in their dispraise, fair words are current coin in a sick-room. Tell your sister that she looks pretty as well as capable in her white apron – even if she doesn't. Tell your mother that the milk-tea was delicious – even if you loathed it. The Lord loveth a cheerful liar, and gratitude is the surest bait for further favours.

Next, cultivate the vanities. Illnesses which spoil the looks are to be avoided. When they have, by negligence on your part, come upon you, by all means forget yourself and your appearance. But in most cases, a little titivation is a pleasantly painless indoor sport for invalids. One friend of mine, recovering from childbirth, too worn and exhausted to read, to knit, to talk much, filled in the intervals between sleeping, eating, and feeding her baby, by learning the art of manicure and making up her face. During her busy life she had never before had time to do this. She emerged from her sick-room with vivid cherry-coloured nails, bright lips to match, and the most amazing eyebrows. Opinions varied about the aesthetic effect of her experiments, but the process had amused her; it cost very little; and her husband disliked it far less than he pretended.

This vanity business not merely provides an agreeable occupation for invalids, it enhances self-respect. I do not know why one should feel more like approaching the tedia of convalescence if one's finger nails have ben enamelled coral – but so it is. The occupational side, however, is important. 'Bed is so boring', many people say. I protest.

In many illnesses the invalid literally has not a minute to himself. There are bed-baths; there are dressings, feedings, massage, injections, wash-outs, little naps, doctors, visitors – and the day is done again. In others, there are quite long periods to be filled in somehow. Now the important thing about leisure is to remember that it is not an ordeal, but a luxury. How many hours in ordinary days dare you lie dreaming? Dreaming of what?

Tastes differ, of course. Some compose laws for ideal republics; some trim non-existent hats; some create perfect lovers; others design petrol-engines. The point is, that there, open and exquisite, lies the whole world of fantasy before you, easy, accessible, and entrance free. For some invalids, reading is possible. For some, knitting. For some wool-work, and for some conversation. Personally I am addicted to Patience (the card kind, I mean). But the important rule is to ration the day's pleasures, to save them up – always to withhold something as a special treat, to establish a kind of gambling discipline – that you won't play another game of *Miss Milligan* until the doctor has been, or eat another grape until after the last dose of medicine. This is not childish. It is a rule based upon long experience – on the old, hedonistic motive for asceticism.

Then there are visitors. The important rule for dealing with visitors is to impress them sufficiently with the severity of your illness without appearing to complain. What you want from them, presumably, is sympathy, flowers, grapes, magnums of champagne, and magazines. What they want from you are feelings of gratified and pleasurable sociability. It has always been considered a work of mercy to visit the sick – however charming and conveniently situated the sick may be. Invalids therefore should play the game. Even if their visitors drink tea at their expense, eat the grapes Uncle Arthur sent them, pour out their troubles in too-vulnerable ears, and otherwise enjoy themselves very much, the invalids must show becoming gratitude for an act of noble charity.

For, after all, illnesses would be very dull without visitors; and the nice ones give us pleasure, while the troublesome ones make us feel superior, so we have it both ways.

As for convalescence – the proper technique is delicate and difficult, but well worth the trouble of achievement. You must steer between the Scylla of making too many demands upon your friends, and the Charybdis of making too few. Remember that convalescence brings certain disadvantages. You may not bathe, nor play tennis, nor ride a motorcycle. You will be unwise to visit Aldershot Tattoo or fly to India. You should not – though Winston Churchill once did it – stand for parliament with an unhealed appendix wound. (He didn't get in, anyway.) But on the other hand, you can claim privileges. You can go to bed early. You can breakfast in your room. You need not travel to the seaside with the children, but can go in lordly isolation, first class if possible, leaving someone else to cope with Bobby when he is sick – as usual – in the carriage. The sound rule here is to see that the privileges outweight the deprivations. For every joy forbidden by the doctor, invent a harmless legitimate indulgence, even if it is only sucking bulls'-eyes. Offer to perform duties which you know that your friends and relatives would never dream of allowing you to do. You will acquire a reputation for generosity with only the smallest risk of inconvenience to yourself. Do not discuss your symptoms with your family, who will by this time be bored by them; but find a nice plump landlady, a greengrocer's wife, or some other sympathetic soul to whom symptoms are a hobby, and pour out the whole tale to her enraptured ears, being prepared in return to receive even more intimate confidences about bad legs and wind. Many a tray has been carried up to the third-floor-back of a seaside lodgings without a murmur, in exchange for a good gossip about kidneys.

As for diagnosis, treatment, and the more scientific side of illness, the safest line is to choose your illness and stick to it – firmly. This is harder than the unsophisticated might imagine. Symptoms are easy. One can feel one's own pains. Temperatures can be taken, blood pressures measured, hearts cardiographed, insides X-rayed. But diagnoses are different. Do not think that absence of all medical knowledge debars acquaintances from diagnosis or from prescription. I began to keep a list once of the illnesses from which my friends told me I was suffering, but when I had covered one foolscap page and half the side of another, I grew tired and gave it up. Friends can be divided into the pro-doctor and anti-doctor types. The former are the more numerous, the latter the more vociferous. Friends who would have you live upon one orange a day; friends who would send you to one German spa and one alone; friends who would have you given a water cure – among them all, it is not hard to lose your head. But be firm. Be polite. And above all, be calm. Remember that this is your illness, and that you have got a right to your own treatment of it. In this world, probably no régime is perfect. But better an erroneous pill than thirty different plasters. Fortunately, we can only die once.

Of course, I could suggest detailed courses of technique for special cases: how to be the most popular patient in a nursing-home; how to be happy in hospital; how to convalesce calmly, and so on. But these may be worked out by intelligent invalids along the broad lines that I have already suggested. The great general rule is to choose your illness wisely, to accept it enthusiastically, and to enjoy it as heartily as your nature will permit.

Good Housekeeping, June 1933

﹏

TABOOS AND TOLERATION

It appears that the most generous-minded and liberal people set limits to their toleration. And these limits seem often very odd. They are always cropping up in most unexpected places. The most inflexible barriers are erected for the least discernible reasons. The other day, for instance, we were looking from the high indented coast of southern Pembrokeshire across the blue bay to Caldy Island. Facing us on the long green shore lay the white Cistercian monastery, a shining focus to that pale and cloudy land lit by the western sun. I commented casually on its peaceful loveliness. It seemed to me then that it might be a good life – that lived within the rigid formal discipline of a religious order. I know how in periods of illness or of other compulsory restriction of all activity, small changes, small beauties, small pleasures, the sun on one's bare hand, a flowering bush, the rough and variable taste of bread – assume immense importance. All sensations acquire a poignancy and significance lost in the huddled complexity of ordinary life. The ordered ritual of religious services, the marshalled processions of the seasons, day and night, winter and summer, enter into experience with a startling clarity of impact. I have even read of the same thing happening to men and women in prison. I entirely believe the statement published by Gandhi last week, that in his days of voluntary silence he achieves a new sense of the significance of speech and a recognizable refreshment of his spirit.

But I imagine that the real value of such retreats from the huge complications of the everyday world are of chief value when they are temporary, when they serve as a time of respite and withdrawal before further efforts. I was not prepared, however, for my rather desultory admiration to be followed by an outburst of indignation from a man in our party. How could I take pleasure in evil things? These monks lured young men, if they had any money especially, into a living death, where they were shut away, imprisoned among neurotic, superstitious, lying, intriguing brethren, until they rotted from morbid introspection and from the futility of a wasted life. The fury of generations of reformers burned in his voice. 'I'm all for freedom', he concluded. 'I don't like State interference. But I'd have every religious order suppressed by law. They shouldn't be allowed.'

Well, well, I thought. Here it is again – that curious, almost chemical disturbance which arises in people when certain subjects are mentioned. Shakespeare knew it. He knew that the incompatibility was something irrational and therefore not amenable to argument, like the physical effect upon some men when they hear bagpipes played. (The quotation, though superbly apt, is too Elizabethan to be given in these pages.) It may arise at the sight of certain kinds of living creatures. I knew a perfectly wholesome, sane, gay and healthy woman, one of the most even-tempered and nerveless whom I have ever met, and she was thrown into a frenzy at the approach of a cat. Frogs, snakes and indeed all reptiles horrify others. A Russian man, of unusual physical courage and unemotional temperament whom I used to know, became almost hysterical if a moth flew into the room. That terror might have been due to an old Russian legend that moths are inhabited by uneasy souls of the dead; but his little daughter, born in England and of an English mother, who never saw her father, and never had heard the legend, inherited precisely this abnormal loathing. Does that throw any light upon the vexed question of the inheritance of acquired characteristics? Does it also throw some light on our sense of racial taboos? The horror which some entirely unprejudiced white men feel at the touch of a

Negro, the distrust of certain liberal-minded Aryans for Jews?

But the revolt comes not only against creatures of alien birth and ancestry. It comes against colours, sounds, habits, and ways of life. The widespread and often inconvenient fear of blood, which makes strong and normally courageous men faint in an operating theatre or at the sight of a street accident; the deep, fierce instinct which fills others with disgust at any sexual behaviour incompatible with a code which they think natural and proper; the sweeping condemnation of an Ulsterman for all Irish Catholics; the superstition of a countryman for a breach of some local law of superstition – peacocks' feathers brought into the house, the wrong number of magpies seen flying together, thirteen guests sitting down to table – are these types of repugnance all really akin, caused by something beyond the watchful but still singularly fallible and fragmentary control of our intelligence? Or can we train ourselves to regard rationally our instinctive recoils and learn to control disgust? How far is it our business to observe with less affection our darling whims of repugnance? I admit that the older I grow, the wilder rise my own ridiculous antipathies. This dislike of the contemplative life, for instance, which, combined with a distrust for papacy and the Roman Catholic Church, so distressed my friend when he looked at Caldy Island, is that also an irradicable antagonism for the Protestant?

It is certainly true that every form of asceticism and every form of withdrawal have at all times in the world's history aroused violent opposition among those who do not share the faiths on which they are founded. I think that this arises partly from fear of the obvious powers of mysticism. At different times and in different places *l'homme moyen sensuel* has watched the Brahmin ascetic wrapped in silent contemplation, protected from pain by a self-developed anaesthesia, enduring, with apparent felicity, tortures unbearable to those who have not also undergone his rigorous preparation. He has watched Christian mystics like St Theresa exercising an administrative capacity entirely incredible in a woman of her physical fragility had she not also been sustained by some faculty which she described as union with God, and which is, to uninitiated onlookers, arrogant and dangerous nonsense. He has seen the strength of the influence exercised by a

St Francis of Assisi, by a John of the Cross, or, in later times, by such men as George Fox and the Quaker saints, who undoubtedly acquired, in positive action as well as in private withdrawal, powers which are a source of envy as well as wonder. He may hear of the ecstasy experienced in the climax of unity by philosophical mystics, from Plotinus to Blake, and may turn away revolted by a mumbo-jumbo, which is all that he can see. And he is afraid – as men were afraid of witches; as, during the French Revolution, the peasants still feared the abbeys that they stormed; he hates what he fears; and he justifies his hatred by assurance of evil. These are short cuts to glory, presumptuous and wicked, allied with all superstition, self-deception, morbidity, spiritual arrogance and folly, he can tell himself. 'Thou shalt not suffer a witch to live', becomes a virtuous interpretation of the rational will. A lurking horror of occultism, a shuddering recoil from the forbidden thing, a repudiation of that criminal descent into the infernal regions of tormented imagination which indeed do exist for those who dare to enter them – these have shaken even the most friendly men out of their usual tolerance. There is reason in their fear. The responsibility for faith is no light one. The warning given by William Kingdon Clifford in his *Ethics of Belief* is based upon no queasy over-scrupulousness.

No one man's belief is in any case a private matter which concerns himself alone. Our lives are guided by that general conception of the course of things which has been created by society for social purposes. Our words, our phrases, our forms and processes and modes of thought are one common property, fashioned and perfected from age to age, an heirloom which every succeeding generation inherits ... Into this, for good or evil, is woven every belief of every man who has speech with his fellows. An awful privilege, an awful responsibility, that we should help to create the world in which posterity will live ... The danger to society is not merely that it should believe wrong things, though that is great enough, but that it should become credulous and lose the habit of testing things and inquiring into them; for then it must sink back into savagery.

There is this entirely respectable dread of falsehood and credulity then, of mankind being led up the garden by faked hopes of happiness or power, which adds authority to the fear of mysticism, and which entered into my friend's outburst against the

Cistercian Abbey on Caldy Island. The argument runs that the contemplative life is either nothing at all – an escape from responsibility into a lethargy, an idle uselessness; in which case to enter a monastery argues either cowardice or silliness; or else there is some power in it – a dark, evil occultism allied with the extravagances of perverse asceticism, and the morbid imaginations of the mentally deranged. In either case, acceptance is complicity in an evil conspiracy to defraud future generations. It is a perfectly sound argument so far as it goes, if all its premises are correct. But are they? During the heyday of nineteenth-century materialism we might have accepted the wholesale condemnation of a life whose whole social action consists in prayer, meditation and use of the powers of the spirit. If indeed thought had no communicable effect, those hours of silent ardour and agony were wasted. The passionate prayers of a Saint Augustine or a Saint Catherine of Siena were, together with the meditations of a Brahmin, or the whirring rattle of a Tibetan monk, a sowing of the wind – futile, ignoble, null. But our more modern psychologists, like our more modern physicists, grow sceptical of our old scepticisms. Year by year they strip us of our assurances. A straight line is no longer the shortest distance between two points; the infiniteness or finitude of the universe remains an unanswered question; the powers of the absent mind, telepathy, foresight, hypnotism and will-transference, though still slightly shadowed and disreputable, are no longer dogmatically denied. Clearly we are still treading clumsily along the frontiers of an unexplored country; its hinterland is lost in mystery; maybe there is very little to be found there. But we should be fools to deny that there is anything. There, indeed, may lie the next great field for human activity, even if its exploration remains a wholly secular adventure. Is there anything really impossible in the idea that some day, trained and gifted psychologists may found, as one of our most valued forms of human activity, colleges of mystics to practise those spiritual exercises, at present discredited and ridiculed, of thought-transference, telepathy, silent meditation, and the other deliberate experiences of the contemplative life?

It is not easy to adjust our inhibitions and taboos to new conceptions of mental activity. We are as shy today about our spirits as our parents were about their bodies, and, having been taught to distrust so many exercises as tampering with the supernatural, it will be an embarrassing shock to us if we discover that, after all, they were perfectly natural, and have no more than television or X-rays to do with superstition or black magic. But the human mind is constantly having to learn new terms for sacrilege and reverence. All long-established customs set up taboos which are only broken with pain and discomfort. The other day a young man, singularly broadminded and generous in most ways, heard of the forthcoming match at the Oval between the women's cricket team that had toured Australia, and a women's team representing the rest of England. Asked what he thought of women playing at the Oval he replied: 'I think it's sacrilege'. So have men thought of dramas played inside cathedrals, of posters stuck up on antique monuments, of Epstein's statuary in any public place, of gramophones played in punts on the upper reaches of the Thames.

The commonplace of today is the sacrilege of yesterday, and we can never grow wholly immune from shocks to our sense of decency; but some knowledge of history may preserve our sense of perspective and fortify us to endure even such sights as a Governor-General drawn from the working classes or a scientist instructing us how to communicate with each other by conscious and deliberate telepathy. Now that Soviet Moscow has sung *God Save the King*, we may even see the Court at St James's Palace sing *The Internationale* without fainting. It is because of this utility of the 'long view' that I regret the passing of landmarks which enable us to realize the transience of our superficial values. For instance, I bemoan the decadence of the real music-hall song and pierrot joke which, however ephemeral, did supply us with a quite unselfconscious index to social values. The modern music-hall with its reiterated rattle of tap dancing, its moaning jazz and its 'hot' tunes galloped to unintelligible words, may stimulate our glands and quicken our heart-beats. I personally have no grudge against it, and enjoy the austere disciplined limbs of well-trained chorus girls moving with automatic precision. But it strikes me as wholly uninformative, whereas the former type of music-hall song, joke and sketch was a rich mine of social values.

Today, only among the more obscure troups of seaside pierrots can we hear the old mellow jokes about mothers-in-law and food and unpleasant smells, songs like Ernie Mayne's 'I can't do the bally bottom button up', jokes like 'Take your feet off the table, Father, and give the cheese a chance', choruses of ripe sociological wisdom such as:

Who goes down the coal mine and brings up the coal?
Who stands in the queue and who brings home the dole?
When the Doctor says 'Twins'
And the nurse, 'Bless my soul' –
Who stands in the hall, gets no credit it all?
 It's a man, every time, it's a man!

The suffragette movement, the Irish independence movement, the divorce reform bills, the war, the slump, unemployment insurance, liquor licensing laws, all the other phenomena of an age are mirrored in such songs. I remember once while studying for the Honours School of Modern History at Oxford I was asked by my tutor to write an essay on 'the social and political movements of the fourteenth century illustrated by its popular songs', and found most illuminating matter in jests about the evil French (with whom we were then at war), the Scots, the Lollards, the extravagant courts, the exacting churchmen, the high taxes. We sang then, it appears, in three languages, all garbled: English, French and Latin. We sang in solo and chorus:

'Tax has tenet us alle
 probat hoc mors tot validorum,
The kyng thereof hade smalle
 fuit in manibus cupidorum,
Hit had harde hansalle,
 dans causam fine dolorum,
Revraunce nede must falle
 propter peccata malorum.

Too political? Well, did you never hear of those government departments, Dilly and Dally, in wartime revues? Did you never hear Gwen Farrar sing the additional verses to 'It ain't gonna rain no more, no more?' As for the two languages, do we not today sing with extraordinary erudition songs in complex American dialect?

Time and Tide ('Notes on the Way'), 18 May 1935

Vera Brittain

A WRITER'S LIFE

Are writers born or made? This question is often asked, and the answer, I think, is that both alternatives are true for different people. An inclination to write shows itself very early in a few fortunate individuals, who are never in doubt what their work in life is to be. Others find themselves impelled to describe some moving period or experience, in terms of which they discover their own talent. For example, it seems probable that the First World War events which caused R.C. Sherriff to produce his famous play, *Journey's End*, were the origin of his subsequent distinguished career. Similarly, it appears to have been Alan Paton's work for the oppressed Negroes of South Africa which inspired him to write his great novel, *Cry, the Beloved Country*.

I was one of the lucky ones for whom an overwhelming impulse towards authorship began in childhood. As soon as I could hold a pen I started to write, and before that I told stories to my brother. I had written five 'novels', illustrated with melodramatic drawings, before I was 11.

Later practice developed on school magazines and in competitions open to schoolgirls and students. My first real triumph came when an essay for a University Extension lecturer won a prize which enabled me to attend an Oxford Summer School. Such tiny successes should not be despised, for they establish the confidence without which no achievement is possible.

More significantly, an examination essay (on the well-worn theme that 'History is the biography of great men') later gained for me an Exhibition at Somerville College, Oxford. Here the weekly essays demanded of Arts students under the tutorial system provide an invaluable discipline. The student learns to say what he or she means lucidly and concisely, and the most determined acquire the art of making a scaffolding, or 'scheme', which eventually becomes the first step in constructing an article, lecture, or book.

I was fortunate again when after college I plunged into freelance journalism; many authors now high in their profession had to endure a longer period in the wilderness than mine. (Alas! it is not so easy to become established as a freelance writer today. Fees are higher but openings are fewer; much is now 'done in the office' for which editors used to look to outside contributors.) Early assignments which together produced a modest living came from the *Manchester Guardian*, the *Yorkshire Post*, *Time and Tide*, and the brilliant weekly review, the *Nation* (later incorporated in the *New Statesman*). I wrote regularly for the *Guardian* for eight years; only the flood of work which followed the publication of my autobiography *Testament of Youth* compelled me to abandon freelance articles.

Testament of Youth was not, as many people imagine, my first book; it was preceded by a small volume of verse, two novels, and two short social studies. Unashamedly I will here confess that I paid fifty pounds towards the publication of my first novel. Such a step is unorthodox, and the advice of literary societies is strongly against it. Nevertheless, I would counsel any young writer confident of the ultimate value of her work, and anxious to cut short the period of frustration, to do as I did if she can raise the cash. My first novel, *The Dark Tide*, brought me seventy-three reviews, including a long and favourable criticism in the *Times Literary Supplement*. This result put me 'on the map', and led to many more freelance articles. The general public may not have been aware of me, but editors and publishers were. Since then I have published twenty-three books. I am at work on a twenty-fourth and have two more planned.

Another question, harder to answer than the one with which I began, is a request to define the qualities most valuable to writers. I would myself put them in this order: (1) humility; (2) imagination; (3) observation; (4) persistence.

Humility involves a readiness to learn from mistakes, rejections and even abuse. The two first are frequent in the early stages; abuse comes later, after a writer is 'established', from those who dislike his or her 'image'. Humility also prevents an overestimate of one's powers and a change in one's behaviour to other people if fame comes. Such fame usually arrives by the grace of God. There has, of course, to be some ability, some achievement, but other writers equally gifted may fail to climb the pinnacle. Great success is nearly always due to a fortunate combination of external events with the chance direction of public taste at the time of publication.

Imagination is essential not only for such obvious needs as the invention of plots and the creation of character, but for the author's ability to achieve identification with the major characters in a biography or novel. Without real imagination, no writer will learn how the apparently trivial (such as the work of a local Council in Winifred Holtby's *South Riding*) can embody the universal.

Observation means a keen realization of the potential value of every experience, however small. A conversation overheard, a flowerbed, a shop-window, or a vivid sunset, all become material for the observant writer.

Persistence – the refusal to be defeated – seems to me even more important than talent. A librarian once showed me the large number of 'two-book authors' in his catalogue; some episode – perhaps a bad review or a time-absorbing event – had nipped the flower of their talent while it was still half-opened. In my own experience, a married woman writer requires persistence more than anything else, owing to the lethal handicap of constant interruptions. Concentration, essential for any intellectual achievement, resembles a ball of knitting wool; if some mischance interrupts the winding process, the job has to start all over again. Small children in particular involve maximum attention to household organization and the planning of one's day.

But organization has its limits even in the best-managed household, so coupled with it must be the self-discipline which enables work to be done whenever and wherever the time is available. There can be no dependence on sound-proof studies; no reliance on 'moods'. Any woman writer who is asked (as I often am): 'What time of day do you write your books?' will answer 'When I can.' Personally I like best the morning hours when my mind is clearest, but for most wives and mothers, mornings are cluttered with 'jobs'. When my children were very young, it was often the late evening before I could sit down to write.

A final frequent question: 'Is all this hard work really worthwhile?' To the dedicated writer, the reply is not difficult. What finally matters is not money or fame, though both are agreeable; not even self-expression, though Somerset Maugham called the writer 'the only free man' because he alone could release himself from his griefs and disappointments by putting them down on paper. Recompense comes from the power of ideas to change the state of the world and even help to eliminate its evils, as the works of Dickens, Tolstoy, Shaw and Wells (to mention only a few) have done, by giving their readers an awareness of what is really happening to mankind, and why. Contemporary writers have the important task of interpreting for their readers this present revolutionary and complex age which has no parallel in history.

Unquestionably writing, spiritually, mentally and physically, is one of the most demanding of occupations, and few authors wholly escape the failures and disappointments which, often unseen, accompany success. But most writers who can look back on a lifetime of rich experience would probably agree with me that few varieties of work are so abundantly rewarding.

Parents' Review, June 1961

✍

THE INFLUENCE OF OLIVE SCHREINER

In a summer garden just before the First World War, a schoolgirl sat engrossed in a recently published book borrowed from her headmistress. Suddenly, with an ecstasy still living in retrospect, she came upon a passage which showed her a world where women would no longer be the second-rate, unimportant creatures that they were then considered, but the equal and respected comrades of men.

Twenty years afterwards, the schoolgirl was to quote that passage in the opening chapter of a book called *Testament of Youth*:

We take all labour for our province!

From the judge's seat to the legislator's chair; from the statesman's closet to the merchant's office; from the chemist's laboratory to the astronomer's tower, there is no post or form of toil for which it is not our intention to attempt to fit ourselves; and there is no closed door we do not intend to force open; and there is no fruit in the garden of knowledge it is not our determination to eat.

This revolutionary paragraph came from Olive Schreiner's *Woman and Labour*, known to my generation as 'the Bible of the Woman's Movement'. To the girl-children of 1911, as to their mothers still struggling for the vote, the message of that book sounded as insistent and inspiring as a trumpet call summoning the faithful to an urgent crusade.

The faithful, of course, were still a minority and the woman who summoned them was a forerunner, her greatness hardly recognized and her personal life a tragedy of misunderstanding, poverty and frustration. In her final years the elderly, eccentric author who came for a short time to England and unpopularly supported the wartime conscientious objectors, created no stir of recognition as she passed through the London streets to some temporary lodging in a shabby boarding-house or third-rate hotel.

Yet today, a hundred years after her birth, Olive Schreiner is coming to be recognized as one of the most remarkable pioneers produced by the nineteenth century. In the eyes of many critics, she ranks as the greatest writer to emerge, up to date, from any Dominion except India. Her literary qualities were inseparable from her capacity for revolutionary thought on all the great issues which still move mankind.

Daring to deal directly with the problems of contemporary life, Olive Schreiner produced in *Woman and Labour* and its predecessor, *The Story of an African Farm*, two of the chief classics of feminism. Like Ibsen's play, *A Doll's House*, these books were milestones on the road to women's emancipation.

For Olive Schreiner the freedom and equality of women was less a political movement than the product of a totally new relationship between the sexes. In *The Story of an African Farm* she wrote of a time, now reached by many of today's young lovers who marry on a basis of shared financial obligations and domestic responsibilities, 'when love is no more bought or sold, when each woman's life is filled with earnest independent labour'.

'Then,' she continued, 'love will come to her, a strange sudden sweetness breaking in upon her earnest work; not sought for, but found.'

Olive Schreiner's influence upon her successors was not confined to the women's revolution. Progress, like peace, appeared to her as indivisible; she saw feminism, socialism, slave emancipation, and the liberation of subject races as fundamentally inseparable from the campaign against war.

In *Trooper Peter Halket of Mashonaland*, she expressed her passionate belief that the cause of women, workers and Negroes was the same. Only Gandhi, in the modern world, has similarly perceived the complex interaction of the different struggles for human freedom, and the fundamental identity of violence in war with the social violence which overwhelms all the victims of power.

Most of us, however, realize that our age, for all its catastrophes of war and death and despite its areas of obstinate reaction, has been a great epoch of material and spiritual liberation. The past half-century has seen freedom from economic fear come to the submerged millions in many countries; freedom from political subjection raise the status of women throughout the world; freedom from racial oppression bring hope to non-white peoples in many communities; freedom from foreign domination release great nations in the East to pursue their own ends.

These immense constructive revolutions have developed, in each case, from the insight of small dedicated minorities drawing their stimulus from one another. Upon them all, whether their members know it or not, the life and work of Olive Schreiner has exercised the vitalizing influence of an organic power.

National Council of Women News (S. Africa), February 1955

WHAT NURSING TAUGHT ME

During the First World War, which the crowded and violent age we live in has now caused to seem so remote, I spent four years as a VAD nurse in a variety of hospitals both at home and abroad. Of the six in which I served, four were military hospitals under the control of the War Office, and two were independent Civilian Hospitals, one in London and one in the provinces.

I am not sure whether military service can justifiably be described as 'national service' in a contemporary sense. But whether or not the two are comparable, I found the 'national service' of those days infinitely preferable to the four months spent under the auspices of voluntary civilian institutions, with their endless series of special traditions and nagging restrictions.

It seems strange that the uncongenial tasks reluctantly assumed so long ago in the name of patriotism should still have their value after thirty years. Such a consequence of 'active service' was certainly one that I never expected. As a student who had just gone up to Oxford with an Exhibition in English Literature, which was the more treasured because it had been worked for and won in the teeth of family opposition, I already cherished private ambitions of becoming a writer. Nursing was definitely the last form of occupation that I should ever have chosen. I had hardly been conscious that nurses existed until the outbreak of war gave them a new and important national status.

The duties assigned to a raw hospital recruit periodically filled me with a boredom and loathing so acute that I dreaded the coming of each new day. This unconstructive attitude persisted until my work took me overseas, first to the Mediterranean and then to the Western Front, and brought me the thrill of unknown lands and vivid new scenes to mitigate the day-by-day routine of cleaning, bed-making, dressings, and bowl-washing.

The young volunteer nurses of the First World War were actually more fortunate in the knowledge that they acquired than their successors of the Second. Even during the height of the 1940–41 air raids, casualties (at any rate in England) never came in so fast as the casualties caused by such great holocausts as the first Battle of the Somme in 1916, the Battle of Passchendaele in 1917, and the Battle of Amiens (the last great German offensive) in the spring of 1918.

Catastrophic as those casualties were from every other standpoint, they brought to the 'untrained' volunteers an experience of surgical nursing which seldom comes even to the trained civilian specialist. With a competence learned in the hard school of experience, the young VADs tackled fractures, haemorrhages, and the dressing of amputations on a scale which the insufficiency of trained Sisters made unavoidable. A young woman who comes on duty one morning, as I did in March, 1918, to find herself in sole charge of forty desperately wounded men of whom at least a quarter need emergency operations, tends ever afterwards to discount the fearsomeness of exacting but less nervewracking experiences.

The amount of foreign service available, with all its colour and informality, to volunteer nurses between 1914 and 1919 was also far greater than that which offered itself between 1939 and 1945. The speed with which the Nazis overran almost the whole Continent of Europe in 1940 reduced the areas of possible overseas service, and compelled most volunteers to serve in civilian hospitals temporarily adapted to the demands of Service ministries or Civil Defence.

It must have been about ten years after I was demobilized in 1919, that I first began to see my period of active hospital service as something more than a disastrous interruption to a promising literary career. In 1929 the process had barely begun by which my war experiences were eventually transformed into the substance of a book, widely read ever since its first appearance in 1933. But a decade after the war I did realize that those experiences were not misfortunes to be deplored, but spiritual lessons to be accepted with gratitude.

Because of them, I 'belonged' to my generation in a way that I could never have done if I had sat out the war in Oxford lecture-rooms. I was part of a fellowship of suffering whose members had learned in a hard school that human beings, whatever their national labels, possess an underlying unity which makes war the sin against the Holy Ghost, and the attainment of reconciliation our generation's reply to the age-long challenge of Calvary.

I had learnt other lessons too, less profound than this great spiritual truth, but more fundamental than the useful mastery of

317

invalid cooking, and the habit of always carrying smelling-salts, an iodine-pencil, and a bandage along with my lipstick and powder-compact in my handbag in case I should find myself on the scene of an accident some valuable minutes before the arrival of doctor or nurse. One of these lessons was the importance, in one's personal life as a prelude to the service of others in sickness or distress, of learning to conquer fear.

When I first went into hospital, I was not only a natural but an ignorant coward. The modern jargon of popular psychology – 'reaction', 'repression', 'anxiety neurosis', 'combat-fatigue', 'battle-hysteria' – had not then become the current coinage of speech which is sometimes more glib than intelligent. But I saw enough cases of what was then called 'shell-shock' to realize the intimate relationship between body and mind, and subsequently to understand the modern psychotherapists' insistence that more people are ill because they are miserable, than miserable because they are ill.

One dark winter evening when I was on night-duty in France, a patient had been brought into our medical ward who could neither move nor speak. Though the doctors could find no physical explanation for his condition, we were obliged to treat him as a case of total paralysis until he was sent down the line – to the care, let us hope, of some specialist better acquainted with the strange vagaries of the human mind than the army doctors at Etaples in 1917.

After that, the text-books could teach me little about the manifestations of conversion-hysteria, though I still had everything to learn about its causes. I acquired this knowledge gradually, my interest deepened by the tragic murder trial of an acquaintance who killed a much-loved wife during one of the periodic fits of amnesia which were the legacy of a bomb explosion on the Western front. By the time I had finished thinking out the implications of that story, I had come to see fear, whether it increases the shock of an individual accident or precipitates the national hysteria which leads to war, as among the mortal enemies of mankind.

I do not remember the exact moment at which I perceived that the mind which fear can anaesthetize and paralyse has within itself the power to discipline and finally eliminate that fear, setting itself free for a life as glorious and spiritually untrammelled as the lives of the saints. 'Always do what you are afraid to do', says an old French proverb. The impulse of a born coward to immunize herself from fear by obeying the proverb, to grasp the nettle danger and out of it pluck the flower safely, dates back to that case of pseudo-paralysis brought into an army hospital in France during a Christmas season over thirty years ago.

I hope, in conclusion, that those who organize our present National Hospital Service have mastered the distinction between essentials and non-essentials which put the overseas medical camps of the First World War into a category quite different from that of its home hospitals staffed by civilians. How often I saw the bright-eyed keenness and youthful readiness to endure, which meant life and hope to wounded men at the back of the front, dissipated in England by perpetual bullying about the details of a uniform which was anyhow out of date, and by a hidebound insistence· upon greater attention to brass sterilizers and metal bed-rails than to the welfare of the patients.

Discipline must exist, of course – but self-discipline voluntarily accepted is always better than discipline dictatorially imposed from above. Some regulations are necessary to the smooth running of a hospital service, but the imparting of confidence to the sick matters more than the number of buttons on a coat, and the conquest of fear in one patient alone has higher value than a hundred newly- polished sterilizers.

Above all other qualities in hospital comes the recognition of humanity – its oneness and its dignity – and the response to its needs. Nothing is harder to retain in the medical service than those human values, nothing easier to acquire than that bright immunity to pity which 'compensates' for horror and pain by a protective armour of callousness, and forgets that the most impaired patient is not merely a suffering body but potentially a triumphant spirit. The doctors and nurses who retain the consciousness of humanity at whatever personal cost will become the stars in the firmament of the National Health Service as surely as they were the lanterns of hope to the sick and wounded of two World Wars.

Chelsea Hospitals Quarterly, January 1950

THE SOMERVILLE SCHOOL OF NOVELISTS

I often wonder how much Somerville College, that famous centre for women's education which is shortly to celebrate the jubilee of its foundation at Oxford, enjoys the reputation of being a 'nursery for novelists'. That this popular reputation is justified even the most austere of dons could hardly deny, for in the eight years between 1915 and 1924 the College has produced as many writers of fiction. Two of them have been best-sellers in both England and the United States, while the names of the others are well known to circulating libraries and their readers. Apart from these young writers, Somerville was also responsible, some years before the war, for that poignant cynic and tragic humorist, Miss Rose Macaulay.

In spite of its high academic standards and difficult entrance examinations, which might well prove more attractive to the future university lecturer than to the potential author, Somerville's record of novelists is not really surprising. In the first place, it has always been what those of our parents who wished us to turn out perfect ladies, and therefore to go elsewhere, were accustomed to describe as 'very mixed'. Provided that she can compete successfully in the entrance examination, and particularly in two tests – the essay and the general paper – for which no amount of previous cramming can prepare, any and every girl who has passed her eighteenth birthday is entitled to become a member of the College.

Religion, again, matters not at all; from its foundation Somerville has been undenominational. On this account it was established as a separate institution from Lady Margaret Hall, with the result that, while the other Oxford women's colleges remained Anglican foundations, Somerville has harboured Catholics, Quakers, Jews, Wesleyans, Parsees, atheists and reformed Hindus. Nationality is unimportant; the well-known Indian lawyer, Miss Cornelia Sorabji, was an early student of the College, while the daughter of a famous German socialist was admitted shortly after the war, a long time before the wind of tolerance had blown the cobwebs of prejudice from the minds of the general public. Class is also a matter of indifference;

ex-elementary-school girls with long records of scholarships are welcomed as eagerly as the daughters of judges, peers and professors. Age presents no difficulties; the mature woman who has taught for years in second-rate schools with the determination to earn enough to pay for a university education, has as good a chance of admission as the callow, confident sixth-form girl whose only recommendation is her brilliant intellectual promise.

In such a community, with its large choice of companions and its wide range of ideas, the inquiring, unconventional mind of the creative writer finds ample opportunity for unrestricted development along its own lines.

At the time when my college days – two periods separated from one another by an interval of war service – first began, the youthful eccentricities of Rose Macaulay had already become a legend. No student was left who remembered her, while the discreet recollections of the older dons were confined to the Senior Common Room, but a college servant of many years' standing was very ready to regale our eager ears with tales of the Somerville celebrity.

No more in those days than in these, it seemed, was Miss Macaulay prepared to take even the most ordinary of human actions, such as getting up and going to bed, for granted. On a cold winter's night, we are told, she would write her weekly essay on the lawn with a lighted candle flickering beside her. At other times, her health in those days not being very robust, she would lie in bed for days together, attended by two or three devoted friends, interminably scribbling on loose sheets of paper, which she would leave lying about the floor or push into her dressing-table until the drawers refused to close. I am not prepared to vouchsafe for the naked truth of these fables. I only know that they led to a temporary outbreak of sleeping on lawns and of distributing manuscripts in disorderly fashion round bedrooms, in the mistaken but persistent belief, common to the young, that by imitating the eccentricities of the great, one somehow acquires their genius as well.

The second group of Somerville novelists – Muriel Jaeger, author of *The Question Mark*, Margaret Leigh, who wrote *The Passing of the Pengwerns*, and Dorothy L. Sayers, the writer of several detective novels – read for their finals during the war. I recollect them vaguely as dominant and important third-years upon whom an obscure and childish 'fresher' was expected to gaze respectfully from afar off. Dorothy Sayers at that time possessed a somewhat wild appearance, and a reputation for extreme peculiarity not altogether justified by occasional epic poems about Oxford and the habit of wearing a red-and-white checked teacloth as an apron. Both she and Muriel Jaeger belonged to an Olympian literary association suitably entitled MAS (Mutual Admiration Society). Another of its members was Elizabeth Murray, Professor Gilbert Murray's beautiful and gifted daughter, whose tragically premature death in 1922 cut short a most promising career.

The spacious days of 1919 to 1921 at Oxford must, I think, remain always vivid to those who were then undergraduates. The university was flooded with a host of war-worn, experienced, rebellious young men in arms against old traditions and restrictions, and insusceptible to discipline by the dons, many of whom knew less of the world than they. At Somerville a handful of us shared their situation as well as their sentiments, and our memories and adventures added vitality to the college's wartime experience of residence in Oriel whilst its own buildings were used as an army hospital.

My second year, 1919 to 1920, was Margaret Kennedy's last. It was the second also of Winifred Holtby, author of *Anderby Wold* and *The Land of Green Ginger*, as well as that of Hilda S. Reid, whose exquisite novel of the Commonwealth period, *Phillida*, was published last year. The three of us contributed, with more fervour than discretion, our opinions to the vivacious *Oxford Outlook*, founded from Balliol by Beverley Nichols and N.A. Beechman to express the spirit of post-war Oxford, and our emotions to the lyrical pages of *Oxford Poetry 1920*. Our last year, when the prospect of finals reduced us to temporary quiescence, was Sylvia Thompson's first.

Rumour has attributed to Margaret Kennedy the announcement to fellow-undergraduates that, after leaving Somerville, she intended to live in the country and write a great novel. Whether or no she thus stated her purpose, so many optimistic Somervillians have proclaimed the same intention that it is very naturally attributed to the writer who has succeeded where the majority fail. At any rate, if she did make it, I can guarantee that her confidence was received with the amused though tolerant scorn that a democratic community of young women metes out with cynical impartiality to ambitious talent and boastful inefficiency. Margaret Kennedy has added lustre throughout two continents to the name of her college, yet when I endeavour to recall her as a fellow-student I can remember only a rainy day, a thin figure clad in mackintosh, felt hat and green scarf, and the fleeting impression of a narrow face, with eyes brooding and stormily reserved. After acquiring a Second in History she disappeared from mind as well as from sight – to take the world by storm five years afterwards.

Of all my fiction-writing contemporaries, Hilda S. Reid was the only one whose peculiarities really resembled, by nature and not by imitation, the legendary habits of Rose Macaulay. Buried in the *Paston Letters* or the *Memoirs of Philippe de Comines*, she frequently forgot to eat her meals or to go to bed, and would doubtless have perished either of starvation or insomnia but for the capable and continuous solicitude of Winifred Holtby. An ex-WAAC forewoman back from France, President of the Somerville Debating Society, member of every college committee and an enthusiastic adherent of all three political parties, Winifred Holtby might well have passed for the female counterpart of Miss Macaulay's pleasant but too-impartial hero in *The Making of a Bigot*. Not unnaturally, she was regarded by Somerville as an unimaginative and efficient committee woman, yet the notes for her first novel, *Anderby Wold*, were already in her desk, and on long solitary walks she would dream for hours of the Yorkshire farmlands where she was brought up as a child. Sylvia Thompson's publishers made much capital out of the fact that she was only 23 when *The Hounds of Spring* was written; I have never understood why the Bodley Head did not give similar publicity to the creation of *Anderby Wold* at 22. It was in every way a profounder book than *The Hounds of Spring*, and, as the work of a young girl, far more remarkable.

Even in her first college year, Sylvia Thompson's popular success was easy for the most casual observer to predict. Her dark beauty and her flair for publicity made her the central figure of a picturesque if somewhat hectic Oxford generation, which was already beginning to revolt against the reflective seriousness of the post-war undergraduate. War-time shadows had vanished and their very memory was unfashionable. The fight for women's degrees had been won, and with victory had passed the need for ultra-staid and exemplary behaviour demanded by authorities fearful of losing the battle at the last fence. What more natural than to profit by these advantages? Unlike her contemporaries, too, Sylvia Thompson came to Somerville with a reputation already in the making. Critics, especially in America, have continually referred to *The Hounds of Spring* as her first book, but while still at school she had written a novel, *The Rough Crossing*, which Basil Blackwell published in 1921 and which received interested notices from several important journals such as *The Times Literary Supplement*.

The only Somerville novelist to take first-class honours was Dorothy Sayers, who gained them in French. Rose Macaulay went down with an Aegrotat (an honours degree without class given to capable students who are not well enough to take all the papers), and the majority of the others took seconds. The nearest to the rare distinction of a first in History was Winifred Holtby, who reached the stage of having her papers taken home by the several examiners. Destined myself for the dull disappointment of a 'safe second' in the same subject, I remember waiting in the chilly hall of the Examination Schools during her forty minutes' viva-voce, at the close of which she reappeared, and informed me with cheerful amusement that she had certainly gone down a class owing to a frivolous generalization about the private life of Henry VIII.

By far the best historical student of us all, Hilda Reid, who has taken seven years to write *Phillida*, succeeded in finishing only enough of her papers to achieve a fourth – another proof of the absurdity of the examination system as a test of rare quality. Sylvia Thompson, at all events, had no use for examinations; her first half-hearted attempt to pass History Previous was made in the year in which I went down, and I am not at all sure that she ever passed either that or anything else.

It certainly cannot matter to her now, any more than our class in 'Schools' has ever mattered to any of us. That is really why I wonder whether Somerville appreciates the popular reputations which so many of its ex-students are winning for themselves. It is the business of a college to instil reverence for university examinations, but it is the nature of the novelist to live in a world where they do not count at all. And it may well be that the future historian, true opponent as he is bound to be of the contrary results of much human effort, will draw attention to Somerville College, Oxford, not for the impressive list of its firsts, but for the remarkable records of its best-selling novelists.

Good Housekeeping, ?[April] 1929

∽

THE SEEING EYE

'Better a house unkept than a life unlived.' So, in a perspicacious sentence, Miss Rose Macaulay once wrote.

I agree with her dictum. Most emphatically I agree. I agree, perhaps, most thoroughly of all when I look round upon the tall, turreted, many-roomed, many-staired eighteenth-century mansions now falling, in London and elsewhere, beneath the builder's hammer to make room for skyscraper hotels and clean, straight, enormous blocks of labour-saving flats. How many generations of women spent narrow, restricted lives of perhaps seventy years in keeping, or seeing that others kept, those natural repositories of dust, with all their angles and corners and passages, tidy and clean? Yet now the houses themselves have become so much useless lumber; the domestic labours of years upon years have vanished into limbo. As for the women who performed them, nobody knows what they lived or worked for, and even their names are forgotten.

Having, like Miss Rose Macaulay, the modern woman's liking for things in their due proportion, I find these reflections very comforting. At all costs, I tell myself, I will not, and certainly need not, join that vast regiment of unremembered women who sacrificed the living of their lives to the keeping of their houses. I happen, it is true, to be married, and therefore burdened with the edifice of housekeeping and domesticity which is still piled, quite unnecessarily, by habit and custom upon the shoulders of every wife and mother. But by nature, by training, by inclination, I am a writer, not a housekeeper. As a professional woman and a bread-winner, it is, I reflect with satisfaction, no part of my duty to pursue the weekly washing from the clothes line to the airing cupboard, or to run my finger along the upper ledges of the shelves in the bathroom.

So far, so good. The theory is sound; if I lived up (or, as some might say, down) to it, I should, perhaps, live in a muddle, but I should be a happy, well-balanced woman, with a literary output at least half as much again as that of the present. My trouble is that I am one of those rare and unlucky monstrosities, a naturally tidy person, to whom the arts of neatness had never to be taught. At school I was one of those unhappy children whose lives are made a torment by being constantly held up as an example to their fellows. No mere sense of duty, but pure unadulterated instinct – inherited from two parents whose militant orderliness has impelled them to experiment one at a time with a vast army of domestic servants in one small flat – caused me to arrange my undergarments in small neat piles within my chest of drawers, and to distribute my exercise books, carefully dusted, in accordance with their sizes and colours beneath the flap of my immaculate form-room desk. Every class for which I was monitor got full marks for tidiness. Every dormitory of which I was head was regularly presented with its termly framed picture 'for neatness and good order'.

This was all quite bad enough, but I might have outlived it if it had not happened that, right on the top of my schooldays, came the war. Too young to have acquired professional qualifications, I became a VAD probationer. For nearly four years it was my patriotic duty to see that floors were swept, windows cleaned, lockers dusted, bowls and bottles polished to the utmost degree of perfection. This thorough and awful training added to my instinct for tidiness an eye as deliberately qualified as any eye could be to detect dust in all its manifestations. My power to 'see dirt' was rapidly developed to its horrible maximum. Over and over again since those years, in every flat, maisonette and house of which I have had charge, I have tried, without the slightest success, to lose this miserable capacity.

Like all naturally neat and therefore exceptional people, I am perpetually surrounded by the legions of the untidy. My husband, for instance, does not notice if the dust lies an inch thick upon his books. The friend who lives with us, though indubitably clean, has a naturally crooked eye. Every housemaid whom I engage imparts to the room that she has just 'done' the appearance of having been recently subjected to a rather devastating earthquake. Every nursemaid who looks after my children seems always to have on hand enough unironed washing to cover the day nursery and both the bathrooms. As for the children themselves, they are apt, like all normal children, to leave their clothes and their toys in every room they are permitted to enter and all over the garden.

And alas! it is all a torment to me. I cannot see a smeared mantelpiece without immediately going in search of some Vim and a rag, or glimpse a garment dropped on the bathroom floor without at once running to pick it up. There are days when only the strongest self-control and the constant repetition of Rose Macaulay's maxim prevent me from leaving the book that I am writing to seek for a duster with which to remove the grit from my papers, or abandoning the article that must be posted by midday in order to attack a clouded mirror with a cloth and some methylated spirit. In despair I am reduced to paraphrasing the cry of the Apostle: 'Who shall deliver me from the burden of this seeing eye?'

The wise books, written by educational specialists with high-sounding qualifications, tell us that we should start very early to inculcate habits of neatness in the young. There are, happily, quite a number of qualities that I should be glad for my son and daughter to inherit from their forbears. I should not object to their being professors like their father, or musicians like their grandfather, or even, if they themselves wished it, to their becoming writers like their mother. But because I want their lives to be as successful, as efficient, as useful and as well-proportioned as any man's or woman's can be, I pray daily that they may be preserved from my instinct for tidiness.

Manchester Guardian, 29 June 1931

327

WINIFRED HOLTBY: A FRIEND'S TRIBUTE

Ten years ago tomorrow Winifred Holtby, the author of *South Riding*, died. Only three months past her thirty-seventh birthday, she was a young victim of Bright's disease, which usually afflicts the elderly. For four years, struggling to finish her last and greatest book despite public demands, the claims of relatives, and almost continuous secret pain, she had managed by sheer willpower to win the race with death. Her obituary notices summed her up as a first-rate journalist, a competent novelist who wrote amusing books of secondary importance, and above all a beautiful personality, selfless, tolerant and humane.

Six months later, *South Riding* appeared, the first representative product of a swiftly maturing talent which might have made her one of the great figures in English letters. With its publication she joined the company of those whose literary reputation, small but secure, rests on the popularity of one famous book. Throughout the reading world this story, and the film based upon it, have come to symbolize that 'second line of defence' which local government puts up against sorrow, poverty, sickness, and other perpetual enemies of man.

In England the original edition of the book sold over 40,000 copies. It was the choice of the British Book Society in the month of its publication, March 1936. The following year Edinburgh University awarded it the annual James Tait Black Memorial Prize for the best novel of 1936. In America, though the theme was unfamiliar, nearly 20,000 copies were sold. Soon after its publication the book was issued in the Albatross Continental edition, and has already been translated into Dutch, Danish, Swedish and Czech. Spanish and French translations are now in preparation, and the story was recently selected as one of the 31 novels included in the 400 carefully chosen books forming the unit-libraries provided by the Army Education scheme.

South Riding has sent many of its readers to visit the churchyard at Rudston where Winifred lies. This village is exquisitely cupped in the surrounding wolds, but it has suffered changes characteristic of many places on our island during the war. In a short story 'Pavements at Anderby', Winifred described the finding of Roman pavements at Rudston. Of the fictitious farmer on whose land the pavements were found, she wrote: 'Beauty and security were his companions until one night when, hearing the first raiders of the Second World War zoom down the East Coast, he rushed out in frenzied anguish and fell under the chance-dropped-bomb that scattered the fine mosaic.'

This description was prophetic. In October, 1943, mistaking the mist-filled wold valley for the Humber, Nazi raiders dumped on the tiny village a load of high-explosives and incendiaries destined for Hull. The Norman church lost its roof and stained-glass windows; a farm close by was shattered; fires raged amid the unprotected houses and fields.

Desolate as the church and graveyard must inevitably appear until the War Damage Commission produces sufficient compensation to redeem the havoc, I do not think that Winifred would have regretted this symbolic participation of her mortal remains in the Second World War. Since 1939 many readers of her books have written saying how thankful I must be that she was spared the terrors of the last six years. But I am not thankful; and this not only for the sake of us, her friends, who in the past decade have realized that, in her own words, 'the dead are most needed, not when they are mourned, but in a world robbed of their stabilizing presence'. I know that she herself, always deeply tormented by what she called 'the horror of immunity', would never have desired to escape from the further instalment of suffering destined for her generation.

Had Winifred lived out her normal span, she would only just have entered her forties when the Second World War broke out. That the war and its needs would have claimed her active mind and responsive spirit I cannot doubt, though it is improbable that she would have joined in propagandist activities. Vehemently as she detested Fascism – a detestation expressed in her vigorous lampoons on Sir Oswald Mosley – her pre-war work for peace rested upon a deeply religious principle and for her consistency and integrity were synonymous.

She saw human beings as we must surely assume that their Maker sees them, in terms first of their essential humanity, and, only secondly as Germans, Japanese, Italians, Indians or Africans.

Hence, unhampered by family ties, she would certainly have been found where danger and suffering, whether of friend or enemy, challenged the strong and free. Perhaps she would have helped the humble in the air-raid shelters of London or Hull; perhaps have gone with the Quakers or the Red Cross to the Far East; perhaps, later, have joined UNRRA in its work of rebuilding the stricken places of the earth.

So I cannot say: 'From this she was spared', but rather: 'Of this she was deprived'. Yet in a deeper sense, she has continued to serve her generation. 'The life was the light of men', wrote St John the Evangelist of One greater than she; and this in a lesser degree is true of every saint and saviour, every standard-bearer of noble values who seeks to enshrine them in daily living. Winifred's courage in adversity, her victorious fight against death for the creation of *South Riding*, completed only a month before the end, have inspired many men and women, both young and older, called by wartime obligations to tread dangerous paths and perform exacting duties.

'So vividly ... has the personality of Winifred Holtby triumphed over the finer artist that a "consecrated egoism" might have produced in her', wrote the distinguished American who directs the work of UNRRA in China, after finding her life-story in the library of an airport where he was delayed by storms, 'that I hardly know whether to regret the spiritual conflict that continually divided her between "the claims of art and the demands of social justice", or to rejoice that she was ... "a typical product of her age", who neither could nor wanted to escape the impact of her age upon her.'

A member even in death of her day and generation, she now surely summons her contemporaries to lay aside the griefs of the war, and face with courage the hard and perilous, yet infinitely hopeful, years which lie ahead.

Yorkshire Post, 28 September 1945

*

THE SMALL HOURS AT THE ADELPHI CENTRE

'OOMPH!'

What was that? Some strange centaur of the night? A tramp snoring in the hedge, unconsciously revealing his alien presence to the solitary watcher in the midnight garden? Then I remember; the pigsty lies on the other side of the shrubs.

From this second fire-watching tour I return to the lighted office; to the reading of *Hamlet* and an article by Max Plowman on death. Gradually the silence of the house merges into an overture of sounds – the creaking of the stairs; the buzzing of flies in the hot kitchen; the subdued trumpeting of elderly slumbers in the dormitory above. An hour later, I go out quietly again through the back door. It is a warm, humid night; the moist smell of earth and the sweetness of the rose-garden pour into the stuffy, blackened passages like water cascading through a cavern.

At first, as indoors, everything seems to be silent. The old house, filled with aged and invalid evacuees bombed out from the East End of London, looms like a black castle against the paler darkness of the sky. The crescent moon has already set, but the stars twinkle blandly, a little blurred by a thin veil of mist. After a few vigilant moments, another faint chorus of sound eclipses the stillness. From the woods echoes the sibilant screech of an owl; the bushes drip-drip, with small methodical thuds; the autumn leaves crackle faintly as they fall on the gravel paths. Far away, in the invisible vault over the sea, sounds the bumping throb of a Nazi aeroplane; the raiders, temporarily too few to destroy English cities, are still active over East Anglia. But tonight the sirens and the guns are silent; no streak of flame, like a falling star above the horizon, marks the funeral pyre of another German boy who has blazed to his death.

At 5.30, the night clouds begin to mass and sink towards the horizon; a colourless light, gradually warming to pale orange, glimmers in the eastern sky. I remember, by contrast, the dawns that I saw while on night duty in 1917 at a Malta hospital; the swift death of the darkness, the sudden leaping of golden sunshine above the violet hills. That was our war, and so, again, is this. Will humanity never learn? The crowing of the cocks, like a sudden challenge to courage, reminds me that the capacity of man is infinite and his spirit immortal.

Essex Ploughshare, October 1941

CHRISTMAS AND FRIENDSHIP

At Christmas time we remember our friends. Every ancient tradition, every annual custom that we have observed from our babyhood upwards, is designed to bring them back to our recollection. Christmas cards, Christmas gifts, Christmas services, Christmas carols and the singing of 'Auld Lang Syne' – all these familiar things are symbols of our loyalty and pledges of our affection.

This year our acts of remembrance will inevitably bring us sadness as well as joy. So many amongst those friends of whose value Christmas reminds us are now far away, and even out of reach. Never, I suppose, in all the world's history, have there been so many broken homes and separated families as we see today. From end to end of Europe men and women – because they belong to conquered countries, despised races and classes, or groups holding minority opinions – are isolated from their friends in gaols and concentration camps.

In our own country, immune for so many centuries from the direct consequences of war, parents are parted from children evacuated to 'reception areas' or overseas; mothers, wives, sisters and sweethearts have lost the cherished companionship of young men now serving in the Army, Navy or Air Force; refugees, cut off from their families in enemy or occupied countries, make the best of dreary lodgings or the fathomless weariness of internment camps; Conscientious Objectors and detained 'suspects' languish in prison; young women are far from home in the Services, in factories, in hospitals or on the land. If those we love are amongst the ranks of the evacuees, the prisoners and internees, or the men and women of the Services, how shall we best keep in touch with them this Christmas time and in the months to come?

It is not an academic question for me. My son and daughter are at school in the United States; my mother, bombed out of her home, is far from London in a Devonshire town; many of my dearest friends are Americans whom I cannot hope to see until the end of the war. I know the ache of longing, the chill fear of forgetting or being forgotten, that loneliness sometimes brings. So let us, for a moment, consider the problem together, with all its difficulties. Let us face the fact that many of our friends are beyond the reach of letters, cut off by enemy occupation or by prison bars; that we can make contact with others only through mails subject to loss or to long delay; that some of us find self-expression difficult and letter-writing a burden. What shall we do to keep the memory of our friends alive in our hearts; to convey to them that we will be loyal and faithful till we meet them again?

In the last war, there was a favourite saying: 'Thoughts are things'. It arose, I suppose, from a dawning realization of telepathy, from the knowledge that it was indeed possible, by the exercise of will, to convey one's thoughts and wishes to another person across the limitations, once thought absolute, of time and space. The consciousness of this possibility gave special point to a sentence written by a boy to the girl whom he loved and from whom he was parted, in a favourite novel of my youth, Olive Schreiner's *The Story of an African Farm*: 'Sometimes such a sudden joy comes over me when I remember that somewhere in the world you are living and working'.

Again and again in my life, I have realized the possibility of conveying, by concentrations of will, that sense of joy and remembrance to someone from whom I have been parted. This 'telepathy' was especially keen between myself and my friend Winifred Holtby, the brilliant young writer who died in 1935. Often, in her letters, she would report a knowledge of my thoughts at a given moment, or answer my inquiries before she could possibly have received the letter which made them. So I ask you to believe that you can convey a sense of companionship to your friends by thinking of them often, by picturing them in your imagination so keenly that their unseen presence will be beside you as you walk alone in country lanes or through city streets.

But if you find this idea too fantastic, there are other, practical ways of keeping in touch. The very act of remembrance will bring back their tastes, their habits and their talents, and help you to write them letters or choose them gifts which will make you as vivid to them as they have become to you. A book which has moved you, or a book token with which to buy it, will convey to a friend the direction of your thoughts; so will a magazine which you read regularly and enjoy. Sometimes, perhaps, it will be possible to arrange a regular exchange of journals. Your comments scribbled down beside a story or article which has appealed to you will tell your friend that the writer has conveyed just what you yourself would like to have said. If your friend is a musician or an artist, the score of a symphony you have heard at a concert, or the reproduction, in one of those inexpensive prints obtainable at art galleries, of a picture that has held some special meaning for you, will convey the same message.

Sometimes, if you find it hard to be articulate or to think of subject-matter for your letters, it is useful to keep a diary beside you and write down small events which have particularly interested you. I suggested this to my son, aged 14, when he constantly wrote me that he had 'no news' and I knew that actually his life was so full that each occurrence jostled the last out of his mind. He took the hint, and his letters describing his American experiences have been fascinating ever since. If your friend is inaccessible by post, this diary of your days will help him to understand better your life during his absence.

If you have both been members of some Church which has counted for much in your friendship, you can often arrange to go to a similar service at the same hour of the same day, to listen to the same radio address or wireless programme, and then exchange impressions. Above all, if your friend is abroad, remember the part that international friendship will play in the world of the future, and try, in your imagination, to reconstruct the society in which he is living from the little that he may be able to tell you. At first, acts of friendship and the rendering of friendly services will alone mitigate the bitter aftermath of war. It is with this knowledge that such organizations as the Fellowship of Reconciliation and the International Voluntary Service for Peace are already training their younger members to play an active part in the work of post-war reconstruction. If the experiences of your absent companion can help you to take some share in this task of healing, the fostering of the friendship between you will contribute to that future peace to which, at Christmas, we dedicate ourselves anew.

Link (Christmas Supplement), December 1941

MY DEBT TO FRIENDS

The Society of Friends and its practical work first impinged on my consciousness between the World Wars. But it was not until 1933, when I published *Testament of Youth*, that I began to have much contact with Quakers.

Although I knew so little of the Society, it seemed to be Friends who best appreciated the lessons of experience which that book tried to convey; Friends who arranged meetings and invited me to speak. I remember especially a lunch-hour gathering in the small Friends Meeting House in Euston Road when even the galleries were crowded, and a moving Sunday evening at Leighton Park where I gave the short address.

After 1936, when I first met Canon H.R.L. Sheppard, I came to know the Society even better. At a large open-air rally near Dorchester, I shared a platform with Dick Sheppard, George Lansbury and Donald Soper under the Chairmanship of Laurence Housman, and was thereby converted from a political exponent of the League of Nations into a Christian pacifist. But though Dick, George Lansbury and I were all Anglicans, the Church of England was seldom responsible for the Peace Pledge Union gatherings at which we appeared. Again it was the Society of Friends which provided the meeting houses, the chairmen and much of the audience.

When war broke out for the second time, I found myself wholly at one with the Friends' Peace Testimony, and began to understand the real cost of bearing witness to an 'inner light'. During those years, apart from the constant endeavour to enshrine convictions in literary work, I found that three 'concerns' demanded a large share of my time. One was the denial of human sacredness by saturation bombing; another the British blockade, with its slow starvation of mothers and children on the Continent; and a third the Indian struggle for freedom.

Each of these preoccupations brought me into close association with a leading Friend. I was soon a member of Corder Catchpool's Bombing Restriction Committee, and through famine relief work met and corresponded with Dr Howard Kershner of the American Friends Service Committee. The Indian challenge won for me the friendship of Agatha Harrison, who by interceding with Mr Amery, then Secretary of State for India, did her best to enable me to accept two successive invitations to attend the All-India Women's Conference as a British delegate. Though she and I alike failed to overcome official obstruction, we both attended the World Pacifist Meeting in 1949–50 after India's liberation, and shared the hut at Sevagram once occupied by Kasturbai Gandhi.

During the war, Corder Catchpool suggested that I should consider becoming a Friend, and we discussed the possibility during a summer weekend which I spent with his family in Hampstead. But eventually I decided against joining the Society. Nevertheless I remained an Anglican somewhat reluctantly, since the Church of England so often seems to me to compromise on the very matters where a true Christian would make a stand.

Why did I remain outside the Society? Like all decisions based on intuition, it is difficult to explain. The problem was partly professional; the work-centred life of a writer so often seems *self*-centred because books have to be written in solitude, and I felt that this form of artistic egotism had little in common with the group-thinking which emerges from the meetings of Friends.

As a writer, too, I felt myself to be dedicated to the service of beauty, which for me is the quality closest to God. 'In the trinity of Truth, Beauty and Goodness,' wrote the late Dr L.P. Jacks, 'Beauty plays the part of the vitalizing element, the other two becoming skeletons when there is no beauty to clothe them in flesh and breathe upon them with the breath of life.'

Sometimes that 'vitalizing element' seemed to be absent from the work and deliberations of Friends. In India I discovered at the Tagore home in Santiniketan that Rabindranath Tagore had found the same lack in Gandhi, who never troubled to read his work and thought poetry irrelevant. In spite of the efforts of C.F. Andrews, the 'hyphen' who linked the two Indian leaders and gave Gandhi Tagore's poems to read on journeys, the Gandhian failure to appreciate beauty meant years of tension between poet and prophet.

But the Society of Friends is changing; the fear of beauty – as the Friends' Fellowship of the Arts testifies – is passing away. My final reason for detachment was perhaps an instinctive

336

consciousness of personal unsuitability. My background, I felt, was too worldly, my tastes too frivolous; it was too late to discard various minor indulgences without a crippling and frustrating measure of dislocation which would undermine my work. The very value that I set on some material attributes of living showed what an inappropriate Friend I should be.

So I remain the denominational hybrid that I once described as 'a Quaker-inclined Anglican married to a Catholic'. But the Society claims my permanent respect and affection; as in the abysmal hours of the war, it lights a beacon in every night. Its members offer an example of purposeful integrity which for truth-seekers both in and outside it is the best form of teaching.

Reynard, March 1956

✍

MEMORIAL QUEUE

On Christmas Day, 1950, King George VI made a broadcast in which he compared the post-war experiences of the British people with the struggle of Christian in *The Pilgrim's Progress*. A few months earlier I had published a biography of John Bunyan, and somewhat diffidently – for the Royal Family do not normally accept gifts from their subjects – I wrote to the King's secretary asking if His Majesty would care to receive a copy. The gracious courtesy of the response went far beyond my most hopeful expectations. His Majesty, I learned, had been 'much touched' by my offer, and after I had sent the book, his secretary wrote again.

'His Majesty wishes me to tell you how pleased he is to accept it, and to say how much he looks forward to reading it.'

The other day, when George VI died, that brief personal episode made me one of the many thousands who treasured some similar memory of the human interest taken by the king in his people and the humble instinctive courtesy by which he expressed it. Their collective memories explained the size and persistence of the immense queue which gathered over three days to pay homage during the King's lying-in-state, and became one of the sights of London.

When the coffin was first brought from Sandringham to Westminster Hall I was moved by a profound impulse, never before experienced in relation to royalty, to spend a moment beside the bier of the kindly, unpretentious man who had accepted my gift. No doubt one of my friends in Parliament or on the Privy Council would arrange for me to visit Westminster Hall when it was closed to the queue already beginning to wait in the piercing February wind. But then I thought: 'No. This is not a time for demanding privileges. If I go at all I will join the queue, share its self-imposed ordeal, and learn to appreciate his people's affection for a monarch who, in the inspired words of an American weekly, "made ordinariness shine".'

During the afternoon, a Westminster policeman told me that two hours were needed to wait in the queue and pass the coffin. I could spare so long only at night, so I returned to Westminster at 7.30 p.m. Although this was the first day of the lying-in-state, the queue already stretched from Westminster for over a mile past Lambeth Bridge along Millbank. Half way across Vauxhall Bridge, I joined the end of it. Behind me more men and women quickly lined up at the rate of two or three hundred every five minutes, though Britain was enduring one of its coldest spells and we had to stand almost motionless in 17 degrees of frost.

When we had only reached Lambeth Bridge, about half way to Westminster, after nearly three hours of slow-motion progress, I began to feel that I should never sustain a further similar period. Several others, defeated by cold feet and aching backs, came to the same conclusion, and at this point left the queue. But after we had crossed the wide bridge, outlined by green lamps shining like emeralds in the frosty darkness, our movement, though still a crawl, was more continuous, and I decided to go on. As we advanced, huddled together for warmth, the full moon, at first red and misty, climbed the sky above the Thames on our right, until it hung clear and bright as an arc-lamp suspended over our heads.

Those long-drawn hours abundantly showed the fortitude, persistence, good humour, and semi-articulate loyalty of the British people. In the queue waited both the old and the young; a couple close beside me had certainly passed 70, and in front of me a small boy and girl from different families indulged in a coy

338

flirtation. Aged about 7 and 8, they exchanged names and addresses, edging back to each other whenever a sudden movement parted them. The boy, lightly clad, mentioned casually that he felt cold, but hardly anybody complained, and no one ill-humouredly, about our slow progress, and no one pushed except when a surge forward of the crowd made pushing unavoidable. Like others, I became acutely conscious of the small, half-seen obstacles in our path; the steps up and down where the kerb began and ended; the trunks of trees growing at the pavement's edge; the stems of the roadside lamps; the municipal dustbins with sloping lids which momentarily provided a welcome rest.

Friendly policemen who assured us that we would get into the Hall though it officially closed at ten provided an encouraging diversion; about 11 p.m. one told me that he had been on duty in that exceptional frost since three in the afternoon. Press photographers with mounted cameras took floodlight pictures of the crowd, provoking cheers and jeers from their good-tempered victims. Towards midnight newspaper-sellers offered copies of the early morning papers, with pictures of ourselves and descriptions of the queue.

By the time my section of it reached the steps of Westminster Hall, Big Ben had chimed half an hour after midnight. White-gloved policemen beckoned us into rows of three and four instead of the single file of the morning. As I caught a glimpse of the distant catafalque beneath the magnificent Gothic roof of the great Hall, I realized that this memorable moment was worth the preceding five hours of endurance. As we drew nearer to the tall ceremonial candles at each corner of the bier, the queue relapsed into a reverent silence, broken only by its muffled footsteps. The flickering flames above the coffin caught the gleam of the jewels in the royal crown, orb, and sceptre. Beside them lay the Queen Mother's wreath of pure white flowers, conspicuous against the deep crimson and yellow of the flag draping the bier. Surrounding it, the Yeomen of the Guard, in their scarlet and gold uniforms, and the Grenadiers, bowed beneath their bearskins over their reversed rifles, stood so motionless that they seemed to be hewn out of wood. Wisps of smoke from the candles drifted over their heads and disappeared into the midnight shadows of the carven roof.

The five hours of waiting had ended in two minutes which no time would banish from the memories of those who had earned their experience. More than any previous occupant of the British throne, the simple devoted man to whom they were paying homage had deserved the tribute of that long cold vigil.

Hindu, 2 March 1952

ʂ

'CLOTHES FOR THE OLDER WOMAN'

As a member of the age-group which will shortly enter the category described in your article 'Clothes for the Older Woman' (Woman's Page, 21 November), I must protest against your contributor's depressing assumption that most of my near-contemporaries have 'rheumatic fingers' and 'bony elbows', need 'comfortable seats' when shopping, and cannot read ordinary notices without spectacles.

Your contributor points out that today a woman aged 60 has 'an average expectation of life of seventeen years', but apparently forgets that this increased expectation is due to prolonged vigour, better diet, more exercise, the conquest of disease, a total revolution in age-perspectives, and a healthy revolt against self-pampering and self-pity. Has she (or perhaps it is he) forgotten the women organizers, MPs, academics, travellers and lecturers working up to 70 and beyond, to say nothing of the vast army of elderly domestic 'helps' tackling heavy household tasks?

Presently (except in country villages or bitter weather) I am not in the least interested in long sleeves, 'sensible' shoes, and 'substantial' underwear, and do not expect to be for quite fifteen years. Dress designers and department stores, it is true, could do far more for the 'older woman', but not by treating her as a wilting invalid.

Letter to the Editor: The Times, 24 November 1955

TRAGIC WATERSHED

'Shooting at Sharpeville' by Ambrose Reeves (Gollancz)

'Since Monday, 21 March, 1960, the name of Sharpeville has become almost a household word around the world', writes the Bishop of Johannesburg in this very moving and courageous book. He adds later: 'History, I believe, will recognize that Sharpeville marked a watershed in South African affairs'.

His report on the Sharpeville shootings should be read by everyone who cares for freedom and justice and values our democratic tradition, for it tells us what happens when that priceless heritage is repudiated or lost.

During a visit to South Africa this summer, I found that every second person had a different opinion about the bishop's decision to return to England in May and to testify regarding the events which he now describes. Few questioned his physical courage, which was well attested by the record of frequent risks voluntarily run, but many doubted his wisdom. Now that I have read his book, I no longer feel any uncertainty that his decision was right. Had he remained in South Africa, his silence would have been the price of immunity from arrest or release from prison. By deporting him when he returned to his diocese last September, the South African Government revealed its fear of his witness. Perhaps the most responsible comment on the bishop's fate was published by the South African Institute of Race Relations in its magazine *Race Relations News* for September 1960:

The Institute views his deportation with concern and deep dismay. As no criminal proceedings have been taken against him it is clear that his deportation cannot be justified on the ground that he has committed any offence ... It is therefore reasonable to conclude that the Bishop was deported because of the forthright views he held and openly expressed on racial questions ... The deportation of the Bishop constitutes a dangerous precedent and represents an abuse of the great executive power which the Government has arrogated to itself.

Before embarking on his main story, the bishop supplies, in a chapter entitled 'Background to Sharpeville', an account of some comparable though less disastrous earlier disturbances. He describes the growth of unrest in the Bafurutse tribe in the western Transvaal, and the increasing tension between the Bapedi and Baptoni peoples of the eastern Transvaal who had lived peacefully as neighbours for seventy-five years. We read also of troubles at Windhoek in South-west Africa, now treated by the South African Government as a fifth province of the Union, instead of a territory previously under a League of Nations Mandate for which South Africa is accountable to the United Nations. The bishop also reports on the riots at Cato Manor outside Durban in June 1959 and February 1960, when nine policemen lost their lives. While he admits African responsibility for this calamitous though rare violence, there is no doubt in his mind where the real liability lies for these disturbances and the later tragedy.

'It must rest', he writes, 'upon those who have created the mass of repressive legislation under which the non-white peoples have to live.'

The bishop's book describes the one-man fight for an official inquiry into the events at Sharpeville which, with a few courageous helpers, he conducted against the Nazi-minded government of Dr Verwoerd. (Two of the lawyers who assisted him were subsequently 'detained' under the emergency regulations which followed the shootings.) We learn how he went to the Baragwanath Hospital outside Johannesburg with a senior lawyer on 22 March and discussed the condition of the casualties with leading members of the medical staff. (Some of those casualties were still there, under police guard, when my husband and I visited the hospital in late July.) Later he interviewed the wounded with his lawyer's help, arranged for attorneys to visit them and for a qualified pathologist to attend the post-mortems on the dead, and finally initiated, with the support of the Consultative Committee of fourteen organizations of which he was chairman, the judicial inquiry that eventually took place.

Many official attempts to frustrate him are also described; they included a preliminary refusal to see him by the deputy commissioner of police who finally gave him a grudging two minutes, and an endeavour to exclude him from the Baragwanath

Hospital. His book, I read in the Johannesburg press, is to be banned in South Africa. It would be interesting to know how he or his publishers obtained the grateful foreword from Chief Luthuli, leader of the African National Congress, for at the end of July the chief was still in Pretoria jail, and my husband and I succeeded in getting a closely-guarded ten minutes' talk with him only after a personal visit to the security police.

Throughout this book, the bishop's statements maintain the quiet and impressive moderation of a detached report. Not once does he mention his own deportation, or the constant threats to his life and welfare (over years, not weeks) which preceded his first departure for England. His publishers, who uncharacteristically leave blank the back and sides of the book's yellow dust-cover, show a similar restraint. The bishop also pays tribute to many white people in Johannesburg and neighbouring towns who supplied food, money and clothing to the victims of the outrage, and to the white women who at short notice drove the grief-stricken relatives of the dead from Sharpeville through police cordons to the magistrate's court in Johannesburg to make their application for the qualified pathologist to attend the post-mortems.

There are no fireworks in this book, no shrill emotions. It is the emotions of the reader which will inevitably be stirred by the bishop's published collection of thirty photographs, and particularly by those which show the mutilated body of a dead African woman lying 150 yards from the fence round the police station which was officially alleged to have been attacked. These pictures prove that most Africans were shot in the back – i.e. as they ran away from the police attacks and not during an attack made by themselves. The Baragwanath Hospital staff subsequently confirmed that the casualties shot in the back amounted to 70% of the total. The reader's feelings are also likely to be aroused by the quiet, factual report of the Commission of Enquiry, and by the extracts in Appendix II from the evidence given before the commission by a number of humble and bewildered African witnesses.

In the chequered history of twentieth-century imperialism, there has been another watershed comparable to Sharpeville; this was the Amritsar tragedy of 13 April 1919, when Britain's General Dyer ordered his soldiers to fire on a helpless crowd of Indians in a public square known as Jallianwalla Bagh. It is surely Amritsar to which Sir Winston Churchill was referring in a 1920 House of Commons speech of which the bishop reminds us, when Sir Winston quoted the memorable words of Lord Macaulay: 'And then was seen what we believe to be the most frightful of all spectacles, the strength of civilization without its mercy.'

By a geographical accident the casualties at Amritsar (379 killed and over 1,000 wounded) were far higher than the Sharpeville casualties, for the square was surrounded by walls on three sides and the military occupied the only exit. The Sharpeville shootings took place in open country; the bishop's photographs show that most of the potential victims could get away, and did. But the Sharpeville pattern of behaviour was the same as the one at Amritsar and the shock to the world's complacency was even worse, for public opinion has grown up quite a little since 1919 in its ideas about the treatment of subject peoples by powerful governments.

Yet, strangely enough, we can look back to Amritsar from Sharpeville with a feeling of hope. The Indian people have never forgotten that tragedy but they have long forgiven it; confronting a different pattern of behaviour, they are now our friends. History today moves swiftly, and it may well be that many people now living will see a different pattern of behaviour come in South Africa, and witness forgiveness by the patient and kindly African people of the massacre of 21 March, 1960.

'Out of that evil event', concludes the bishop, 'good may yet come if those in South Africa turn from the bitterness of the past, believing that God has some better thing in store for all the peoples of their country than the way of apartheid, which has shown all too clearly that it is a way of death and not of life.'

John O'London's, 8 December 1960

∽

CASUALTY

The moment you enter a casualty department, you become the

living equivalent of a suitcase at an airport terminal travelling along a conveyor belt. If the process is interrupted, it has to start all over again. An injudicious visit to the lavatory during the two-hours' wait can mean that you lose your place in the queue for X-ray photographs. There is, however, infinite variety in your progress from the basement to the department of the all-powerful

who receive your 'pictures'.

oken and where, how long

must return for the next

mn cold.

are no priorities. No one

or a Fellow of the Royal

get no more attention than

njured foot with whom you

'ound floor' awaiting the

nd only a broken left arm

nyself to banish impatient

e at home, and concentrate

ng-room is a middle-aged

usly swollen bandaged leg,

t-blue hat jauntily perched

irl with steel crutches, in a

the clinic she follows a

graceful, slender youth, who skilfully manoeuvres his wooden walking-sticks across the polished floor.

At each stage of your prolonged journey comes impartial questioning and a new record of 'particulars' (your age, residence, occupation, purpose, and behaviour at the time of the accident). Only once did my replies evoke a slight smile of surprise from the laconic young interne who was examining my arm. 'And how did you fall?'

'I was crossing Northumberland Avenue to go to St Martin's Church. Some builders doing repairs had left a pole outside the gutter, and in the dark I tripped over it and fell flat.'

'Did you lose consciousness?'

'Oh, no. I just lay in the road for a minute or two and a kind young man helped me up.'

'And then I suppose you went home?'

'No, I didn't. I went on to St Martin's and gave my talk.'

Like the skilful doctors who look so juvenile, the clerks, nurses, and women radiographers are all kind and efficient. Years ago, in *Testament of Youth*, I wrote, rather bitterly, about the 'bright immunity from pity' of the Bart's sisters in charge of wards filled with the wounded of the First World War. But later I had to record that on the Western Front I was obliged to develop the same immunity myself, and came to realize that pity is a luxury which those in attendance, month after month and year after year, on the sick and suffering have to forgo if they are to retain enough sanity to do their job.

All the same, I think I have perceived more imaginative sympathy in the young professional women of today than in the Sisters of the First London General Hospital, Camberwell. Perhaps, having grown so much older, I am myself more tolerant. Perhaps they are better qualified for their work and, being more confident, can spare time to be gentle.

Nevertheless, one feels the same relief in encountering the spontaneous kindness characteristic of the working man and woman. 'Hard on you not being able to do up your coat on a cold morning like this,' benevolently comments the hospital lift man, who must have seen hundreds of broken arms. But nothing quite equals the courtesy, so often justly commended, of the London taxi-driver.

'Take your time – there's no hurry,' quietly insists the driver who took me to the hospital, when I hand him my purse to help himself to the fare that I can only extract with difficulty.

'Sure you're all right?' asks his colleague (summoned by a magnificent Jamaican commissionaire) who drives me home. As considerately as a porter at Claridge's expecting a bumper tip, he helps me out of the taxi and escorts me between the cars parked at the entrance to my flat.

It is worth while being a casualty to be reminded how human common humanity can be.

Guardian, 29 November 1966

THE KIND OF GOD I BELIEVE IN

This article is bound to appear naïve to its more scholarly readers, for though I can absorb with profit books by such well-known religious writers as Canon Raven and Dr G.H.C. Macgregor, I have no theological training whatsoever. All I can attempt to do – and it is difficult enough – is to explain as best I can the changing convictions about God of an ordinary intelligent person during the course of a relatively long life.

It is easiest to begin by saying what I cannot accept. First, I do not believe in the anthropomorphic Old Testament deity by whom I imagine that few devout people are now convinced, though he was held over the children of my generation as the source of some awful potential retaliation if we misbehaved.

Secondly, I have no faith in a God whose authority has to be sustained by the periodic introduction of supernatural magic; that is, by the contravention of natural laws which in any rational and spiritual universe must be assumed to have been laid down by Himself. The law of cause and effect always seems to me to be an essential part of God's operations, and I remain unimpressed by effects which appear to be produced without their normal cause. Hence, while I can believe in a God who expresses Himself in varying degrees through all human beings but especially through His saints such as Isaiah, Buddha, St Francis of Assisi, and Gandhi, and at maximum through Jesus Christ, my belief in an in-dwelling God does not depend upon such beautiful miracles as the virgin birth or even the resurrection. For me the resurrection is a lovely parable of the reawakening of faith in their own mission among the disciples at first demoralized and overwhelmed by the tragedy of the crucifixion. I can think of many reasons for the restoration of courage and determination to a group of dedicated men other than the return of their lost leader from the grave. The life and teaching of Jesus seems to me to provide enough evidence that God exists without a supernatural beginning and end, and I find the resurrection as irrelevant as the nativity.

Hence I do not believe that when my mortal body dies it will rise again. Nor do I anticipate any form of immortality for my soul (whatever precisely that may be), though in view of the amazing discoveries of this century, I would not be arrogant enough to deny the possibility that in one dimension or another my consciousness may continue. I have a completely open mind on the subject, but in any case my faith in God does not depend on whether or not my friends and I are destined for some variety of future existence.

What kind of God then do I believe in, and why? The best description of Him that I can find is no more remote than the familiar mystical opening words of St John's Gospel: 'In the beginning was the Word, and the Word was with God, and the Word was God. In Him was life, and the life was the light of men. And the light shineth in darkness and the darkness comprehended it not.' Could anything express more clearly than those last six words the tragedy of mankind in every age, but especially, perhaps, in our own?

For the Greeks, that brilliant and rational people, the Word – Logos – meant the immanent wisdom, the indwelling spirit of truth and goodness perpetually in conflict not so much with evil as with blindness; with the uncomprehending darkness which encompasses the hearts of men if they make no attempt to find and obey the God within themselves. It is this spirit of wisdom, this intrinsic but not automatic power of goodness, that God means for me.

Through many years I did not believe that God existed in these or any other terms. As a schoolgirl adversely impressed by conventional Sunday observances and the pharisaical behaviour of the Anglican clerics in the small provincial town where we lived, I responded with enthusiasm to the rationalism of Olive Schreiner, Havelock Ellis, and W.E. Henley ('I am the Captain of my Fate, I am the Master of my Soul'). That stoical creed sustained me throughout the First World War, in which my male contemporaries were deceived into giving up their promising young lives and I could find no evidence for a beneficent God. This outlook continued until, in 1936, I met Canon Dick Sheppard of St Martin's and became a pacifist. From the words and works of that great, good and suffering man, and from the pacifist creed which I came perforce to embrace, it gradually dawned upon me that the goodness and wisdom of God, though always there for our inspection and example, cannot function to transform the universe without the co-operation of man.

Perhaps if I had known Dick for longer than twelve months – he died, too soon, in 1937 – I might have taken less than nine more years to come to the convictions that I now hold. I can probably best explain the kind of God I believe in by describing the simple experience through which the fact of His existence eventually – and I think finally – became a certainty in my mind. This certainty began to grow in, of all places, Parliament Square on VE Day (8 May) 1945, and worked itself out in the weeks that followed.

That warm, sunny afternoon I went to Whitehall to hear the announcement that the war in Europe was over, and deliberately stood on almost the exact spot in which, as a young Red Cross nurse with my friends all gone, I had 'celebrated' Armistice Day in 1918. But this time the humble civilians on the pavement amongst whom I stood did not burst into noisy rejoicing; too many had seen their fellow citizens killed and their homes destroyed. They had acquiesced – though not always willingly – in such evil deeds as obliteration bombing and the starvation of Europe, but they had also endured with patience much wrong done to them by others. Suddenly I had an overwhelming impression of their essential goodness – a goodness which could transform the world if they worked with the God within them instead of blindly joining His enemies.

And then came the strange experience which defeats even now my power to describe it in words. I only knew that out of the humiliations, errors and confusions of the war just ending had emerged a certainty so immense that the sad record of human fallibility acquired a totally new perspective. Walking stoically up Whitehall at the close of the first war, I had felt no conviction of any divine principle, any Easter morning, any meeting again. Now, walking up Whitehall with London's long ordeal at an end, I became deeply aware that during the past five years my attitude had changed.

I could not yet believe in the Easter morning or the meeting again; I did not expect to recover my beloved dead in any future conceivable by human intelligence. But of the existence of a benign rule, a spiritual imperative behind the anarchy caused by man's wilful folly, I was now fully assured; the youthful lampless endurance of the first war had been replaced by a mature conviction. Like the girl student in Norman Macowan's play *Glorious Morning*, I knew that God lived, and that the sorrow and suffering in the world around me had come because men refused to obey His laws. The self-interested policies which had driven mankind to the edge of the abyss seemed to me to supply incontrovertible testimony that an opposite policy – the way of God, the road of the Cross – would produce an opposite result.

I did not, and do not, regard Him as omnipotent in any supernatural or automatic sense, but only with the co-operation of the creature whom He made in his image and endowed with free will. So far, throughout the centuries of human history, that co-operation has been rejected by all but a few, and I know clearly that its refusal may continue until man ends his life on earth with the weapons of his own invention. But today, even at this late hour, it is still attainable; it lies in the divine potentialities with which we, sinners as we are, have been invested by the mere fact of our humanity. And once it is attained, but only then, God's kingdom will come and we shall build Jerusalem on earth as it is in Heaven.

Kingsway: The magazine of the West London Mission, Winter, 1961

Notes

These notes are not intended to provide an exhaustive list of all the people, places and events mentioned in the articles, but it is hoped that the following details will be of interest and assistance to the reader. For brevity Winifred Holtby and Vera Brittain are referred to by their initials.

Page	Line	
3	25	**Hilda Stewart Reid** (1898–1982): A first-year friend of WH's at Somerville in 1917, and from 1919, when Winifred returned after war service with the WAAC, until her death. Published *Ashley Hamel*, a novel (1939), and with VB edited *Pavements at Anderby* (1937), a posthumous collection of short stories by WH.
7	31	**The League of Nations** represented the new idealism in international relations, and was an important feature of the Treaty of Versailles which followed the German defeat in the First World War. In January 1919 the peace conference unanimously adopted a resolution for its creation, and the Covenant of the League was worked out by a committee of six members. It stipulated that members were to afford each other mutual protection against aggression; to submit disputes to arbitration or inquiry; and to abstain from war until three months after an award. It also provided for a permanent secretariat to be established in Geneva. The Treaty of Versailles was ratified by the German government in July, and subsequently by France, Great Britain, Italy and Japan, but it was never ratified by the United States. Following the Italian invasion of Ethiopia in October 1935, the League of Nations voted the application of sanctions against Italy, but could not agree to apply the oil sanction, which might have proved decisive. Addis Ababa was occupied by

351

Page	Line	
		the Italian forces in May 1936. After a final meeting in Geneva in April 1945, the League of Nations was dissolved, and its assets transferred to the United Nations.
7	33	**Sarah Gertrude Millin** (1889–1968): South African novelist, and friend of WH and VB. Wrote the lives of *Rhodes* (1933) and *Smuts* (1936).
8	35	**Six Point Group**: This feminist body was 'inaugurated in February 1921, under the chairmanship of Viscountess Rhondda, to work for six closely connected objects – pensions for widows, equal rights of guardianship for married parents, the improvement of the laws dealing with child assault and the position of the unmarried mother, equal pay for teachers and equal opportunities for men and women in the Civil Service' (VB, *Testament of Experience*). VB and WH joined the group (which also of course worked generally for the feminist cause) in 1922, and this led to their association with *Time and Tide*, the 'independent non-party weekly', feminist in orientation, established by Lady Rhondda (1883–1958) in 1920. WH and VB were on the Six Point Group's Executive Committee.
9	36	**Jean F. McWilliam** (1881–1963): Somerville undergraduate 1903–06. During the First World War was the Commandant of a WAAC Signals Unit at Huchennville, to which WH was posted as hostel forewoman in September 1918. Emigrated to South Africa in 1920, and was, first, Lecturer in English at Rhodes University College, Grahamstown, and subsequently Head Mistress of Pretoria High School for Girls. She edited with Mrs Holtby *Letters to a Friend* (1937), a selection of the letters written to her by WH between 1920 and 1935.
10	2	**Viscountess Rhondda** (1883–1958): A suffragette. Founded *Time and Tide* in 1920. Her unorthodox sympathies were on the political right. Published her autobiography *This Was My World* in 1933. A friend and colleague of WH.
11	24	**Stella Benson** (1892–1933): Novelist friend of WH. *Tobit Transplanted* (1931) won the Femina Vie Heureuse prize.
12	32	**Monica Whately**: She stood unsuccessfully as Labour candidate in the 1929 General Election (the first after full suffrage), in which the Conservatives under Baldwin were replaced by a minority Labour administration led by Ramsay MacDonald. VB, who with WH had joined the Labour Party in 1924, worked enthusiastically for Whately, and the latter's energy and eloquence 'created a stimulating contest which dramatized the purpose of the long suffragist campaign' (VB, *Testament of Experience*).
22	10	**Olive Schreiner** (1855–1920): Noted South African pacifist,

Page	Line	
		feminist, and author of *The Story of an African Farm* (1883), which deeply influenced VB's early development. *Woman and Labour* (1911) was an influential contribution to the feminist demand for equality.
22	15	**ICU**: The Industrial and Commercial Workers' Union of South Africa. Founded in Cape Town in 1919. WH was primarily responsible for the appointment in 1928 of William Ballinger, a 34-year-old Scottish trade unionist, as an independent adviser.
22	30	**Colonel Josiah Clement Wedgwood** (1872–1943): MP for Newcastle-under-Lyme 1906-1942. Liberal until 1919; accepted the Labour Whip in May 1919 but from 1931 sat as an Independent Labour MP. Chairman of the Committee on House of Commons Records 1929.
24	26	**Sir Percy Harris** (1876–1952): Liberal MP for South-West Bethnal Green 1922–45. After coming to London from Somerville in 1922 WH worked and spoke for him during two general elections.
25	29	**Henry Noel Brailsford** (1873–1958): Editor of the *New Leader* 1922–26. Leader-writer successively to the *Manchester Guardian*, *Tribune*, *Daily News* and the *Nation and Athenaeum*. Joined Independent Labour Party 1907. Author of some 16 books.
47	4	**Eva Hubback** (1886–1949): Principal, Morley College; Member of London County Council Education Committee and Chairman of LCC Schools Sub-Committee. Educated Newnham College, Cambridge; Economics Tripos, Part II, 1908, Class I. Publications include 'The Population of Britain'.
48	6	**Sir William Schwenck Gilbert** (1836–1911): Playwright and humorist, whose collaboration with Sir Arthur Sullivan produced an unforgettable series of ever-popular operas.
48	33	**Lord Birkenhead** (1872–1930): MP (Unionist) Walton Division of Liverpool 1906–18. Attorney-General 1915–19; Lord Chancellor 1919–22; Secretary for India 1924–28. Prolific author whose books include two volumes of *Famous Trials* (1926 & 1928).
52	24	**Margaret Grace Bondfield** (1873–1953): Member of Parliament and trade union leader; as Minister of Labour in MacDonald's second administration she was the first British woman cabinet minister. Staunch supporter of adult suffrage.
60	25	**Sir Alfred Hopkinson** (1851–1939): MP (Unionist) for Combined English Universities 1926–29.
64	37	**William John Brown** (1894–1960): Secretary, Civil Service

Page	Line	
		Clerical Association, 1919–42. Labour MP for West Wolverhampton in 1929; resigned Labour Whip in March 1931; sat as Independent Labour MP until defeated in October 1931.
67	21	**George John Gordon Bruce, 11th Lord Balfour,** (1883–1967): One of the two Treasurers of the Open Door Council from 1926, and Vice-President of the Fawcett Society from *c.* 1960.
67	22	**Mrs Cecil (Ada Elizabeth) Chesterton** (1870–1962): Journalist, philanthropist and author of many books, including *In Darkest London* (1926), based on her experiences among the destitute and homeless. Set up Cecil Houses where homeless women could obtain decent food and accommodation for a small payment, and later Cecil Residential Clubs for the low-paid and aged.
67	22	**Mrs Elizabeth Abbott**: Chairman of the Open Door Council.
67	22	**Open Door Council**: The Council was founded in 1926 (with representatives, including Lady Rhondda, from feminist organizations) to oppose protective legislation based solely on sex and to press for recognition of the right of all women to paid work.
67	23	**Alison Neilans** (1884–1942): Worked for women's suffrage; head of the political department of the Women's Freedom League; General Secretary for nearly 30 years of the Association for Moral and Social Hygiene (now the Josephine Butler Society).
73	15	**Dame Millicent Garrett Fawcett** (1847–1929): A prominent non-militant (suffragist) leader of the movement for women's suffrage and educational reformer. One of the founders of Newnham College.
73	15	**Mrs Ray Strachey** (1887-1940): Active but non-militant participant in the campaign for votes for women. Published in 1928 her classic work *The Cause: A Brief History of the Women's Movement.* Married Oliver Strachey, brother of Lytton.
75	18	**Elizabeth Garrett Anderson, MD** (1836–1917): One of the first English women to enter the medical profession. Mayor of Aldeburgh 1908–9; the first woman to be a mayor.
75	18	**Agnes Garrett**: Suffragette supporter and speaker. Sister of Elizabeth Garrett Anderson.
75	21	**The Rt Hon. Henry Fawcett** (1833–1884): Blind Liberal statesman and economist. Professor of Political Economy at Cambridge.
75	29	**Josephine Butler**: An early feminist and social reformer,

Page	Line	
		Josephine Butler (1828–1906) led a campaign for the repeal of the Contagious Diseases Acts of the 1860s which enabled police in some urban areas to terrorize women after declaring them to be 'common prostitutes'.
76	12	**Flora Robson** (1902–84): Popular and highly regarded stage and film actress.
76	18	**Charles Vernon France** (1868–1949): A popular actor who began his career in Rochdale in 1891.
77	23	**M. Dupont** and his daughters are characters in the H.G. Wells novel *Men Like Gods* published in 1923.
79	9	**Sir Herbert Austin** (1866–1941): English motor car manufacturer. Pioneered the small car, and marketed in 1921 the 'Austin 7'.
80	5	**St John Ervine**: An Irish novelist and dramatist (1883–1971), best known for *The First Mrs Fraser* (1928), he also wrote critical and political studies (on Oscar Wilde and G.B. Shaw among others). A friend too of WH's.
80	30	**Dr Marie Carmichael Stopes** (1880–1958): A pioneer in the campaign for birth control, and the author of many books on the subject. Opened the first birth control clinic in the British Empire in 1921.
84	5	**Sir Oswald Mosley** (1896–1980): Resigned from 1929 Labour government and founded the British Union of Fascists in 1932; during the Second World War he was imprisoned.
90	14	**Earl Baldwin of Bewdley** (1867–1947): Leading Conservative politician between the two world wars. Prime Minister 1923–24, 1924–29 and 1935–37.
90	17	**Dame Ethel Smyth** (1858–1944): Composer, writer and feminist. Composed 'The March of the Women', the battle song of the WSPU. Wrote four books of autobiography.
93	18	**Sir Edward Grey** – later 1st Viscount Fallodon (1862–1933): Foreign Secretary 1905–16. Chancellor of Oxford University 1928–33.
93	28	**WSPU**: Women's Social and Political Union. Founded in Manchester in 1903 by the indomitable suffragette leader, Mrs Pankhurst.
98	9	**incompleteness of the English franchise**: The Electoral Reform Act of 1918 enfranchised all women aged at least 30, but full equality with men (voting at 21) was not achieved until 1928, through the Equal Franchise Act.
98	15	**political party**: The Labour Party, founded in 1900.
98	38	**woman representative, League of Nations Assembly**: Mrs H.M. Swanwick (1864–1939), feminist, socialist and worker for world peace, was appointed a British delegate to the

Page	Line	

League of Nations in 1924.

99   5   **Margery Fry; Oxford Statute**: Margery Fry (1874–1958), pacifist and feminist, was Principal of Somerville College 1926–31. In 1927 a University Statute, narrowly approved, limited women students at Oxford to 840, about a sixth the number of men students.

100   1   **Mrs Pankhurst**: Emmeline Pankhurst (1858–1928) founded the Women's Social and Political Union (WSPU), the militant wing of the movement for women's suffrage, in 1903 and led the battle for the vote. VB heard her speak in Lady Rhondda's house a few months before her death.

100   14   **headmistress**: Louise Heath-Jones (d. 1931), the founder of St Monica's School, a private boarding-school for girls, south of London, attended by VB for four years.

100   17, 18   **Cat and Mouse Act**: The Prisoners' Temporary Discharge for Ill-Health Act of 1913 was intended to avoid the creation of suffragette martyrs by ensuring temporary release for those whose lives were endangered by a hunger-strike (which had become an important weapon in the suffrage campaign).

100   35   **Rokeby Venus**: This famous painting of a female nude by Velasquez, hanging in the National Gallery, was slashed on 10 March 1914 by the suffragette Mary Richardson. 'Poor artist and genius!' VB wrote in her diary that day. 'What has he done that the rancour and spite of a political maniac should be vented on his creation!'

102   34   **Christabel Pankhurst; exile in Paris**: the 'cool, calculating' eldest of Emmeline Pankhurst's three daughters (1880–1958), she played a very prominent role in the suffrage battle, and edited the WSPU periodical *The Suffragette*. When in 1912 her mother and Mrs Pethick-Lawrence were on hunger-strike in prison, she fled to Paris ('Where is Christabel?') to reorganize the WSPU.

103   8   **Mrs Pethick-Lawrence**: Emmeline Pethick-Lawrence (1867–1943), a close friend of Mrs Pankhurst and, with her husband Frederick (whose biography VB published in 1963), a leading suffragist; she was excluded from the WSPU in 1912 by Emmeline and Christabel Pankhurst as they embarked on a policy of extreme militancy.

103   9   **'General' Drummond**: A pugnacious Scot nicknamed 'the General', Flora Drummond (d. 1949) was a very active member of the WSPU, imprisoned on one occasion for entering 10 Downing Street with a petition for the Prime Minister.

103   36   **Emily Wilding Davison; Lady Constance Lytton**: Tragic figures of the suffrage battle, Emily Davison (b. 1872) died three days after throwing herself in front of the king's horse during the 1913 Derby; and Lady Constance Lytton (1869–1923) suffered very serious physical damage when, disguised as 'Jane Warton, a seamstress', she was forcibly fed eight times in prison before her identity was discovered.

104   3,   **Annie Kenney; 'Charlie' Marsh; Vida Goldstein**: Three
4   militant suffragettes. Annie Kenney (1879–1953) was a mill-girl who became a devoted follower of Christabel Pankhurst, and the only working-class woman among the WSPU leadership; Charlotte Marsh (b. 1887) was forcibly fed in prison and was cross-bearer at the head of the huge funeral procession for Emily Davison; Vida Goldstein (1869–1949), an Australian feminist, made a speaking tour of England in 1911 and campaigned for women's suffrage and international peace for several years in Europe.

104   19   **Olive Schreiner's allegory**: See *The Story of an African Farm*, Part II, Chapter 2 ('Waldo's Stranger').

106   14   **task of making feminism social**: In 1951, VB added the following note to her copy of the article: 'Feminism became *social* with the coming of the Welfare State. The triumph of the Labour movement in 1945 was also the victory of social feminism.'

108   25   **Mrs Sidney Webb**: Beatrice Webb (1858–1943), a very influential social reformer, Fabian and historian.

109   1,   **Lord Phillimore; Lord Balfour of Burleigh**: Reformist
7   Peers: the 1st Baron Phillimore (1845–1929), a distinguished legal expert, Lord Chief Justice of Appeal 1913–16; the 11th Baron Balfour of Burleigh (1883–1967), a prominent bureaucrat.

109   12,   **Conferences; Industrial Women's Organizations; National**
14   **Union of Societies for Equal Citizenship**: The Conference called by NUSEC (originally the important, non-militant National Union of Women's Suffrage Societies) confirmed its opposition to protective legislation for women; while the Women's Trade Union Conference reaffirmed support for protective legislation and attacked the Open Door Council's policy.

109   15   **Doris Stevens; Miss Wilkinson**: Doris Stevens was a leading American feminist (18192–1963). Ellen Wilkinson, a cotton-worker's daughter, was a socialist, union-organizer and feminist (1891–1947); elected a Labour MP in 1924, she led the Jarrow march of the unemployed in 1938, and in 1945 was appointed Minister of Education in Attlee's Labour Government.

Page	Line	
109	30	**Dr Marion Phillips**: A political activist and Labour MP (1881–1932), she was appointed Chief Woman Officer of the Labour Party in 1918.
109	33	**Barbara Drake**: Wrote several influential socialist and feminist books, including *Women in Trade Unions* (1921).
111	18	**Our candidate**: Monica Whately.
111	24	**The division**: St Albans in Hertfordshire; the Conservative majority at the previous election was over 9,000.
112	34	**Mrs Despard**: Charlotte Despard (1844–1939), a socialist and leading suffragist; she left the WSPU to found the Women's Freedom League in 1903, and in 1918 stood unsuccessfully as a Labour candidate in the General Election.
115	1	**Mrs Dora Russell**, *Hypatia*: The second wife of Bertrand Russell, Dora Russell (b. 1894) founded with him the progressive school Beacon Hill, and published the lively feminist polemic *Hypatia* in 1925 (VB's 'little extravaganza' *Halcyon, or the Future of Monogamy*, published in 1929, is a similar work).
116	13	**Dr Gregory**: A Scottish physician and Professor of Medicine at Aberdeen and Edinburgh, he published *A Father's Legacy to his Daughters* in 1774.
116	31	**Professor Wieth-Knudsen**: A Danish economist, composer and writer (b. 1878).
118	18	**John Langdon-Davies**: A journalist (1897–1971), he was a war correspondent in the Spanish Civil War and founded the Foster Parents Scheme for European Children.
118	19	**W.L. George; Anthony Ludovici**: Their 'impertinent' works include *The Story of Woman* (1925) by George (1882–1926) and *Lysistrata* (1924) by Ludovici (1882–1971).
119	24	**Hannah More**: A religious writer and reformer (1745–1833), she published such books as *Practical Piety* (1811) and *Christian Morals* (1813).
120	3	**Mrs Gaskell's** *Life of Charlotte Brontë*: Elizabeth Gaskell (1810–85) was a close friend of Charlotte Brontë (1816–55), and the biography of her fellow-novelist is a classic. VB's quotations are from Volume One, Chapter XIII.
121	5	**three great books; brother and sisters**: *Jane Eyre* was published before the deaths of Branwell in September 1848, of Emily (stubbornly refusing, in the spirit of her *Wuthering Heights*, to allow a doctor to be called) in December, and of Anne in May 1849; *Shirley* (after whom VB named her daughter) and *Villette* appeared soon afterwards.

Page	Line	
125	7	**Sir James Purves-Stewart**: A prominent physician and medical writer (1869–1949).
132	17	**Matrimonial Causes Bill**: Mrs Eirene White's Bill, which would have established seven years' separation as sufficient ground for divorce, failed to pass its third reading.
133	3	**Miss Pankhurst**: (Estelle) Sylvia Pankhurst (1882–1960) was active in the WSPU 1903–14, but – 'shy, conscientious, excessively sensitive to suffering' – she disagreed with the policies of her mother and sister Christabel; unlike them, she remained a pacifist during the First World War and worked in the slums of London's East End to alleviate the suffering of the poor.
134	26	**National Health Insurance**: The Act of 1911 was not substantially changed until the National Health Service was set up in 1946.
135	14	**the late Minister of War in the first Labour Government**: Stephen Walsh (1859–1929); born in Liverpool 'in humble circumstances', he was admitted as a foundling to the Kirkdale Industrial School and Orphanage.
136	11	**Rachel and Margaret McMillan**: Scottish educational reformers, pioneers of child welfare and of open-air nursery schools. Rachel McMillan (1859–1917) worked in the slums of London 1902–13 with her sister Margaret (1860–1931), establishing in 1908 the first school clinic in London, and in 1913 the Rachel McMillan Open Air Nursery School. Largely through their efforts, nursery schools were incorporated by statute in the British educational system in 1918. Margaret McMillan's *Education through the Imagination* (1904) and *The Nursery School* (1919) were influential books.
136	13	**Sir George Newman**: An eminent physician and writer (1870–1948); his Yale Lectures were published under the title *Citizenship and the Survival of Civilisation* in 1928.
136	20	**C3 population**: 'C3' was the lowest classification of physical fitness in the First World War; 'inferior; extremely unfit'.
136	34	**Dr Cyril Burt; LCC**: Although some findings of the psychologist Sir Cyril Burt (1883–1976) have been questioned, the figures issued by the London County Council broadly indicate the serious effects of poor health care on the mental development of children in London slums during the 1920s.
145	2	**German women's losses**: When he came to power in 1933, Hitler's attack on Germany's serious unemployment problem included the removal of 'several groups from the labour market– the Jews, the socialists, the pacifists and, of

Page	Line	

course, the women' (VB, speech on 'Anti-Feminism in Europe'). Apart from suffering the strong social pressures of a 'back-to-the-kitchen' movement, women were barred from professions such as teaching.

145   8   **'eternal vigilance'**: Semi-quotation from a famous speech made in 1790 by John Curran (1750–1817).

146   6, 7   **Mrs Owen; Mrs Harriman**: Ruth Bryan Owen (1885–1954), first woman member of Congress from Florida and US Minister to Denmark 1933–36; Florence Borden Harriman (1870–1967), US Minister to Norway 1937–40.

148   5   **Ralph Ingersoll**: American editor and publisher (b. 1900); his *Report on England* appeared in 1940.

151   6   **Amy Johnson; Caroline Haslett**: Amy Johnson, the famous aviator (1904–41), whose solo flight half-way round the world (from Croydon to Darwin) in 1930 – the first by a woman – made her an international celebrity; Caroline Haslett (1895–1957), an engineer who founded the Women's Engineering Society in 1919 to establish women in the profession.

151   15, 16   **Thelma Cazalet; Mr Eden**: Thelma Cazalet Keir (b. 1899), Conservative MP for Islington 1931–45, fought for women's issues like equal pay; the British statesman and Prime Minister Anthony Eden, Earl of Avon (1897–1977), was Foreign Secretary in Churchill's War Cabinet 1940–45.

155   5   **Irene Savidge**: Was charged with Sir Leo Money on uncorroborated police evidence of behaving in Hyde Park 'in a manner reasonably likely to offend against public decency'. Both were acquitted, and as a result of intense parliamentary and public protest a tribunal was set up to investigate the case. A bizarre aspect was the undisclosed medical evidence given in court by the defence counsel, Sir Henry Curtis Bennett, but undoubtedly confirming that Miss Savidge (aged 22) was *virgo intacta*!

155   5   **Miss O'Malley**: Was charged at Bow Street Police Court in May 1928 as a common prostitute soliciting in Southampton Row. The case was dismissed by the Magistrate, Mr Graham-Campbell, with the laconic observation that 'Having regard to the short time the officers have known her, and the medical evidence that she was *virgo intacta*, I should not be justified in finding she is a common prostitute'. There was strong criticism of the police for their failure to make any attempt to obtain evidence of annoyance, and justifiable concern as to 'what would have been the result if this woman had been married and so unable to produce this medical certificate'.

Page	Line	
155	10	**Katherine Mayo** (1868–1940): American writer; author of the controversial book *Mother India* (1927), and *The Face of Mother India* (1935), etc.
155	10	**Judge Ben Lindsey:** Associated for twenty-six years with the Juvenile and Family Court of Denver, Colorado. His book, *The Revolt of Modern Youth* (1928), maintaining that a social revolution was taking place, caused considerable perturbation.
156	6	**Dr Norman Haire** (1892–1952): Australian-born sexologist, gynaecologist and obstetrician. Settled in England in 1919, and took an active part in the early birth-control movement.
156	24	**Lord Parmoor** (1852–1941): Leader of the House of Lords 1929–31.
162	14	**Harold J. Laski** (1893–1950): Professor of Political Science, University of London, and connected for many years with the London School of Economics. Author of numerous books on political subjects.
162	22	**John Scanlon:** A miner's son who after working briefly in the pits became a skilled ship's plater on the Clyde. Wrote pamphlets for the Clydeside workers' movement, and freelance articles for the Glasgow socialist newspaper *Forward*. After the war he became the secretary to the Wallsend Labour Party, and subsequently election agent for Sir Patrick Hastings, who, on being elected, engaged him as his parliamentary secretary. In a caustic prefatory note to *The Decline and Fall of the Labour Party* (1932) he remarks that 'few of the characters in this book are real people; they are mostly politicians'!
163	25	**Sir Charles Blake Cochran** (1872–1951): Theatrical manager, and producer of innumerable highly successful plays and revues in London and New York.
165	28	**Norman Angell:** Pseudonym of the journalist Ralph Lane (1872–1967), best known for his extremely influential *The Great Illusion* (1910), which argued that war is irrational and ruins conqueror and conquered alike. A founder of the UDC and winner of the Nobel Peace Prize in 1933, he later opposed pacifism and supported rearmament.
165	28	**Lord Beaverbrook** (1879–1964): British newspaper owner who controlled the *Daily Express*, *Sunday Express*, and *Evening Standard*, which propagated his various political campaigns.
165	28	**Major Francis Yeats-Brown** (1886–1944): Soldier and author. Served with the 17th Cavalry, Indian Army; in France with the 5th Lancers; and in Mesopotamia with the

Page	Line	
		Royal Flying Corps. Published highly successful *Bengal Lancer* in 1930.
165	29	**Robert Mennell**: A Quaker, who as a conscientious objector suffered solitary confinement during the First World War. Chapter XII of *Cry Havoc!* consists of a wide-ranging argument about pacifism between Mennell and Yeats-Brown, who held diametrically opposite points of view.
165	30	**Sir (James) Arthur Salter** (1881–1975): Economist and politician. General Secretary of Reparations Commission 1920–22; Parliamentary Secretary to the Ministry of Shipping till 1941; Minister of State for Economic Affairs 1951–52, etc. Author of *The United States of Europe* (1933).
166	30	**UDC**: The Union of Democratic Control, founded in 1914 with the conviction that democratic control of foreign policy would keep Britain out of war, developed into a leading anti-war organization in the 1920s (it had 2,000 members in 1927). Ramsay Macdonald and J.A. Hobson were among its supporters.
167	2	**Earl Herbert Henry Asquith** (1852–1928): Liberal Prime Minister 1908–15, and Coalition Prime Minister with the Conservatives 1915–16.
172	36	**Arabella Susan Lawrence** (1871–1947): Labour MP for North East Ham, 1923–24 and 1926–31. Parliamentary Secretary Ministry of Health 1929–31.
172	36	**Rt Hon. Ellen C. Wilkinson** (1891–1947): Labour MP for Middlesborough East, and for Jarrow from 1924. Minister of Education 1945. Various publications, including the Jarrow epic *The Town That Was Murdered* (1939).
172	38	**Viscountess Nancy Witcher Astor** (1879–1964): The first woman MP to take her seat in the House of Commons in 1919.
173	1	**Mrs Margaret Wintringham** (d. 1955): Independent Liberal MP, Louth Division, 1921–24.
173	1	**Lady Lucy Edith Pelham Noel-Buxton** (1888–1960): Labour MP for North Norfolk 1930–31, and for Norwich 1945–50.
173	16	**Red Flags in London**: In England and Wales in 1933 the official total of unemployed was 2½ million. In November of that year the National Government introduced a complex and large-scale piece of legislation covering all able-bodied unemployed from 14 to 65, which one MP described as 'a jig-saw puzzle of 63 clauses'. The benefit rates – which had been reduced by 10% two years earlier – remained unchanged. As one contemporary critic put it,

the 'real storm centre' was the proposal to set up the Unemployment Assistance Board, working through its own officials, and the establishment of a cumbersome tripartite administration – the Labour Exchange, the Public Assistance Committees, and the new Board. It was also proposed to set up a self-supporting contributory Insurance Fund, and there was a considerable outcry against saddling the Fund with an annual debt repayment charge of £5,500,000, designed to pay off in about forty years the total deficit incurred in times of exceptional expenditure.

Three hundred and seventy hunger marchers trekked from Glasgow to London to lobby their MPs and to attend the Hyde Park rally, and they were joined by further contingents from Newcastle, Plymouth, Manchester, Sheffield, Cardiff, Derby, Yarmouth, Brighton and Chatham. The meeting was held in drizzling rain on a gloomy Sunday, 23 February 1934, and a resolution was passed calling for the complete and unconditional withdrawal of the Unemployment Bill, the abolition of the Means Test, and full maintenance for all the unemployed, the last to be a charge on the National Exchequer.

The march was organized, *The Times* reported, 'by the Communists and fragmentary sections of the ILP'. The official Labour Party appears to have been embarrassed by the rally, and one commentator remarked that 'Transport House feels that the Reds – which its officials dislike quite as fervently as they dislike Blacks – are exploiting the unemployed all too effectively.'

Conservative MPs were among those protesting that 2*s*. a week was a wholly inadequate sum to support a dependent child, and the Hyde Park rally was fuelled by the widely publicized suicide a fortnight before of a Mrs Hickley of Hampstead who had been unable to face any longer the strain of feeding three adults and three children on 21*s*. 6*d*. a week. At the inquest a doctor gave evidence that she was suffering from starvation.

173	27	**Sir George Ambrose Lloyd** (1879–1941): President of Navy League from 1930; Chairman of British Council from 1937; Colonial Secretary May 1940 to February 1941.
173	27	**Lord Trenchard** (1873–1956): Marshall of the RAF, and often known as 'The father of the Air Force'. Commissioner Metropolitan Police 1931–35.
174	25	**Harry Pollitt** (1890–1960): Secretary, Communist Party 1929–56, and Chairman from 1956.

Page	Line	
174	25	**Tom Mann** (1856–1941): General Secretary of the Amalgamated Society of Engineers 1918–21. Socialist and trade unionist.
175	30	**Rt Hon. James Ramsay MacDonald** (1866–1937): Prime Minister in first two Labour Governments 1924 and 1929–31, and in Coalition Government 1931–35.
176	37	**John McGovern** (1887–1968): Labour MP for Glasgow Shelleston 1930, and Independent Labour Party Member from 1931.
177	18	**Sir Herbert Samuel** (1870–1963): Leader of the Liberal Party in the House of Commons 1931–35; Home Secretary 1916 and 1931–32. MP for Darwen Division of Lancashire 1929–35.
177	31	**General James Barry Munnik Hertzog** (1866–1942): South African Prime Minister 1924–39. In September 1939 refused to follow Britain in declaring war against Hitler, was defeated in Parliament and resigned.
180	8	**Professor D.D.T. Jabavu**: Professor of Classics at the Native University College at Fort Hare. Took active lead in the campaign against the Representation of Natives Bill and The Native Trust and Land Bill, and in 1935 in convening an All-African National Convention.
180	23	**DORA**: Defence of the Realm Act. An Act originally promulgated in 1914 under the Government's Emergency Powers to prevent people communicating with the enemy or obtaining information for that purpose.
180	34	**Sir Edward William Macleay Grigg** (1879–1955): Governor and C.-in-C. Kenya colony 1925–30. Joint Parliamentary Under-Secretary of State to the War Office 1940–42.
180	36	**Lieut. Col. Leopold Charles Maurice Stennett Amery** (1873–1955): Secretary of State for the Colonies 1924–29. Conservative MP for Birmingham Sparkbrook 1918–45.
181	15	**Kikuyu**: Bantu-speaking people inhabiting an area south-west of Mount Kenya and north of Nairobi. Agriculturists, with cattle their predominating concern, and maize and sorghum their principal crops.
181	15	**Masai (or Maasai)**: Nilo-Hamitic-speaking people of East Africa occupying an area extending from Mount Kilimanjaro to Mount Kenya. Originally nomadic pastoralists whose meals, religious observances, livelihood, etc., were based on cattle. In translation their standard greeting is 'I hope your cattle are well'.
181	23	**Field-Marshal The Rt Hon. Jan Christiaan Smuts** (1870–1950): South African soldier and statesman. Prime Minister 1919–24. Prime Minister, Foreign Minister and

Page	Line	
		Minister of Defence 1939–48. Helped to launch League of Nations, and was later associated with the United Nations.
186	18	**Piet Gert Wessels Groebler** (1873–1942): Minister of Lands in the first South African Nationalist Cabinet, and Minister of Native Affairs 1933–38.
186	24	**Lord Delamere** (1870–1931): Pioneer of British colonization in East Africa.
188	32	**Norman Leys, MD, DPH**: Spent 20 years in East Africa, and 15 in writing *Kenya* (1924). Also wrote *A Lost Chance in Kenya* (1931). The father of Winifred's almoner friend, Nannice Leys.
188	32	**William McGregor Ross**: Author of *Kenya From Within: A Short Political History* (1927).
189	28	**Rt Hon. Cecil John Rhodes** (1853–1902): Acquired considerable fortune in diamond mining enterprises in Kimberley. Member of the Cape Legislature in 1881, and Cape Premier in 1890 and 1896. He was at the head of the British South Africa Chartered Company which annexed the vast amount of territory originally named Rhodesia, now Zimbabwe. Retired from political life after the highly controversial Jameson Raid in 1895.
189	32	**Sir James Gordon McDonald** (1867–1942): A pioneer of Rhodesia, now Zimbabwe, and closely associated with Rhodes. Author of *Rhodes: A Life*.
190	4	**Matabele**: A mixed people of largely Zulu origin. Defeated by the Boers in Transvaal in 1837. Withdrew to the Matopo Hills where their chief kraal was established at Bulawayo. Overthrown by the British South Africa Company's forces in 1893–4.
190	17	**Sir William Harcourt** (1827–1904): Statesman. Urged inquiry into Jameson Raid. As member of the Committee in 1897 he made a searching examination of Cecil Rhodes but defended the Committee's report from radical attack.
190	37	**Viscount John Morley** (1838–1923): Statesman and writer. MP 1883–95 and 1896–1908. Secretary of State for India 1905–10. Author of biographies of Gladstone, Cromwell, Voltaire, Richard Cobden, etc.
190	38	**James Louis Garvin** (d. 1947): Editor of *The Observer* 1908–42. Published *The Life of Joseph Chamberlain* in 3 volumes.
191	36	**Oswald Spengler** (1880–1936): German scientist and historical philosopher. Main work *The Decline of the West* (English translation 1926–29). Greeted with enthusiasm the rise of the German National Socialists but the Hitler régime could not digest his pessimistic doctrine and his

Page	Line	
		main work was suppressed.
192	3	**Fridtjof Nansen** (1861–1930): Norwegian explorer famous for his North Polar expedition 1893. Active in Russian famine relief 1921. Nobel Prize for Peace 1922.
192	3	**Albert Schweitzer** (1875–1965): Doctor of Theology, music critic and organist who became a Doctor of Medicine in order to devote his life to missionary work in Equatorial Africa. Nobel Prize for Peace 1952.
193	32	**Eduard Beneš** (1884–1948): Czechoslovak statesman, and co-founder with Thomas Masaryk of the Czech Republic. President 1935–38 and 1940–48.
194	13	**Rt Hon. Louis Botha** (1863–1919): Commander-in-Chief of Boer forces from 1900. He was Premier of Transvaal 1907–10.
197	36	**Charles James Fox** (1749–1806): Entered Parliament at 19. Throughout William Pitt's 17-year Premiership he was his most formidable adversary, favouring American Independence, denouncing the Slave Trade, and advocating Parliamentary Reform.
200	15	**Ralph Iron**: The pseudonym under which Olive Schreiner published *The Story of an African Farm* in two volumes in January 1883. In the 1887 edition Olive Schreiner's name was given in brackets beneath the original pen-name.
200	20	**Havelock Ellis**: Although known now mainly for his analysis of sexuality, Havelock Ellis (1859–1939) also wrote several 'philosophical' books.
202	1, 2	**Army Sister; youthful VAD**: The Sister is called 'Hope Milroy' in *Testament of Youth*, whose Chapter VIII ('Between the Sandhills and the Sea') narrates the events of this article; VB joined the women's Voluntary Aid Detachments (formed to assist the professional military nursing services) in 1915, at the age of 21.
204	14	**Lord Haig**: Douglas Haig, Earl of Bermersyde (1861–1928), was Commander-in-Chief of the British forces in France from December 1915.
205	33	**Pangbourne**: In Berkshire on the Thames.
206	10	**Woman and Labour**: The quotation is from Chapter IV ('Woman and War').
206	31	**Nurse Cavell**: Edith Cavell (b. 1865), a nurse, was arrested and executed by the Germans in 1915 for helping fugitive French and English soldiers.
206	32	**The Well of Loneliness**: By Radclyffe Hall (1880–1943), a lesbian, this novel was published, and suppressed for 'indecency', in 1928; VB reviewed it sympathetically and defended it in court, and her last published book, 40

Page	Line	
		years later, was *Radclyffe Hall: A Case of Obscenity?*
207	7, 9	**contemporaneous German war novels; Journey's End**: The most famous and influential of these recently published novels was Erich Maria Remarque's *All Quiet on the Western Front*; *Journey's End* (1929) by R.C. Sherriff (1896–1975) was based on the author's First World War experiences.
207	13	**May Wedderburn Cannan** (b. 1893). She published a collection of poems, *In War Time* (from which VB quotes), and a novel, *The Lonely Generation*.
207	26,34	**Death of a Hero, All Else is Folly**: Both anti-war books were published in 1929, the first by Richard Aldington (1892–1962), the second by Peregrine Acland (b. 1891).
208	24,28	**John, Shirley**: VB's two children, John and Shirley Catlin (the prominent politician Shirley Williams) were born in 1927 and 1930 respectively.
209	16	**Mafeking, Ladysmith**: The siege and relief of these South African towns were celebrated events of the Boer War (1899–1902).
209	22	**my young brother**: Captain Edward Brittain was killed in action on the Italian front in June 1918.
209	29	**Kingsley's heroes**: Charles Kingsley (1819–75), author of *The Water Babies*, retold classical myths for children in his popular *The Heroes* (1856).
211	12	**Wyndham Lewis**: Writer and painter (1884–1957), he was a war-artist during the First World War.
211	24	**Hitler**: Although in 1932 Adolf Hitler (1889–1945) had not yet been appointed Chancellor, he had published *Mein Kampf*, his Nazi Party had grown rapidly, and the collapse of the German economy from 1929 had made him a political force.
212	33	**occupied areas of Germany**: The Versailles Treaty (1919) demilitarized these areas and placed them under temporary Allied (mainly French) control.
213	1	**G.D.H. Cole** (1889–1959): Was a university teacher who became a leading socialist thinker and writer, contributing frequently to the *New Statesman*. Chairman of Fabian Society 1939–46. Numerous publications include *A History of Socialist Thought*.
213	19, 20	**writer of satires; Cry Havoc!**: The first was WH, whose satirical *Mandoa, Mandoa!* had come out earlier in 1933; the second, published in July 1933, was a highly emotional, popular and influential anti-war tract ('not so much a book as a scream', said one reviewer) by the journalist Beverley Nichols (1898–1983), who had been VB's contemporary at Oxford.

Page	Line	
214	26	**Hugh Dalton**: Economist and statesman (1877–1962), he was a Labour Party MP (later Chancellor of the Exchequer), strongly anti war in the late 1920s.
215	30	**What Would be the Character of a New War?**: Published in 1931, this 'enquiry' comprises a series of sober essays by international experts attempting, through analysis of military and other relevant factors, to show how destructive large-scale warfare had become. The essays were collected by the Inter-Parliamentary Union, a body of parliamentarians seeking to secure international co-operation and peace.
216	11	**Aveluy Wood**: Near Thiepval, and between Albert and Bapaume, this wood was laid waste during the five-month Battle of the Somme (1916), in which there were well over a million casualties.
217	27	**Women's International League**: Founded during the International Women's Conference at The Hague in 1915, to work for international peace and freedom.
217	29	**Storm Jameson**: A prolific novelist from Yorkshire (b. 1897), she was a close friend of VB's during the 1930s, when she was a leading pacifist; *No Time Like the Present* is an autobiographical account of the First World War period.
219	4	**Dr Maude Royden**: Prominent as a feminist and Christian activist (1876–1956), she was a pioneering woman preacher and, in the 1930s, a crusader for peace.
219	18	**League of Nations Union; the Anti-War Movement**: The LNU, an organization with obvious internationalist ideals, was founded in 1918, and in the late 1920s became the most influential anti-war group in Britain (with a membership in 1931 of over 400,000). The AWM, a Communist-controlled organization founded in 1932, was renamed the British Movement against War and Fascism in 1934, but soon afterwards dissolved.
220	6	**No More War Conference**: Annual conference of the No More War Movement, a pacifist body established in 1921 (by 1927 it had about 3,000 members) and later absorbed by the PPU.
220	7	**Wickham Steed**: Journalist, editor and lecturer (1871–1956), he became a well-known broadcaster on world affairs 1937–47.
221	25, 26	**Sir Ronald Ross; Lord Lister**: Eminent physicians. Ross (1857–1932) led a medical expedition to West Africa in 1899 and won the Nobel Prize for his work on controlling malaria; Lister (1827–1912) established antiseptic surgery in 1865.

Page	Line	
223	36	**President Wilson**: The reference is to the role of President Woodrow Wilson (1856–1924) in advocating the formation of the League of Nations.
224	38	**Manchuria; Abyssinia**: The inefficacy of the League of Nations as an international authority was demonstrated when the Japanese invaded Manchuria (now north-east China) in 1931 and the Italians under Mussolini attacked Abyssinia (Ethiopia) in 1935.
225	4	**Dr L.P. Jacks**: A philosopher (1860–1955), he was Principal of Manchester College, Oxford, and editor of the *Hibbert Journal*; in 1934 he published *The Revolt against Mechanism*, an influential book.
225	16	**Headway**: LNU periodical.
225	30	**blunder of Versailles**: VB was one of the many who considered that the Treaty of Versailles (1919) was responsible, especially through its humiliation of Germany, for the rise of Hitler and of Fascism.
226	2	**Winston Churchill**: The great statesman (1874–1965) was First Lord of the Admiralty when he made this speech.
227	25	**Rush-Bagot agreement**: Negotiated by the American Richard Rush (1780–1859) and the Englishman Charles Bagot (1781–1843) in 1817 – with the approval of President James Monroe and Robert Castlereagh, the British Minister of War – this agreement demilitarized the Great Lakes.
227	29	**Cobden Treaty**: Richard Cobden (1804–65), political economist and advocate of free trade, concluded this commercial treaty with France, 'based on tariff reduction and the expansion of trade'.
228	14	**Spanish War**: Civil war in Spain between Fascist and Republican forces raged from 1936 to 1939; overwhelmingly the writers who responded to the *Left Review*'s questionnaire were supporters of the Republican cause, only small minorities supporting Franco's Fascists or advocating neutrality.
229	4	**Left Book Club**: Founded by Victor Gollancz in 1936 to resist the rise of Fascism and Nazism; its left-wing membership opposed any deal with Hitler.
229	9	**Chamberlain**: British Prime Minister 1937–40, Neville Chamberlain (1869–1940) tried to avert war by appeasing Hitler in the Munich Agreement of September 1938.
229	23, 24	**Clemenceau; Lloyd George; Sir John Simon**: Three architects of the Treaty of Versailles. Georges Clemenceau (1841–1929), the French premier, was bitterly hostile to Germany; David Lloyd George (1863–1945), the British Prime Minister, was a dominant figure at the conference;

Page	Line	
		and Sir John Simon (1873–1954), who was Home Secretary during the war, negotiated for Britain on the disarmament of Germany.
230	12	**Czechoslovakia**: Sudetenland, the northern border area of Czechoslovakia, was ceded to Germany without Czech consent, as part of Chamberlain's 'bargain' with Hitler.
232	2	**worldwide calamity**: On the typescript of this article VB commented: 'Written 3 September 1939, between 11.0 a.m. and 1 p.m.' – that is, as Great Britain declared war.
233	3	**Dick Sheppard**: Canon H.R.L. Sheppard (1880–1937) was a deeply admired Anglican priest who, as its Vicar, made St Martin-in-the-Fields (Trafalgar Square, London) a centre of humanitarian service and of religious broadcasting. A powerfully influential pacifist, he founded the PPU in 1935.
233	32	**Peace Pledge Union**: Major British pacifist organization, founded in July 1935 by Dick Sheppard after a meeting of signatories to the pledge he had publicized ('I renounce war and never again, directly or indirectly, will I support or sanction another'); in 1940, at its peak, the PPU had some 136,000 members.
234	7	**National Peace Council**: Set up in 1904 as an umbrella organization, it organized an Annual Peace Congress and circulated petitions (like the one of 1938–9 calling for an international peace conference).
234	10	**Testament of Youth**: The description of the effects of mustard gas occurs about half-way through Chapter VIII ('Between the Sandhills and the Sea').
235	15	**New Forest**: Earlier in 1939, VB had bought a cottage in the countryside near the New Forest, Hampshire, as a 'retreat' from London, and did much of her writing there.
239	8, 9	**Lord Haw-Haw; Dr Goebbels**: William Joyce, nicknamed 'Lord Haw-Haw' (1906–1946), made notorious propaganda broadcasts to Britain on German radio during the war and was afterwards executed for treason; Dr Goebbels (1897–1945) was the Nazi Minister of Propaganda.
240	13	**Heinrich von Treitschke**: A prominent historian and German nationalist (1834–96) whose ideas strongly influenced Nazi policy.
241	12	**Food Relief Campaign**: The PPU's Food Relief Campaign, like the Famine Relief Campaign (chaired by the Bishop of Chichester) and the Friends, worked hard for the relief of those starving in Europe as a result of war conditions and the policy of blockading German-controlled ports. VB's pamphlet *One of These Little Ones* (1943) was an attempt to rouse public opinion against the blockade.

Page	Line	
243	28	**Brendan Bracken**: A Conservative politician (1901–58) who had been Churchill's Private Secretary, he was Minister of Information 1941–45; the quotation is from a statement he made to the press while visiting Canada (19 August 1943).
244	23	**George Orwell**: VB's argument with the well-known novelist, journalist and political writer (1903–50) was provoked by his attack, in his column in the *Tribune* (26 May 1944), on *Seed of Chaos*, her recently published tract against the British Government's policy, from 1942, of area-bombing. During 1944 VB also addressed a long, carefully argued article to the question of whether or not war can be humanized, since this was a source of contention among pacifists and other workers for peace during the war.
245	13	**Prof. A.L. Goodhart**: Arthur L. Goodhart, an eminent legal expert and writer (1891–1978), was Professor of Jurisprudence at Oxford University 1931–51.
247	11	**Victor Gollancz**: Prominent left-wing publisher and writer (1893–1967), he warned about Fascism and Nazism in several publications of the 1930s; after the war he organized Save Europe Now, to relieve starvation in Germany, and the Association of World Peace (now War on Want).
247	26	**Nicolas Berdyaev**, *The Meaning of History*: A Russian religious philosopher (1874–1948) expelled from Russia in 1922, he was concerned with the 'problem of freedom'.
249	2	**Dictate of Constantine**: In AD 313, the Emperor Constantine made Christianity the official religion of the Roman Empire, and thereafter pacifism was abandoned by the Church as a central tenet.
249	10	**'Lebensraum'**: 'Living-space'; territory desired for a nation's development.
249	14	**San Francisco**: The international conference of 50 Allied nations held at San Francisco April–June 1945 established the United Nations and the International Court of Justice.
250	22	**VE Day**: 8 May 1945 (Victory in Europe).
251	38	**Dresden, 300,000 died**: Eye-witness accounts of the effects of mass-bombing were unreliable in the estimates of numbers of casualties, partly because of their unprecedented scale – Max Hastings in his *Bomber Command* (1979) concludes that the fire-bombing of Dresden killed 'a minimum of 30,000 and perhaps as many as 100,000 people'.
252	29	**death of President**: Franklin Delano Roosevelt (1882–1945), President of the United States from 1933, died

Page	Line	
		a month before Germany's surrender, and was succeeded by Harry S. Truman (1884–1972), who took the decision to drop the first atom-bombs in August 1945.
253	13, 18	**Field-Marshal Kesselring; Sir Arthur Harris**: Albrecht Kesselring (1885–1960) directed the German air-attack during the Battle of Britain in 1940; Sir Arthur Harris (1892–1984), Commander-in-Chief of the RAF's Bomber Command 1942–5, directed the policy of area-bombing which laid waste many German cities.
253	22, 25	**general election; Clement Attlee; H.J. Laski**: In the 1945 election, Churchill and the Conservative Party were ousted by the Labour Party under Clement Attlee (1883–1967), who had served as Deputy Prime Minister in the coalition War Cabinet. Harold Laski (1893–1950), Professor of Political Science at the University of London, was a member of the Labour Party Executive Committee and author of several controversial books.
253	26, 34	**war with Japan; massacre bombing**: Japan did not surrender until September 1945. Before atom-bombs were dropped on Hiroshima and Nagasaki in August, Japanese cities were heavily bombed by the American Air Force (in a single raid on Tokyo over 80,000 people were killed, many more than died from air-attack in England throughout the war).
256	16	**Trooper Peter Halket of Mashonaland**: This 'parable' bitterly attacked the imperialist Cecil Rhodes and racist violence in Southern Africa.
256	34	**Spinoza**: Dutch philosopher (1632–77), whose theories are expounded in his *Ethics*.
257	2	**Marshall Aid**: Named for its originator, General George Marshall (1880–1959), this scheme supplied US material and financial aid to Europe after the war.
257	11	**USSR mourning; Malenkov**: Stalin, Russia's 'great dictator', died in 1953, and was succeeded for two years by Malenkov.
259	18	**Quaker community**: The religious Society of Friends was formed in the seventeenth century; strongly pacifist in orientation, it also participates through its Peace Committee (established in 1888) in the work of other peace movements.
259	25	**Bombing Restriction Committee; Corder Catchpool**: A Friend, Catchpool (1883–1953) became a leading pacifist and treasurer of the PPU; in 1941 he founded the Committee for the Abolition of Night Bombing, which the following year became the BRC; VB was a leading member,

Page	Line	

and her *Seed of Chaos* was one of several BRC publications.

259 27 Fellowship of Reconciliation; *Massacre by Bombing*: A Christian pacifist organization founded in 1914, the FOR developed into an international movement, its American branch becoming the dominant pacifist movement there. *Massacre by Bombing* was the title of the American edition of *Seed of Chaos*, published by the FOR some months before the British edition; a group of prominent Protestant leaders supported it with a 'call to repentance', and President Roosevelt was one of those who attacked them publicly.

259 31 Dr Felix Morley: Distinguished American journalist (b. 1894), editor of the *Washington Post* 1933–40, he was awarded the Pulitzer Prize for editorial writing in 1936.

260 31 David Low: Cartoonist (1891–1963) who became famous for his political cartoons in the London *Evening Standard* 1927–50.

261 23 Dr Bell: The Rt Rev. George Bell (1883–1958), Bishop of Chichester 1929–58, was one of the most outspoken and effective critics of area-bombing and the blockade during the war.

262 14 Gandhi; Civil Disobedience: Mohandas (Mahatma) Gandhi, Indian nationalist and social reformer (1869–1948); his advocacy of non-violence and a policy of civil disobedience achieved Indian independence, and deeply influenced social and political activists in the West.

262 18 Campaign for Nuclear Disarmament: The CND was founded in 1958 to 'press for a British initiative to reduce the nuclear peril and to stop the armaments race'; it gained international attention up to 1964 (the final Rally of the 1962 Aldermaston March attracted a crowd of 150,000 to Hyde Park), but the movement waned somewhat until the battle against installation of Cruise missiles revived it strongly in the early 1980s.

264 15 Lord Coleraine: James Bonar Law, Baron Coleraine (b. 1931); his letter to *The Times* (15 September 1961) complained about 'the mischief of the ageing adolescents who comprise "The Committee of 100" and who seem bent on loosing on us a nuclear war'.

264 15, 19 The Committee of 100; Lord Russell: Bertrand Russell, the eminent philosopher, writer and social critic (1872–1970), was leader of the Committee of 100, an offshoot of the CND formed in 1960 to publicize the anti-nuclear cause through mass civil disobedience (in September 1961, over 1,000 people were arrested during a sit-down protest in

Page	Line	

Trafalgar Square). He *did* 'end up with a statue' – but in Red Lion Square, not Westminster.

276 **9** **Lovat Dickson** (b. 1902): Writer and publisher. Books include *Richard Hillary* (1950), *H.G. Wells* (1969), two volumes of autobiography, etc. Managing Director of Lovat Dickson Ltd, Publishers, 1932–38; Director Macmillan & Co. 1941–64; and Pan Books 1946–64.

276 **11** **Rudyard Kipling** (1865–1936): Poet and novelist, who was awarded Nobel Prize 1907.

277 **1** **John Buchan** (1875–1940): Author of *The Thirty Nine Steps* and biographies of Sir Walter Scott, Julius Caesar, etc. Governor-General of Canada 1935–40.

277 **7** **Professor William James** (1842–1910): Professor of Philosophy at Harvard University. Author of *Principles of Psychology* (1892), the famous *The Varieties of Religious Experience* (1902), *The Meaning of Truth* (1909), etc.

277 **25** **Robert Louis Stevenson** (1850–1894): Scottish essayist, novelist and poet. Author of *Treasure Island* (1883), and *Dr Jekyll and Mr Hyde* and *Kidnapped* (1886), he lived in voluntary exile in Samoa from 1889 until his death.

278 **22** **Stephen Hawes** (d. about 1523): English poet. Author of the allegorical *Passetyme of Pleasure, or History of Graunde Amoure and la Bel Pucel*.

282 **27** **Helen Wills** (later Helen Wills Moody) (b. 1905): American tennis star and one of the all-time greats. World record holder of eight Wimbledon singles titles.

282 **29** **Samuel Butler** (1835–1902): Author of originality, best known for *Erewhon*, *Erewhon Revisited*, and *The Way of All Flesh*.

282 **29** **Sir Edmund Gosse** (1849–1928): Poet and critic. Acclaimed for his *History of Eighteenth Century Literature* and *History of Modern English Literature*.

286 **7** **Reginald Cheyne Berkeley** (1890–1935): English dramatist.

286 **30** **Eamon de Valera** (1882–1975): Commandant in Irish uprising, Easter 1916; death sentence commuted, released General Amnesty 1917. MP for Down, Northern Ireland, 1921–29, and South Down 1933–37. President of Ireland 1959–73.

287 **2** **Luigi Pirandello** (1867–1936): Italian dramatist and novelist, many of whose works have been translated into English. Nobel Prize for Literature 1934.

287 **2** **Sean O'Casey** (1883–1964): Irish dramatist of remarkable power. Plays include *Juno and the Paycock*, *The Silver Tassie* and *Red Roses for Me*.

Page	Line	
287	11	**James Spenser**. *Limey: An Englishman Joins the Gang*, edited and with an introduction by H. Kingsley (1933).
288	18	**Diana Wynyard** (1906–1964): Principally stage actress. Played Gertrude in *Hamlet* and Portia in *The Merchant of Venice* when with the Shakespeare Memorial Theatre Company.
288	19	**Clive Brook** (1887–1974): Popular film and stage actor. Made 102 films in England and Hollywood, including *Cavalcade*.
288	21	**Una O'Connor** (1893–1959): Stage and film actress. Appeared in both stage and film versions of *Cavalcade*.
290	17	**Alexander Pushkin** (1799–1837): National poet of Russia. Died of wounds received in a duel.
291	28	**Dorothy Richardson** (1872–1957): Novelist. Introduced stream-of-consciousness technique into English fiction. Author of *Pilgrimage*, a sequence of novels.
292	4	**Naomi Mitchison** (b. 1897): Writer of fiction and non-fiction. Author of more than 30 books, including *The Corn King and the Spring Queen*, *The Bull Calves*, *The Cleansing of the Knife*, etc. Tribal Mother to Bakgatla, Botswana, since 1963.
294	11	**How to Enjoy Bad Health**: The anecdote in this article which WH attributes to 'one young woman of my acquaintance' whose specialist informed her that she was unlikely to recover from the disease afflicting her, was, in fact, based on her own personal experience. As VB reveals in *Testament of Friendship*, after the consultation Winifred immediately telephoned H.G. Wells, 'the unknown hero of her youth', who invited her to tea. No doubt to allay the anxiety of her family and friends, who might well have realized that she was writing about herself, Winifred tacked on the disingenuous red herring of the specialist having made an erroneous diagnosis.
294	20	**WAAC**: The Women's Army Auxiliary Corps, in which WH served 1918–19.
302	13	**Taboos and Toleration**: Early in 1935, with less than nine months to live, WH took refuge in the Yorkshire seaside resort of Hornsea in order to work uninterruptedly on her posthumously published novel *South Riding*. At the end of April she travelled south to join VB for a fortnight's holiday in Tenby on the south coast of Pembrokeshire, and here she wrote some of her last 'Notes on the Way' for *Time and Tide*. Across the bay on Caldy Island the white Cistercian monastery – which she vividly describes as 'a shining focus to that pale and cloudy land lit by the western

Page	Line	
		sun' – provided the inspiration for this article.
305	2	**George Fox** (1624–1691): Founder of the Society of Friends.
305	21	**William Kingdon Clifford** (1845–79): Mathematician and metaphysician. Fellow of Trinity College, Cambridge.
308	3	**Ernie Mayne**: Popular music-hall comedian. Made first appearance in London in 1892. His best known numbers included 'She Pushed Me Into the Parlour' and 'Ten Little Fingers, Ten Little Toes'.
308	35	**Gwen Farrar** (1899–1944): Actress and vocalist. Best known through her music-hall partnership with Norah Blaney.
310	12	**Alan Paton**, *Cry, the Beloved Country*: Writer, educationalist and President of the South African Liberal Party until it was proscribed in 1968, Paton (b. 1903) published his moving novel of protest against apartheid in 1948.
314	11	**Woman and Labour**: The quotation is from Chapter IV ('Woman and War').
314	34	**The Story of an African Farm**: The quotation is from Part II, Chapter 4 ('Lyndall') of this novel (1883).
317	26	**book, widely read**: *Testament of Youth*.
318	29	**tragic murder trial**: Leonard Lockhart, who had been badly shell-shocked in the First World War, killed his wife in a suicide pact as the Second World War loomed; he was found 'guilty but insane'. In *Account Rendered* (1944), VB transposed Lockhart's story into fiction.
320	2	**Somerville Jubilee**: Named after Mary Somerville, a great scientist of the nineteenth century, Somerville College, Oxford, was founded in 1879.
320	12	**Rose Macaulay**: Novelist, travel-writer, essayist, pacifist (1881–1958), Rose Macaulay is well known for such books as *The Pleasure of Ruins* (1953) and *The Towers of Trebizond* (1956).
320	33	**Cornelia Sorabji**: An eminent Indian barrister and feminist (1866–1954), she was at Somerville 1889–92.
321	12	**my college days**: VB read English Literature at Somerville 1914–15 before leaving to become a VAD; she returned to read Modern History 1919–21.
321	36, 38	**Muriel Jaeger; Margaret Leigh; Dorothy Sayers**: Muriel Jaeger (d. 1969) published several other novels, including *Retreat from Armageddon* (1936), as did Margaret Leigh. Dorothy Sayers (1893–1957) became internationally famous for her Lord Peter Wimsey detective stories; she also translated Dante's *Divine Comedy* and wrote Christian apologetics.

Page	Line	
322	23, 33	**Margaret Kennedy; Sylvia Thompson**: Margaret Kennedy, novelist and playwright (1896–1967), is best remembered for her lively comedy *The Constant Nymph* (1924). Sylvia Thompson (1902–68) followed *Hounds of Spring* (1925) with several other novels.
322	31	**Oxford Poetry 1920**: VB co-edited and contributed to this collection of undergraduate poetry at the invitation of its publisher Basil Blackwell.
324	4	**women's degrees won**: From 1920 women were permitted to receive Oxford degrees.
327	4	**The friend who lives with us**: WH.
330	6	**UNRRA**: The United Nations Relief and Rehabilitation Administration (1943–47) organized a programme of international aid, especially for refugees and inhabitants of the war-ravaged countries.
330	20	**distinguished American**: Benjamin Kizer (b. 1878), a prominent lawyer, was director of UNNRA's China Office 1944–46.
330	32	**Adelphi Centre**: On the initiative of John Middleton Murry (then editor of the *Adelphi* magazine) and a group of fellow socialists and pacifists, a London house was bought in 1935 and used as a centre to promote socialism through educational activities. Later the centre was extended by the addition of Max Plowman's country home at Langham in East Anglia, and during the Second World War the centre was used, under the aegis of the PPU, to shelter conscientious objectors and working-class evacuees.
331	4	**Max Plowman**: Literary critic and poet (1883–1941), he succeeded Middleton Murry as editor of the *Adelphi*, and was secretary of the PPU 1937–38; a very influential pacifist (he published *The Faith Called Pacifism* in 1936), he died suddenly at Langham a few months before VB wrote this article there.
332	31	**son and daughter in the United States**: VB remained in London through most of the war (including the blitz), but John and Shirley Catlin were sent to live in the United States for four years, 1940–44 (mainly with VB's friend Ruth Gage Colby).
333	17	**The Story of an African Farm**: The quotation (slightly inaccurate) is from Waldo's letter to Lyndall, Part II, Chapter 11.
335	15	**George Lansbury; Donald Soper; Laurence Housman**: Prominent pacifists. Lansbury, politician and social activist (1859–1940), was Leader of the Labour Party 1931–50; Donald (later Lord) Soper (b. 1903) became a Methodist

Page	Line	
		minister and renowned public speaker; Housman was a well-known dramatist, poet and artist, as well as feminist and pacifist (1865–1959).
335	36	**Dr Howard Kershner**: Journalist and broadcaster (b .1891), he was director of relief for the American Friends 1939–42.
336	1, 7	**Agatha Harrison; Sevagram; Kasturbai Gandhi**: Harrison (d. 1954) was secretary of the India Conciliation Group and worked for Indian independence. At the village Sevagram, Gandhi established his final ashram (centre of religious instruction). His wife Kasturbai (1869–1944) took no part in politics.
336	29, 31	**Rabindranath Tagore; Santiniketan; C.F. Andrews**: The internationally admired Indian poet Tagore (1861–1941) founded a 'university', Visva-Bharati, at Santiniketan, and came to believe that cultural and social reform were more important for India than political freedom. Andrews, an educationalist (1871–1940), had close connections with both Gandhi (about whom he published several books) and Tagore (for whom he taught at Santiniketan).
337	15	**King George VI** (b. 1895): He became king on the abdication of his brother Edward VIII in 1936, and gained national respect and affection for his unassuming courage and compassion during the war.
337	18	**biography of John Bunyan**: *In the Steps of John Bunyan* (1950).
341	3, 5	**Sharpeville; Bishop of Johannesburg**: In 1960, 69 Africans were killed and nearly 200 wounded when police fired on a crowd protesting against apartheid regulations. The Rt Rev. Ambrose Reeves (1899–1980), Bishop of Johannesburg 1949–61, held various clerical posts in England after being deported from South Africa, and was President of the Anti-Apartheid Movement from 1970.
342	21	**Dr Verwoerd**: Implacable exponent of apartheid (1901–66), he was Prime Minister of South Africa 1958–66.
343	3	**Chief Luthuli**: A leader of non-violent resistance to apartheid, Albert Luthuli (1899–1967) won the Nobel Prize for Peace 1960.
345	33	**St Martin's Church**: Until this accident started the physical and mental decline that ended in her death in 1970, VB maintained a very close association with St Martin-in-the-Fields, the church at Trafalgar Square linked with Dick Sheppard and, through the memorial service in 1935, with WH.

Page	Line	
346	6	**Bart's sisters**: VB disguised St Bartholomew's Hospital (the oldest London hospital) as 'St Jude's'; see *Testament of Youth*, Chapter IX ('This Loneliest Hour').
347	4	**Canon Raven; Dr G.H.C. Macgregor**: Both were Professors of Divinity and expounded Christian pacifism. The books VB probably had in mind are *The Theological Basis of Christian Pacifism* (1952) by Canon Charles Raven (1885–1964), and *The New Testament Basis of Pacifism* (1936) by Prof. G.H.C. Macgregor (1892–1963).
348	29	The well-known poem of Henley (1848–1903) quoted by VB is 'Invictus', from *Echoes*.
350	3	**Norman Macowan's** *Glorious Morning*: Actor and playwright (1877–1961), he wrote *The Blue Lagoon* (1920) as well as *Glorious Morning* (1938).

Books by
Winifred Holtby

FICTION

Anderby Wold, John Lane at The Bodley Head 1923; Virago Press 1981
The Crowded Street, John Lane at The Bodley Head 1924; Virago Press 1981
The Land of Green Ginger, Jonathan Cape 1927; Virago Press 1983
Poor Caroline, Jonathan Cape 1931; Virago Press 1985
Mandoa, Mandoa!, William Collins 1933; Virago Press, 1982
South Riding, William Collins 1936 & Fontana Paperbacks 1954 *et seq.*
Truth Is Not Sober (short stories), William Collins 1934
Pavements at Anderby (short stories; edited by H.S. Reid and Vera Brittain), William Collins 1937

CRITICISM

Virginia Woolf: A Critical Study, Wishart 1932

SATIRE

Eutychus, or The Future of the Pulpit, Kegan Paul 1928
The Astonishing Island, Lovat Dickson 1933

SOCIOLOGY

A New Voter's Guide to Party Programmes, Kegan Paul 1929
Women, John Lane at The Bodley Head 1934

POETRY

The Frozen Earth, William Collins 1935

DRAMA

Take Back Your Freedom (with revision by Norman Ginsbury), Jonathan Cape 1939

LETTERS

Letters to a Friend (edited by Alice Holtby and Jean McWilliam), William Collins 1937

Selected Letters of Winifred Holtby and Vera Brittain (edited by Vera Brittain and Geoffrey Handley-Taylor), Brown & Sons, Hull 1960

Books by Vera Brittain

AUTOBIOGRAPHY

Testament of Youth, Victor Gollancz 1933; Virago Press 1978
Testament of Experience, Victor Gollancz 1957; Virago Press 1979
Chonicle of Youth: Vera Brittain's War Diary 1913–17 (edited by Alan Bishop),
    Victor Gollancz 1981

BIOGRAPHY

Testament of Friendship: The Story of Winifred Holtby, Macmillan 1940; Virago
    Press 1980
In the Steps of John Bunyan (USA, *Valiant Pilgrim*), Rich and Cowan 1950
Pethick-Lawrence: A Portrait, George Allen & Unwin 1963
Envoy Extraordinary: A Study of Vijaya Lakshmi Pandit, George Allen & Unwin
    1965

FICTION

The Dark Tide, Grant Richards 1923
Not Without Honour, Grant Richards 1924
Honourable Estate, Victor Gollancz 1936
Account Rendered, Macmillan 1945; Virago Press 1982
Born 1925, Macmillan 1948; Virago Press 1982

HISTORY

Women's Work in Modern England, Noel Douglas 1928
The Story of St Martin's, Pitkin 1951
Lady Into Woman: A History of Women from Victoria to Elizabeth II, Andrew
    Dakers 1953

The Women at Oxford: *A Fragment of History*, George G. Harrap 1960
The Rebel Passion: *A Short History of Some Pioneer Peace-Makers*, George Allen & Unwin 1964

TRAVEL

Thrice A Stranger: New Chapters of Autobiography, Victor Gollancz 1938
Search After Sunrise, Macmillan 1951

POETRY

Verses of a VAD, Erskine Macdonald 1918
Poems of the War and After, Victor Gollancz 1934

LETTERS

Selected Letters of Winifred Holtby and Vera Brittain (edited by Vera Brittain and Geoffrey Handley-Taylor), Brown & Sons, Hull 1960

MISCELLANEOUS

Halcyon, or The Future of Monogamy, Kegan Paul 1929
England's Hour, Macmillan 1941; Futura Paperback 1981
Humiliation with Honour, Andrew Dakers 1942
One of These Little Ones … A Plea to Parents and Others for Europe's Children, Andrew Dakers 1943
Seed of Chaos: What Mass Bombing Really Means, New Vision Publishing Co. 1944
Above All Nations (An anthology with George Catlin and Sheila Hodges), Victor Gollancz 1945
On Becoming a Writer, Hutchinson 1947
Radclyffe Hall: A Case of Obscenity?, Femina Books 1968

Index